to JUDAISM

A Textbook and Reader

JACOB NEUSNER

WESTMINSTER/JOHN KNOX PRESS
Louisville, Kentucky

Book design by Publishers' WorkGroup

First edition

Published by Westminster/John Knox Press
Louisville, Kentucky

This book is printed on acid-free paper that meets the American National Standards Institute Z39.48 standard.

PRINTED IN THE UNITED STATES OF AMERICA

2 4 6 8 9 7 5 3

Library of Congress Cataloging-in-Publication Data

Neusner, Jacob, 1932–
    An introduction to Judaism : a textbook and reader / Jacob Neusner.
        p.   cm.
    Includes bibliographical references and index.
    ISBN 0-664-25348-2

    1. Judaism—History.   2. Judaism—United States—Customs and practices.   3. Judaism—Sacred books.   I. Title.
BM157.N47   1992
296—dc20   91-34830

An Introduction to Judaism

An Introduction

Contents

Anthology for Chapters Six to Nine
Rabbinic Judaism: Its Formative History
and Holy Books

Anthology for Chapters Ten and Eleven
Rabbinic Judaism:
Law, Philosophy, Mysticism, and Theology

Part Three
The Jewish People and the Torah

Anthology for Part Three
How Encyclopedias Define Judaism

Acknowledgments

Emil L. Fackenheim, "The Human Condition after Auschwitz." © 1971 by Emil Fackenheim. Reprinted by permission. Originally published in *The Human Condition after Auschwitz: A Jewish Testimony a Generation After* (Syracuse, N.Y.: Syracuse University, the B. G. Randolph Lectures in Judaic Studies, April 1971).

William Scott Green, "Old Habits Die Hard: Judaism in *The Encyclopedia of Religion*," *Critical Review of Books in Religion* 1989 (Atlanta: Scholars Press for Journal of the American Academy of Religion and Journal of Biblical Literature, 1989), pages 23–40. Not subject to copyright.

Ben Halpern, "The Jewish Consensus," *The Jewish Frontier* (September 1962), pages 9–13. © 1962 by the *Jewish Frontier*. Reprinted by permission of *Jewish Frontier*.

Excerpt from "The Mystical Element in Judaism" by Abraham J. Heschel from *The Jews: Their History, Culture, and Religion,* edited by Louis Finkelstein. © 1949, 1955 by Louis Finkelstein. Reprinted by permission of HarperCollins Publishers, Inc.

Louis Jacobs, "Judaism," *Encyclopaedia Judaica* (Jerusalem: Keter Publishing Co., 1971), 10:383–86. © 1971 Keter Publishing Co. Reprinted by permission of Macmillan Co., New York.

Isadore Twersky, "The Shulhan Arukh: Enduring Code of Jewish Law," *Judaism* 1967 16:141–58. © 1967 by American Jewish Congress.

Reprinted by permission of the American Jewish Congress. Originally published in *Judaism*, vol. 16, no. 2 (Spring 1967), 141–58. Footnotes are omitted.

Jack Wertheimer, "Recent Trends in American Judaism," from *The American Jewish Yearbook*. Selection: pages 63, 75–82, 96–97, 107–10, 114–17, 124–34, 161–62. Reprinted by permission of Basic Books, Inc., Publishers, New York.

A Word to the Student: Why Study Judaism?

Practiced through most of recorded history, Judaism has not only exercised a powerful influence on Christianity and Islam, the two most influential religions of humanity past or present, but it has also shown us how through religion people have worked together to meet crises and answer urgent questions. In Judaism we see how religion shapes the life of a single social group, the Jews; Judaism provides a fine example of how religion can be public, not private, and shared, not only personal. Not all Jews practice Judaism, but all who practice Judaism are Jews, that is, they are regarded as members of the Jewish community or the people, "Israel." Hence in Judaism we study the intimate relationship between religion and a particular society.

But there is another reason for people who want to study religion in general to study Judaism. Most Americans are Christians, so when they study Christianity or Western civilization, which is Christian, they study what they regard as their own religion and heritage. But when they want to study a religion other than the one which they grew up in and know best, Judaism is a fine candidate, because Judaism is familiar yet somewhat exotic. There are approximately six million Jews in North America, including more than five million in the United States, and more than 80 percent say that they practice Judaism. Clearly, a great many people know Jews, and nearly everyone knows about Judaism. Because of this familiarity, Judaism is accessible. Were it as strange to Americans as Buddhism or Islam, about which, until very recently, few of us had any direct knowledge at all, studying Judaism would present an obstacle course of odd names, writings of which we might not make sense, and a history involving holy men with unintelligible names and nations that fought over religious questions that mean nothing at all to us. But Judaism uses some of the same writings as does Christianity because the Old Testament of Christianity is the written Torah of Judaism.

But even while near at hand and familiar, Judaism is also exotic. That is for two reasons. First, the two things that everybody knows about Judaism—(1) it is the religion of the Old Testament; and (2) it is the religion of the Jews and pretty much the same thing as their culture or their history—are both right and wrong. Judaism is much more than the religion of the Old Testament, just as Christianity is much more than the religion of the New Testament. And, second, Judaism is not only a culture or a history. It is a religion that takes over the history and culture of the Jewish people and re-presents them in a thoroughly transformed way. In Judaism we see how a religion defines its world.

In this introduction to Judaism, I take it for granted that readers are interested in Judaism because real people—whom we know and with whose problems we can identify—practice that religion. So first we will consider the real religion in the here and now of our own country: Judaism in North America, as practiced by Americans and Canadians who are Jews. That means I introduce Judaism by starting not at its beginnings, in remote historical times and distant places, but in its immediate and contemporary expression as the religion of (some) Americans. Part One of this book describes Judaism in the world today and in North America in particular. I begin here not only because this book is addressed to Americans and Canadians but also because the largest single body of practitioners of Judaism in the world today are North Americans. The percentage of North American Jews who declare that they are Jews by reason of religion is far greater than the proportion of the Jewish population of the State of Israel that sees itself as Jews by reason of religion (most of the Jewish population of the State of Israel regards itself as Jews by nationality rather than by religion), and, of course, far larger than the Jewish population of any other country. So to examine Judaism as a religion that affects people, seeking a reasonably coherent and cogent case, North Americans provide us with the best example.

How, in fact, do people we know practice this religion? The

answer to that question cannot address a stale catalogue of things that books say: Jews believe this, Jews do that. Instead of turning to descriptions of what Judaism teaches and requires, therefore, we shall consider what Jewish Americans actually do because they are Jews and wish to practice Judaism. And when we consider this, it must be in terms of how we define the way in which a religion lives. The answer here is simple: religion changes people, and it does so in particular through its rites, which have the power to transform a person or a circumstance—a place, an occasion. Religion tells us that we are something else, something more, than we thought we were; and when Jewish Americans engage in a rite of Judaism, it changes and enchants them. So in Part One we survey some of the more important occasions of transcendence that affect Jewish Americans at home, in the family, in the synagogue, and in the Jewish community.

But knowing how its faithful live tells us only half of the story of what a religion is. The other half of the story, in the case of Judaism, is told to us in the holy books that Judaism reveres and calls "the Torah," meaning God's will and word for the here and now. In Part Two we shall learn how Judaism took shape as people responded to extraordinary crises in their everyday political and religious lives. We shall see that these crises presented questions that had to be answered and that were answered through responses deemed self-evidently true and immediately relevant by the people who responded to those answers. These questions and answers were set forth in holy books, from the Five Books of Moses (the Pentateuch: Genesis, Exodus, Leviticus, Numbers, and Deuteronomy) to the Mishnah, the Midrash, and the two Talmuds. And yet, even when we understand how a religion took shape, we still do not know where, when, and why it flourished as it did, or why it met competition within its own chosen community. So in addition to understanding the beginning of a religion, we must understand its success, when it succeeded, and its failure, when it failed. Part Two addresses the birth of Judaism, Judaism's long period of cogency, and the formation, in modern times, of a variety of alternatives to the Judaism that had predominated for so long. And that brings us back to the Judaism we know, the one that thrives in North America, requiring us to define Judaism in light of both its contemporary expression here and its long and remarkably cogent history. Holding the pieces together is the challenge of definition, and that is where we end.

If this book succeeds, you will not only know a great deal more about Judaism. You also will have a different, and perhaps richer, conception of what religion is and does. Judaism can serve as an example of religion, for every particular religion we study should be asked to teach us general truths about religion. What is it that we learn about religion in general from Judaism in particular? Let me specify three propositions about religion that Judaism in particular offers for people to consider.

1. Religion explains particularly well the progress of humanity through the cycle of life, from birth to death. That is why we begin our study of Judaism with an account of living Judaism, the way in which real people are changed—transformed, enchanted—by the rites of Judaism. Contemporary Judaism contains a very powerful argument on behalf of this proposition: all of us are many things in a context of diverse commitments, that is, in a society where we can be part of an undifferentiated mass when we so choose (at mass sports events, for instance, or watching television) and also different from everybody else when we want to be. Jews choose to be different only on some very distinctive occasions which, we now know, define them in the affairs of home and family: where we live, as we pass through the years allotted to us. Judaism is perceived in the world at large as not a strong religion, because Jews do not go to synagogue in the massive numbers that Christians go to church. But when we realize that when Jews marry other Jews, it is (so far as anyone knows) mostly in a religious rite, that most Jews who reach puberty celebrate a bar or bat mitzvah, that most Jews celebrate those rites of Judaism that involve the home and family, such as Passover, that most Jews are buried in accord with the rites of Judaism, we are forced to see Judaism quite differently. We observe a religion that works its power of enchantment within the framework of home and family life. That means that a religion that sets forth dietary laws that some Judaisms reject altogether and most Jews, of whatever Judaism, ignore most of the time also makes some demands that most people obey. The reason, I maintain, is that Judaism explains particularly well the life of the individual and the family, and from that fact I generalize that religion works well when it comes to living in the here and now. This is the topic of Part One.

2. Religion serves particularly well to help a defeated society endure defeat. As we shall see, the Judaism that has predominated

for nearly two thousand years is the one that took shape after the destruction of the Second Temple of Jerusalem in the year 70 B.C.E. All of its canonical writings beyond the Hebrew Scriptures took shape from the second century forward. And the power of that Judaism—the self-evident truth that the believers have imputed to it—derives from its capacity to answer a very particular question: What next? Judaism tells us that when religion works, it works best because of its peculiar kind of power. That is not to suggest, in the line of Marx, that religion is the opiate of the masses, or, like Nietzsche, that some religions (he spoke of Christianity) really are for slaves. On the contrary, it is to suggest that religion offers the best explanation for the human condition because the human condition, if groups live long enough, is more often one of defeat and disappointment than of victory and triumph. That is my thesis in Part Two.

3. The third lesson I learn from Judaism is that religion is always historical, and yet it invariably thrives in the acutely contemporary world. That is to say, religion transforms the past into something memorable and the present into an occasion for celebrating past events. Religion speaks of history but is never historical. Judaism teaches those lessons because, while described as a historical religion, most of the "facts of history" that are supposed to dictate the faith of Judaism never happened at all, did not happen in the way in which Judaism says they did, or, if actual events, did not mean to everybody who knew about them what they self-evidently meant to Judaism. So the "facts of history" turn out to be the constructs from which the faith is composed. But the composition of the faith forms an acutely contemporary task, for it happens in the intensely-present-tense of this morning. Judaism says that in so many words when it speaks of how, at Passover, each person is to see himself or herself as redeemed, personally, from Egypt: and that can be only in the here and now. The deepest layers of contemporary Judaic consciousness, bearing the memories of murder and transforming them into "Holocaust," form the foundations of a conception of today's world order, a conception that dictates how people relate to their neighbors and what they want of their nations as well. That accounts for the ending point of this book: defining Judaism.

That much then: What Judaism teaches us about religion in general is three theses. First, religion informs the life of home and family, and, whatever its power in the social order and the life of nations, derives its strength from the intimate and fragile bonds of child to mother and father. Second, religion is for the losers, who by religion in time are turned into, if not the winners, then at least the survivors—the ones who get to tell the story later on. And third, religion turns history into the reality of the moment, reshaping a received past into the materials for a usable future. Commonly speaking of events in a long-dead past, religion in fact means to frame a message for this morning and for me in particular. But, as we shall see even in Part One, the most striking trait of Judaism is its capacity to make me see myself as though I were something that no this-worldly evidence tells me that I am: part of the family and holy people, Israel, that begin with Abraham and Sarah in remote antiquity. These three lessons that Judaism teaches stand in contrast with the point at which I began: the power of religion in world affairs. As evidence for my proposition that religion is the most powerful force in humankind I adduced the capacity of religion to cause war and disrupt the life of regions and nations. And yet I offered as generalizations about religion propositions about the humble affairs of home and family, community and near-at-hand society.

Were we to speak of Christianity or Buddhism or Shinto or Islam, were we to interrogate religion in Papua New Guinea or in the Celebes or in Bali or in Morocco, we might produce other generalizations. But I am confident that wherever we should turn for our facts about religions, we should end up with these generalizations everywhere. And therein lies the fundamental lesson that Judaism, in particular, offers: religion matters in the world order—whether as a medium for disruption and as disruption, as in times past, or as a way for different persons to conduct a dialogue, as in times to come—because, to begin with, religion makes a difference in the home and family. But Judaism is a religion that, through time, found itself speaking not to a nation in its land or to a powerful and important social group within society at large but, mainly, to humble folk—mothers, fathers, and their children. We learn from Judaism how a religion can speak in particular to the family in the here and now of their immediate condition: this morning, to an "us" that assembles around a common table. So we come first to Judaism at home, through the year and the life cycle, and only later turn to Judaism in books, through its long history starting at virtually the beginning of recorded time.

PART ONE

THE JEWISH PEOPLE: JUDAISM IN THE WORLD TODAY

1

Judaism at Home: Through the Year

GRACE AFTER MEALS

Christians say grace before meals. When Jews wish to say a prayer in connection with eating, the prayer is in two parts, a blessing for bread before eating ("Blessed are you, Lord our God, ruler of the world, who brings forth bread from the earth"), and then a substantial "blessing for food" (*birkat hammazon*), which is recited after the meal has been completed. Christians very commonly make up a blessing for the occasion. The Judaic liturgy, by contrast, invokes not the here and now but all of time and eternity, a kind of précis of the entire theology of Judaism. In America, Grace after Meals is often said at public events, for example, at synagogue and community meals, where young people gather in youth groups and summer camps, not to mention at all meals eaten by Orthodox Jews and by some Conservative Jews and rabbis. It is neither the most nor the least common rite. Since Grace after Meals addresses a common occasion and at the same time transforms the routine into an extraordinary experience, we begin our encounter with living Judaism here.

On routine weekdays, one psalm prefaces the Grace; on Sabbaths and festivals, another psalm is sung. The two—quite naturally—form a match and a complement. Let us consider them in sequence. First, the psalm for every day:

> By the rivers of Babylon we sat down and wept, when we remembered Zion. . . . If I forget you, O Jerusalem, let my right hand wither away, let my tongue cling to the roof of my mouth

if I do not remember you, if I do not set Jerusalem above my highest joy. (Ps. 137:1, 5)

Now the psalm for the Sabbath or a festival:

When the Lord brought back those that returned to Zion, we were like dreamers. Our mouth was filled with laughter, our tongue with singing. Restore our fortunes, O Lord, as the streams in the dry land. They that sow in tears shall reap in joy. (Ps. 126:1–2, 4–5)

The contrast tells the story. On weekdays, we are in the here and now of exile; on the Sabbath or a festival, we refer to the then and there of Zion as the world of redemption and salvation. The eating of the meal involves more than an individual's eating food. It involves us—the group—with history and destiny and invokes the specific moments—time past on weekdays, time future on holy days—that make the group distinctive, with a destiny all its own. So the setting of the meal tells me I am more than who I thought I was when I sat down because I was hungry. It identifies the hunger with one historical moment, the satisfaction with another. I was hungry and I ate and had enough. We hungered but were fed and will have enough. From the *I* and the here and now, the occasion of the meal has moved me to the *we* of time and eternity. From the individual's experience of hunger and satiation, I draw inferences about the encounter with calamity and renewal, today and the Sabbath, this life and the coming age. The psalms chosen as prelude to the Grace after Meals set the scene. Now to the action.

To understand the occasion and the setting, we must recall that in classical Judaism the table at which meals were eaten was regarded as the equivalent of the sacred altar in the Temple. Judaism taught that each Jew before eating had to attain the same state of ritual purity as the priest in the sacred act of making a sacrifice. So in the classic tradition the Grace after Meals is recited in a sacerdotal circumstance. The Grace is in four principal paragraphs, moving from the here and now to the time to come, from the meal just eaten to the messianic banquet. We start with the ordinary and say what is required: thanks for a real meal in today's world:

Blessed art Thou, Lord our God, King of the Universe, who nourishes all the world by His goodness, in grace, in mercy, and in compassion: He gives bread to all flesh, for His mercy is everlasting. And because of His great goodness we have never lacked, and so may we never lack, sustenance—for the sake of His great Name. For He nourishes and feeds everyone, is good to all, and provides food for each one of the creatures He created.

Blessed art Thou, O Lord, who feeds everyone.

The first of the four principal paragraphs leaves us where we were: at the table at which we ate our meal. It effects no transformation, for it does not claim that we are someone other than who we knew we were when we began the meal, and it does not say that we are located somewhere else. More to the point, the statement does not claim that we have eaten other than ordinary food, grown anywhere. It does say the unexceptional thought that God has given food, which any religious person may affirm. The reason is that the food is not transformed, any more than we are.

Now comes the first unanticipated statement:

We thank Thee, Lord our God, for having given our fathers as a heritage a pleasant, a good and spacious land; for having taken us out of the land of Egypt, for having redeemed us from the house of bondage; for Thy covenant, which Thou has set as a seal in our flesh, for Thy Torah which Thou has taught us, for Thy statutes which Thou hast made known to us, for the life of grace and mercy Thou hast graciously bestowed upon us, and for the nourishment with which Thou dost nourish us and feed us always, every day, in every season, and every hour.

For all these things, Lord our God, we thank and praise Thee; may Thy praises continually be in the mouth of every living thing, as it is written, *And thou shalt eat and be satisfied, and bless the Lord thy God for the good land which He hath given thee.*

Blessed art Thou, O Lord, for the land and its food.

We have moved from what we have eaten to where we have eaten. But that introduces a dissonant note: Where am I, and who am I? I am no longer merely someone who has eaten a meal. My thanks go for more than the food. Now I refer to a "good and spacious land," meaning only what Judaism knows as the Land of Israel; to "us," not me; to "our fathers"; to having been taken "out of the land of Egypt," having been redeemed from slavery; to a covenant in "our flesh"; to Torah and statutes; and on and on, down to land and food.

A considerable realm of being has taken over everyday reality. I am no longer what I thought: a hungry man who has eaten lunch. Now, on the occasion of a cheese sandwich, I invoke the entire sacred history of Israel, the Jewish people, from the exodus from Egypt to the circumcision of my penis. All invoked for a single occasion, a meal that has changed my condition from one of hunger to one of satisfaction. And that is the very meaning of the transformation, through the enchantment of the statements at hand, of every meal—or, for the generality of Jews, many public and communal meals—into the reenactment of the former and present condition of Israel, the holy people.

Not only so, but the occasion points toward the end as well:

> O Lord our God, have pity on Thy people Israel, on Thy city Jerusalem, on Zion the place of Thy glory, on the royal house of David Thy Messiah, and on the great and holy house which is called by Thy Name. Our God, our Father, feed us and speed us, nourish us and make us flourish, unstintingly, O Lord our God, speedily free us from all distress.
>
> And let us not, O Lord our God, find ourselves in need of gifts from flesh and blood, or of a loan from anyone save from Thy full, generous, abundant, wide-open hand; so we may never be humiliated, or put to shame.
>
> O rebuild Jerusalem, the holy city, speedily in our day. Blessed art Thou, Lord, who in mercy will rebuild Jerusalem. Amen.

The climax refers to Jerusalem, Zion, David, the Messiah, the Temple—where God was sustained in times past; then to dependence on God alone, not on mortals; and to the rebuilding of Jerusalem. All of these closely related symbols invoke the single consideration of time at its end: the coming of the Messiah and the conclusion of history as we now know it. The opening psalms have prepared us for this appeal to the endtime: exile on weekdays, return to Zion on Sabbaths and holy days.

The fourth paragraph of the Grace after Meals returns us to the point where we began—thanks for lunch:

> Blessed art Thou, Lord our God, King of the Universe, Thou God, who are our Father, our powerful king, our creator and redeemer, who made us, our holy one, the holy one of Jacob, our shepherd, shepherd of Israel, the good king, who visits His goodness upon all; for every single day He has brought good, He does bring good, He will bring good upon us; He has rewarded us, does reward, and will always reward us, with grace, mercy and compassion, amplitude, deliverance and prosperity, blessing and salvation, comfort, and a living, sustenance, pity and peace, and all good—let us not want any manner of good whatever.

Of the four paragraphs of the Grace after Meals, the first and the fourth, which multiply prayers for future grace alongside thanks for goodness now received, begin and end in the here and now. The two in the middle invoke a different being altogether.

I have eaten an ordinary meal in the here and now. I invoke the entire history of Israel, refer to the holy land and food produced there, and so transform a cheese sandwich into a foretaste of eternity in the land of God's choosing for me. I eat anywhere, nowhere in particular, but am located by the sacred words in some one place. Eating is turned paradoxically into a locative experience, identifying my right place with somewhere else than where I now am. Where I eat has no bearing, any more than has what I eat, on what has really happened. For I was hungry and now am satisfied; and in that experience, in my very natural and fleshly body, I have lived out the life of time and eternity. The transformation of the ordinary into the unusual effected by the rehearsal of holy land and sacred history moves present time and perceived space from now to then. In seeing matters in this way, Judaism perceives things as other than they are. And that mode of thought, we shall see time and again, characterizes the Judaic experience of the everyday.

To conclude: What has happened at the meal is simple. The diner was hungry and ate—a commonplace, entirely secular action. But the experience of hunger and of eating is turned, through the medium of words, into an encounter with another world of meaning altogether. The rite, an act of thought and imagination, transforms time and space, moving us from nowhere in particular to a particular place, changing me and all of us from the here and the now into the social entity of the past and the future then. The words we say change the world of the *I* by telling me I am more than in the here and now and live more than in the perceived present, because I am more than a mere *I* but part of a larger *we*—all because of words I say when I eat lunch.

THE PASSOVER SEDER

The single most widely practiced rite of Judaism in North America requires family and friends to sit down for supper. The meal consumed with ceremony turns people into something other than what they think they are, and puts them down square in the path of an onrushing history. In the presence of symbols both visual and verbal, in the formation of family and friends into an Israel redeemed from Egypt, people become something else—a wonder worked by words.

At the festival of Passover, or *Pessah*, which coincides with the first full moon after the vernal equinox, Jewish families gather around their tables for a holy meal. There—speaking in very general terms— they retell the story of the exodus from Egypt in times long past. With unleavened bread and sanctified wine, they celebrate the liberation of slaves from Pharaoh's bondage. At this rite, a single formula captures the moment—here we begin, if we are to understand how the *we* of the family becomes the *we* of Israel, how the eternal and perpetual coming of spring is made to mark a singular moment, a one-time act on the stage in the unfolding of linear time:

> For ever after, in every generation, *every Israelite must think of himself or herself as having gone forth from Egypt.* (italics added)

A curious passage indeed! It is one thing to tell Jews to think of themselves in one way, rather than in some other. It is quite a different thing to explain why Jews respond to the demand—and they do respond.

What, for nearly all Jews all over the world, makes plausible the statement "*We* went forth . . ."? And why do people sit down for supper and announce, "It was not only our forefathers that the Holy

One, blessed be He, redeemed. *Us, too, the living,* He redeemed together with them"? I cannot imagine a less plausible statement, a more compelling invitation to derision and disbelief. We were not there. Pharaoh has been dead for quite some time. Egypt languishes in the rubbish heap of history. Wherein the enchantment? Why us? Why here? Why now? The answer derives from the power, within Judaism, through enchantment to transform the here and now into an intimation of the wholly other. In seeing the everyday as metaphor, we perceive that deeper layer of meaning that permits us to treat as obvious and self-evident the transforming power of comparison, of simile applied to oneself: Let's pretend, and What if? and Why not?

When things are not the way they seem, it is because we have already concluded that beyond the here and now there must be a something else. That is how metaphor does its work. And this enchantment can, I think, occur only because the family and friends now assembled have in mind and imagination already transformed themselves. Then they can be told to change and instructed in their roles. If we review the provocative themes of the script for the drama, we may pick out those components of the everyday that are subjected to transformation.

One theme stands out, which I may state in this way: we, here and now, are really living then and there. So, for example:

> *We* were slaves of Pharaoh in Egypt and the Lord our God brought us forth from there with a mighty hand and an outstretched arm. And if the Holy One, blessed be He, had not brought our fathers forth from Egypt, then we and our descendants would still be slaves to Pharaoh in Egypt. And so, even if all of us were full of wisdom, understanding, sages and well informed in the Torah, we should still be obligated to repeat again the story of the exodus from Egypt; and whoever treats as an important matter the story of the exodus from Egypt is praiseworthy.

And again:

> This is the bread of affliction which our ancestors ate in the land of Egypt. Let all who are hungry come and eat with us, let all who are needy come and celebrate the Passover with us. This

year here, next year in the land of Israel; this year slave, next year free people.

And yet a third statement:

> This is the promise which has stood by our forefathers and stands by us. For neither once, nor twice, nor three times was our destruction planned; in every generation they rise against us, and in every generation God delivers us from their hands into freedom, out of anguish into joy, out of mourning into festivity, out of darkness into light, out of bondage into redemption.

Enchantment is not subtle. As though the implicit premise were not clear, let us revert to the point at which we began and hear it stated in so many words:

> For ever after, in every generation, *every Israelite must think of himself or herself as having gone forth from Egypt.* For we read in the Torah: "In that day thou shalt teach thy son, saying: All this is because of what God did for me when I went forth from Egypt." It was not only our forefathers that the Holy One, blessed be He, redeemed; us too, the living, He redeemed together with them, as we learn from the verse in the Torah: "And He brought us out from thence, so that He might bring us home, and give us the land which He pledged to our forefathers." (italics added)

There is nothing subtle about rites of transformation. We are never left in doubt about *who* we are now supposed to be, or *where*, or *when*, or *why*.

If the Passover seder banquet enchants the everyday experience of people under pressure, transforming what is personal and private into what is public and shared, nothing in the unfolding of the seder rite focuses upon that one message. As with *Kol Nidre* ("All vows . . ."; a formula releasing worshipers from vows made to God in the past year), in which the words speak of one thing, the music of something else, so here the words speak of many things, only sometimes coming to the main point. But the main point remains present throughout, because that one theme, the exodus of Israel from Egypt, remains at the fore. The word *seder* means "order," and the sense is that a

sequence of actions takes place as prescribed. Here is the order of the
seder. The word *matzoh* refers to unleavened bread. What we shall see
is a disjuncture between words and deeds, between declarations and
inner sentiments. To make this clear I have divided the order into the
gestures, on the one side; the recitation of words, indented and in
italics, on the other:

Deeds
 words
first washing of the hands
eating of the parsley
breaking of the middle cake of matzoh
 recital of the narrative (Haggadah)
second washing of the hands
 grace for bread
breaking and dividing up of topmost piece of matzoh
eating of bitter herb dipped in *charoset* (chopped nuts, wine)
eating of bitter herb with matzoh
meal
eating of the *afikomon* (a piece of matzoh eaten to mark the end
 of the meal)
 Grace after Meals
 Hallel (recitation of Pss. 113–18)
 closing prayer

The curious picture emerges of two quite separate occasions,
running side by side but not meeting. Were we to describe the banquet on the basis of this catalogue, we should expect a recitation
much engaged by attention to hand washing, the eating of parsley,
the breaking and disposition of pieces of unleavened bread—in all,
raising and lowering, breaking and hiding and eating, pieces of matzoh. We should then be unprepared for the reality of the seder rite,
which involves an enormous flow of words. Not only so, but the
introit of the rite focuses upon the ritual aspect of the meal, not on
the narrative:

Why has this night been made different from all other nights?
On all other nights we eat bread whether leavened or unleavened, on this night only unleavened; on all other nights we eat
all kinds of herbs, on this night only bitter ones; on all other

nights we do not dip herbs even once; on this night, twice; on all other nights we sit at the table either sitting or reclining, on this night we all recline.

In point of fact, none of these questions, addressed by the youngest present to the presiding officer, is ever answered. Instead we get the following (I italicize the operative words):

We were slaves of Pharaoh in Egypt; and the Lord our God brought us forth from there with a mighty hand and an outstretched arm. And if the Holy One, blessed be He, had not brought our fathers forth from Egypt, then surely we, and our children, and our children's children, would be enslaved to Pharaoh in Egypt. *And so, even if all of us were full of wisdom and understanding, well along in years and deeply versed in the tradition, we should still be bidden to repeat once more the story of the exodus from Egypt; and he who delights to dwell on the liberation is one to be praised.*

Now we shift from the symbols present to the occasion commemorated and celebrated; and a considerable "narrative" makes us forget the pillow and the parsley and the matzoh and remember Pharaoh and Egypt. This narrative is composed of bits and pieces which all together do not flow together at all, a citation and exegesis of some verses of Scripture, some games, prayers, snatches of stories, hymns. Made up of incoherent liturgies, joining together varieties of essentially unrelated material, the so-called narrative does tell this story, and I take it to form the centerpiece of the whole:

Long ago our ancestors were idol-worshipers but now the Holy One has drawn us to his service. So we read in the Torah: And Joshua said to all the people, "Thus says the Lord, God of Israel: From time immemorial your fathers lived beyond the river Euphrates, even to Terah, father of Abraham and of Nahor, and they worshiped idols. And I took your father Abraham from beyond the river and guided his footsteps throughout the land of Canaan. I multiplied his offspring and gave him Isaac. To Isaac I gave Jacob and Esau. And I set apart Mount Seir as the inheritance of Esau, while Jacob and his sons went down to Egypt."

I remind you where we are: sitting around a table; family and friends at a banquet. The advent of our idol-worshiping ancestors hardly pertains to the occasion. All of it is deeply relevant to those present, for it says who they (really) are, and for whom they really stand. They in the here and now stand for "our ancestors"—Abraham, Isaac, and Jacob. That is the first part.

Here is the second, and more important, part (the key words are italicized):

> Blessed is *he who keeps his promise to Israel, for the Holy One set a term to our bondage,* fulfilling the word which he gave our father Abraham in the covenant made between the divided sacrifice: Know beyond a doubt that your offspring will be *strangers in a land that is not theirs,* four hundred years they shall serve and suffer. But in the end I shall pronounce judgment on the oppressor people and your offspring shall go forth with great wealth.

We are dealing with people who respond to the description of their circumstance here: strangers in a land that is not theirs, indeed! That is bad sociology—and, for the free Jews of the Western democracies, worse politics. But in here, in the heart, it not only rings true; it is true: *strangers in a land that is not theirs,* not because the neighbors are enemies, but because the Jews are different from the neighbors, and that suffices. Canada and America are as much theirs as anyone else's, but still: *strangers in a land that is not theirs.* They could, of course, migrate to a land that *is* theirs (within its civil myth)—namely, the State of Israel. But they do not—and yet they say, "This year slaves here, next year free in Jerusalem." There is a jarring unreality to the entire drama. Through the natural eye, one sees ordinary folk, not much different from their neighbors in dress, language, or aspirations. The words they speak do not describe reality, and are not meant to. When Jews say of themselves, "We were the slaves of Pharaoh in Egypt," they know they never felt the lash; but through the eye of faith, that is just what they have done. It is *their* liberation, not merely that of long-dead forebears, they now celebrate.

Here lies the power of the Passover banquet rite to transform ordinary existence into an account of something beyond. Ordinary existence imposes its tensions. Jews are different from Gentiles, and thus are defined as Jews. But now, in the transformation at hand, to be a Jew means to be a slave who has been liberated by God. To be Israel means to give eternal thanks for God's deliverance. And that deliverance is not at a single moment in historical time. Transformed into a permanent feature of reality, it is made myth: that story of deep truth that comes true in every generation and is always celebrated. Here again, events of natural, ordinary life are transformed through myth into paradigmatic, eternal, and ever-recurrent sacred moments. In terms I have used before, the everyday is treated as paradigm and metaphor. Jews think of themselves as having gone forth from Egypt, and Scripture so instructs them. God did not redeem the dead generation of the exodus alone, but the living, too—especially the living. Thus, the family states:

> Again and again, in double and redoubled measure, are we beholden to God the All-Present: that He freed us from the Egyptians and wrought His judgment on them; that He sentenced all their idols and slaughtered all their first-born; that He gave their treasure to us and split the Red Sea for us; that He led us through it dry-shod and drowned the tyrants in it; that He helped us through the desert and fed us with the manna; that He gave the Sabbath to us and brought us to Mount Sinai; that He gave the Torah to us and brought us to our homeland—there to build the Temple for us, for atonement of our sins.

Israel was born in historical times. Historians, biblical scholars, and archeologists have much to say about that event. But to the classical Jew, their findings, while interesting, have little bearing on the meaning of reality. The redemptive promise that stood by the forefathers and "stands by us" is not a mundane historical event but a mythic interpretation of historical, natural events. Oppression, homelessness, extermination—like salvation, homecoming, renaissance—are this-worldly and profane, supplying headlines for newspapers. The myth that a Jew must think of himself or herself as having gone forth from Egypt, and as being redeemed by God, renders ordinary experience into a moment of celebration. If "us, too, the living, He [has] redeemed," then the observer witnesses no longer only historical people in historical time, but an eternal return to sacred time.

2

Judaism
in the Family:
Through the Cycle of Life

THE RITE OF CIRCUMCISION

The words of enchantment in the case of Judaism transform the birth of the child from a private and personal happening in the natural family to a public and momentous event in the life of the supernatural family of Israel on earth and of God in heaven. That rite of enchantment frames a deed and the words said at its doing, and in attendance are not only family and friends of the here and now but one who was present at the original deed. Specifically, in the case of a boy child, a minor surgical rite, of dubious medical value, becomes the mark of the renewal of the agreement between God and Israel, the covenant carved into the flesh of the penis of every Jewish male— and nothing less. The beginning of a new life renews the rule that governs Israel's relationship to God. So the private joy is reworked through words of enchantment—once more, sanctification—and so transformed into renewal of the community of Israel and God.

Once more, we are not only in the here and now: we are in another time, another place. We not only perform the ritual—cutting the flesh, manipulating the blood, drinking the wine—we translate the deeds into other dimensions altogether. And at issue, above all, is not the *I* but the *we*, the transformation radical beyond all other changes.

The rite of passage of circumcision in Judaism involves, therefore, a most personal moment, the birth of a child because of the private sexual relation of the mother and the father and the personal travail of the mother. That most individual occasion, the beginning of a person's life, links in a concrete way to specific moments and personalities in the public and supernatural life of Israel. On a Jewish son is performed a surgical operation in the name of the faith, by cutting off the foreskin of the penis and calling the rite *berit milah*: the covenant (*berit*) effected through the rite of circumcision (*milah*). Berit milah seals with the blood of the infant son the contract between Israel and God, generation by generation, son by son.

Circumcision must take place on the eighth day after birth, normally in the presence of a quorum of ten adult males. Commonly, it is done in the home, not in the hospital; and crowded into a few rooms will be relatives and friends. There is nothing private or merely surgical about the operation. The contemporary practice of having a surgical operation in no way carries out the rite of circumcision. For what changes the matter is not only circumstance. It is the formula, the words of blessing that form the counterpart to the Grace after Meals, the medium of enchantment that transforms the birth of a child to an individual couple into an event heavy with meaning: a metaphor for something more, for something that transcends.

But that deep significance is psychologically quite natural. For no moment in the passage of life from birth to death so touches a parent as does the birth of a child. Questions of past and future weigh heavily on the present. The parent looks backward, toward family perhaps for a time—as young people find expedient—neglected, and directs hopes forward, toward a future of perfection to be realized by the child, a perfection unattained by the parents themselves and likely unattainable by any mortal: so great is the power of dreaming. Fathers and mothers now become grandparents; siblings, uncles and aunts: a new social entity takes shape around the new person. When, on such an occasion, Judaism intervenes, exhausted mother and happy, confused father will do pretty much whatever they are told in the name of a blessing for the child—if only *mazel tov* (under a good star).

There are four aspects by which the operation is turned into a rite. When the rite begins, the assembly and the mohel together recite the following:

> The Lord spoke to Moses saying, Phineas, son of Eleazar, son of Aaron, the priest, has turned my wrath from the Israelites by displaying among them his passion for me, so that I did not wipe

out the Israelite people in my passion. Say therefore I grant him my covenant of peace.

Commenting on this passage, Lifsa Schachter, a Jewish writer, states, "Phineas is identified with zealously opposing the . . . sins of sexual licentiousness and idolatry. He is best known for an event which occurred when the Israelites, whoring with Moabite women in the desert, were drawn to the worship of Baal-Peor. . . . Phineas leaped into the fray and through an act of double murder . . . quieted God's terrible wrath."

Second, in looking around the room where the rite takes place, we notice that a chair is set called the "chair of Elijah": thus, the rite takes place in the presence of a chair for Elijah, the prophet. The newborn son is set on that chair, and the congregation says, "This is the chair of Elijah, of blessed memory." Elijah, having complained to God that Israel neglected the covenant (1 Kings 19:10–14), comes to bear witness that Israel observes the covenant of circumcision. Then, before the surgical operation, a blessing is said. Third, after the operation, a blessing is said over a cup of wine.

Let me take up each of these matters and explore their meaning. To understand the invocation of Elijah, for whom we set a chair, we first recall the pertinent biblical passage:

Suddenly the word of the Lord came to him: "Why are you here, Elijah?"

"Because of my great zeal for the Lord the God of hosts," he said. "The people of Israel have forsaken your covenant, torn down your altars, and put your prophets to death with the sword. I alone am left, and they seek to take my life."

The answer came: "Go and stand on the mount before the Lord."

For the Lord was passing by: a great and strong wind came rending mountains and shattering rocks before him, but the Lord was not in the wind; and after the wind there was an earthquake, but the Lord was not in the earthquake; and after the earthquake fire; but the Lord was not in the fire; and after the fire a still small voice.

When Elijah heard it, he muffled his face in his cloak and

went out and stood at the entrance of the cave. Then there came a voice: "Why are you here, Elijah?"

"Because of my great zeal for the Lord God of hosts," he said. "The people of Israel have forsaken your covenant, torn down your altars, and put your prophets to death with the sword. I alone am left, and they seek to take my life." (1 Kings 19:10–14)

This passage stands behind the story told in a medieval document, *Pirqe Rabbi Eliezer,* that Elijah attends the rite of circumcision of every Jewish baby boy:

The Israelites were wont to circumcise until they were divided into two kingdoms. The kingdom of Ephraim cast off from themselves the covenant of circumcision. Elijah, may he be remembered for good, arose and was zealous with a mighty passion, and he adjured the heavens to send down neither dew nor rain upon the earth. Jezebel heard about it and sought to slay him.

Elijah arose and prayed before the Holy One, blessed be he. The Holy One, blessed be he, said to him, *"Are you better than your fathers* (1 Kings 19:4)? Esau sought to slay Jacob, but he fled before him, as it is said, *And Jacob fled into the field of Aram* (Hosea 12:12).

"Pharaoh sought to slay Moses, who fled before him and he was saved, as it is said, *Now when Pharaoh heard this thing, he sought to slay Moses. And Moses fled from the face of Pharaoh* (Ezek. 2:15).

"Saul sought to slay David, who fled before him and was saved, as it is said, *If you save not your life tonight, tomorrow you will be killed"* (1 Sam. 19:11).

Another text says, *And David fled and escaped* (1 Sam. 19:18). Learn that everyone who flees is sad.

Elijah, may he be remembered for good, arose and fled from the land of Israel, and he betook himself to Mount Horeb, as it is said, *and he arose and ate and drank* (1 Kings 19:8).

Then the Holy One, blessed be he, was revealed to him and said to him, "What are you doing here, Elijah?"

He answered him saying, "I have been very zealous."

The Holy One, blessed be he, said to him, "You are always zealous. You were zealous in Shittim on account of the immorality. For it is said, *Phineas, the son of Eleazar, the son of Aaron the priest, turned my wrath away from the children of Israel, in that he was zealous with my zeal among them* (Num. 25:11).

"Here you are also zealous, By your life! They shall not observe the covenant of circumcision until you see it done with your own eyes."

Hence the sages have instituted the custom that people should have a seat of honor for the messenger of the covenant, for Elijah, may he be remembered for good, is called the messenger of the covenant, as it is said, *And the messenger of the covenant, whom you delight in, behold he comes* (Mal. 3:1).

So, too, the "messenger of the covenant" is the prophet Elijah, and he is present whenever a Jewish son enters the *covenant* of Abraham, which is circumcision. God ordered Elijah to come to every circumcision so as to witness the loyalty of the Jews to the covenant. Elijah, then, serves as the guardian for the newborn, just as he raised the child of the widow from the dead (1 Kings 17:17–24). Along these same lines, as the seder table of Passover, a cup of wine is poured for Elijah, and the door is opened for Elijah to join in the rite. Setting a seat for Elijah serves to invoke the presence of the guardian of the newborn and the zealous advocate of the rite of the circumcision of the covenant. Thus, celebrating with the family of the newborn are not "all Israel" in general, but a specific personage indeed. The gesture of setting the chair silently sets the stage for an event in the life of the family not of the child alone but of all Israel. The chair of Elijah, filled by the one who holds the child, sets the newborn baby into Elijah's lap. The enchantment extends through the furnishing of the room; what is not ordinarily present is introduced, and that makes all the difference.

We move, third, from gesture to formula, for a blessing is said after the rite itself. That is, the mohel takes the knife and cuts the foreskin, and then these words are said by the father:

Praised are You . . . who sanctified us with Your commandments and commanded us to bring the son into the covenant of Abraham our father.

The explicit invocation of Abraham's covenant turns the concrete action in the here and now into a simile of the paradigm and archetype: I circumcise my son just as Abraham circumcised Isaac at eight days, and Ishmael. What I do is like what Abraham did. Things are more than what they seem. Then I am a father, like Abraham, and—more to the point—my fatherhood is like Abraham's.

The operation done, the wine is blessed, introducing yet a further occasion of enchantment:

> Praised are You, Lord our God, who sanctified the beloved from the womb and set a statute into his very flesh, and his parts sealed with the sign of the holy covenant. On this account, Living God, our portion and rock, save the beloved of our flesh from destruction, for the sake of his covenant placed in our flesh. Blessed are You . . . who makes the covenant.

The covenant is not a generality; it is specific, concrete, fleshly. It is, moreover, meant to accomplish a specific goal—as all religion means to attain concrete purposes—and that is to secure a place for the child, a blessing for the child. By virtue of the rite, the child enters the covenant: he joins that unseen "Israel" that through blood enters an agreement with God. Then the blessing of the covenant is owing to the child. For covenants or contracts cut both ways.

After the father has recited the blessing—"who has sanctified us by his commandments and has commanded us to induct him into the covenant of our father, Abraham"—the community of ten males responds: "Just as he has entered the covenant, so may he be introduced to Torah, the *huppah* [marriage canopy] and good deeds."

Schachter interprets those "others" who are present as follows:

> In the presence of Elijah . . . *Torah*—as against idolatry; in the presence of Phineas . . . *huppah*, as against sexual licentiousness; in the presence of Abraham . . . to *good deeds: For I have singled him out that he may instruct his children and his posterity to keep the way of the Lord by doing what is just and right.* (Gen. 18:18)

THE BAR OR BAT MITZVAH

The single most important rite in contemporary North American Judaism is the celebration of puberty—for boys, among the Orthodox;

for boys and girls, among Conservative, Reform, and Reconstructionist Jews, which is to say nearly all Jews. Upon reaching the age of puberty (for males, thirteen; for females, twelve or thirteen), a child is called for the first time to the Torah—an event known as *bar* or *bat mitzvah* for male or female, respectively. *Bar* means "son," and *bat*, "daughter," with the sense of being subject to; and *mitzvah* means "commandment."

The matter is very simple. The young person is called to the Torah, recites the blessing required prior to the public proclamation of a passage of the Torah, and reads that passage (or stands as it is read). When the Torah lection of the week has been read, the congregation proceeds to a passage of the prophets. The young person reads that passage for the congregation. That is the rite—no rite at all.

It is no rite simply because nothing is done on this occasion that is not done by others on the same occasion. The young person is treated no differently from others on this Sabbath, or last week, or next week. He or she simply assumes a place within the congregation of adult Jews, is counted for a quorum, and is expected to carry out the religious duties that pertain. The young person is not asked to imagine himself or herself in some mythic state or setting, such as Eden or Sinai or the Jerusalem of the Messiah's time. The family of the young person does not find itself compared to "all Israel," and no stories are told about how the young person and the family reenact a mythic event such as the exodus from Egypt. No one is commanded to see himself or herself as if this morning he or she was born, crossed the Red Sea, entered the Promised Land, or did any of those other things that the dual Torah invokes on enchanted occasions of personal transformation.

It is, on the whole, a rather bloodless and impersonal transaction, because what changes is merely status in respect to responsibility. Becoming a bar mitzvah or a bat mitzvah means that one is subject to the requirement of carrying out religious deeds, that one bears responsibility for himself or herself. That simple transaction— coming for the first time as an adult to assume the rights and responsibilities of maturity—forms the single most powerful occasion in the life of the maturing young Jew and his or her family. It is prepared for, celebrated elaborately, looked back upon as a highlight of life. And, as is clear, it is a moment left without enchantment, just as is death (a point I shall discuss shortly).

Only upon achieving intelligence and self-consciousness, normally at puberty, is a Jew expected to accept the full privilege of mitzvah (commandment) and to regard himself or herself as *commanded* by God. But that sense of "being commanded" is impersonal and not imposed by the invocation of any myth. The transaction is neutral: it involves affirmation and assent, confirmation and commitment. But there is no bower, no Eden, no family at table reading a received rite. Judaism perceives the commandments as expressions of one's acceptance of the yoke of the kingdom of heaven and submission to God's will. That acceptance cannot be coerced, but requires thoughtful and complete affirmation. The bar or bat mitzvah is thus assuming for the first time full responsibility before God to keep the commandments. The calling of the young Jew to the Torah and the conferring upon him or her of the rights of a full member of the community ratify what has taken place but effect neither a change in status of the individual nor, even less, a significant alteration in the condition of the community.

THE MARRIAGE CEREMONY

No greater joy marks life than the beginning of a marriage, the moment of perfect illusion. The bride plans to change the groom; the groom hopes the bride will never change: grand illusion. We say words that legitimate what aforetime was not. That change in a this-worldly sense is merely legal, a change in personal status and consequent property rights and obligations. But, in the enchantment of Judaism, the words transform not only the relationship in law but also the participants (in our Western context) in love. In this way, as in the imaginative rereading of the birth of a boy baby, the *we* of you and I becomes the *us* of the social entity. But what *us* and which entity?

Entry into the imaginative world created by the rite of marriage is made easy by the human condition. For, just as the Grace after Meals turns a natural and common experience into the enactment and celebration of another place and time and world altogether, so does the rite of the huppah turn one thing into something else. The words said after a meal affect the personal and merely physical, while those that change the public union of two private persons call upon encompassing eternity. Yet, in the case of the Grace, it is from hunger to satisfaction, from exile to redemption; and in the case of the wedding, it is from the here and the now to Eden past and Zion redeemed at the end of time—perfection to perfection. Still, the experience that all of us have, now changed into a metaphor for something other, is different from the transformation of hunger and satisfaction into the paradigm of the human condition of Israel's suffering and solace.

The enchantment transforms the space, the time, the action, and the community of the *I* of the groom and the *I* of the bride. The space is contained by the huppah (marriage canopy or bower), which (rightly done) is constructed under the open sky: a contained space of heaven representing heaven. The time? It is now in the beginning. When else could it be? The action, then, invokes creation, the making of a new Eden. The community of the two *I's* becoming one *we* is the couple changed into the paradigm of humanity, beginning with Adam and Eve. Stripped down to essentials, the union of woman and man becomes the beginning of a new creation, the woman becoming Eve; the man, Adam. In this way is realized the prophecy of the snake in Eden, as explained by the great medieval Bible interpreter Rashi (1040–1105). When the snake says, "But God knows that as soon as you eat of it, your eyes will be opened and you will be like God" (Gen. 3:5), the meaning, according to Rashi, is that you will become "creators of worlds." At the marriage rite a new world begins: a family, a social entity, humanity at the beginning of new creation of life.

The rite comes to a climax in the Seven Blessings (*sheva berakhot*). But it unfolds in stages, beginning before the couple reaches the marriage canopy and ending long afterward. Seen in sequence, the rite follows this pattern: (1) the bride's veil is put in place by the groom; (2) the ketubah (marriage contract) is witnessed; (3) under the huppah, erusin (betrothal); (4) under the huppah, nissuin (marriage).

If we walk through the rite, stopping at its principal stages, we come first to the touching moment when the groom places the veil over the bride's face, prior to entering under the marriage canopy, and makes the following statement to her:

> May you, our sister, be fruitful and prosper. May God make you as Sarah, Rebecca, Rachel, and Leah. May the Lord bless

you and keep you. May the Lord show you favor and be gracious to you. May the Lord show you kindness and grant you peace.

The blessing of the groom for the bride invokes the matriarchs of Israel—a detail we need not find surprising. Rachel makes her appearance in the Seven Blessings; and as soon as we speak of Abraham, we think of Sarah; so, too, Isaac and Rebecca, Jacob and Leah and Rachel.

In focusing upon the drama, we should not lose sight of the occasion. The wedding takes place in the here and now; and in Judaism, we do not lose sight of practical considerations. The bride is not only Eve, she is also a woman who bears responsibility to her husband; and the groom, Adam, is also going to go back to work next week. The task of rite is not only to transform but also to underline reality. In the case of the huppah, the rite of marriage, a legal transaction goes forward, the formation of a social entity, a family, in which the rights and obligations of each party have to reach the expression and guarantee of a contract. In the case of the marriage ceremony, a marriage contract, a ketubah, is appropriately signed and delivered from the groom to the bride's possession, and is the first stage in the process. A précis of the ketubah follows:

> This ketubah witnesses before God and man that on the _____ day of the week, the _____ of the month _____, in the year 57____, the holy covenant of marriage was entered between bridegroom and his bride, at _____. Duly conscious of the solemn obligation of marriage the bridegroom made the following declaration to his bride: "Be consecrated to me as my wife according to the laws and traditions of Moses and Israel. I will love, honor and cherish you; I will protect and support you; and I will faithfully care for your needs, as prescribed by Jewish law and tradition." And the bride made the following declaration to the groom: "In accepting the wedding ring I pledge you all my love and devotion and I take upon myself the fulfillment of all the duties incumbent upon a Jewish wife."

The Aramaic language of the ketubah specifies the legal standing of the husband's obligation to the wife. In order to pay what is owing to her should he divorce her, or in order to provide for her if he dies before she does, the husband pledges even the shirt on his back. No one is playing games.

To understand the next stage in the rite—between the signing of witnesses on the ketubah and the recitation of the Seven Blessings—we have to call to mind the law of Judaism. That law knows a two-stage process: one called erusin; the other, nissuin. We may roughly represent these stages as betrothal, then marriage. The union of a couple takes place in two stages: erusin, in which the woman is sanctified, or designated as holy, to a particular man; and nissuin, in which the actual union is consecrated through the Seven Blessings. In ancient times, these stages took place in an interval of as much as a full year, with the rite of designation separated from the consummation by twelve months. But, in our own day, the wedding rite encompasses both.

Erusin is carried out under the marriage canopy as bride and groom drink of a cup of wine and say this blessing:

> Blessed are You, our God, King of the world, who creates the fruit of the vine.
>
> Blessed are You, Lord our God, King of the world, who has sanctified us by his commandments and commanded us concerning proper sexual relations, forbidding to us betrothed women but permitting to us married women through the rites of the huppah and sanctification. Blessed are You, Lord, who sanctifies his people Israel through the marriage canopy and the rite of sanctification.

Then the bridegroom gives a ring to the bride, with this formula:

> Behold you are sanctified to me by this ring in accord with the tradition of Moses and Israel.

That concludes the chapter of the rite known as erusin, which we may translate, with less than exact accuracy, as betrothal.

Then come the Seven Blessings. The climax of the rite of Adam and Eve, of you and me as Israel in Jerusalem beyond time, comes in the recitation of Seven Blessings (*sheva berakhot*) over a cup of wine. Here is the first of those seven transforming statements of sanctification, which the rabbi or the cantor says over a cup of wine:

Praised are You, O Lord our God, King of the universe, Creator of the fruit of the vine.

The rite takes place over the cup of wine; the enchantment begins by turning the wine into something else than what it has been.

Then comes the first action, invoking through words the world of Eden:

Praised are You, O Lord our God, King of the universe, who created all things for your glory.

Praised are You, O Lord our God, King of the universe, Creator of Adam.

Praised are You, O Lord our God, King of the universe, who created man and woman in his image, fashioning woman from man as his mate, that together they might perpetuate life. Praised are You, O Lord, Creator of man.

In the second, third, and fourth blessings, the sequence of three is perfectly realized: first, creation of all things; then, creation of man; then creation of man and woman in God's image. These words invoke a world for which the occasion at hand serves as metaphor. "We now are like them then"—this is what is at stake.

Israel's history begins with creation—first, the creation of the vine, symbol of the natural world. Creation is for God's glory. All things speak to nature, to the physical as much as the spiritual, for all things were made by God. In Hebrew, the third blessing ends with, "who formed the *Adam*." All things glorify God; above all creation is Adam. The theme of ancient paradise is introduced by the simple choice of the word *Adam*, heavy with meaning. The myth of human-kind's creation is rehearsed: man and woman are in God's image, together complete and whole, creators of life, "like God." Woman was fashioned from man together with him to perpetuate life. And, again, "blessed is the creator of Adam." We have moved, therefore, from the natural world to the archetypical realm of paradise. Before us we see not merely a man and a woman, but Adam and Eve.

The enchantment works its wonder by identifying the moment at hand, by telling us what we are like—that is, what is really happening. And under the circumstances formed by that mode of metaphorical thought, the reality that generates meaning is the *out there* of "man and woman in His image," Eden, creation. The *in here*—bride and groom wondering whether this is really true—then matches the *out there*. The world is truly a stage; the men and women, truly players. But here, in the fifth blessing, one actor takes two roles at once:

> May Zion rejoice as her children are restored to her in joy. Praised are You, O Lord, who causes Zion to rejoice at her children's return.

A jarring intrusion: Zion comes uninvited. No one mentioned her. But, as we saw in the Grace after Meals ("If I forget you, O Jerusalem") and given the standing of Zion as metaphor simultaneously for the resolution of Israel's exile and the human condition of suffering, who can find surprising the entry of this new character, this persona?

This Adam and this Eve also are Israel, children of Zion the mother, as expressed in the fifth blessing. Zion lies in ruins, her children scattered. Adam and Eve cannot celebrate together without thought to the condition of the mother, Jerusalem. The children will one day come home. The mood is hopeful yet sad, as it was meant to be, for archaic Israel mourns as it rejoices and rejoices as it mourns. Quickly then, back to the happy occasion, for we do not let mourning lead to melancholy. "Grant perfect joy to the loving companions," for they are creators of a new line in mankind—the new Adam, the new Eve—and of their home: May it be the garden of Eden. And if joy is there, then "praised are you for the joy of bride and groom."

The joy of the moment gives a foretaste of the joy of restoration, redemption, return. Now the two roles become one in that same joy: first Adam and Eve, groom and bride; Eden, then, the marriage canopy now:

> Grant perfect joy to these loving companions, as You did to the first man and woman in the Garden of Eden. Praised are You, O Lord, who grants the joy of bride and groom.

That same joy comes in the metaphors of Zion the bride and Israel the groom.

In the seventh blessing, the joy is not in two but in three masks: Eden then; marriage party now; and Zion in the coming age:

Praised are You, O Lord our God, King of the universe, who created joy and gladness, bride and groom, mirth, song, delight and rejoicing, love and harmony, peace and companionship. O Lord our God, may there ever *be heard in the cities of Judah and in the streets of Jerusalem voices of joy and gladness, voices of bride and groom, the jubilant voices of those joined in marriage under the bridal canopy, the voices of young people feasting and singing.*

Here the words in italics allude to the vision of Jeremiah, when all seemed lost, that Jerusalem, about to fall and lose its people, will one day ring with the shouts not of the slaughtered and the enslaved but of the returned and the redeemed. Hence, this concluding blessing returns to the theme of Jerusalem, evoking the tragic hour of Jerusalem's first destruction. When everyone had given up hope, supposing with the end of Jerusalem had come the end of time, only Jeremiah counseled renewed hope. With the enemy at the gate, he sang of coming gladness:

Thus says the Lord:
In this place of which you say, "It is a waste, without man or beast," in the cities of Judah and the streets of Jerusalem that are desolate, without man or inhabitant or beast,
There shall be heard again the voice of mirth and the voice of gladness, the voice of the bridegroom and the voice of the bride, the voice of those who sing as they bring thank-offerings to the house of the Lord. . . .
For I shall restore the fortunes of the land as at first, says the Lord. (Jer. 33:10–11)

The closing blessing is not merely a literary artifice or a learned allusion to the ancient prophet. It defines the exultant, jubilant climax of this acted-out myth: Just as here and now there stand before us Adam and Eve, so here and now in this wedding, the olden sorrow having been rehearsed, we listen to the voice of gladness that is coming. The joy of this new creation prefigures the joy of the Messiah's coming, hope for which is very present in this hour. And when he comes, the joy then will echo the joy of bride and groom before us. Zion the bride, Israel the groom, united now as they will be reunited by the compassionate God—these stand under the marriage canopy.

But enchantment is just that. In the end, we are who we are: real man, real woman, and the bridal canopy, which stands for heaven and for Eden, is a prayer shawl stretched on four poles. Groom and bride rejoice not as metaphor but as fact. Then (in the received tradition), immediately leaving the canopy, they head for bed, then for celebration. In the innocent world in which sexual relations commence after the marriage, a rite known as *yihud*, solitary converse of bride and groom all by themselves for the first time, is provided for, and to this the conclusion to the final blessing refers:

> Praised are You, O Lord, who causes the groom to rejoice with his bride.

These Seven Blessings say nothing of private people and of their anonymous falling in love. Nor do they speak of the community of Israel, as one might expect on a public occasion. Lover and beloved rather are transformed from natural to mythical figures. The blessings speak of archetypical Israel, represented here and now by the bride and groom. All becomes credible not by what is said but by what is felt: that joy, that sense of witness to what we ourselves experience are the two ingredients that transform. The natural events of human life—here, the marriage of ordinary folk—are by myth heightened into a reenactment of Israel's life as a people. In marriage, individuals stand in the place of mythic figures, yet remain, after all, a man and a woman. What gives their love its true meaning is their acting out the myth of creation, revelation, and redemption, here and now embodied in that love. But in the end, the sacred and the secular are united in most profane, physical love.

The wedding of symbol and everyday reality—the fusion and confusion of the two—these mark the classical Judaic enchantment that turns into metaphor the natural and human sentiment, the joy of marriage. Invoking creation, Adam and Eve, the Garden of Eden, and the historical memory of the this-worldly destruction of an old, unexceptional temple, the private is turned public, the individual made paradigm. Ordinary events, such as a political and military defeat or success, are changed into theological categories, such as divine punishment and heavenly compassion. If religion is a means of ultimate transformation, rendering the commonplace into the paradigmatic, changing the here and now into a moment of eternity and of eternal return, then the marriage liturgy serves to exemplify what is *religious* in Judaic existence. Time, space, action as these touch the passage of life lived one by one, the meal, the birth, the marriage—all are transformed through community, by which, we now realize, Judaism means the communion of the ages, the shared being of all who have lived in Israel and as Israel.

DEATH AND BURIAL

Puberty and death, stages in the life cycle, for different reasons and in different ways do not undergo that metamorphosis that turns a moment from what it merely seems to be into some other reality. In the Judaic transformation of the everyday, puberty and death remain pretty much untouched. In the language I have used, they stand for not *as if* but merely for an *is*. No metaphor from the corporate experience of Israel fetched from beyond the here and now—no Elijah, no Adam and Eve, no slaves in Egypt—enchants the everyday. In death, I die—*I*, not *we*. Nothing intervenes to turn the stark fact into something other than it is: the end of the life of an individual. No Moses, no Elijah, no David come to join the flights of angels that carry me to my rest. When I reach the age of responsibility for carrying out religious duties, I personally become responsible. No Phineas, no freed slaves join in celebration. I am changed; the occasion is not.

That is not to say, in the case of death, there are no rules everywhere applicable. Quite to the contrary, there are ample *halakhot* (rules) for death; and today there are customs that dictate what we do, and do not do, to celebrate the coming of the age of responsibility that marks a young man as a bar mitzvah and a young woman as a bat mitzvah. The importance of the rules for death and burial impresses people who otherwise observe little or nothing of the *halakhah* (law or rule). When I was a student at the Jewish Theological Seminary, the one set of rules we had to learn well concerned death and burial, because—as our teacher, Boaz Cohen, told us—these are the ones you will certainly apply. There are rules—but no myth. An event in the cycle of life—whether death or puberty—profoundly affects the individual and the family but is left unchanged by a mythic account.

A review of the rites of death shows us that all things focus upon the individual, his or her condition; and it is, I claim, for that very reason that we invoke no transforming metaphor. At the onset of death, the dying Jew says a confession:

> My God and God of my fathers, accept my prayer. . . .
>
> Forgive me for all the sins which I have committed in my lifetime. . . .
>
> Accept my pain and suffering as atonement and forgive my wrongdoing for against You alone have I sinned. . . .
>
> I acknowledge that my life and recovery depend on You.
>
> May it be Your will to heal me.
>
> Yet if You have decreed that I shall die of this affliction,
>
> May my death atone for all sins and transgressions which I have committed before You.
>
> Shelter me in the shadow of Your wings.
>
> Grant me a share in the world to come.
>
> Father of orphans and Guardian of widows, protect my beloved family. . . .
>
> Into Your hand I commit my soul. You redeem me, O Lord God of truth.
>
> Hear O Israel, the Lord is our God, the Lord alone.
>
> The Lord He is God.
>
> The Lord He is God.

What is important in the confession in comparison with other critical rites of passage is its silence, for what the dying person does not invoke tells us more than what is said. To state matters very simply, there is not a word before us—excluding only the final three lines—that cannot be said by any Gentile who believes in God, sin, atonement, judgment, and reconciliation—which is to say, by any Christian or Muslim. The concluding sentences identify the dying person with the holy community and its faith. But they, too, do not call to witness—to name familiar spirits—the slaves in Egypt, Adam and Eve, Elijah, or even the divine Judge seated before an open book and inscribing the fate of each person.

Nor does the halakhah require a gesture to suggest otherwise. Everything that is done concerns the corpse. Little invokes that transforming metaphor that makes of a meal a celebration of freedom; of an out-of-door picnic, a commemoration of Israel's wandering in the wilderness; of a surgical operation, a mark of eternal loyalty to God engraved in the flesh. The corpse is carefully washed and always protected. The body is covered in a white shroud, then laid in a coffin and buried. Normally burial takes place on the day of death or on the following day.

The burial rite at the graveside is laconic. The prayers that are said are exceedingly brief. One prayer that is commonly recited is as follows:

The dust returns to the earth, as it was, but the spirit returns to God, who gave it. May the soul of the deceased be bound up in the bond of life eternal. Send comfort, O Lord, to those who mourn. Grant strength to those whose burden is sorrow.

It is common to intone the prayer El Male Rahamim ("O God full of Compassion"):

O God, full of compassion and exalted in the heights, grant perfect peace in your sheltering presence, among the holy and pure, to the soul of the deceased, who has gone to his eternal home. Master of mercy, we beseech you, remember all the worthy and righteous deeds that he performed in the land of the living. May his soul be bound up in the bond of life. The Lord is his portion. May he rest in peace. And let us say, Amen.

The body is placed in the grave. Three pieces of broken pottery are laid on eyes and mouth as signs of their vanity. A handful of dirt from the Land of Israel is laid under the head. The family recites the *kaddish*, an eschatological prayer of sanctification of God's name, a prayer that looks forward to the messianic age and the resurrection of the dead. The prayer expresses the hope that the Messiah will soon come, "speedily, in our days," and that "he who brings harmony to the heavens will make peace on earth." The words of the mourner's kaddish exhibit the remarkable trait that they, too, remain silent, appealing to no metaphor, not even referring to death itself. The following is said by the mourners in what was the vernacular when the prayer was composed:

> May the great name [of God] be magnified and sanctified in the world which [God] created in accord with his will.
> And may his kingdom come in your life and days, and in the life of all the house of Israel, speedily, promptly.
> And say, Amen.

The community says:

> May the great name be blessed for ever and all eternity.

The mourner continues:

> May the holy name of the blessed one be blessed, praised, adored, exalted, raised up, adorned, raised high, praised,
> Yet beyond all of those blessings, songs, praises, words of consolation, which we say in this world.
> And say, Amen.

The community says "Amen." Then the mourner continues:

> May great peace [descend] from heaven, [and] life for us and for all Israel.
> And say, Amen.

The community says "Amen." Now the following, said by the mourner, comes in Hebrew:

> He who makes peace in the heights will make peace for us and for all Israel.
> And say, Amen.

The community says "Amen."
    The family of the deceased as well as the assembled then shovel dirt onto the body until the grave is filled. Then two lines are formed, leading away from the grave, and the mourners all say the following blessing:

> May the Omnipresent comfort you among the other mourners
> of Zion and Jerusalem.

The appeal to Zion and Jerusalem, of course, refers to the Temple of old, which people mourn until the coming restoration—thus, a messianic and eschatological reference, the only one.

The mourners remain at home for a period of seven days and continue to recite the memorial kaddish for eleven months. The life cycle for the private individual is simple, but for the individual as part of Israel, God's holy people, it is rich, absorbing, and encompassing. Life is lived with people, God's people, in God's service. And yet we discern no appeal to presences other than God's, no metamorphosis of death into something more. All things stand for other things, but death stands for itself.

Yet not entirely. For death does diminish the community, and the social entity has a stake in the matter. To state the matter simply, let me ask a question: What will happen when we all die? Will Israel end, too? So far as death happens to the individual, the rite takes note of the individual alone. But so far as death presents doubts to the ongoing community, the rite, too, proposes to take up and transform the event: hence, the one aspect in which the received Judaism proposes to treat death as metaphor. Death stands for eternal life, and death invokes the metaphor of the resurrection of the dead. Death is transformed both in deed and in doctrine by the belief in the resurrection, and that belief is tied to the final judgment at which Israel attains its ultimate salvation at the end of time. In that critical detail in which death engages the ongoing community, the corporate community makes its statement, also affecting the individual and the family. Then, and only then, while the dirt is real dirt, the dead body is turned from a mere corpse into more than mortal matter: a metaphor of the life to come.

That is a matter of both deed and doctrine, way of life and worldview. Death does not mark the end of life. In God's time, the dead will live again. The resurrection of the dead stands for the thoroughgoing metamorphosis of a this-worldly experience: death stands for the opposite, for life eternal. In halakhah, the transformation takes the form of a particular and strict rule against autopsy or any disfiguring of the corpse. The dead will live; therefore, the body must be preserved, so far as it can be, for the coming resurrection.

The counterpart in the study of Torah—that is, the component of the worldview that comes to the fore—requires us to uncover proof not that the dead will live but that the doctrine of the resurrection of the dead rests upon Scripture, which is to say that that doctrine was revealed by God in the Torah and not merely by reason, let alone human hope or fantasy.

3

Judaism
in the Synagogue

THE WORLD OF THE SYNAGOGUE:
DAILY PRAYER

The conception of prayer characteristic of Judaism derives from the Temple and its priesthood and offerings. This prayer continues the offerings of the altar to God. Now the priesthood in the book of Leviticus represented those offerings in a very particular way, and that representation predominates in the Mishnah, ca. 200 C.E., and in its exegetical continuations in the Tosefta, the Talmud of the Land of Israel, and the Talmud of Babylonia, ca. 300–600 C.E. In these definitive documents (discussed further in Part Two), the priestly conception of the Temple cult shaped the synagogue activity of prayer. That conception treated the offerings of the altar in the Temple in Jerusalem (the "tent of meeting" of the books of Exodus, Leviticus, and Numbers) as responses to God's command: This you shall do. The language is simple: "The Lord spoke to Moses saying, Speak to the children of Israel and say to them. . . ." The command addressed the community as a whole through the priesthood.

Specifically, the community of Israel was to offer on the altar a daily whole-offering, dawn and dusk; and the obligation of that whole-offering rested on the holy people as a whole. The Mishnah carried forward that conception in its definition of the half-shekel offering that every Jew was to pay to the Temple as one's personal share in the corporate cost of the everyday whole-offerings. The half-shekel from each man—no more, no less—was owing, since the obligation rested on each one. Then the priests acted in behalf of Israel as a whole, carrying out the public and common obligation.

Scripture contained other conceptions of prayer, but none of divine service. Scriptural books most certainly recognize personal prayer of petition and intercession. Hannah's prayer in 1 Sam. 2:1, "My heart exults in the Lord, I have triumphed through the Lord. . . . I rejoice in your deliverance"; the meditations of Jeremiah; the numerous personal prayers in Psalms (for example, "The Lord is my shepherd, I shall not want")—all of these testify to the broad recognition that prayer as such spoke for the individual. The cult, for its part, made equal provision for individual offerings: for example, sin offerings to expiate unwitting sin, guilt offerings, free-will offerings, thank offerings, and peace offerings. But the community owed the daily whole-offering and its Sabbath and festival counterparts; and, by that analogy, obligatory prayer was incumbent in particular upon the corporate community of holy Israel.

The conception of public worship as obligatory, of owing quite independent of the feelings and attitudes of the private individual, contradicts a common view, characteristic of one wing of Protestant communions but not of the apostolic, historical, and Reformation Protestant churches, or of the Roman Catholic or Orthodox churches. It is the view that prayer is personal, expresses deepest emotions validated (or invalidated) within the individual heart, and is not primarily public, though people may do it together. God calls to each, and the individual responds to the call, each one, one by one. Prayer takes place not as public performance of duty—recitation in common of the required words, sacrifice for the community at large, the carrying out of objective obligations—but responds to the heart and is the outpouring of the heart. Therefore, prayer starts in private and only then is shared. This conception of prayer is the opposite of an obligation incumbent on the community, in that the community hardly forms a significant component of the transaction—except after the fact. Within this conception, prayer is something that individuals do by themselves and that they feel; it is not duty but grace, not obligatory but optional in the deepest sense. Specifically, prayer, when possible, constitutes the human response to grace. From this point of view, mechanically saying the words—whether of the Hail Mary, or the Our Father, or the Shema that says "Hear, O Israel"—makes no difference in heaven or on earth. But the priests of the ancient Temple and their continuators, the rabbis of the Mishnah and the Talmud and down to our own time, see prayer as public and communal. The premise is that corporate society bears obligations to heaven, a part of which society as a whole carries out by saying the right words and making the right gestures.

The recitation of public prayers, obligatory on the community (as well as on the individual), encompasses three important matters: recitation of the creed, petition for the needs and welfare of the community and the individual, and the situation or identification of the community in its larger setting. Accordingly, we find ourselves on a tour through the world that Judaism composes for Israel: world-view, way of life, larger theory of who is Israel. I cannot imagine a more systematic or orderly exposition of that enchanted world precipitated by the recitation of the right words in the right way at the right time. The Shema ("Hear, O Israel, the Lord our God, the Lord is one") presents the creed, hence the view of the world in its entirety. The Prayer of Supplication, or Eighteen Benedictions (Heb., *Shemoneh esré*), covers the everyday needs of the community viewed in its own terms. The concluding prayer, *Alenu* ("It is our duty . . ."), a prayer of departing for the world, then states the theory of Israel to which the worldview of the Shema and the way of life outlined in the Eighteen Benedictions refer.

Evening and morning, Israel individually and communally proclaims the unity and uniqueness of God. The proclamation is preceded and followed by blessings. The whole constitutes the credo of the Judaic tradition. It is "what the Jews believe." Components recur everywhere. The three elements of the creed cover creation, revelation, and redemption: that is to say, God as creator of the world, God as revealer of the Torah, God as redeemer of Israel. The recital of the Shema is introduced by a celebration of God as Creator of the world. (All references are to Jules Harlow, *Liturgy and Ritual, Day of Atonement Prayers*.)

Creation of the World, Attested by Sunrise, Sunset

[In the morning, the individual, in community or not, recites these preliminary benedictions.]

Praised are You, O Lord our God, King of the universe.
You fix the cycles of light and darkness;

You ordain the order of all creation;
You cause light to shine over the earth;
Your radiant mercy is upon its inhabitants.
In Your goodness the work of creation
Is continually renewed day by day. . . .
O cause a new light to shine on Zion;
May we all soon be worthy to behold its radiance.
Praised are You, O Lord, Creator of the heavenly
bodies.

[The corresponding prayer in the evening refers to the setting of
the sun.]

Praised are You. . . .
Your command brings on the dusk of evening.
Your wisdom opens the gates of heaven to a new day.
With understanding You order the cycles of time;
Your will determines the succession of seasons;
You order the stars in their heavenly courses.
You create day, and You create night,
Rolling away light before darkness. . . .
Praised are You, O Lord, for the evening dusk.

Morning and evening, Israel responds to the natural order of the
world with thanks and praise of God who created the world and who
actively guides the daily events of nature. Whatever happens in nature
gives testimony to the sovereignty of the Creator. And that testimony
is not in unnatural disasters but in the most ordinary events: sunrise
and sunset. These, especially, evoke the religious response to set the
stage for what follows.

For Israel, God is not merely creator but purposeful creator. The
works of creation serve to justify and to testify to Torah, the revelation of Sinai. Torah is the mark not merely of divine sovereignty but
of divine grace and love, source of life here and now and in eternity.
So goes the second blessing:

Revelation of the Torah, as the Expression of
God's Love for Israel

Deep is Your love for us, O Lord our God;
Bounteous is Your compassion and tenderness.

> You taught our fathers the laws of life,
> And they trusted in You, Father and king,
> For their sake be gracious to us, and teach us,
> That we may learn Your laws and trust in You.
> Father, merciful Father, have compassion upon us:
> Endow us with discernment and understanding.
> Grant us the will to study Your Torah,
> To heed its words and to teach its precepts. . . .
> Enlighten our eyes in Your Torah,
> Open our hearts to Your commandments. . . .
> Unite our thoughts with singleness of purpose
> To hold You in reverence and in love. . . .
> You have drawn us close to You;
> We praise You and thank You in truth.
> With love do we thankfully proclaim Your unity.
> And praise You who chose Your people Israel in love.

Here is the way in which revelation takes concrete and specific form in the Judaic tradition: God, the Creator, revealed His will for creation through the Torah, given to Israel, God's people. That Torah contains the "laws of life."

In the Shema, Torah—revelation—leads Israel to enunciate the chief teaching of revelation:

> Hear, O Israel, the Lord our God, the Lord is One.

This proclamation of the Shema is followed by three Scripture passages. The first is Deut. 6:5–9:

> You shall love the Lord your God with all your heart, with all your soul, with all your might.

And further, one must diligently teach one's children these words and talk of them everywhere and always, and place them on one's forehead and arm, on doorposts and gates. The second Scripture is Deut. 11:13–21, which emphasizes that, if Jews keep the commandments, they will enjoy worldly blessings; but that, if they do not, they will be punished and disappear from the good land God gives them. The third is Num. 15:37–41, the commandment to wear fringes on the corners of one's garments. These fringes—which are today attached to the prayer shawl worn at morning services by Conservative and Reform Jews and to a separate undergarment worn for the same purpose by Orthodox Jews—remind the Jew of *all* the commandments of the Lord.

The proclamation is completed and yet remains open; for, having created humanity and revealed His will, God is not unaware of events since Sinai. Humanity is frail; and in the contest between the word of God and the will of humanity, Torah is not always the victor. We inevitably fall short of what is asked of us, and Jews know that their own history includes divine punishment for human failure time and again. The theme of redemption, therefore, is introduced. Redemption—in addition to creation and revelation, the third element in the tripartite worldview—resolves the tension between what we are told to do and what we are able actually to accomplish. In the end it is the theme of God, not as Creator or Revealer, but God as Redeemer that concludes the twice-daily drama:

Redemption of Israel Then and in the Future

You are our King and our father's King,
Our redeemer and our father's redeemer.
You are our creator. . . .
You have ever been our redeemer and our deliverer.
There can be no God but You. . . .
You, O Lord our God, rescued us from Egypt;
You redeemed us from the house of bondage. . . .
You split apart the waters of the Red Sea,
The faithful you rescued, the wicked drowned. . . .
Then Your beloved sang hymns of thanksgiving. . . .
They acclaimed the King, God on high,
Great and awesome source of all blessings,
The everliving God, exalted in His majesty.
He humbles the proud and raises the lowly;
He helps the needy and answers His people's call. . . .
Then Moses and all the children of Israel
Sang with great joy this song to the Lord:
Who is like You, O Lord, among the mighty?
Who is like You, so glorious in holiness?
So wondrous your deeds, so worthy of praise!

The redeemed sang a new song to You;
They sang in chorus at the shore of the sea,
Acclaiming Your sovereignty with thanksgiving:
The Lord shall reign for ever and ever.
Rock of Israel, arise to Israel's defense!
Fulfill Your promise to deliver Judah and Israel.
Our redeemer is the Holy One of Israel,
The Lord of hosts is His name.
Praised are You, O Lord, redeemer of Israel.

Redemption is both in the past and in the future. That God not only creates but also redeems is attested by the redemption from Egyptian bondage. The congregation repeats the exultant song of Moses and the people at the Red Sea, not as scholars making a learned allusion but as participants in the salvation of old and of time to come. Then the people turn to the future and ask that Israel once more be redeemed. But redemption is not only past and future. When the needy are helped, when the proud are humbled and the lowly are raised—in such commonplace, daily events redemption is already present. Just as creation is not only in the beginning but happens every day, morning and night, so redemption is not only at the Red Sea but every day, in humble events. Just as revelation was not at Sinai alone but takes place whenever people study Torah, whenever God opens their hearts to the commandments, so redemption and creation are daily events. We note once more that, while the individual may recite these prayers, the affirmation concerns the entire social entity, holy Israel.

The great cosmic events of creation in the beginning, redemption at the Red Sea, and revelation at Sinai—these are everywhere, every day, near at hand. Israel views secular reality under the aspect of eternal, ever recurrent events. What happens to Israel and to the world, whether good or evil, falls into the pattern revealed of old and made manifest each day. Historical events produce a framework in which future events will find a place and by which they will be understood. Nothing that happens cannot be subsumed by the paradigm.

Creation, the exodus from Egypt, and the revelation of Torah at Sinai are commemorated and celebrated, not merely to tell the story of what once was and is no more, but rather to recreate out of the raw materials of everyday life the "true being"—life as it was, always is, and will be forever. At prayer, Israel repeatedly refers to the crucial elements of its corporate being, thus uncovering the sacred both in nature and in history. What happens in the proclamation of the Shema is that the particular events of creation—sunset, sunrise— evoke in response the celebration of the power and the love of God, of God's justice and mercy, and of revelation and redemption.

The immense statement of the creed in the Shema gives way to the second of the three required components of obligatory public worship; that is, prayers of petition, or supplication, which directly address God with requests. What the community asks for—always in the plural—concerns the public welfare and covers matters we should today assign to the category of public policy as much as of personal need. In the morning, noon, and evening, these weekday prayers of petition comprise the Eighteen Benedictions. Some of these, in particular those at the beginning and the end, recur in Sabbath and festival prayers.

The prayer of petition is said silently. Each individual prays by and for himself or herself, but together with other silent, praying individuals. The Eighteen Benedictions are then repeated aloud by the prayer leader, for the prayer is both private and public, individual and collective. To contemplate the power of these prayers, imagine a room full of people, all standing by themselves yet in close proximity, some swaying this way and that, all addressing themselves directly and intimately to God in a whisper or in a low tone. They do not move their feet, for they are now standing before the King of kings, and it is not meet to shift and shuffle. If spoken to, they will not answer. Their attention is fixed upon the words of supplication, praise, and gratitude. When they begin, they bend their knees—so, too, toward the end; and at the conclusion, they step back and withdraw from the Presence. These, on ordinary days, are the words they say. The introductory three paragraphs define the One to whom petition is addressed: (1) the God of the founders, who is (2) omnipotent and (3) holy. The text of the three opening benedictions follows:

The Founders

Praised are you, Lord our God and God of our fathers, God of Abraham, God of Isaac, and God of Jacob, great, mighty, revered God, exalted, who bestows lovingkindness and is master of all things, who remembers the acts of loyalty of the founders and who in love will bring a redeemer to their descendants for his great name's sake. King, helper, savior and shield, praised are you, Lord, shield of Abraham.

God's Power

You are powerful forever, Lord, giving life to the dead. You are great in acts of salvation. You sustain the living in loyalty and bring the dead to life in great mercy, holding up the falling, healing the sick, freeing the prisoners, and keeping faith with those who sleep in the dirt. Who is like you, Almighty, and who is compared to you, King who kills and gives life and brings salvation to spring up? And you are reliable to give life to the dead. Praised are you, Lord, who gives life to the dead.

God's Sanctity

We shall sanctify your name in the world just as they sanctify it in the heights of heaven. . . . Holy, holy, holy is the Lord of hosts, the whole earth is full of his glory.

On weekdays petitionary prayer follows (the topic in italics is followed by the text of the prayer). The phrase "Praised are you" marks the conclusion of the blessing at hand:

Wisdom–Repentance

You graciously endow man with intelligence;
You teach him knowledge and understanding.
Grant us knowledge, discernment, and wisdom.
Praised are You, O Lord, for the gift of knowledge.

Our Father, Bring Us Back to Your Torah

Our King, draw us near to Your service;
Lead us back to You truly repentant.
Praised are You, O Lord who welcomes repentance.

Forgiveness–Redemption

Our Father, forgive us, for we have sinned;
Our King, pardon us, for we have transgressed;
You forgive sin and pardon transgression.
Praised are You, gracious and forgiving Lord.

Behold Our Affliction and Deliver Us

Redeem us soon for the sake of Your name,
For You are the mighty Redeemer.
Praised are You, O Lord, Redeemer of Israel.

Help Us—Bless Our Years

Heal us, O Lord, and we shall be healed;
Help us and save us, for You are our glory.
Grant perfect healing for all our afflictions,
O faithful and merciful God of healing.
Praised are You, O Lord, Healer of His people.

O Lord our God! Make this a blessed year;
May its varied produce bring us happiness.
Bring blessing upon the whole earth.
Bless the year with Your abounding goodness.
Praised are You, O Lord, who blesses our years.

Gather Our Exiles—Reign Over Us

Sound the great shofar to herald [our] freedom;
Raise high the banner to gather all exiles;
Gather the dispersed from the corners of the earth.
Praised are You, O Lord, who gathers our exiles.

Restore our judges as in days of old;
Restore our counselors as in former times;
Remove from us sorrow and anguish.
Reign over us alone with lovingkindness;
With justice and mercy sustain our cause.
Praised are You, O Lord, King who loves justice.

Humble the Arrogant—Sustain the Righteous

Frustrate the hopes of those who malign us;
Let all evil very soon disappear;
Let all Your enemies be speedily destroyed.
May You quickly uproot and crush the arrogant;
May You subdue and humble them in our time.
Praised are You, O Lord, who humbles the arrogant.

Let Your Tender Mercies, O Lord God, Be Stirred

For the righteous, the pious, the leaders of Israel,
Toward devoted scholars and faithful proselytes.
Be merciful to us of the house of Israel;
Reward all who trust in You;
Cast our lot with those who are faithful to You.
May we never come to despair, for our trust is in You.
Praised are You, O Lord, who sustains the righteous.

Favor Your City and Your People

Have mercy, O Lord, and return to Jerusalem, Your city;
May Your Presence dwell there as You promised.
Rebuild it now, in our days and for all time;
Reestablish there the majesty of David, Your servant.
Praised are You, O Lord, who rebuilds Jerusalem.

Bring to Flower the Shoot of Your Servant David

Hasten the advent of the Messianic redemption;
Each and every day we hope for Your deliverance.
Praised are You, O Lord, who assures our deliverance.

O Lord, Our God, Hear Our Cry!

Have compassion upon us and pity us;
Accept our prayer with loving favor.
You, O God, listen to entreaty and prayer.
O King, do not turn us away unanswered,
For You mercifully heed Your people's supplication.
Praised are You, O Lord, who is attentive to prayer.

O Lord, Our God, Favor Your People Israel

Accept with love Israel's offering of prayer;
May our worship be ever acceptable to You.
May our eyes witness Your return in mercy to Zion.
Praised are You, O Lord, whose Presence returns to Zion.

Our Thankfulness

We Thank You, O Lord our God and God of our fathers,
Defender of our lives, Shield of our safety;

Through all generations we thank You and praise You.
Our lives are in Your hands, our souls in Your charge.
We thank You for the miracles which daily attend us,
For Your wonders and favor morning, noon, and night.
You are beneficent with boundless mercy and love.
From of old we have always placed our hope in You.
For all these blessings, O our King,
We shall ever praise and exalt You.
Every living creature thanks You and praises You in truth.
O God, You are our deliverance and our help. Selah!
Praised are You, O Lord, for Your Goodness and Your glory.

Peace and Well-Being

Grant peace and well-being to the whole house of Israel;
Give us of Your grace, Your love, and Your mercy.
Bless us all, O our Father, with the light of Your Presence.
It is Your light that revealed to us Your life-giving Torah,
And taught us love and tenderness, justice, mercy, and peace.
May it please You to bless Your people in every season,
To bless them at all times with Your fight of peace.
Praised are You, O Lord, who blesses Israel with peace.

The first two petitions pertain to intelligence. Israel thanks God for mind: knowledge, wisdom, discernment. But knowledge is for a purpose, and the purpose is knowledge of Torah. Such discernment leads to the service of God and produces a spirit of repentance. We cannot pray without setting ourselves right with God, and that means repenting for what has separated us from God. Torah is the way to repentance and to return. So knowledge leads to Torah, Torah to repentance, and repentance to God. The logical next stop is the prayer for forgiveness. That is the sign of return. God forgives sin; God is gracious and forgiving. Once we discern what we have done wrong through the guidance of Torah, we therefore seek to be forgiven. Sin leads to affliction. Affliction stands at the beginning of the way to God; once we have taken that way, we ask for our suffering to end. We beg redemption. This is then specified. We ask for healing, salvation, a blessed year. Healing without prosperity means we may suffer in good health or starve in a robust body. So along with the prayer for healing goes the supplication for worldly comfort.

The individual's task is done. But what of the community? Health and comfort are not enough. The world is unredeemed. Jews are enslaved, in exile, and alien. At the end of days, a great shofar (ram's horn) will sound to herald the Messiah's coming—as is now besought. Israel at prayer asks first for the proclamation of freedom, then for the ingathering of the exiles to the Promised Land. Establishing the messianic kingdom, God needs also to restore a wise and benevolent government, good judges, good counselors, and loving justice. Meanwhile Israel finds itself maligned. As the prayer sees things, arrogant men hating Israel hate God as well. They should be humbled. And the pious and righteous—the scholars, the faithful proselytes, the whole House of Israel that trusts in God—should be rewarded and sustained. Above all, remember Jerusalem. Rebuild the city and dwell there. Set up Jerusalem's messianic king, David, and make him prosper. These are the themes of the daily prayer: personal atonement, good health, and good fortunes; collective redemption, freedom, the end of alienation, good government, and true justice; the final and complete salvation of the land and of Jerusalem by the Messiah. At the end comes a prayer that prayer may be heard and found acceptable; then an expression of thanksgiving, not for what may come but for the miracles and mercies already enjoyed morning, noon, and night. And at the end is the prayer for peace—a peace that consists of wholeness for the sacred community.

The third of the three components of the communal worship draws the community outward into the world. When Jews complete any service of worship, they mark its conclusion by making a statement concerning themselves in the world: the corporate community looking outward. Every synagogue service concludes with a prayer prior to going forth, called Alenu, from its first word in Hebrew. Like the exodus, the moment of the congregation's departure becomes a celebration of Israel's God, a self-conscious, articulated rehearsal of Israel's peoplehood. But now it is the end, rather than the beginning, of time that is important. When Jews go forth, they look forward:

> Let us praise Him, Lord over all the world;
> Let us acclaim Him, Author of all creation.
> He made our lot unlike that of other peoples;
> He assigned to us a unique destiny.
> We bend the knee, worship, and acknowledge

The King of kings, the Holy One, praised is He.
He unrolled the heavens and established the earth;
His throne of glory is in the heavens above;
His majestic Presence is in the loftiest heights.
He and no other is God and faithful King,
Even as we are told in His Torah:
Remember now and always, that the Lord is God;
Remember, no other is Lord of heaven and earth.
We, therefore, hope in You, O Lord our God,
That we shall soon see the triumph of Your might,
That idolatry shall be removed from the earth,
And false gods shall be utterly destroyed.
Then will the world be a true kingdom of God,
When all mankind will invoke Your name,
And all the earth's wicked will return to You.
Then all the inhabitants of the world will surely know
That to You every knee must bend,
Every tongue must pledge loyalty.
Before You, O Lord, let them bow in worship,
Let them give honor to Your glory.
May they all accept the rule of Your kingdom.
May You reign over them soon through all time.
Sovereignty is Yours in glory, now and forever.
So it is written in Your Torah:
The Lord shall reign for ever and ever.

SABBATHS OF CREATION,
FESTIVALS OF REDEMPTION

The great theologian Abraham Joshua Heschel has spelled out
the human transformation accomplished by the Sabbath:

Judaism is a religion of time aiming at the sanctification of
time. Unlike the space-minded man to whom time is unvaried,
iterative, homogeneous, to whom all hours are alike . . . , the
Bible senses the diversified character of time. There are no two
hours alike. Every hour is unique and the only one given at the
moment, exclusive and endlessly precious. Judaism teaches us
to be attached to holiness in time, to be attached to sacred

events, to learn how to consecrate sanctuaries that emerge from the magnificent stream of a year. The Sabbaths are our great cathedrals, and our Holy of Holies is a shrine that neither the Romans nor the Germans were able to burn. . . . Jewish ritual may be characterized as the art of significant forms in time, as architecture of time. Most of its observances . . . depend on a certain hour of the day or season of the year. . . . The main themes of faith lie in the realm of time. We remember the day of the exodus from Egypt, the day when Israel stood at Sinai; and our Messianic hope is the expectation of a day, of the end of days.[1]

Contrast the Sabbath and the occasion of Passover. Passover is once a year, not every week. Passover stands in judgment against others—the outsider—and gives resonance to legitimate resentment. Passover is like a love affair—intense but brief. The Sabbath stands in judgment upon us as human beings and calls into question the things that should merely engage but, in fact, overwhelm us. That is why, at sunset on the eve of the seventh day, words do not create worlds, except for a tiny sector of Israel, that special entity of Orthodoxy. The magic works only when people want it to. The Sabbath is like a marriage that is ordinary and lasts for years. A love affair is what it is—but on the basis of the Sabbath, one can build one's life, and many do.

The Sabbath lays down a judgment on the fundamental issues of our civilization and, specifically, demands restraint, dignity, reticence, and silent rest—not commonplace virtues. If, therefore, the transformation of time, the centerpiece of the life of Judaism, occurs for only a few, the reason is not obsolescence but the opposite: excessive relevance. The Sabbath touches too close to home, ripping the raw nerve of reality. It calls into question the foundations of the life of one dimension only, asking how people can imagine that what they see just now is all there is. The Judaic vision, which perceives things to be not what they seem, blinds with too much light on the Sabbath. Circumcision is once in a while; the meal is eaten, mostly, without benefit of blessing, except on cultic occasions; the huppah for the fortunate is once or, at most, twice, and it is hard to pretend we are Adam and Eve anyhow; and the Passover is but once a year and, in all the hocus-pocus of removing leaven and eating matzoh, easy in its cultic complexity. But the Sabbath and, in its wake, the festivals and the Days of Awe—these are another matter. They question. They disrupt. They condemn. And they take place every week—or, with the festivals, more often—turning one place into another and one time into another.

The Sabbath celebrates the completion and perfection of creation, that is, of nature:

> When the heaven and earth were done, and all their array, when God had finished the work that he had been doing, then he rested on the seventh day from all the work that he had done. Then God blessed the seventh day and made it holy, because on it God desisted from all of the work of creating in which he had been engaged. (Gen. 2:1–3)

This account of the first Sabbath stands in judgment on those who, like God, create but, unlike God, never rest, who deny themselves occasion to admire and enjoy. I can find no more penetrating judgment upon the human condition than the Sabbath's: one can have too much, enjoy too little, and so care about things that do not count:

> Inner liberty depends upon being exempt from domination of things as well as from domination of people. There are many who have acquired a high degree of political and social liberty, but only very few are not enslaved to things. This is our constant problem—how to live with people and remain free, how to live with things and remain independent.[2]

The words that at sunset on Friday transform the world and bring into being a different world do their work only when we want them to. But no message can find a less endearing welcome than one that questions the one-sidedness of the life of things and material achievement. The Sabbath speaks of transcendent things, of life with God and in God, in ways in which the more concrete celebration of freedom does not. For the Sabbath penetrates into the heart of commonplace being, while Passover addresses the merely social and political. Societies do well with the latter kind of problem, working to change matters to suit them through the power of the will. In a world that celebrates deed, not deliberation, that reckons value in what is weighed and measured, how can words create the intangible world of time?

> We cannot solve the problem of time through the conquest of space, through either pyramids or fame. We can only solve the problem of time through sanctification of time. To men alone time is elusive; to men with God time is eternity in disguise. This is the task of men: to conquer space and sanctify time. We must conquer space in order to sanctify time. All week long we are called upon to sanctify life through employing things of space. On the Sabbath it is given us to share in the holiness that is in the heart of time.[3]

From the issue of intellect we turn to the everyday: Why not ask the question that the Sabbath answers? Heschel's account of that question—Are things merely what they seem to be?—cuts to the core of that Judaic perspective that denies that the everyday is all there is:

> In our daily lives we attend primarily to that which the senses are spelling out for us: to what the eyes perceive, to what the fingers touch. Reality to us is thinghood, consisting of substances that occupy space; even God is considered by most of us a thing. The result of our thinginess is our blindness to all reality that fails to identify itself as a thing, as a matter of fact. This is obvious in our understanding of time, which, being thingless and insubstantial, appears to us as if it had no reality.[4]

The words that precipitate the world of the Sabbath invoke the day both as a memorial of creation and as a remembrance of the redemption from Egypt. The primary liturgy of the Sabbath is the reading of the Scripture lesson from the Torah in the synagogue service. So the three chief themes of the Judaic system—creation, revelation, and redemption—are combined in the weekly observance of the seventh day. The Sabbath works more than through words: it is the creation also of one's actions and omissions in making of time a different world. The Sabbath is protected by negative rules: one must not work; one must not pursue mundane concerns. But the Sabbath is also adorned with less concrete but affirmative laws: one must rejoice; one must rest.

How to make and keep the Sabbath? All week long I look forward to it, and the anticipation enhances the ordinary days. Usually, by Friday afternoon, those who keep the Sabbath will have bathed, put on their Sabbath garments, and set aside the affairs of the week. At home, the family—husband, wife, children, or whoever stands for family—will have cleaned, cooked, and arranged the finest table. It is common to invite guests for the Sabbath meals. The Sabbath comes at sunset and leaves when three stars appear Saturday night. After a brief service, the family comes together to enjoy its best meal of the week—a meal at which particular Sabbath foods are served. In the morning comes the Sabbath service—including a public reading from the Torah, the Five Books of Moses, and prophetic writings—and an additional service in memory of the Temple sacrifices on Sabbaths of old. Then home for lunch and commonly a Sabbath nap, the sweetest part of the day. As the day wanes, the synagogue calls for a late afternoon service, followed by Torah study and a third meal. Then comes a ceremony, *havdalah* (separation)—effected with spices, wine, and candlelight—between the holy time of the Sabbath and the ordinary time of weekday. I do not mean to suggest that this idyllic picture characterizes all Sabbath observance, nor do I believe (though many Jews do) that the only way to sanctify the Sabbath is in the received way I have described. Reform Judaism has displayed the wisdom to honor, as an act of sanctification of the time of the Sabbath, a variety of abstinences and actions. But, in the main, the Sabbath works its wonder when people retreat into family—however they understand family—and take leave of work and the workaday world.

This simple, regular observance has elicited endless praise. To the Sabbath-observing Jew, the Sabbath is the chief sign of God's grace:

> For thou has chosen us and sanctified us above all nations, in love and favor has given us thy holy Sabbath as an inheritance.

So is sanctified the Sabbath wine. Likewise in the Sabbath-morning liturgy:

> You did not give it [Sabbath] to the nations of the earth, nor did you make it the heritage of idolators, nor in its rest will unrighteous men find a place.

> But to Israel your people you have given it in love, to the seed of Jacob whom you have chosen, to that people who sanctify the Sabbath day. All of them find fulfillment and joy from your bounty.
>
> For the seventh day did you choose and sanctify as the most pleasant of days and you called it a memorial to the works of creation.[5]

Here again we find a profusion of themes, this time centered upon the Sabbath. The Sabbath is a sign of the covenant. It is a gift of grace, which neither idolators nor evil people may enjoy. It is the testimony of the chosenness of Israel. And it is the most pleasant of days. Keeping the Sabbath *is* living in God's kingdom:

> Those who keep the Sabbath and call it a delight will rejoice in your kingdom.

So states the additional Sabbath prayer. Keeping the Sabbath now is a foretaste of the redemption: "This day is for Israel light and rejoicing." As the afternoon prayer affirms, the rest of the Sabbath is:

> A rest granted in generous love, a true and faithful rest. . . .
> Let your children realize that their rest is from you, and by their rest may they sanctify your name.

That people need respite from the routine of work is no discovery of the Judaic tradition. But that the way in which Jews accomplish this routine change of pace may be made the very heart and soul of spiritual existence is the single absolutely unique element in Judaic tradition. The word *Sabbath* simply renders the Hebrew *Shabbat*; it does not translate it, for there is no translation. In no other tradition or culture can an equivalent word be found. Certainly those who compare the Sabbath of Judaism to the somber, supposedly joyless Sunday of the Calvinists know nothing of what the Sabbath has meant and continues to mean to Jews.

What, precisely, does the Sabbath expect of us? And how, if we say the words and mean them, do we find the Sabbath as the answer and the way of life of the ordinary person? Heschel answers these questions when he describes the Sabbath as a work of art:

Labor is a craft, but perfect rest is an art. It is the result of an accord of body, mind and imagination. . . . The seventh day is a palace in time, which we build. It is made of soul, of joy and reticence. In its atmosphere a discipline is a reminder of adjacency to eternity. Indeed, the splendor of the day is expressed in terms of abstentions, just as the mystery of God is more adequately conveyed . . . in the categories of negative theology which claims that we can never say what he is, we can only say when he is not.

Heschel finds in the Sabbath "the day on which we are called upon to share in what is eternal in time, to turn from the world of creation to the creations of the world."[6]

From this brief description of what the Jew actually does on the seventh day, we can hardly come to understand how the Sabbath can have meant so much as to elicit such words as those of the Jewish prayerbook and of Rabbi Heschel. Those words, like the negative laws of the Sabbath—not to mourn, not to confess sins, not to repent, not to do anything that might lead to unhappiness—describe something only the participant can truly comprehend and feel. Only a family whose life focuses upon the Sabbath week by week, year by year, from birth to death, can know the sanctity of which the theologian speaks, the sacred rest to which the prayers refer. The heart and soul of the Judaic tradition, the Sabbath, cannot be described; it can only be experienced. For the student of religions, it stands as that element of Judaism that is absolutely unique and therefore a mystery. It forms the heart of the enchanted life of Judaism: where and how and why Judaism is a religion, not merely a social entity, or a politics, or a culture, or a way of life. For transformation speaks not of external things but of a change at the very core of being: there is religion; there, in the language of Judaism, is the Torah; there we meet God; there we become like God: "in our image, after our likeness."

The festivals, too, mark the passage of time: not of the week but of the seasons. These seasons of sanctification and celebration are three: *Sukkot,* the week following the first full moon after the autumnal equinox, alluded to in classical sources as the "Festival," the one above all others; *Pessah,* or Passover, the week following the first full moon after the vernal equinox; and *Shavuot,* or the Feast of Weeks, seven weeks later. Each festival both celebrates and commemorates:

celebrating an event in nature, commemorating an event in Israel's sacred history.

Sukkot, the Feast of Tabernacles, marks the end of agricultural toil. The fall crops by then are gathered in from field, orchard, and vineyard. The rainy season in the Holy Land of Israel—and, in North America, the winter—is about to begin. It is time both to give thanks for what has been granted and to pray for abundant rains in the coming months. Called "festival of the ingathering," Sukkot is the celebration of nature. But the mode of celebration, also after the fact, commemorates a moment in Israel's history—specifically, the wandering in the wilderness. Then the Israelites lived not in permanent houses but in huts or shedlike stalls, or booths. At a time of bounty, it is good to be reminded of the travail of men and women and their dependence upon heavenly succor, which underlines the message of the Sabbath. The principal observance of the Festival is still the construction of a frail hut, or booth, for temporary use during the festival. Here, in warmer climates, Jews eat their meals out of doors. The huts are covered over with branches, leaves, fruit, and flowers, but light shows through, and, at night, the stars are visible.

This brings us back to Passover. But now we see the festival in its own setting, rather than in ours. We know the words, and I have explained why people so say them as to make a world. But what world do they call into being? Passover is the Jewish spring festival, and the symbols of the Passover seder—hard-boiled eggs and vegetable greens, lying on a plate on the seder table but curiously neglected in the Passover narrative—are not unfamiliar in other spring rites. Here, however, the spring rite has been transformed into a historical commemoration. The natural course of the year, while important, is subordinated to the historical events remembered and relived on the festival. Called the "Feast of Unleavened Bread" and the season of our freedom, the Passover festival preserves ancient rites in a new framework.

It is, for example, absolutely prohibited to make use of leaven, fermented dough, and the like. The agricultural calendar of ancient Canaan was marked by the grain harvest, beginning in the spring with the cutting of barley and ending with the reaping of the wheat approximately seven weeks later. The farmers would get rid of all their sour dough, which they used as yeast, and old bread as well as any leaven from last year's crop. The origins of the practice are not clear, but it is beyond doubt that the Passover taboo against leaven was connected with the agricultural calendar. Just as the agricultural festivals were historicized, much of the detailed observance connected with them was supplied with historical "reasons" or explanations. In the case of the taboo against leaven, widely observed today even among otherwise unobservant Jews, the reason was that the Israelites, having to leave Egypt in haste, had therefore to take with them unleavened bread, for they did not have time to permit the bread to rise properly and be baked. Therefore we eat the matzoh, unleavened bread.

The Feast of Weeks, Shavuot, or Pentecost, comes seven weeks after Passover. In the ancient Palestinian agricultural calendar, Shavuot marked the end of the grain harvest and was called the "Feast of Harvest." In Temple times, two loaves of bread were baked from the wheat of the new crop and offered as a sacrifice—the firstfruits of the wheat harvest. So Shavuot came to be called "the day of the firstfruits." Judaism added a historical explanation to the natural ones derived from the land and its life: the rabbis held that the Torah was revealed on Mount Sinai on that day and celebrated it as "the time of the giving of our Torah." Nowadays, in Reform and Conservative synagogues, the confirmation or graduation ceremonies of religious schools take place on Shavuot.

The three historical-agricultural festivals pertain, in varying ways and combinations, to the themes I have already considered. Passover is the festival of redemption and points toward the Torah revelation of the Feast of Weeks; the harvest festival in the autumn celebrates not only creation but especially redemption. Like the Sabbath, these festivals take ordinary people and turn them into Israel; they profane time and sanctify it. The same reason that accounts for the neglect of the Sabbath explains the limited popularity of the Festival, Sukkot; the Feast of Weeks, Shavuot; and the observance of Passover other than its banquet, on the one side, and (far less commonly) the bread taboo, on the other. But at stake in holy time is holiness, the transformation of a world by reason of an occasion; and if God counts and weighs and takes account of numbers, then what does God make of Israel anyhow? In the comparison of size as of space, no magic works. But to change life—that is true enchantment. And the Sabbath and its counterpart festivals transform life through the reordering of time and space, the reconciliation of action and community at rest.

For if the Grace after Meals reaches into the commonplace experience of hunger and satisfaction, if the rites of circumcision and of the huppah serve to transform joy from personal to public existence, then what shall we say of the Sabbath? Among the words that make things different, those of the Sabbath speak to the heart of matters: the human condition of having too much and keeping too little. That dilemma is to be resolved through the enchantment of sanctification. In the transformation of working day to Sabbath, humanity completes creation and, like God, rests on the seventh day, so sanctifying it. The human condition that asks, What are we, what is our worth? finds its answer on the Sabbath: We are like God, and we are worth the world.

THE DAYS OF AWE:
STANDING BEFORE GOD FOR JUDGMENT

The New Year, Rosh Hashanah, and the Day of Atonement, Yom Kippur, together mark days of solemn penitence, at the start of the autumn festival season. These, in the prayers said on the occasion, are solemn times. The words of the liturgy specifically create a world of personal introspection, individual judgment. The turning of the year marks a time of looking backward. It is melancholy, like the falling leaves, but hopeful—as with the pennant and the World Series' losers; next year is another season.

The answer of the Days of Awe concerns life and death, which take mythic form in affirmations of God's rule and judgment. The words create a world aborning, the old now gone, the new just now arriving. The New Year, Rosh Hashanah, celebrates the creation of the world: *Today the world is born.* The time of new beginnings also marks endings: *On the New Year the decree is issued: Who will live and who will die?* At the New Year—so the words state—humanity is inscribed for life or death in the heavenly books for the coming year; and on the Day of Atonement, the books are sealed. The world comes out to hear these words. The season is rich in celebration. The synagogues on that day are filled—whether with penitents or people who merely wish to be there hardly matters. The New Year is a day of remembrance on which the deeds of all creatures are reviewed. The principal themes of the words invoke creation, and God's rule over creation; revelation, and God's rule in the Torah for the created world; and redemption, God's ultimate plan for the world.

On the birthday of the world God made, God asserts sovereignty, as in the New Year Prayer:

> Our God and God of our Fathers, Rule over the whole world in Your honor . . . and appear in Your glorious might to all those who dwell in the civilization of Your world, so that everything made will know that You made it, and every creature discern that You have created him, so that all in whose nostrils is breath may say, "The Lord, the God of Israel is King, and His kingdom extends over all."[7]

Liturgical words concerning divine sovereignty, divine memory, and divine disclosure correspond to creation, revelation, and redemption. Sovereignty is established by creation of the world. Judgment depends upon law: "From the beginning You made this, Your purpose known." And therefore, since people have been told what God requires of them, they are judged:

> On this day sentence is passed upon countries, which to the sword and which to peace, which to famine and which to plenty, and each creature is judged today for life or death. Who is not judged on this day? For the remembrance of every creature comes before You, each man's deeds and destiny, words and way.

These are strong words for people to hear. As life unfolds and people grow reflective, the Days of Awe seize the imagination: I live, I die, sooner or later it comes to all. The call for inner contemplation implicit in the mythic words elicits deep response.

The theme of revelation is further combined with redemption; the ram's horn, or shofar, which is sounded in the synagogue during daily worship for a month before the Rosh Hashanah festival, serves as a thread of unity connecting daily worship and the New Year:

> You did reveal yourself in a cloud of glory. . . . Out of heaven you made them [Israel] hear Your voice . . . amid thunder and lightning You revealed yourself to them, and while the shofar sounded You shined forth upon them. . . . Our God and God of our fathers, sound the great shofar for our freedom. Lift up the

ensign to gather our exiles. . . . Lead us happily to Zion Your
City, Jerusalem the place of Your sanctuary.

The complex themes of the New Year, the most "theological" of Jewish holy occasions, thus weave together the tapestry of a highly
charged moment in a world subject to the personal scrutiny of a most
active God.

What of the Day of Atonement? Here, too, we hear the same
answers, see the unfolding of a single process of transformation of
secular into sacred time. Of the Days of Awe, the most personal,
solemn, and moving is the Day of Atonement, Yom Kippur, the Sabbath of Sabbaths. It is marked by fasting and continuous prayer. On it,
the Jew makes confession:

> Our God and God of our fathers, may our prayer come before
> You. Do not hide Yourself from our supplication, for we are not
> so arrogant or stiff-necked as to say before You, "We are righ-
> teous and have not sinned." But we have sinned.
> We are guilt laden, we have been faithless, we have robbed. . . .
> We have committed iniquity, caused unrighteousness, have
> been presumptuous. . . .
> We have counseled evil, scoffed, revolted, blasphemed.

The Hebrew confession is built upon an alphabetical acrostic, as if
God, who knows human secrets, will, by making certain every letter
is represented, combine them into appropriate words. The very alpha-
bet bears witness against us before God. Then:

> What shall we say before You who dwell on high? What shall
> we tell You who live in heaven? Do You not know all things,
> both the hidden and the revealed? You know the secrets of
> eternity, the most hidden mysteries of life. You search the inner-
> most recesses, testing men's feelings and heart. Nothing is con-
> cealed from You or hidden from Your eyes. May it therefore be
> Your will to forgive us our sins, to pardon us for our iniquities,
> to grant remission for our transgressions.

A further list of sins follows, composed on alphabetical lines.
Prayers to be spoken by the congregation are all in the plural: "For

the sin which we have sinned against You with the utterance of the lips . . . for the sin which we have sinned before You openly and secretly." The community takes upon itself responsibility for what is done in it. All Israel is part of one community, one body; and all are responsible for the acts of each. The sins confessed are mostly against society, against one's fellowmen; few pertain to ritual laws. At the end comes a final word:

> O my God, before I was formed, I was nothing. Now that I have been formed, it is as though I had not been formed, for I am dust in my life, more so after death. Behold I am before You like a vessel filled with shame and confusion. May it be Your will . . . that I may no more sin, and forgive the sins I have already committed in Your abundant compassion.

While much of the liturgy speaks of "we," it focuses primarily on the individual, from beginning to end. The Days of Awe speak to the heart of the individual, telling a story of judgment and atonement. So the individual Jew stands before God: possessing no merits, yet hopeful of God's love and compassion. If that is the answer, can there be any doubt about the question? I think not. The power of the Days of Awe derives from the sentiments and emotions aroused by the theme of those days: What is happening to me? Where am I going?

JEWISH LAW AND LEARNING:
HALAKHAH AND STUDY OF THE TORAH

Halakhah (law or rule) defines. It governs whether or not people want it to. That is, the norms of the group precede individual or family in the definition of the way of life, and the individual or the family does not make decisions except within the consensus of the community formed, from of old, in the halakhah. For the community—nation, people, society, whatever the social entity is called—transcends the individual and the family, coming before, continuing afterward, and it dictates the circumstance of enchantment and transformation, lending credibility to what is mere magic when done by an individual alone.

Accordingly, rules held in common turn individuals and families into a community. Then, but only then, the enchantment of rite transforms the shared experience of the community, asking questions urgent not to individual or family primarily, but to the community first of all: questions of culture and value, of work and leisure; of all together, for instance. Second, the group expresses its sense of self in a worldview formed on a shared imagination, a pretense of *as if* held in common. For the *as if* becomes the *is* only when enough people join in the drama—when the audience is on stage, so to speak. Short of community, a vision of a community held only by radically isolated individuals or by mere aggregates of families frames the perspective of the sect or the commune or the ghetto. All three have in common the defining of the self against the other, a reliance on the outsider to lend credibility to the sect's or the commune's or the ghetto's isolation and fantasy of isolation. With these matters clear, we ask ourselves how, in the circumstance of a corporate society, Judaism spelled out the worldview and the way of life in which the corporate, not only the private, rites worked their magic.

The way of life of corporate, holy Israel finds definition in halakhah, by which people state (after the fact mostly) those rules that describe the life they lead. In halakhah they record the actions that turn one thing into something else: the sexual union of man and woman into a contracted relationship sanctified by heaven, for example; the preparation of food into the consecration of the meal; or the saying of words into prayer. Halakhah, therefore, constitutes the way of life that, prior to and beyond the experience of family, forms out of families a corporate, holy community, Israel in God's sight. When people think of law, they ordinarily imagine a religion for book-keepers, who tote up the good deeds and debit the bad and call the result salvation or damnation, depending on the outcome. But when we speak of life under the halakhah law, we mean life in accord with the halakhah, the rules and regulations of the holy life. The mythic structure built upon the themes of creation, revelation, and redemption finds expression not only in synagogue liturgy, but especially in concrete, everyday actions or action symbols—that is, deeds that embody and express the fundamental mythic life of the classical Judaic tradition. So far as the formula or incantation is carried by the blessing or prayer, the gesture of enchantment takes form in halakhah. Judaism transforms the ordinary into the holy through both, and the rite on the remarkable occasion takes second place behind the ritualization of the everyday and commonplace—that is to say, the sanctification of the ordinary.

The word *halakhah*, as is clear, is normally translated as "law," for the halakhah is full of normative, prescriptive rules about what one must do and refrain from doing in every situation of life and at every moment of the day. But since halakhah derives from the root *halakh*, which means "go," a better translation would be "way." The halakhah is the "way": the way man or woman lives life; the way man or woman shapes the daily routine into a pattern of sanctity; the way man or woman follows the revelation of the Torah and attains redemption. For the Judaic religious encounter, this way is absolutely central. Belief without the expression of belief in the workaday world is of limited consequence. In referring to the enchanted world beyond and within the faith or the Torah, the purpose of revelation is to create a kingdom of priests and a holy people. The foundation of that kingdom, or sovereignty, is the rule of God over the lives of humanity. For the Judaic tradition, God rules much as people do—by guiding others on the path of life, not by removing them from the land of living. Creation lies behind; redemption in the future; Torah is for here and now. To the classical Jew, Torah means revealed law or commandment, accepted by Israel and obeyed from Sinai to the end of days.

The spirit of the Jewish way (halakhah) is conveyed in many modes, for law is not divorced from values but rather concretizes human beliefs and ideals. The purpose of the commandments is to show the road to sanctity, the way to God. In a more mundane sense, a fourth-century rabbi has provided a valuable insight:

> Rava said, "When a person is brought in for judgment in the world to come, that person is asked, 'Did you deal in good faith? Did you set aside time for study of Torah? Did you engage in procreation? Did you look forward to salvation? Did you engage in the dialectics of wisdom? Did you look deeply into matters?' "[8]

Rava's interpretation of Scripture—"and there shall be faith in thy times, strength, salvation, wisdom and knowledge" (Isa. 33:6)—gives us a glimpse into the life of the Jew who followed the way of Torah. The first consideration was ethical: did the Jew conduct affairs faithfully? The second was study of Torah, not at random but every day, systematically, as a discipline of life. Third came the raising of a family, for celibacy and abstinence from sexual life were regarded as sinful; the full use of a woman's and a man's creative powers for the procreation of life was a commandment. Nothing God made was evil. Wholesome conjugal life was a blessing. But, fourth, merely living day by day according to an upright ethic was not sufficient. It is true that people must live by a holy discipline, but the discipline itself was only a means; the end was salvation. Hence the pious people were asked to look forward to salvation, aiming their deeds and directing their hearts toward a higher goal. Wisdom and insight completed the list, for without them, the way of Torah was a life of mere routine, rather than a constant search for deeper understanding.

The halakhah in detail meant to make a main point, and the literature of the halakhah, beginning with the Talmud, articulated that point clearly. One formulation of the entire Torah—law and theology alike—is attributed to Hillel, a first-century authority:

> What is hateful to yourself do not do to your fellowman. That is the whole Torah. All the rest is commentary. Now go and study.[9]

The saying assigned to Hillel was neither the first nor the last to provide a pithy definition of the Torah or Judaism. In the definition attributed to him, we see that, from among many available verses of Scripture, the selected model is Lev. 19:18: "You shall love your neighbor as yourself: I am the Lord." This commandment summarized everything.

Still a further definition of the purpose of the halakhah as it defines the religious duties, or commandments, incumbent on all Jews as corporate Israel, derives from later rabbis of the Talmud. Thus, Simlai expounded:

> Six hundred and thirteen commandments were given to Moses, three hundred and sixty-five negative ones, corresponding to the number of the days of the solar year, and two hundred and forty-eight positive commandments, corresponding to the parts of man's body.
>
> David came and reduced them to eleven: *A Psalm of David* (Psalm 15). *Lord, who shall sojourn in thy tabernacle, and who shall dwell in thy holy mountain?* (i) *He who walks uprightly and* (ii) *works righteousness and* (iii) *speaks truth in his heart and* (iv) *has no slander on his tongue and* (v) *does no evil to his fellow and* (vi) *does not take*

up a reproach against his neighbor, (vii) *in whose eyes a vile person is despised but* (viii) *honors those who fear the Lord.* (ix) *He swears to his own hurt and changes not.* (x) *He does not lend on interest.* (xi) *He does not take a bribe against the innocent.* . . .

Isaiah came and reduced them to six (Isaiah 33:25–26): (i) *He who walks righteously and* (ii) *speaks uprightly,* (iii) *he who despises the gain of oppressions,* (iv) *shakes his hand from holding bribes,* (v) *stops his ear from hearing of blood* (vi) *and shuts his eyes from looking upon evil, he shall dwell on high.*

Micah came and reduced them to three (Micah 6:8): *It has been told you, man, what is good, and what the Lord demands from you,* (i) *only to do justly and* (ii) *to love mercy, and* (iii) *to walk humbly before God.*

Isaiah again came and reduced them to two (Isaiah 56:1): *Thus says the Lord,* (i) *Keep justice and* (ii) *do righteousness.*

Amos came and reduced them to a single one, as it is said, *For thus says the Lord to the house of Israel. Seek Me and live.*

Habakkuk further came and based them on one, as it is said (Habakkuk 2:4), *But the righteous shall live by his faith.*[10]

This long passage illustrates in both form and substance the essential attributes of definitions of the halakhah seen all together, with the Hebrew Scriptures as the source of authoritative teaching. But the Scriptures are not cited in a slavish, unimaginative way; rather, they are creatively used as the raw material for the rabbi's own insights.

The power of that vision of *as if,* when extended to Scripture, transforms Scripture into the Judaic system at hand. The direction of life under the law—the corporate life of Israel defined in concrete terms—is the search for God; and the good life consists of that search—"The righteous man shall live by his faith"—for, in Hebrew, the word for "faith" is *emunah,* meaning "trust," "loyalty," "commitment." Thus, what keeps a person alive, what renders the life of the family real and meaningful, is trust in and loyalty to God, to which the holy community, Israel, is called all together and all at once. The appeal to Scripture alerts us to the definitive trait of the framing of the worldview embodied by the way of life of the halakhah—that is, appeal to Scripture or, in the language of Judaism, to Torah. So as we move from way of life to worldview, we remain within the same enchanted circle of the faith: Torah defining way of life; Torah, properly read, framing worldview. The way of life transforms action into mitzvah, religious deeds done in compliance with God's will, and the worldview transforms thought into Talmud Torah—that is, Torah study—seeing the workaday world as a metaphor for God's view of matters.

In examining the practice of reforming the *is* into the *as if,* I noted the emphasis upon Torah, study of Torah, interest in finding in the written and oral parts of the Torah (which we know as the Hebrew Scriptures and the Mishnah and Talmud, respectively) not merely what is there but what is there for us. That interest forms an entry into the theory behind the transformation of the everyday into the extraordinary. It consists in reading life as a metaphor for a reality beyond, for—in the language of Scripture—seeing humanity as simile for God: "in our image, after our likeness." The power of halakhah to transform details of the everyday derives from the authority of the social imagination to reread the everyday into a set of events in the paradigm of Scripture, and also to rewrite Scripture—the Torah—into a series of accounts of the reality with which the everyday is to be compared.

NOTES

1. Abraham J. Heschel, *The Sabbath* (New York: Farrar, Straus, 1948), pp. 216–17.

2. Abraham J. Heschel, cited in Fritz A. Rothschild, *Between God and Man* (New York: Harper, 1959), p. 222.

3. Ibid., p. 229.

4. Ibid., p. 215.

5. *The Jewish Prayerbook.* Unless otherwise noted, all such quoted material in this chapter is from this source.

6. Rothschild, *Between God and Man,* p. 218.

7. Mahzor, liturgy for the Days of Awe.

8. Babylonian Talmud tractate Shabbat, p. 31A.

9. Ibid.

10. Babylonian Talmud tractate Mikkot 24A.

4

How People Practice
Judaism in America:
The Jewish People and
the Jewish Faith

THE TWO JUDAISMS
OF AMERICA

As we have seen, the Day of Atonement, the Passover seder, the marriage ceremony, the burial rite, and other celebrations of home and family are significant for the vast majority of Jewish Americans, Canadians, West Europeans, Brazilians, Argentinians, Australians, and South Africans. The political issues of Jewish corporate life, typified by work on behalf of Soviet Jewry and concern with the State of Israel, engage the same vast majority, inspiring vivid energies, deep emotions. The first set of rites derives from the Judaism of the dual Torah; the political work from the Judaism of Holocaust and Redemption.

These two Judaisms, each with its own symbolic system and appeal to a story of who we are and what on that account we must do, coexist side by side in the lives of the middle range of Jewry. In the hearts of Jews of Reform, Conservative, middle-class Orthodox, Reconstructionist, or, for that matter, humanist commitment—whether those Jews are members of a synagogue or unaffiliated—these two Judaisms evoke profound and life-transforming affections, attitudes, and emotions. The one serves home and family; the other, the corporate community. A simple statement of their ubiquity suffices. When one Jew marries another Jew, it is virtually unheard of for them to have a civil, not a Judaic, religious marriage—a rite that derives from the Judaism of the dual Torah. The sign of the other Judaism, that of Holocaust and Redemption, proves equally one-sided:

deep concern for the State of Israel, profound response to the tale of
the destruction of European Jewry between 1933 and 1945. When
we discern the power and influence of these two Judaisms and
understand how they work, we shall see how and why Jewish Americans, Canadians, West Europeans, Brazilians and Argentinians, Australians and South Africans constitute—in varying ways, to be sure—
a singular people on earth.

THE JUDAISM
OF HOME AND FAMILY

When I refer to the two Judaisms of American Jewry, I do not
mean that small segment of the Jewish-American world who find
their way to the synagogue twice a day, study the Torah morning and
night, live out their lives wholly within the Judaism of the dual
Torah. That sector of Jewry, self-segregated and rightly self-assured,
raises no questions about religiosity. It is pious in the profound and
rich sense of Judaism. Synagogues of that sector of Jewry, mostly
Orthodox, are crowded on weekdays and require two, three, or more
worship services on the Sabbath. While these Jews (in the main)
remain aloof from the appeal of Holocaust and Redemption, for them
Judaism encompasses the whole of life and commitment; and both
the private and the familial, and also the civic and the public, life of
Jewry join in a single entity, defined within the Torah in two parts,
oral and written, which God handed over to Moses at Mount Sinai.
No study has suggested that the observant Orthodox compose so
much as one-tenth of the Jews of North America, although in a few
major cities, such as New York City or London, the proportion is
perhaps double. The bulk of Jewish Americans, Canadians, West Europeans, Latin Americans, South Africans, and Australians do not live
within the disciplines of the Torah. While in North America most of
the Jews (nonobservant in the Orthodox sense) do not affiliate with
the Orthodox community, they do in Western Europe and the European communities of South Africa and Australia; but the picture does
not change. Jews integrated into the values and civilization of the
West have a dual Judaism—the one for the home, the other for
the life of public discourse; and it is that Judaism that shapes and
defines the lives of nearly all Jews in the West, those who are not
fully observant in the Orthodox definition.

But it would be a mistake to see as fundamentally secular ordinary Jewish Americans and Canadians and West Europeans, Brazilians and Argentinians, Australians and South Africans, living not in segregation but culturally wholly integrated among their Gentile, mostly Christian neighbors. I shall show that these Jews—like their neighbors in some ways, unlike them in others—respond to the crises of life and history by invoking a very particular story of who they are. This story speaks not of mere facts but talks of God's actions and demands. Thus in secular America and Canada lives a people who, in the inner vision of heart and soul, at times dwells alone in splendid encounter with God. Integrated in clothing and language, commonly in food and neighborhood, in work and rest, they are God's people; and, in their own way, these Canadians and Americans listen to God's voice and act together to sanctify the lives that God has given them.

Two Judaisms flourish in the vast middle range of the socially integrated Jewries of the West: one for home and family; one for the shared life of the corporate community. The Judaism found compelling in the private life derives from the Judaism of the dual Torah, oral and written, that took shape in late antiquity, the first seven centuries of the Common Era, and reached its definitive statement in the Talmud of Babylonia. That Judaism not only flourished, as the normative and paramount system, into the nineteenth century but now, on the eve of the twenty-first century, continues to impart shape and structure on the ongoing life of the synagogue, to its liturgy, its holy days and festivals, its theology, its way of life and worldview.

THE JUDAISM
OF HOLOCAUST AND REDEMPTION

The second Judaism came on the scene only in the aftermath of the Second World War and the rise of the State of Israel. I call this the Judaism of Holocaust and Redemption, because it is a Judaic system that invokes, as its generative worldview, the catastrophe of the destruction by Germany of most of the Jews of Europe between 1933 and 1945 and the creation, three years afterward, of the State of Israel. This Judaism, too, has its way of life, its religious duties, its public celebrations. It is communal, stressing public policy and practical action. It involves political issues; for example, policy toward the State of Israel, government assistance in helping Soviet Jews gain freedom, and, in the homelands of the Jewish Americans, Canadians, Britons, or French, matters of local politics as well. The first of the two Judaisms flourishes in the synagogue, as I have said; and the second, in the streets. The one is private, the other public; the one personal and familial, the other civic and communal.

Let me spell out the worldview and way of life of this other Judaism that has the power to transform civic and public affairs in Jewry as much as the Judaism of the dual Torah enchants and changes the personal and familial ones. In politics, history, society, Jews in North America respond to the Judaism of the Holocaust and Redemption in such a way as to imagine they are someone else, living somewhere else, at another time and circumstance. That vision transforms families into an Israel, a community. The somewhere else is Poland in 1944 and the earthly Jerusalem, and the vision turns them from reasonably secure citizens of America or Canada into insecure refugees finding hope and life in the Land and State of Israel. Public events commemorate, so that *we* were there in "Auschwitz," which stands for all the centers where Jews were murdered; and *we* share, too, in the everyday life of that faraway place in which we do not live but should, the State of Israel. That transformation of time and of place, no less than the recasting accomplished by the Passover seder or the rite of berit milah or the huppah, turns people into something other than what they are in the here and now.

The issues of this public Judaism, the civil religion of North American Jewry (and not theirs alone), are perceived to be political. But the power of that Judaism to turn things into something other than what they seem, to teach lessons that change the everyday into the remarkable—that power works no less wonderfully than does the power of the other Judaism to make me Adam or one of the Israel who crossed the Red Sea. The lessons of the two Judaisms are, of course, not the same. The Judaism of the dual Torah teaches about the sanctification of the everyday in the road toward the salvation of the holy people. The Judaism of Holocaust and Redemption tells me that the everyday—the here and the now of home and family— ends not in a new Eden but in a cloud of gas; that salvation lies today, if I will it, but not here and not now. And it teaches me not only not to trouble to sanctify, but also not even to trust, the present circumstance.

The closing prayer, Alenu ("who has not made us like the nations of the world"), bears the redeeming message that, in the end, the nations of the world will become like us in worshiping the one true God, Creator of heaven and earth. The task incumbent on me because of the Judaism of Holocaust and Redemption, its Alenu, leads me toward a humanity in the image not of the divine but of the demonic. The great theologian of the Judaism of Holocaust and Redemption, Emil Fackenheim, has often maintained that the Holocaust produced an eleventh commandment "Not to hand Hitler any more victories." The commanding voice of Sinai gave Ten Commandments; the commanding voice of Auschwitz, that eleventh. The ten call for us to become like God in the ways in which the image of God may be graven upon us human beings: by keeping the Sabbath and honoring the other and having no other gods but God. The eleventh tells us what we must not do; it appeals to us not to love God but to spite a man. Thus politics transforms.

The Judaism of Holocaust and Redemption supplies the words that make another world of this one. Those words, moreover, change the assembly of like-minded individuals into an occasion for the celebration of the group and the commemoration of their shared memories. Not only so, but events defined, meetings called, moments identified as distinctive and holy, by that Judaism of Holocaust and Redemption, mark the public calendar and draw people from home and family to collectivity and community—those events, and, except for specified reasons, not the occasions of the sacred calendar of the synagogue; that is, the life of Israel as defined by the Torah. Just as in the United States religions address the realm of individuals and families, but a civil religion—Thanksgiving, the Fourth of July, the rites of politics—defines public discourse on matters of value and ultimate concern, so the Judaism of the dual Torah forms the counterpart to Christianity, and the Judaism of Holocaust and Redemption, as I said, constitutes Jewry's civil religion.

Let me now define in detail this other and competing Judaism, and explain its political program. Only then shall we be able to assess the impact, upon the received Judaism, of the civil religion comprised by Holocaust and Redemption. The "Holocaust" of the Judaism of

Holocaust and Redemption refers to the murder of six million Jewish children, women, and men in Europe from 1933 through 1945 by Nazi Germany. The "Redemption" is the creation of the State of Israel. Both events constitute essentially political happenings: a government did the one; a state and government emerged from the other. And both events involved collectivities acting in the realm of public policy. The worldview of the Judaism of Holocaust and Redemption stresses the unique character of the murders of European Jews, the providential and redemptive meaning of the creation of the State of Israel. The way of life of the Judaism of Holocaust and Redemption requires active work in raising money and political support for the State of Israel. Different from Zionism, which holds that Jews should live in a Jewish state, this system serves in particular to give Jews living in America a reason and an explanation for being Jewish. This Judaism, therefore, lays particular stress on the complementarity of the political experiences of mid-twentieth-century Jewry: the mass murder in death factories of six million of the Jews of Europe, and the creation of the State of Israel three years after the end of the massacre. These events together are seen as providential. The system as a whole presents an encompassing myth, linking one event to the other as an instructive pattern, as I said, and moves Jews to follow a particular set of actions, rather than other sorts, as it tells them why they should be Jewish. In all, the civil religion of Jewry addresses issues of definition of the group and the policies it should follow to sustain its ongoing life and protect its integrity.

The Judaism of Holocaust and Redemption affirms and explains in this-worldly terms the Jews' distinctiveness. It forms, within Jewry, a chapter in a larger movement of ethnic assertion in America. Attaining popularity in the late 1960s, the Judaism of Holocaust and Redemption became popular at the same time that movements for black rights, Italo-American and Polish-American affirmation, feminism, and movements for self-esteem without regard to sexual preference attained prominence. That movement toward the rediscovery of difference responded to this assimilation into American civilization and its norms. Once people spoke English without a foreign accent, they could think about learning Polish, or Yiddish, or Norwegian. It then became safe and charming. Just as when black students demanded what they deemed ethnically characteristic food, so Jewish students discovered they wanted kosher food. In that context, the

LABYRINTH BOOKS

536 W 112TH STREET   NEW YORK NY 10025
TEL 212 865 1588   FAX 212 865 2749

books@labyrinthbooks.com www.labyrinthbooks.com

M-F 9-10 SAT 10-8 SUN 11-7

Judaism of Holocaust and Redemption came into sharp focus, with its answers to unavoidable questions deemed related to public policy: Who are we? Why should we be Jewish? What does it mean to be Jewish? How do we relate to Jews in other times and places? What is "Israel," meaning the State of Israel, to us, and what are we to it? Who are we in American society? These and other questions form the agenda for the Judaism of Holocaust and Redemption.

The power of the Judaism of the Holocaust and Redemption to frame Jews' public policy—to the exclusion of the Judaism of the dual Torah—may be shown very simply. The Holocaust formed the question; redemption, in the form of the creation of the State of Israel, the answer, for all universal Jewish public activity and discourse. Synagogues, except for specified occasions, appeal to a few, but activities that express the competing Judaism appeal to nearly everybody. That is to say, nearly all American Jews identify with the State of Israel and regard its welfare as more than a secular good: as a metaphysical necessity, as the other chapter of the Holocaust. Nearly all American Jews are not only supporters of the State of Israel; they also regard their own "being Jewish" as inextricably bound up with the meaning they impute to the Jewish state.[1] In many ways, every day of their lives these Jews relive the terror-filled years in which European Jews were wiped out—and every day they do something about it. It is as if people spend their lives trying to live out a cosmic myth, and, through rites of expiation and regeneration, accomplished the goal of purification and renewal. Access to the life of feeling and experience—to the way of life that makes one distinctive without leaving the person terribly different from everybody else—emerged in the Judaic system of Holocaust and Redemption. The Judaism of Holocaust and Redemption presents an immediately accessible message, cast in extreme emotions of terror and triumph, its round of endless activity demanding only spare time. That Judaism realizes in a poignant way the conflicting demands of Jewish Americans to be intensely Jewish, but only once in a while, and provides a means of expressing difference in public and in politics while not exacting much of a cost in meaningful everyday difference from others.

In addition to the Judaism of the dual Torah, therefore, Jewish North and Latin Americans, Western Europeans, Australians, and South Africans share a transforming perspective, which imparts to their public vision, as much as to their private vision, a different set of spectacles from those worn by everybody else in the sheltering society of America or Canada. There is not only a Jewish-ethnic, but a Judaic-religious corporate experience out there; and, while it self-evidently does not lead to the synagogue, it does enchant vision and change perspective and persons. There are myths and rites to which people respond, even though they are not those of the received Judaism. And, as I shall suggest, the Judaic system that takes the place, in the life of the community at large, of the received Judaism indeed occupies its share of the place reserved for the unique, the self-evident truths beyond argument.

JUDAISM AT HOME AND
JUDAISM IN PUBLIC:
THE CIVIL RELIGION OF
AMERICAN JEWS

When we ask why the bifurcation between the personal and the familial, subjected to the Judaism of the dual Torah, perceived as religion; and the public and civic, governed by the Judaism of Holocaust and Redemption, perceived as politics—we turn outward. For the explanation lies in the definition of permissible difference in North America and the place of religion in that difference. Specifically, in North American society, defined as it is by Protestant conceptions, it is permissible to be of a different religion, but religion is a matter that is personal and private. Hence, Judaism as a religion encompasses what is personal and familial. The Jews as a political entity, then, put forth a separate system, one that concerns not religion, which is not supposed to intervene in political action, but public policy. Judaism in public policy produces political action in favor of the State of Israel, Soviet Jewry, or other important matters of the corporate community. Judaism in private affects the individual and the family and is not supposed to play a role in politics at all. That pattern conforms to the Protestant model of religion, and the Jews have accomplished conformity to it by creating two Judaisms. A consideration of the Protestant pattern, which separates not the institutions of church from the activities of the state, but the entire public polity from the inner life, will show us how to make sense of the presence of the two Judaisms of North America.

Here in Protestant North America, people commonly see religion as personal and private. Prayer, for example, speaks for the individual. No wonder, then, that those enchanted words and gestures that Jews adopt transform the inner life, recognize life's transitions, and turn them into rites of passage. It is part of a larger prejudice that religion and rite speak to the heart of the particular person. What can be changed by rite, then, is first of all personal and private, not social, not an issue of culture, not affective in politics, not part of the public interest. What people do when they respond to religion, therefore, affects an interior world—a world with little bearing on the realities of public discourse: what, in general terms, we should do about nuclear weapons; or, in terms of Judaism, how we should organize and imagine society. The transformations of religion do not involve the world, or even the self as representative of other selves, but mainly the individual at the most unique and unrepresentative. If God speaks to me in particular, then the message, by definition, is mine—not someone else's. Religion, the totality of these private messages (within the present theory), therefore, by definition, does not make itself available for communication in public discourse. Religion plays no public role. It is a matter not of public activity but of what people happen to believe or do in private, a matter mainly of the heart.

But the public life of Jewry, reaching religious statement in Judaism, is not trivial, not private, not individual, not a matter only of the heart. Religion is public, political, social, economic. Religion as a powerful force in shaping politics and culture, economic action, and social organization finds its counterpart, within Jewry, as we shall see, in the power of the community of the Jews to generate a Judaism.

Nothing humanity has made constitutes a less personal, a less private, a less trivial fact of human life than religion. Religion, however, is understood in Protestant North America as being individual and subjective: how I feel all by myself, not what I do with other people. The prevailing attitude of mind identifies religion with belief, to the near exclusion of behavior. Religion is understood as a personal state of mind or an individual's personal and private attitude. When we study religion, the present picture suggests, we ask not about society but about self, not about culture and community but about conscience and character. Religion speaks of individuals and not of groups: of faith and its substance, and, beyond faith, of the things that faith represents: faith reified; hence, religion. William Scott Green, professor of religion at the University of Rochester, further comments in more general terms:

> The basic attitude of mind characteristic of the study of religion holds that religion is certainly in your soul, likely in your heart, perhaps in your mind, but never in your body. That attitude encourages us to construe religion cerebrally and individually, to think in terms of beliefs and the believer, rather than in terms of behavior and community. The lens provided by this prejudice draws our attention to the intense and obsessive belief called "faith," so religion is understood as a state of mind, the object of intellectual or emotional commitment, the result of decisions to believe or to have faith. According to this model, people have religion but they do not do their religion. Thus we tend to devalue behavior and performance, to make it epiphenomenal and of course to emphasize thinking and reflecting, the practice of theology, as a primary activity of religious people. . . . The famous slogan that "ritual recapitulates myth" follows this model by assigning priority to the story and to people's believing the story, and makes behavior simply an imitation, an aping, a mere acting out.[2]

Now, as we reflect on Green's observations, we recognize what is at stake: it is the definition of religion—or, rather, what matters in or about religion—emerging from Protestant theology and Protestant religious experience.

For when we lay heavy emphasis on faith to the exclusion of works, on the individual rather than on society, on conscience instead of culture; when we treat behavior and performance by groups as less important, and thinking, reflecting, theology, and belief as more important, then we are adopting as normative for academic scholarship convictions critical to the Protestant Reformation. Judaism and the historical, classical forms of Christianity, Roman Catholic and Orthodox, place emphasis at least equally on religion as a matter of works and not of faith alone, on behavior and community as well as belief and conscience. Religion is something that people do, and they do it together. Religion is not something people merely *have*, as individuals. Since the entire civilization of the West, from the fourth century on, carried forward the convictions of Christianity, not about the individual alone but about politics and culture, we may hardly find surprising the Roman Catholic conviction that religion flourishes not alone in heart and mind but in eternal social forms: the church; in former times, the state as well.

A community of interest and experience such as the Jews comprise will self-evidently appeal to shared values that give expression to common experience, explaining in a single way how diverse individuals and families find it possible to see things in so cogent a manner: this way, not that. The issue, therefore, is not whether a Judaism forms the center, but *which* Judaism. What is important in understanding where and how Judaism is a religion, and where it is not, is this: the two Judaisms coexist, the one in private, the other in public. The Judaism of the dual Torah forms the counterpart to religion in the Protestant model, affecting home and family and private life. The Judaism of Holocaust and Redemption presents the counterpart to religion in the civil framework, making an impact upon public life and policy within the distinctive Jewish community of North America. The relationships between the two Judaisms prove parlous and uneven, since the Judaism of home and family takes second place in public life of Jewry—and public life is where the action takes place in that community.

Not only so, but the Judaism of the dual Torah makes powerful demands on the devotee, for example, requiring him or her to frame emotions within a received model of attitudes and appropriate feelings. The Judaism of Holocaust and Redemption, by contrast, provides ready access to emotional or political encounters, easily available to all—by definition. The immediately accessible experiences of politics predominate. The repertoire of human experience in the Judaism of the dual Torah presents, by contrast, as human options the opposite of the immediate. In this Judaism, Jews receive and use the heritage of human experience captured, as in amber, in the words of the dual Torah. Thus, in public life, Jews focus their imaginative energies upon the Holocaust and their eschatological fantasies on the "beginning of our redemption" in the State of Israel. Two competing Judaisms—the one that works at home, the other in public—therefore coexist on an unequal basis, because the one appeals to easily imagined experience, the other to the power of will to translate and transform the here and the now into something other.

The Judaism of Holocaust and Redemption speaks of exclusion and bigotry, hatred and contempt, and asks us, therefore, to imagine ourselves in gas chambers. All of us have known exclusion (although many suppress the knowledge). No Jew can imagine himself or herself to be utterly like "everyone else," because the beginning of being a Jew is, by definition, to be different because one is a Jew—whatever the difference may mean. Accordingly, the Judaism of Holocaust and Redemption addresses an experience that is common and by definition accessible to all Jews. The Judaism of the dual Torah speaks of God and humanity in God's likeness, after God's image. It calls up the experience of exile and redemption, appealing to corners of experience that, for us as we are, prove empty. The Judaism of the dual Torah demands sensibility, intellect, understanding; it asks us to build bridges from who we are to what the Torah tells us we may become. Not everyone musters the inner energy to imagine, and many do not. No wonder, then, that the Judaism of Holocaust and Redemption enjoys priority over the Judaism of the dual Torah—except in those corners of life, in those private moments of intense personal experience, at which the Torah, and only the Torah, serves to tell us what is happening to us. The competition, as I said, is unequal, because the one Judaism reaches into that sore surface of Jewish life—that is, being different by reason of being Jewish; while the other plumbs the depths of our being human in God's image: not the same thing at all.

And yet—

And yet—if I may make my judgement explicit—the Judaism of the Holocaust and Redemption, with its focus upon the "out there" of public policy and its present preeminence, offers as a world nightmares made of words. Its choice of formative experiences and its repertoire of worthwhile human events impose upon Jews two devilish enchantments. First, the message of Holocaust and Redemption is that difference is not destiny but disaster—if one trusts the Gentiles. Second, the expressions of Holocaust and Redemption—political action, letters to public figures, pilgrimages to grisly places—leave the inner life untouched but distorted. Being Jewish in that Judaism generates fear and distrust of the other, but does not compensate by an appeal to worth and dignity for the self. The Judaism of Holocaust and Redemption leaves the life of individual and family untouched and unchanged. But people live at home and in family. Consequently, the Judaism of Holocaust and Redemption, in ignoring the private life, makes trivial the differences that separate Jew from Gentile. People may live a private life of utter neutrality, untouched by the demands of the faith, while working out a public life of acute segregation. The Judaism of Holocaust and Redemption turns on its head the wise policy of the reformers and enlightened of the early nineteenth century: a Jew at home, a citizen "out there." Now it is an undifferentiated American at home, a Jew in the public polity.

The Judaism of the dual Torah, for its part, proves equally insufficient. Its address to the self and family to the near exclusion of the world beyond leaves awry its fundamental mythic structure, which appeals to history and the end of time, to sanctification and the worth of difference. Viewed whole, each of its components at the passage of life and the passing of one's own life—the disposition of birth, marriage, aging, for example; the encounter with difference—makes sense only in that larger context of public policy. Separating the private and familial from the public and communal distorts the Judaism of the dual Torah. Ignoring the individual and the deeply felt reality of the home leaves the Judaism of Holocaust and Redemption strangely vacant: in the end, a babble of tear-producing, but unfelt, words; a manipulation of emotions for a transient moment. The Judaism of the Holocaust and Redemption is romantic. The Judaism of the dual Torah accomplishes the permanent wedding of Israel, the Jewish people, to God. The one is for hotels; the other, for the home. But both Judaisms speak to our heart—the divided heart today.

NOTES

1. I do not mean to suggest that American Judaism constitutes a version of Zionism. Zionism maintains that Jews who do not live in the Jewish state are in exile: there is no escaping that simple allegation, which must call into question that facile affirmation of Zionism central to American Judaism. Zionism further declares that Jews who do not live in the State of Israel must aspire to migrate to that nation or, at the very least, raise their children as potential emigrants: American Judaism chokes on this position. Zionism holds, moreover, that all Jews must concede—indeed, affirm—the centrality of Jeru-

salem, and of the State of Israel, in the life of Jews throughout the world. Zionism draws the necessary consequence that Jews who live outside of the State of Israel are in significant ways less "good Jews" than the ones who live there. Now all of these positions, commonplace in Israeli Zionism and certainly accepted—in benign verbal formulations, to be sure—by American Jews, contradict the simple facts of the situation of American Jews and their Judaism. First, they do not think that they are in exile: their Judaism makes no concession on that point. Second, they do not have the remotest thought of emigrating from America to the State of Israel—even though on ceremonial occasions they may not protest when Israelis declare such to be their duty.

2. Personal letter, 17 January 1985.

THE JEWISH PEOPLE: JUDAISM IN THE WORLD TODAY

Recent Trends
in American Judaism

JACK WERTHEIMER

The decade of the 1980s witnessed a series of acrimonious confrontations between the leaders of various religious denominations within American Jewry. Some observers have voiced concern that American Jewry will soon be riven into contending camps that do not recognize each other's legitimacy as Jews. Others maintain that such a polarization has already come to pass; that a deep divide separates Orthodox from non-Orthodox Jews, with only a relatively small population of modern-Orthodox and right-wing Conservative Jews seeking to bridge the divide. And still others view the present confrontations as merely a passing stage in the continuing evolution of a distinctly American version of Judaism.

The time period under discussion spans the two decades from the late 1960s to the late 1980s. This has been an era of perceptible change in patterns of behavior among American Jews, particularly in the religious sphere. Beginning in the mid-1960s, the agenda of American Jewish life shifted significantly in the wake of new social trends and reassessed priorities. In short, the changing character of Jewish life in America necessitated shifts within organized religious institutions, which in turn set off new chains of events. To set into bolder relief the far-reaching shifts that have occurred of late in the religious sphere, it would be well to begin with a brief consideration of Jewish religious life in the middle decades of the twentieth century.

THE RELIGIOUS BEHAVIOR OF AMERICAN JEWS

An examination of the religious behavior of the masses of American Jews provides a convenient point of departure for a consideration of developments in American Judaism since the mid-1960s. The key sources of data on the religious behavior of American Jews are population studies. In the decade from 1977 to 1987, over fifty such studies were conducted under the auspices of local federations of Jewish philanthropies for the purpose of compiling profiles of the Jewish populations they serve. Virtually every large Jewish community has been surveyed, as have a considerable number of middle-size and small communities.[1] Included in these surveys are a series of questions pertaining to religious life: denominational affiliation, synagogue membership and attendance, selected measures of ritual observance, and intermarriage patterns. While these studies provide rich materials on contemporary trends, only a few such surveys exist from mid-century that can serve as a basis for comparative analysis. Still, when possible, comparisons will be made, taking account of, among other things, earlier surveys, as well as the National Jewish Population Study of 1970–71.[2]

Denominational Preferences

Recent population studies indicate that the preponderant majority of American Jews continue to identify with one of the denominations of American Judaism, albeit at varying rates and in declining numbers (see Table 1). When asked how they identify their denominational preference, over two-thirds of Jews in all communities for which we have data indicated that they are either Reform, Conservative, or Orthodox. This kind of self-identification does not necessarily translate into synagogue membership or religious observance, but it indicates that the majority of American Jews accept some kind of religious label. However, compared to the National Jewish Population Study of 1970–71,[3] which found that only 14 percent of American Jews eschewed a denominational preference, it appears that in the 1980s a rising percentage of Jews do not identify with one of the religious movements. For the most part, it is only in smaller Jewish communities that approximately 85 percent of Jews accept a denominational label. By contrast, in the larger centers of Jewish population it is far more common for Jews to see themselves as "just Jewish" or without a religious preference.

The rejection of a denominational label by 23 percent of New York Jews, 28 percent of Los Angeles Jews, 30 percent of Miami Jews, 20 percent of Chicago Jews, and 22 percent of Philadelphia Jews is

TABLE 1.
DENOMINATIONAL SELF-IDENTIFICATION (PERCENT)

Community	Year of Study	Orthodox	Conservative	Reform	No Preference/ Other
Atlanta, Ga.	1983	5	42	37	16
Atlantic City, N.J.	1985	6	46	29	15
Baltimore, Md.	1985	20	35	29	16
Boston, Mass.	1985	4	33	42	21
Chicago, Ill.	1982	6	35	39	20[a]
Cleveland, Ohio	1981	9	39	47	5
Denver, Colo.[d]	1981	7	28	35	30
Hartford, Conn.	1981	6	38	40	16
Kansas City, Kan.	1985	7	38	38	16
Los Angeles, Calif.	1979	6	30	34	30
MetroWest, N.J.	1986	6	38	34	20
Miami (Dade County, Fla.)	1982	11	35	24	30
Milwaukee, Wisc.	1983	7	27	52	14
Minneapolis, Minn.	1981	5	53	32	10
New York, N.Y.	1981	13	35	29	23
Palm Beach County, Fla.	1987	2	43	3	25
Philadelphia, Pa.	1984	5	41	25	22[b]
Pittsburgh, Pa.	1984	13	44	37	6
Richmond, Va.	1983	8	42	36	14
Rochester, N.Y.	1980	12	36	42	10
St. Louis, Mo.	1982	8	26	52	14
St. Paul, Minn.	1981	7	55	27	11
Scranton, Pa.	1984	31	48	20	
Seattle, Wash.	1979	16	30	46	8
Tampa, Fla.	1980	2	43	41	14
Washington, D.C.	1983	4	35	41	18[c]
Worcester, Mass.	1987	6	29	49	16

Source: Unless otherwise noted, tables are based on the studies listed in n. 1. Atlantic City and St. Paul data are from the Boston Study, p. 154.
[a]Includes "Traditional."
[b]Includes 1.5 percent Reconstructionist; 7 percent "Traditional."
[c]Includes 3 percent Reconstructionist.
[d]Does not include converts.
Note: Figures rounded to nearest whole number.

particularly noteworthy, given that these are the five largest Jewish communities in the United States and encompass close to 60 percent of the national Jewish population. (See Table 2 for a ranking by size of the larger Jewish communities and their approximate populations when last surveyed.)

Table 1 illustrates the wide fluctuation in strength of the various denominations. Each of the major movements can claim great strength in particular communities. When we take the size of communities into account, it is possible to evaluate the relative strength of each denomination. (In most surveys, Reconstructionists were deemed numerically neglible and therefore were not listed separately. Even in

TABLE 2.
LARGEST U.S. JEWISH COMMUNITIES

Community	Jewish Population	Community	Jewish Population
New York, N.Y.	1,742,500	Middlesex County, N.J.	39,350
Los Angeles, Calif.	500,870	Oakland, Calif.	35,000
Chicago, Ill.	248,000	San Diego, Calif.	35,000
Miami (Dade County,		Monmouth County, N.J.	33,600
Fla.)[a]	241,000	Central New Jersey	32,000
Philadelphia, Pa.	240,000	Denver, Colo.	30,000
Boston, Mass.	170,000	Houston, Tex.	28,000
Washington, D.C.	157,335	Southern New Jersey	28,000
MetroWest, N.J.	111,000	Hartford, Conn.	26,000
Baltimore, Md.	92,000	Milwaukee, Wis.	23,900
San Francisco, Calif.	80,000	Delaware Valley, Pa.	23,000
Cleveland, Ohio	70,000	Minneapolis, Minn.	23,000
Detroit, Mich.	70,000	Kansas City, Mo.	22,100
Bergen County, N.J.	69,300	Cincinnati, Ohio	22,000
Ft. Lauderdale, Fla.	60,000	Dallas, Tex.	22,000
Orange County, Calif.	60,000	New Haven, Conn.	22,000
South Broward, Fla.	60,000	Seattle, Wash.	19,500
Atlanta, Ga.	50,000	Northern New Jersey	19,000
Phoenix, Ariz.	50,000	Buffalo, N.Y.	18,500
Palm Beach County, Fla.	45,000	San Jose, Calif.	18,000
Pittsburgh, Pa.	45,000	Tucson, Ariz.	18,000
Rockland County, N.Y.	40,000	Rhode Island	17,500
South County, Fla.	40,000	Columbus, Ohio	15,000

Source: Executive Summary, Kansas City study. See n. 1.
[a] American Jewish Year Book 1988, p. 229.

Philadelphia, where the central institutions of the Reconstructionist movement are located, only 1.5 percent of respondents identified with Reconstructionism.)

A high level of identification with Orthodoxy is confined largely to New York. Even in New York, Orthodox allegiance is concentrated mainly in the boroughs of Brooklyn and the Bronx and is relatively weak in Manhattan. (Twenty-seven percent of heads of Jewish households in Brooklyn identified as Orthodox compared to 8 percent in Manhattan.)[4] The numerical strength of Orthodoxy in the largest Jewish community of the United States gives that movement a visibility that belies its actual size. In point of fact, some demographers contend that the percentage of Jews who identify as Orthodox has declined to under 10 percent in the late 1980s.[5]

Identification with Conservative Judaism continues at a high level in every Jewish community, but the dominance of the movement is now challenged by Reform in quite a number of localities. In some areas, such as Philadelphia and Minneapolis–St. Paul, Conservatism has maintained formidable strength. It also holds the allegiance of a high percentage of Jews in Sunbelt communities, both in areas where older Jews retire, such as southern Florida, and in burgeoning communities such as Atlanta. Nationally, the Conservative movement still commands the allegiance of a plurality of Jews, albeit a shrinking plurality.

The main beneficiary of Orthodox and Conservative losses seems to be the Reform movement (as well as the group of Jews with no preference). This is evident in Boston, for example, where, between 1965 and 1985, individuals who identified themselves as Orthodox declined from 14 percent to 4 percent, and as Conservative from 44 percent to 33 percent, while the percentage of those who identified as Reform rose from 27 percent to 42 percent, and the "no preference" group increased from 5 percent to 14 percent. Reform continues to exhibit great popularity in its traditional areas of strength—the Midwest and South—but is gaining many new adherents throughout the nation. Just as the middle decades of the twentieth century witnessed dramatic numerical gains by the Conservative movement, the closing decades of the century appear as a period of particular growth for Reform Judaism. Indeed, some Reform leaders contend that their movement has already outstripped Conservatism. However, most demographers of American Jewry argue otherwise. On the basis of

recent population studies, Barry Kosmin, director of the North American Jewish Data Bank, estimated in 1987 that American Jews were
divided as follows: 2 percent Reconstructionist, 9 percent Orthodox,
29 percent Reform, 34 percent Conservative, and 26 percent "other"
or "just Jewish."[6]

To refine such figures and project likely trends for the near-term
future, it is useful to examine patterns among generational and age
groups. A dozen studies of Jewish communities provide data on the
identification of various age groupings within each of the religious
denominations. Among Jews who identify themselves as Orthodox, a
consistent pattern emerges: higher percentages of Orthodox Jews are
in the 18- to 34-year-old group than in middle-aged groupings; but
the highest percentages of Orthodox Jews in any age category are
over age 65. This suggests both a source of future strength and future
weakness for Orthodoxy. Unlike the other denominations, Orthodoxy
is retaining the allegiance of its young and even showing a modest
increase in attractiveness to younger Jews. By contrast, surveys conducted shortly after World War II repeatedly found that younger Jews
from Orthodox homes intended to abandon an Orthodox identification. As a denomination with more adherents in the childbearing
years than in middle age, Orthodoxy can expect an infusion of new
members through the birth of children to its younger population. But
even as it maintains its attractiveness to its youth, Orthodoxy will
have to contend with ongoing losses through the death of its older
population, a group that is considerably more numerous than its
youth population. In virtually every community for which data are
available, with the notable exception of New York, between two and
three times as many Orthodox Jews are over age 65 as are between
ages 18 and 45. Thus, despite higher birthrates, Jews who identify as
Orthodox are not likely to increase in the near future.

Adherents of Conservative Judaism form a different pattern. Self-
identification with Conservatism is stronger among middle-aged
groups than among younger or older groups. In some communities,
the largest segment of Conservative Jews is aged 35 to 44 and in
others 45 to 64; but the percentage of Conservative Jews aged 18 to
35 is smaller than in either of the other two age categories. The
apparent attrition among younger members constitutes the greatest
demographic challenge facing the Conservative movement. At present
it is unclear whether the movement has been unable to retain the

allegiance of many of its youth, or whether children who grow up in Conservative families defer identifying with the movement until they have children of their own, in which case population studies conducted in the early 1990s should reveal a rise in the percentage of Conservative Jews in the younger age categories.[7] Which of these explanations holds true will determine whether the Conservative movement will age or retain a youthful character.

Of all the denominations, Reform maintains greatest stability across the age spectrum, with the exception of the oldest age cohorts. In virtually every community there are approximately as many Reform Jews in the younger age grouping (18 to 35) as in middle-aged groupings. This would indicate the success of the movement either in retaining its youth or in recruiting younger Jews from the other denominations. From a numerical point of view, it is immaterial how Reform recruits its younger members, but it would still be interesting to know whether young people are attracted from within, or whether Reform is recruiting from outside its ranks.

DENOMINATIONAL LIFE:
REFORM JUDAISM

The most visible evidence of significant shifts in Jewish religious life may be observed in the new policies and procedures adopted by the various Jewish denominations. All of the movements have been challenged by their own constituents to respond to new social concerns, and in turn each movement has been forced to react to the new directions taken by other groups on the religious spectrum. As a result, all four major movements in American Judaism have adopted radically new programs that could not have been envisioned at midcentury.

Since the mid-1960s the official position of the Reform movement regarding a range of religious practices and ideological issues has been shaped by two seemingly contradictory impulses. On the one hand, Reform has sanctioned a number of radical departures from traditional practice: it was the first to ordain women as rabbis and cantors; it steadfastly refused to place sanctions on rabbis who officiated at mixed marriages; and most dramatically, it unilaterally redefined Jewish identity. On the other hand, the Reform movement has reintroduced or signaled its willingness to tolerate many religious practices that had been rejected in the past; in many temples men now don skullcaps and prayer shawls, kosher meals are prepared, and Hebrew usages have been reinstated. Reform, then, is changing in both directions—toward a more radical break with traditional practices and toward an unprecedented openness to traditional teachings.

This eclecticism has been made possible by a rethinking of the basic Reform position. Whereas Reform Judaism was formerly a movement that on principle said "no" to some aspects of the Jewish tradition, it is now a movement that is open to all Jewish possibilities, whether traditional or innovative. The guiding principle of Reform today is the autonomy of every individual to choose a Jewish religious expression that is personally meaningful. The result is a Judaism open to all options and therefore appealing to a broad range of Jews— including those who have long felt disenfranchised, such as homosexuals and Jews married to non-Jews. The dilemma this raises for the Reform movement is one of limits, of boundaries. If the autonomy of the individual prevails above all else, what beliefs and practices unite all Reform Jews? Is there, then, a model Reform Jew? And is there anything a Reform Jew can do that places him or her beyond the pale of acceptable behavior? Thus far, Reform Judaism has been unable to answer these questions.

The Abandonment of Ideology

Not surprisingly, the issues that have prompted the most intense debate in the Reform movement have revolved around questions of definition and boundary. As noted above, the reintroduction of some rituals during the 1950s already engendered debate over the future direction of Reform, with some prominent rabbis expressing concern that the movement was losing its way and becoming less distinctive. The debate became considerably more vociferous as Reform Judaism instituted several radical new changes during the 1970s. Three issues especially sparked controversy: the introduction of a new prayer book to replace the venerated *Union Prayer Book* that had done service for eighty years; the decision of growing numbers of Reform rabbis to officiate at mixed marriages; and the desire of the movement to produce an updated platform to replace earlier ideological statements. In each case, Reform was torn between respect for the autonomous choice of the individual and the need to define a clear-cut position; and in each case, the former concern triumphed over the latter.

DENOMINATIONAL LIFE:
ORTHODOX JUDAISM

During the past quarter century, two major trends have marked the development of Orthodox Judaism in America. First Orthodoxy has achieved an unprecedented degree of respectability in the eyes of both non-Orthodox Jews and non-Jews. Where once Orthodox Judaism had been written off as a movement of immigrants and poor Jews, it is now regarded as a denomination with staying power and appeal to Jews from across the religious spectrum. As sociologist Charles Liebman has noted, "This is the first generation in over two hundred years—that is, since its formulation as the effort by traditional Judaism to confront modernity—in which Orthodoxy is not in decline."[8] Even though Orthodoxy is not growing numerically, its comparative stability, particularly as measured by the ability to inculcate a strong sense of allegiance among its young, has given the movement significant credibility and dynamism. Indeed, the movement's programs, particularly with regard to youth, are being increasingly imitated by the other denominations.

The second trend that characterizes Orthodoxy is the shift to the right in the thinking and behavior of Orthodox Jews. Orthodox Jews today observe ritual commandments more punctiliously than at mid-century; they regard rabbinic authorities who adjudicate Jewish law in a conservative manner with more favor than they do more liberal rabbis; and in their attitudes toward non-Orthodox Jews they tend to be more exclusivist than before. Both the emergence of a stronger Orthodoxy and the movement's shift to the right have reshaped relations between Orthodox and non-Orthodox Jews.

Problems of Definition

Considerable difficulties inhere in any discussion of the Orthodox world. Like their counterparts in other religious movements, Orthodox Jews do not share a single articulated theology, let alone movement ideology. Where Orthodoxy differs, however, is in the degree of intolerance displayed by different sectors of the same movement toward each other. This is evident in the expressions of dismay that modern Orthodox Jews voice about "the black hats"—more right-wing Orthodox types[9]—moving into their neighborhoods.[10] Right-wing Orthodox rabbis often seek to delegitimate their

more moderate Orthodox counterparts,[11] while the right-wing Orthodox press reserves its greatest scorn for the policies of moderate
Orthodox groups.[12] Even on the Orthodox right, different Hasidic
groups have battled with each other. The student of Orthodoxy is
thus faced with the question of whether Orthodoxy can truly be
viewed as a coherent and united movement.

Further, Orthodoxy is institutionally fragmented in a manner
not paralleled within the other movements. Whereas Reform, Reconstructionist, and Conservative Judaism have within them a single
organization of congregations, a single rabbinic organization, and a
single institution for the training of rabbis, Orthodoxy has a multiplic-
ity of organizations for each of these purposes.[13] Such institutional
diffusion has apparently not hindered Orthodoxy but has created difficulties for the students of Orthodox life—particularly in determining
who speaks for Orthodoxy. There are many conflicting voices.

The whole issue of authority is more complicated in Orthodoxy
than in the other denominations. In some ways, Orthodox Jews are
the most likely to accept the opinion of a rabbi as authoritative on
matters pertaining to Jewish living. Indeed, some Orthodox Jews go
so far as having their rabbis decide for them sensitive financial and
professional matters, and even personal family questions, such as
whom to marry and how many children to bring into the world. At
the same time, Orthodox synagogues are less dependent on a rabbinic
elite to guide their fortunes than are those of other denominations.
Pulpit rabbis have less status in the Orthodox world than in any other
segment of the Jewish community, and most Orthodox institutions
rely heavily on lay rather than rabbinic leadership.

Sociologists have attempted to identify the major groupings
within Orthodoxy by using various analytic schemata. In a pioneering
study published in the *American Jewish Year Book*, Charles Liebman
differentiated between the "uncommitted Orthodox," the "modern
Orthodox," and the "sectarian Orthodox."[14] The first were either East
European immigrants who, out of inertia rather than religious choice,
identified as Orthodox, or individuals who had no particular commitment to Jewish law but preferred to pray in an Orthodox synagogue.
The modern Orthodox "seek to demonstrate the viability of the
halakhah for contemporary life . . . [and also] emphasize what they
have in common with all other Jews rather than what separates
them." The sectarians are disciples of either *roshei yeshivah* (heads of

yeshivahs) or Hasidic rebbes (Hasidic holy men), whose strategy it is to isolate their followers from non-Orthodox influences.

In contrast to Liebman's ideological scheme, sociologist William Helmreich utilizes behavioral measures to differentiate sectors of the Orthodox world.[15] Helmreich describes three separate groups—the "ultra-Orthodox," by which he means primarily Hasidic Jews; the "strictly Orthodox," referring to the products of Lithuanian-type yeshivahs transplanted in America; and the "modern Orthodox," by which he means Jews who look to Yeshiva University and its rabbinic alumni for leadership. Each group has its own norms of behavior, particularly with regard to secular education for children, the inter-action between men and women, and even the garb they wear, for example, the knitted *kippah*, the black velvet yarmulke, or the Hasidic *streimel*. Helmreich's contribution is to draw attention to the "yeshi-vah world" of the strictly Orthodox, a world that, as we will see, is transforming American Orthodoxy.

In a forthcoming study, sociologists Samuel Heilman and Steven M. Cohen speak of the "nominal Orthodox," the "centrist Orthodox," and the "traditionalist Orthodox."[16] The authors claim that Orthodox Jews, regardless of where they are situated on the religious spectrum, share with each other a high degree of similarity in what they regard as required ritual observances, belief in God and divine revelation, disagreement with potentially heretical ideas, feelings of bonding with other Orthodox Jews, and political conservatism on specific issues; in all of these areas, Orthodox Jews have more in common with each other than with non-Orthodox Jews. While this essay will take note of the severe strains within the Orthodox movement, it does accept the premise that there are important religious beliefs and behaviors that unite Orthodox Jews and set them apart from non-Orthodox Jews.

Why the Revival?

How so we account for Orthodoxy's impressive rebound in recent decades? What factors prompted the emergence of programs for Orthodox revitalization? And why do they seem to succeed?

Perhaps the key to Orthodox success has been its educational institutions. As noted above, Orthodoxy began to invest heavily in all-day religious schools at mid-century. In 1940 there were only thirty-five Jewish day schools in America, scattered in seven different communities, but principally located in the metropolitan New York area. Within the next five years the number doubled, and day schools could now be found in thirty-one communities. The postwar era witnessed an even more impressive surge, so that by 1975 there was a total of 425 Orthodox day schools, including 138 high schools, with a total enrollment of 82,200. It is estimated that by the 1980s approximately 80 percent of all Orthodox children were enrolled in day schools.[17]

Day schools serve the Orthodox community as the key instrument for formal education and socialization. With at least half of each day devoted to Jewish studies, day schools have the luxury of teaching students language skills necessary for Hebrew prayer and the study of Jewish texts in their original Hebrew or Aramaic, as well as ample time to impart information on the proper observance of rituals. Equally important, day schools provide an environment for building a strong attachment to the Orthodox group: they prescribe proper religious behavior and impart strong ideological indoctrination; and they create an all-encompassing social environment where lifelong friendships are made. According to one study of a leading Orthodox day school, even students from non-Orthodox homes developed a strong allegiance to Orthodoxy due to their ongoing exposure to the school's programs. Moreover, the majority of students were as religiously observant or even more observant than their parents.[18] At mid-century, the proliferation of day schools was creating a quiet revolution that few contemporaries noticed. By the 1970s and 1980s, Orthodoxy began to reap the benefits of its educational investments.[19]

Complementing the day-school movement is a series of other institutions designed to socialize the younger generation of Orthodox Jews. Orthodox synagogues of various stripes have introduced separate religious services for the young people as well as a range of social, educational, and recreational programs to provide an Orthodox environment while the youth are not in school. In addition, Orthodox groups have invested heavily in summer camps, which provide an all-embracing Orthodox experience during vacation months. Beyond that, it has become the norm for Orthodox teenagers to spend some time in Israel, again in an Orthodox ambience.

A second factor in the revitalization of Orthodoxy was the participation of Orthodox Jews in the postwar economic boom that brought unparalleled affluence to Americans in general. Like their counterparts in the other denominations, Orthodox Jews in increasing numbers acquired college and graduate degrees and entered the professions. These occupations freed Jews from the need to work on the Sabbath, thereby eliminating a conflict between economic necessity and religious observance that had bedeviled traditionally minded Jews in earlier periods. Thanks to their newfound affluence, Orthodox Jews could afford to send their offspring to day schools, from kindergarten through high school, and to pay for summer camps and trips to Israel for their children. In general, Orthodox Jews were now able to partake fully of American life even while adhering to traditional observances. The link between religious traditionalism and poverty and the backward ways of the Old World had been broken.[20]

An important consequence of this new affluence has been the ability of Orthodox Jews to insulate themselves more effectively from the rest of the Jewish community. With their host of synagogues, day schools, recreational programs, restaurants, summer camps, and the like, Orthodox Jews, in their largest centers of concentration, can live in separate communities that rarely interact with the larger Jewish populace. Even within the structures of existing communities, Orthodox Jews have obtained the right to separate programs geared to their own needs, or Jewish communal organizations tacitly set aside special resources for the sole use of Orthodox Jews.[21] Living in separate communities that insulate them from the larger Jewish community has helped to foster an élan among Orthodox Jews and a belief, particularly conveyed to the young, that the Orthodox community constitutes the saving remnant of American Judaism.

A series of developments in the broader American society has also given an important boost to Orthodoxy. Particularly during the 1960s and early 1970s, when experimentation and rebellion appeared to be the order of the day, those who were repelled by the new social mores found solace in the stability of Orthodoxy. More recently, the comparatively lower rates of divorce and substance abuse in the Orthodox grouping have encouraged many Jews to perceive Orthodox Judaism as a bulwark against social instability. At the same time, the openness of American culture has made it possible for Jews to identify with Orthodoxy without the need to defend their distinctive ways. As Charles Liebman has noted, "The very absence of rigid ideational and cultural structures which characterizes modernity, the undermining of overarching moral visions, and the celebration of plural beliefs and styles of life, invite culturally deviant movements."[22]

Finally, Orthodoxy has achieved increased stability in recent decades because it has policed its community more rigorously and has defined its boundaries ever more sharply. Where once a great range of behaviors was tolerated and the Orthodox movement contained a large population of nominal adherents, Orthodox Jews today are far less tolerant of deviance. Far more than any other movement in American Judaism, Orthodoxy—in its various permutations—has set limits and defined acceptable and unacceptable behavior. This has a twofold psychological impact. First, it attracts individuals who want to be given explicit guidelines for proper behavior, rather than shoulder the burden of autonomy that is the lot of modern individuals. Second, it sharpens the group's boundaries, thereby providing adherents with a strong feeling of community and belonging.[23]

DENOMINATIONAL LIFE: CONSERVATIVE JUDAISM

Far more than the other denominations, Conservative Judaism has experienced severe turmoil, at times even demoralization, during the past quarter century. In part, this is the result of the letdown following the end of the Conservative movement's era of heady growth in the 1950s and 1960s. Equally important, Conservative Judaism has experienced turmoil because forces both within and outside the movement have confronted it with provocative new challenges. Conservatism had managed to paper over serious ideological differences within its ranks during the boom years, but by the late 1960s and early 1970s, internal dissent intensified and new alliances were being forged within the movement to press for change. With each step taken toward ideological and programmatic clarification, one faction or another of the Conservative coalition has felt betrayed.

In addition, Conservative Judaism's once enviable position at the center of the religious spectrum has turned to a liability as American Judaism has moved from an era of relative harmony to intense polarization. As the conflict between Reform on the left and Orthodoxy on the right has intensified, the Conservative movement, as the party of the center, has found itself caught in a crossfire between two increasingly antagonistic foes, and hard-pressed to justify its centrism. As Ismar Schorsch, chancellor of the Jewish Theological Seminary, has noted, the center "must produce an arsenal of arguments for use against both the left and right which, of necessity, often include ideas that are barely compatible."[24]

Strains in the Conservative Coalition

The Conservative movement has long been based on a divided coalition. Writing at mid-century, Marshall Sklare noted the gap between the masses of Conservative synagogue members and the rabbinic and lay elites of the movement.[25] Whereas the elites shared similar standards of religious practice and a common ideological commitment, the masses of synagogue members were unaware of Conservative ideology and often were only minimally observant. According to Sklare's analysis, "Conservatism represents a common pattern of acculturation—a kind of social adjustment—which has been arrived at by lay people. It is seen by them as a 'halfway house' between Reform and Orthodoxy."[26]

Even within the elite there was a considerable distance between the seminary "schoolmen" and the rabbis in the field. As one of the rabbis bitterly put it: "Certain members of our faculty . . . have put us in shackles and in bonds . . . so that we cannot move. . . . [This] is humiliating to us. . . . [They] laugh at us as ignoramuses . . . [and imply] that we have been graduated as social workers and not as rabbis for humanity."[27] This statement draws attention to lack of empowerment and legitimacy accorded by the seminary's faculty to its students during the first half of this century. But the gap within the Conservative elite also consisted of a tacit understanding concerning the division of labor within the movement. As Neil Gillman, a professor of theology at the seminary observes:

> All of the groundbreaking Conservative responsa on synagogue practice [and] Sabbath observance . . . came out of the Rabbinical Assembly. . . . For its part, the Seminary Faculty remained within the walls of scholarship. It issued no responsa. If anything, it maintained a stance of almost explicit disdain toward all of this halakhic activity. . . . This relationship was actually a marriage of convenience. The Faculty could cling to its traditionalism, secure in the knowledge that the real problems were

being handled elsewhere. The Rabbinical Assembly looked at its teachers as the hallmark of authenticity, holding the reins lest it go too far.[28]

The gap between the seminary and the rabbinate was symbolized by the maintenance of separate seating in the seminary's own synagogue until the 1980s, even as virtually every rabbi ordained by the institution served in a congregation that had instituted mixed seating of men and women.

By the late 1960s and early 1970s, the long-standing "discontinuities and conflicts" within the Conservative movement, to use Sklare's formulation, had grown more aggravated. First, there was the gap between the rabbis and their congregants. This issue was directly confronted by Hershel Matt in the mid-1970s in a letter to his congregants explaining why, after twenty-eight years in the rabbinate, he had decided to leave the pulpit: "The present reality is that affiliation with a congregation or even election to the Board or to committees does not require any commitment" to the primary purpose of a synagogue—"seeking to live in the holy dimension of Jewish life . . . trying to accept the obligation and joy of worshipping God, . . . trying to learn Torah from the rabbi."[29] A decade later, a younger colleague of Matt's, Shalom Lewis, published an essay describing the loneliness of the Conservative rabbi:

> The loneliness we suffer is not necessarily social but spiritual. We might bowl, swim, and *kibbitz* with the best of them, but we are still in another world entirely. We quote Heschel and no one understands. We perform *netilat yadayim* and our friends think we're rude when we are momentarily silent. . . . We walk home, alone, on Shabbos. I am blessed with a wonderful social community, but I have no spiritual community in which I have companions.[30]

Conservative rabbis have for decades bemoaned their inability to convince the masses of their congregants to live as observant Jews. In 1960, at a time of most rapid growth for the Conservative movement, Max Routtenberg noted the "mood and feeling among many of us that our achievements touch only the periphery of Jewish life and that our failures center around the issues that concern us most as

rabbis and as Jews."[31] Almost two decades later, Stephen Lerner characterized the problem even more bluntly: "The major problem is that
we have been or are becoming a clerical movement. We have no
observant laity and even our lay leadership is becoming removed
from the world of the traditional family."[32] In the intervening years,
the journals and national conventions of the Conservative rabbinate
repeatedly addressed this issue, and rabbis voiced their concern that
the movement "had become less identifiable" and was in danger of
"los[ing] its force and becom[ing] of less and less consequence on the
American Jewish scene."[33] The mood in Conservatism was aptly
captured by one rabbi who remarked to his colleagues that "self-
flagellation appears to be the order of the day for the leadership of
Conservative Jewry."[34]

The observations of leading sociologists further added to the
pessimistic mood. Early in 1972, Marshall Sklare published an essay
titled "Recent Developments in Conservative Judaism" designed to
update his study of 1953. As read by the editor of *Conservative Judaism*,
Sklare "offered a thesis that the Conservative movement at the zenith
of its influence, has sustained a loss of morale," attributable to "the
emergence of Orthodoxy, the problem of Conservative observance,
and the widespread alienation among Conservative young people."[35]

Charles Liebman and Saul Shapiro, in a survey conducted at the
end of the 1970s and released at the 1979 biennial convention of
the United Synagogue, came up with strong evidence to substantiate
the thesis of the Conservative movement's decline.[36] Liebman and
Shapiro found that almost as many young people reared in Conservative synagogues were opting for no synagogue affiliation as were
joining Conservative congregations. Further, they contended that
among the most observant younger Conservative families, particularly as defined by *kashrut* observance, there was a tendency to "defect"
to Orthodoxy. Here was evidence of a double failing: a movement
that had invested heavily in Jewish education in the synagogue setting seemingly did not imbue its youth with a strong allegiance to the
Conservative synagogue; and rabbis who themselves had rejected
Orthodoxy found their "best" young people—including their own
children—rejecting Conservatism for Orthodoxy.

In truth, many of the best of Conservative youth were choosing
a path other than Orthodoxy, one which would have a far more
profound effect on the movement than denominational "defections."

Beginning in the early 1970s, products of Conservative synagogues, youth movements, Ramah camps, and the seminary were instrumental in the creation of a counterculture movement known as *"havurah Judaism."*[37] Although Conservative Jews did not completely monopolize the havurah movement, they played key roles as founders, theoreticians, and members. The first person to suggest the applicability of early rabbinic fellowships as a model for the present age was Jacob Neusner, who had been ordained at the seminary.[38] The first and perhaps most influential of all havurot was founded in Somerville, Massachusetts, in 1968 by a group of Ramah and seminary products under the leadership of Arthur Green, a rabbi ordained at the seminary. The guiding force in the founding of the New York Havurah, as well as the journal *Response*, was Alan Mintz, who had earlier served as the national president of United Synagogue Youth (USY). Finally, the books that served as primers of havurah Judaism, the *Jewish Catalogs*,[39] were compiled by products of Conservative youth programs.

Richard Siegel, one of the editors of *The Jewish Catalog*, provided the following analysis of the link between havurah Judaism and the Conservative movement, when he was invited to address the national convention of the Rabbinical Assembly:

> Ramah created a new Jewish lifestyle. . . . A group of discontents was created [due to experimentation at Ramah], a group of people who had a vision of something different from what went on in synagogues. . . . In essence, it was an internal development within the Conservative movement which had within it the seeds of internal contradiction, and its own destruction, in a way. The Conservative movement was unable to absorb . . . to meet the religious needs of a group of young people.[40]

For Siegel, then, it was the intense experience of participating in a Jewish religious community at Camp Ramah that prompted the emergence of the havurah movement as a substitute for what young people regarded as the formal and sterile atmosphere of the large Conservative synagogue. As Susannah Heschel put it to another group of Conservative rabbis: "The movement has succeeded too well in educating its children, because these children feel they have no proper place in Conservative life."[41]

In the short term, Heschel was correct in noting the alienation of some of these youth from Conservative synagogues. But there is substantial evidence to indicate that in the 1980s many of the formerly disaffected, including those who continue to worship within the havurah setting, increasingly participate in Conservative life: they send their children to Solomon Schechter schools and Ramah camps; they identify with the liturgy and ideology of Conservatism; and most importantly, they have moved from the periphery to the center of Conservatism's institutional life. It is this last development which accounts in large measure for the turbulence within Conservative Judaism in recent years. Put simply, leadership in the Conservative movement, its national institutions, synagogues, rabbinate, and various organizational arms, has passed into the hands of men and women who were reared in the pews of Conservative synagogues and socialized in its Ramah camps and USY programs. That transition has brought dislocation and turmoil to the Conservative movement for over a decade.

The biographies of recent Conservative leaders tell much of the story. When Gerson D. Cohen assumed the chancellorship of the Jewish Theological Seminary of America (JTS) in 1972, he brought with him years of experience as an early participant in the Ramah experiment. His successor, Ismar Schorsch, shared such experiences and is himself the son of a Conservative rabbi. Equally important, the Conservative rabbinate has been recruiting ever growing percentages of its members from Conservative homes. During the first half of the twentieth century, the preponderant majority of rabbinical students at JTS were drawn from Orthodox families and educational institutions. Since then, the percentage of such students has dwindled, so that hardly any current rabbinical students come from the Orthodox community. Instead, close to one-third are either from Reform backgrounds or unaffiliated families, or are converts to Judaism, while the other two-thirds are products of the Conservative movement.[42] The seminary faculty, too, has been replenished with American-born Jews, who for the most part have been educated in Conservative institutions.

The new elite of the Conservative movement differs from its predecessors of earlier generations in two significant ways. Today's leaders regard the world of Orthodoxy as alien, and are far less emotionally tied to it. Accordingly, they feel fewer constraints in setting their own course. Second, and even more important, the new elite of the Conservative movement is far more prepared to put into practice the logical consequences of Conservative ideology. It is particularly significant that many of the new elite had experience in Ramah camps, because Ramah, as one observer noted, "is the battleground par excellence for Conservative Judaism, where theory and practice must and do meet. . . . [Only Camp Ramah] constantly turn[ed] to the central educational institution, the JTS, to ask what are the permissible limits of experimentation in Jewish prayer? What are the permissible limits of Shabbat observance? What precisely is the role of women in Conservative Jewish life?"[43] Precisely because it created a total Jewish environment, Ramah provided a setting in which to explore what it means to live as a Conservative Jew on a day-to-day basis. Products of Ramah, accordingly, have been prepared to put Conservative ideology into action once they have assumed roles of leadership within the movement.

As the Conservative elite has changed in character, the structure of alliances within the Conservative coalition has shifted dramatically. The "schoolmen" described by Marshall Sklare in the mid-1950s now include some women, but even more important, include home-grown products with strong ties to the Conservative movement and no allegiances to Orthodoxy. The same is true of the rabbinate and organizational leadership. Thus, coalitions for change cut across the movement, rather than remain solely in one sector, as had long been the case. The issue of women's ordination, which has agitated Conservative Judaism for a decade, has served as the symbol of change and the catalyst for further realignment within the movement.

Women's Ordination as Symbol and Catalyst

Although Conservative Judaism had long accepted the mixed seating of men and women in synagogues and, since the 1950s, had increasingly celebrated the coming of age of girls in Bat Mitzvah ceremonies, it was only in the early 1970s that more far-reaching questions concerning the status of women in religious life were addressed by the movement. A group of Conservative feminists, members of Ezrat Nashim[44]—a Hebrew pun referring to the separate women's gallery in traditional synagogues, but also implying a pledge to provide "help for women"—pressed its agenda at the convention of the Rabbinical Assembly (RA) in March 1972, by holding a "counter-session" to which only women—wives of rabbis—were invited. The group demanded the following of the RA: that women be granted membership in synagogues; be counted in a *minyan*; be allowed to participate fully in religious observances; be recognized as witnesses before Jewish law; be allowed to initiate divorce; be permitted to study and function as rabbis and cantors; and be encouraged to assume positions of leadership in the Jewish community. These demands drew special attention because they were put forward by self-proclaimed "products of Conservative congregations, religious schools, the Ramah Camps, LTF (Leaders Training Fellowship), USY, and the seminary."[45]

Until a detailed history of Jewish feminism is written, it will not be possible to determine how many Conservative women actually supported these demands. What is clear, however, is that they evoked a sympathetic response within the Conservative rabbinate. This can be seen in the ever-increasing attention paid to the women's issues in both the journal and the convention proceedings of the Conservative rabbinate, beginning shortly after the aforementioned Rabbinical Assembly convention. In terms of action, in 1973 the Rabbinical Assembly's committee on Jewish law and standards adopted a *takka-nah* (legislative enactment) permitting women to be counted as part of a minyan. The next year, the same committee considered whether women could serve as rabbis and as cantors, and whether they could function as witnesses and sign legal documents. Supporters of women's equality concluded that the minority opinions on these matters provided a sufficient basis for change in the status of women.[46]

When news about the decision on counting women in a minyan became public knowledge through articles in the general press, Conservative opponents of "egalitarianism"—the term that came to be applied to the equal treatment of women—began to organize. The decision had placed such rabbis on the defensive with their own congregants. How could individual rabbis committed to traditional role differences between men and women in the synagogue continue to justify their stance when a takkanah permitting the counting of women in the minyan had been passed by the legal body of the Conservative rabbinate? The action of the law committee, it was argued, undermined the authority of the individual rabbi. Further-

more, opponents contended, the committee had assumed an unprecedented role as an advocate of change. In short order, rabbis opposed
to the decisions of the law committee organized a body initially known
as the Ad Hoc Committee for Tradition and Diversity in the Conservative Movement and subsequently renamed the Committee for Preservation of Tradition within the Rabbinical Assembly of America. Thus,
even before the issue of women's ordination was formally raised, the
battle lines were drawn within the Conservative rabbinate.[47]

Despite bitter divisions among its membership over questions of
women's status, the Rabbinical Assembly assumed a leadership role in
advocating a decision on women as Conservative rabbis. At its annual
convention in 1977, the RA petitioned the chancellor of the seminary
to "establish an interdisciplinary commission to study all aspects of
the role of women as spiritual leaders in the Conservative Movement." Chancellor Cohen acceded to this petition and selected four-
teen individuals, evenly divided between rabbinic and lay leaders, to
serve on the commission. The commission heard testimony around
the country based on a variety of perspectives, including halakhah,
ethics, economics, sociology, psychology, and education. From the
outset, however, it had committed itself to a guideline that "no rec-
ommendation would be made which, in the opinion of the members
of the Commission, . . . would contravene or be incompatible with
the requirements of Halakhah as the latter had been theretofore
observed and developed by the Conservative Movement." Within two
years, the commission concluded its work; it presented the RA with a
majority opinion supported by eleven members, urging the JTS to
admit women to the Rabbinical School, and a minority report issued
by three members opposing such action.[48]

The majority, in its report, contended that since the role of the
contemporary rabbi "is not one which is established in classical Jewish texts . . . [there is] no specifiable halakhic category which can be
identified with the modern rabbinate." The halakhic objections to the
ordination of women "center around disapproval of the performance
by a woman of certain functions. Those functions, however, are not
essentially rabbinic, nor are they universally disapproved, by the
accepted rules governing the discussion of Halakhah in the Conservative Movement."

The minority report, in contrast, argued that the key halakhic
issues had not been resolved to the satisfaction of many Conservative

Jews, as well as Jews outside of the movement "who may be affected by practices in connection with testimony relating to marriage and divorce." The minority expressed concern that the ordination of women would drive opponents of egalitarianism out of the Conservative movement.

Once the commission reported its findings back to the Rabbinical Assembly, attention turned to the faculty of the seminary. During the course of the commission's hearings, Chancellor Cohen had shifted his position from a desire to maintain the status quo to enthusiastic support of women's ordination. He took it upon himself to bring the matter before the faculty of the seminary within one year, an undertaking that itself precipitated further controversy. It was not at all clear from seminary rules of procedure that the faculty was empowered to decide on admissions policies. Some argued that only talmudists on the faculty should have a right to decide; others objected to any faculty participating on the ground that admissions policies were a purely administrative matter; and still others claimed that halakhic questions had not been resolved satisfactorily, and therefore, no decision could be taken by the seminary. In December 1979 the matter was brought before the faculty, but was tabled indefinitely so as to avoid a sharp split.[49]

Pressure for action on the ordination issue continued to mount, particularly within the Rabbinical Assembly. A number of women of Conservative background who had studied for the rabbinate at the Reform and Reconstructionist seminaries pressed for admission to the Rabbinical Assembly. The official organization of Conservative rabbis now was placed in the position of possibly admitting women who were as qualified as many male candidates ordained by non-Conservative institutions, even as the movement's own seminary refused to ordain women as rabbis. The issue came to a head in 1983, when Beverly Magidson, a rabbi ordained at the Hebrew Union College, successfully demonstrated her qualifications for admission to the Rabbinical Assembly (RA). Like all candidates for admission not ordained by JTS, Magidson needed the support of three-fourths of the rabbis present at the convention in order to gain admission; in fact she received the support of a majority. Some supporters of Magidson's admission opted to vote against her on the grounds that a woman ordained by the seminary should be the first female admitted to the RA. Others felt that such a momentous decision should be reserved for a convention that drew a broader cross-section of the membership (the convention met in Dallas, and attendance was lower than usual). But it was clear from the vote of 206 in favor to 72 opposed that it was only a matter of time before a woman rabbi would be admitted to the RA and that the seminary could no longer defer a decision.[50]

In the fall of 1983, Chancellor Cohen once again brought the issue of women's ordination before the faculty. In the interval, several of the staunchest opponents of women's ordination had left the faculty, and Professor Saul Lieberman, an intimidating figure even after his retirement from the faculty, had passed away. Clearly outnumbered, most other opponents of women's ordination, principally senior members of the rabbinics department, refused to attend the meeting. By a vote of 34 to 8, with one abstention, on October 24, 1983, the faculty voted to admit women to the Rabbinical School. By the following fall, nineteen women were enrolled in the Rabbinical School; one of them, Amy Eilberg, was ordained in May 1985, on the basis of her academic attainments during years of graduate studies.[51]

The protracted and bitterly divisive debate over women's ordination went beyond the issue of women's status in Judaism to the broader questions of movement definition. Predictably, given the centrism of the Conservative movement, advocates of opposing positions branded their opponents as either radical Reformers or Orthodox obstructionists. This was particularly evident during the debate over Magidson's application for admission to the RA. Opponents explicitly stated that if the RA voted affirmatively, "we are going to be publicly identified with the Reform movement";[52] supporters argued that by rejecting Magidson, "we will be subjecting ourselves to ridicule. . . . Our own communities and our congregants will lump us with Orthodox intransigents."[53]

Whereas earlier controversial decisions, such as the law committee's stance on the permissibility of driving to synagogue on the Sabbath, affected only individual Jews, the ordination of women as rabbis directly affected all segments of Conservative Jewry. Congregations eventually would have to decide whether to hire a woman as a rabbi; members of the Rabbinical Assembly would have to decide whether they could accept women as equals, particularly as witnesses in legal actions; and members of the seminary faculty would have to decide whether they could participate in the training of women as rabbis. Once ordained as rabbis, women would assume a central role in the Conservative movement, a role that could not be ignored.

CONCLUSION

In concluding this report on trends in American Judaism since the 1970s, it is appropriate to ask what they portend for the future of American Jewry. For the most part, the debate between sociologists of the American Jewish community revolves around the health of Jews as an ethnic group, and relatively little is said about the religious dimension of Jewish life. This is understandable, given the propensity of sociologists to focus on quantitative measures and on the survival of Jews as a viable and forceful group on the American scene. In light, however, of the uncertain future of ethnicity as an enduring bond within American society and the reemergence of religion as a powerful factor, the condition of American Judaism needs to be reevaluated. This question takes on particular importance for Jews, since Judaism has traditionally provided its adherents with patterns of behavior and reasons for identification that go beyond ethnicity, with a Jewish content that has motivated them to remain distinctive.[54]

The current debate between sociologists pits "transformationists" against "assimilationists," with the former arguing that American Jewry is undergoing dramatic changes that are transforming but not weakening Jewish life, whereas the latter perceive the changes within Jewish life as portents of decline and eventual assimilation into the fabric of American society.[55] Recent trends in American Judaism provide evidence to bolster both positions. Certainly American Judaism has been transformed in recent decades: all of the religious movements have repositioned themselves on questions of ideology and, to a large extent, also practice. New movements of religious renewal have emerged that have particularly attracted young Jews. Indeed, there are more options for religious expression and more tolerance for religious pluralism than in any previous era in American Judaism. Moreover, there is a great curiosity today about religious expression, as distinct from the associational character of much of Jewish life in earlier decades of the century.

Simultaneously, demographic data suggest diminishing involvement in Judaism among the masses of American Jews. Surveys conducted during the 1980s show a decline in the percentages of Jews who identify with any religious denomination. And compared to surveys conducted two decades ago, lower percentages of Jews attend synagogues with any regularity, keep kosher, or light Sabbath candles weekly. Most ominously, the rate of mixed marriage has skyrocketed

in the past two decades, and is highest among the youngest Jews.
Efforts to cope with this unprecedented challenge—which relates to
the very transmission of Jewish identity—color all aspects of Jewish
religious life.

All of these patterns suggest that in the religious sphere, a bipolar
mode is emerging, with a large population of Jews moving toward
religious minimalism and a minority gravitating toward greater participation and deepened concern with religion. The latter include
newly committed Jews and converts to Judaism, whose conscious
choice of religious involvement has infused all branches of American
Judaism with new energy and passion; rabbinic and lay leaders of the
official denominations, who continue to struggle with issues of continuity and change within their respective movements; and groups of
Jews who are experimenting with traditional forms in order to
reappropriate aspects of the Jewish past. These articulate and vocal
Jews have virtually transformed American Judaism during the past
two decades. At the same time, an even larger population of American Jews has drifted away from religious participation. Such Jews
have not articulated the sources of their discontent but have "voted
with their feet," by absenting themselves from synagogues and
declining to observe religious rituals that require frequent and ongoing attention. To a great extent, their worrisome patterns of attrition have been obscured by the dynamism of the religiously involved.
It remains to be seen, therefore, whether the transformation of American Judaism wrought by the committed minority during recent
decades will sustain its present energy and inspire greater numbers of
Jews to commit themselves to a living Judaism.

NOTES

1. The following population studies conducted under the auspices of
local federations of Jewish philanthropies were utilized in the compilation
of data for this section (relevant page numbers for data on religious issues
follow). All data cited in this section are taken from these reports, unless
noted otherwise. (I thank Jeffrey Scheckner, Administrator, North American
Jewish Data Bank, for graciously making these studies available to me.)
Atlanta: *Metropolitan Atlanta Jewish Population Study: Summary of Major Findings*,
Atlanta Jewish Federation, 1983, pp. 8–9. Baltimore: Gary A. Tobin, Jewish
Population Study of Greater Baltimore, Associated Jewish Charities and Wel-
fare Fund, 1985, sect. 6 and *Summary Report*, pp. 21–32. Boston: Sherry Israel,

Boston's Jewish Community: The 1985 CJP Demographic Study, Combined Jewish Philanthropies of Greater Boston, 1985, chap. 3. Chicago: Peter Friedman, *A Population Study of the Jewish Community of Metropolitan Chicago*, Jewish Federation of Metropolitan Chicago, 1982, pp. 42–45. Additional data that did not appear in the published report were generously provided to the author by Dr. Mark A. Zober, Senior Planning and Research Associate at the Jewish United Fund of Metropolitan Chicago. Cleveland: Ann Schorr, *From Generation to Generation*, and *Survey of Cleveland's Jewish Population*, Jewish Community Federation of Cleveland, 1981, pp. 42–49. Dade County, Fla.: Ira M. Sheskin, *Population Study of the Greater Miami Jewish Community*, Greater Miami Jewish Federation, 1982, pp. 157–211, 227–244. Denver: Bruce A. Phillips, *Denver Jewish Population Study* and *Supplement to the Denver Jewish Population Study*, Allied Jewish Federation of Denver, 1981, pp. iii–iv, 44–55; and pp. 14–25, respectively. Hartford: *Highlights from the Greater Hartford Jewish Population Study*, Greater Hartford Jewish Federation, 1981, p. 8. Kansas City: Gary A. Tobin, *A Demographic Study of the Jewish Community of Greater Kansas City: Executive Summary*, Jewish Federation of Greater Kansas City, 1985, pp. 3–19, 36–41. Los Angeles: Steven Huberman and Bruce A. Phillips, *Jewish Los Angeles: Synagogue Affiliation. Planning Report*, Jewish Federation Council of Greater Los Angeles, 1979, pp. 3–32, 37–51. Also Bruce A. Phillips, "Los Angeles Jewry: A Demographic Portrait," *AJYB* 1986, vol. 86, pp. 126–95. MetroWest, N.J.: Michael Rappeport and Gary A. Tobin, *A Population Study of the Jewish Community of MetroWest, New Jersey*, United Jewish Federation of MetroWest, N.J., 1985, pp. 61–96. Milwaukee: Bruce A. Phillips and Eve Weinberg, *The Milwaukee Jewish Population: Report of a Survey*, Milwaukee Jewish Federation, 1984, pp. iv, 1–17. Also *Summary Report*, pp. 1–5. Minneapolis: Lois Geer, *Population Study: The Jewish Community of Greater Minneapolis*, Federation for Jewish Service, 1981, chap. 5, pp. 1–19. Also *Executive Summary*, pp. 8–9. Nashville: Nancy Hendrix, *A Demographic Study of the Jewish Community of Nashville and Middle Tennessee*, Jewish Federation of Nashville and Middle Tennessee, 1982, p. 20. New York: Steven M. Cohen and Paul Ritterband, *The Jewish Population of Greater New York, A Profile*, Federation of Jewish Philanthropies of N.Y., 1981, pp. 22–34. Additional data were provided to me directly by Paul Ritterband. Palm Beach County, Fla.: Ira M. Sheskin, *Jewish Demographic Study*, Jewish Federation of Palm Beach County, 1987, pp. 101–40. Philadelphia: William Yancey and Ira Goldstein, *The Jewish Population of the Greater Philadelphia Area*, Federation of Jewish Agencies of Greater Philadelphia, 1983, pp. 109–162, 172–208. Phoenix: Bruce A. Phillips and William S. Aron, *The Greater Phoenix Jewish Population Study: Jewish Identity, Affiliation, and Observance*, Greater Phoenix Jewish Federation, 1983, pp. 3–10. Pittsburgh: Ann Schorr, *Survey of Greater Pittsburgh's Jewish Population*, United Jewish Federation of Greater Pittsburgh, 1984, sect. 4. Also *Community Report*, pp. 6–15. Richmond: Ann Schorr, *Demographic Study of the Jewish Community of Richmond*, Jewish Federation of Richmond, 1984, pp. 9, 30–31, 42–48. Rochester: Gary A. Tobin and Sylvia B. Fishman, *The Jewish Population of Rochester, N.Y. (Monroe County)*, Jewish Community Federation of Rochester, N.Y., 1980, pp. i–iii, 19–33. St.

Louis: Gary A. Tobin *A Demographic and Attitudinal Study of the Jewish Communi-*
ty of St. Louis, Jewish Federation of St. Louis, 1982, pp. iv–viii, 23–42. Scran-
ton: *Demographic Census,* typescript report by Mrs. Seymour Bachman,
Scranton-Lackawanna Jewish Federation, 1984. Seattle: James McCann with
Debra Friedman, *A Study of the Jewish Community in the Greater Seattle Area,*
Jewish Federation of Greater Seattle, 1979, pp. 8–11, 67–73. Tampa: Ray
Wheeler, *A Social and Demographic Survey of the Jewish Community of Tampa,*
Florida, Tampa Jewish Federation, 1980, pp. 60–66. Washington, D.C.: Gary
A. Tobin, Janet Greenblatt, and Joseph Waksberg, *A Demographic Study of the*
Jewish Community of Greater Washington, 1983, United Jewish Appeal Federa-
tion of Greater Washington, D.C., 1983, pp. 25, 39, 97–101, 139–50. Worces-
ter: Gary A. Tobin and Sylvia Barack Fishman, *A Population Study of the Greater*
Worcester Jewish Community, Worcester Jewish Federation, 1986, pp. 91–112.

2. The results of the National Jewish Population Study were published
in a series of pamphlets issued by the Council of Jewish Federations and
Welfare Funds during the 1970s.

3. See *Jewish Identity: Facts for Planning,* pp. 2–4.

4. Steven M. Cohen and Paul Ritterband, "The Social Characteristics of
the New York Area Jewish Community, 1981," *American Jewish Year Book*
(hereafter *AJYB*) 1984, vol. 84, p. 153 and table 3.3.

5. Barry Kosmin, "Facing Up to Intermarriage," *Jewish Chronicle* (London), July 24, 1987.

6. Ibid.

7. A strong case for the defection scenario has been made by Charles
Liebman and Saul Shapiro in "A Survey of the Conservative Movement:
Some of Its Religious Attitudes," unpublished paper, Sept. 1979, p. 22. Steven
M. Cohen has argued that identification is tied to family status. See "The
American Jewish Family Today," *AJYB* 1982, vol. 82, pp. 145–53.

8. Charles S. Liebman, "Orthodoxy Faces Modernity," *Orim* (Spring
1987): 13.

9. The term "right-wing Orthodox," despite its problematic nature, is
used in the present discussion because it is common parlance. The category
roughly approximates the "sectarian Orthodox" identified by Liebman, the
"traditionalist Orthodox" identified by Heilman and Cohen, and the "strictly-
Orthodox" and "ultra-Orthodox" identified by Helmreich. See the discussion
that follows.

10. For an interesting account of such fears in one modern Orthodox
community, see Edward S. Shapiro, "Orthodoxy in Pleasantdale," *Judaism*
(Spring 1985): 170.

11. See, for example, the views of Rabbi Moses Feinstein, who differentiated between *shomrei mitzvot,* observers of the commandments, and the
community of "God-fearers," sectarians; and Ira Robinson, "Because of Our
Many Sins: The Contemporary Jewish World as Reflected in the Responsa of
Moses Feinstein," *Judaism* (Winter 1986): 38–39.

12. The most important English-language periodical of the Orthodox
right is the *Jewish Observer,* which espouses the views of Agudath Israel. Its

approach has been characterized by one modern Orthodox writer as one of "unrelieved negativism. Rather than articulating its own positive approach to issues, it is in most instances content merely to inveigh against positions adopted by others." David Singer, "Voices of Orthodoxy," *Commentary* (July 1974): 59.

13. Orthodox rabbinic organizations include the Rabbinical Council of America, Agudath HaRabbonim, the Rabbinical Alliance of America, Agudath Ha'Admorim, and Hitachduth HaRabbonim HaHaredim. (See M. L. Raphael, *Profiles in American Judaism*, p. 155.) Among synagogue bodies there are the Union of Orthodox Jewish Congregations of America and the National Council of Young Israel. On the various rabbinical seminaries, aside from Yeshiva University's Rabbi Isaac Elchanan Theological Seminary, see William Helmreich, *The World of the Yeshiva: An Intimate Portrait of Orthodox Jewry* (New York, 1982).

14. Charles Liebman, "Orthodoxy in American Jewish Life," *AJYB* 1969, pp. 21–98.

15. William Helmreich, *World of the Yeshiva*, pp. 52–54.

16. Samuel C. Heilman and Steven M. Cohen, *Cosmopolitans and Parochials: Modern Orthodox Jews in America*, forthcoming.

17. For data on the proliferation of day schools and the rise in enrollments, see Egon Mayer and Chaim Waxman, "Modern Jewish Orthodoxy in America: Toward the Year 2000," *Tradition* (Spring 1977): 99–100. For more recent estimates, see Alvin I. Schiff, "The Centrist Torah Educator Faces Critical Ideological and Communal Challenges," *Tradition* (Winter 1981): 278–79.

18. Joseph Heimowitz, "A Study of the Graduates of the Yeshiva of Flatbush High School" (Ph.D. diss., Yeshiva University, 1979), pp. 102–3.

19. Two surveys illustrating higher levels of education and observance among younger Orthodox Jews are Egon Mayer, "Gaps Between Generations of Orthodox Jews in Boro Park, Brooklyn, N. Y.," *Jewish Social Studies* (Spring 1977): 99; and Heilman and Cohen, *Cosmopolitans and Parochials*, chap. 5.

20. Charles Liebman noted this shift in the economic status of Orthodox Jews already in the mid-1960s ("Changing Social Characteristics of Orthodox, Conservative and Reform Jews," *Sociological Analysis* (Winter 1966): 210–22). See also Bertram Leff's study of the occupational distribution of Young Israel members, cited in Gershon Kranzler, "The Changing Orthodox Jewish Community," *Tradition* (Fall 1976): 72 n.8; almost two-thirds of male members were professionals.

21. In New York City, for example, Jewish Ys reserve special times for Orthodox Jews who require sex-segregated swimming. Other federation agencies sponsor special clinics and programs for Orthodox Jews, such as a program for developmentally handicapped Orthodox youth.

22. See Liebman, "Orthodoxy Faces Modernity," pp. 13–14.

23. On the treatment of deviance within the Orthodox setting, see Egon Mayer, *From Suburb to Shtetl: The Jews of Boro Park* (New York, 1979), pp. 134–35; Helmreich, *World of the Yeshiva*, chap. 8; and Jeffrey Gurock, "The Orthodox Synagogue," in Wertheimer, ed., *The American Synagogue* (New York, 1987), pp. 37–84.

24. Ismar Schorsch, "Zacharias Frankel and the European Origins of Conservative Judaism," *Judaism* (Summer 1981): 344.

25. Marshall Sklare, *Conservative Judaism: An American Religious Movement* (Glencoe, Ill., 1953), p. 229.

26. Ibid., p. 229. See also Elliot N. Dorff, *Conservative Judaism: Our Ancestors to Our Descendants* (New York, 1977), esp. pp. 110–57.

27. Sklare, *Conservative Judaism*, p. 190.

28. Neil Gillman, "Mordecai Kaplan and the Ideology of Conservative Judaism," *Proceedings of the Rabbinical Assembly* (hereafter "*Proceedings of the RA*"), 1986, p. 64.

29. "On Leaving the Congregational Rabbinate," *Beineinu* (Nov. 1975): 6–7.

30. "The Rabbi Is a Lonely Person," *Conservative Judaism* (Winter 1983–84): 40–41.

31. Max Routtenberg, quoted by William Lebeau, "The Rabbinical Assembly Faces the Seventies," *Proceedings of the RA*, 1970, p. 99.

32. "2001: Blueprint for the Rabbinate in the Twenty-first Century," *Proceedings of the RA*, 1979, p. 122.

33. William Greenfeld, quoted by Hillel Silverman in *Proceedings of the RA*, 1970, p. 111.

34. See Jordan S. Ofseyer's contribution to the symposium discussion in *Conservative Judaism* (Fall 1972): 16.

35. Stephen C. Lerner, in his introduction to a symposium responding to Sklare's critique, which was entitled, significantly, "Morale and Commitment," *Conservative Judaism*, Fall 1972, p. 12. Sklare's essay forms the concluding chapter in the revised edition of his book (New York, 1972), pp. 253–82.

36. Liebman and Shapiro, "Survey of the Conservative Movement"; and Saul Shapiro, "The Conservative Movement" (unpublished, dated Nov. 13, 1979). For critiques of the survey design and its assumptions, see Harold Schulweis, "Surveys, Statistics and Sectarian Salvation," *Conservative Judaism* (Winter 1980): 65–69; and Rela Geffen Monson, "The Future of Conservative Judaism in the United States: A Rejoinder," *Conservative Judaism* (Winter 1983–84): esp. 10–14.

37. Stephen C. Lerner, "The Havurot," *Conservative Judaism* (Spring 1970): 3–7; William Novak, "Notes on Summer Camps: Some Reflections on the Ramah Dream," *Response* (Winter 1971–72): 59. See also the symposium on Ramah in *Conservative Judaism* (Fall 1987), which points up the relationship between the camping movement and havurah Judaism.

38. Jacob Neusner, *Contemporary Judaic Fellowship in Theory and Practice* (New York, 1972).

39. Richard Siegel, Michael Strassfeld, and Sharon Strassfeld, comps. and eds., *The Jewish Catalog* (Philadelphia, 1973); Sharon Strassfeld and Michael Strassfeld, comps. and eds., *The Second Jewish Catalog* (Philadelphia, 1976); idem, *The Third Jewish Catalog* (Philadelphia, 1980).

40. "Futuristic Jewish Communities," *Proceedings of the RA*, 1974, p. 80.

41. Susannah Heschel, "Changing Forms of Jewish Spirituality," *Proceedings of the RA*, 1980, p. 146.

42. Aryeh Davidson and Jack Wertheimer, "The Next Generation of Conservative Rabbis," in *The Seminary at 100*, ed. Nina Beth Cardin and David W. Silverman (New York, 1987), p. 36. Other essays in the volume also point up the ability of the Conservative movement to recruit from within; see, for example, Burton I. Cohen, "From Camper to National Director: A Personal View of the Seminary and Ramah," pp. 125–34.

43. Robert Chazan, "Tribute to Ramah on Its 25th Anniversary," *Beineinu* (May 1973): 31.

44. Alan Silverstein, "The Evolution of Ezrat Nashim," *Conservative Judaism* (Fall 1975): 44–45.

45. Ibid.

46. Mayer Rabinowitz, "Toward a Halakhic Guide for the Conservative Jew," *Conservative Judaism* (Fall 1986): 18, 22, 26, 29; see also Aaron H. Blumenthal, "The Status of Women in Jewish Law," *Conservative Judaism* (Spring 1977): 24–40.

47. Rabbi I. Usher Kirshblum headed these two committees; his correspondence with rabbinic colleagues, spanning the period from 1975 until 1983, is in the Archives of Conservative Judaism, at the Jewish Theological Seminary of America.

48. The "Final Report of the Commission for the Study of the Ordination of Women as Rabbis" was compiled by Gordon Tucker, executive director of the commission, and is printed in *The Ordination of Women as Rabbis: Studies and Responsa*, ed. Simon Greenberg (New York, 1988), pp. 5–30. See also the position papers of seminary faculty members in the Greenberg volume. Several of the most forceful papers presented in opposition to women's ordination are not included in Greenberg's volume but appeared in a booklet entitled "On the Ordination of Women as Rabbis" (JTS, mimeo, early 1980s). See esp. the papers of David Weiss Halivni, Gershon C. Bacon, and David A. Resnick.

49. On the background to the faculty vote of 1979, see David Szonyi, "The Conservative Condition," *Moment* (May 1980): esp. 38–39.

50. For the debate over Magidson's application, see *Proceedings of the RA*, 1983, pp. 218–51.

51. See Francine Klagsbrun, "At Last, A Conservative Woman Rabbi," *Congress Monthly* (May–June 1985): 11; and Abraham Karp, "A Century of Conservative Judaism," *AJYB* 1986, vol. 86, pp. 3–61.

52. David Novak, in *Proceedings of the RA*, 1983, p. 223.

53. Aaron Gold, in ibid., p. 237.

54. For a contrary view stressing only the "structural" factors that account for Jewish identification, see Calvin Goldscheider and Alan Zuckerman, *The Transformation of the Jews* (Chicago, 1984).

55. Two penetrating analyses of the debate between "assimilationists" and "transformationists" are presented in Cohen, *American Assimilation or Jewish Revival?* pp. 1–18; and Charles S. Liebman, *Deceptive Images: Toward a Redefinition of American Judaism* (New Brunswick, 1988), pp. 61–73.

The Jewish Religious
Experience in America:
The Problem of Interpretation

JACOB NEUSNER

The study of religions in America, including American Judaism, presents a curious irony. We have a great many answers, much information. We have yet to state the questions. That is, our knowledge of the facts about various religious groups is considerable. We confidently narrate the history of religious movements, the biography of important religious figures, the story of religious institutions. These are answers. But what is the question? To the degree that historical studies limit themselves to the positivist agendum, prefer to talk about matters readily defined in measurable terms, reduce religion to its visible expressions, the available facts do fit the issues under study. Social scientists, of course, find the present agendum congenial, for it reduces the religious question to the answers produced by hard facts, opinions that can be counted, institutions which can be accurately described. When, therefore, we speak of American Judaism, the sociologists take for granted we are talking with them.

The religious question, however, is not wholly answered by positivist methods and results. To take one instance, even when we know the history of Hebrew Union College, its founders, budgets, curricula, and the like, we have not exhausted all that we ought to want to know about that history, its meaning and implications for the study of American Judaism. Indeed, I wonder, when we have completed our description of the founders and later leaders, the professors and students, the work of alumni, whether we have properly interpreted even these readily accessible facts. For several matters still elude us. First, why do people do what they do? What larger issues are present in their minds? Second, what do they imagine they do? What transcendent conception occupies their thoughts, gives meaning to their actions? Third, how do these two matters, the mind and imagination of participants, compare and relate to the work of others? I refer not solely to other Jews, who did not participate in founding Hebrew Union College and whose conception of Jewish religiosity was not the same as the founders', but also to other Americans, busy at the same time with a curiously similar set of programs and intentions.

I use as an example the history of Hebrew Union College because of the claim characteristic of Reform Judaism from Isaac Mayer Wise's day to our own to constitute "American Judaism," and because that claim reveals a very considerable set of aspirations, beliefs, and unarticulated conceptions well outside the capacity of the social scientists and their quantifications. But matters cannot rest within the limits of our example, which is meant to exemplify a larger thesis: a very considerable problem has yet to be defined and investigated by students of American Jewish history, and that is the religious one. By religious I do not mean solely the history of religious institutions, solely the biographies of religious people, solely the opinions on questions deemed to be of religious nature held by people polled by social scientists. These are part of the matter. I also do not mean only the catalogue of religious books and theological essays, both for the masses and for the religious elite, produced in this country, although that catalogue also contributes interesting data.

The larger question is, What is *religious* about the American Jews? What is not merely Jewish, but also *Judaic* about them? And what is *American* about what we regard as their religion? My purpose is to define those questions and to lay out an agendum, to suggest appropriate data for inquiry into questions and data which, I believe, have not been carefully explored to date.

Let me state my conclusion at the outset. I think the investigation of the nature of Jewish religion in America requires far more attention than has been given to the creative expressions of Jews speaking as, and for, anything but typical Jews. A group of people of remarkably homogeneous origins entering into the warp and woof of American culture continues to exhibit remarkably homogeneous traits, a detailed consensus of beliefs and behavior. These traits find ready and measurable definition in politics, in economics, and in social life. But they also have to be examined in their most subtle, and, I think, most authentic guise. When individuals, thinking themselves unique and private, represent and exemplify the group, what do they tell us about the inner life and perceptions of that group? Individuals who do so are, I believe, primarily the poets, the writers, the scholars, the creators of mind and of intellect.

Those traits characteristic and definitive of the whole—of "American Judaism"—by contrast should not be located chiefly among the people who aim and claim to begin with to express and exemplify them, because these latter people, all too self-conscious, say what they think should be said, express what they anticipate will be, if not conventional, at least deemed significant, define matters in commonplace, banal terms. They lead us not to the inner realities but to the outward banalities. Jewish religious thinking, for example, takes place among theologians whose ideas are formed in response to the classical literature and who therefore define the religious-theological problems in terms familiar in other non-American, non-modern settings. The theologians, with noteworthy exceptions, supply rather gross testimony either to the continuities of the classical tradition, or to the self-conscious and therefore contrived revisions of the classical tradition in response to external and superficial stimuli.

When, for example, we ask about the state of Jewish religious thinking about the Holocaust, we have remarkably limited choice of answers, represented by well-meaning sentimentalists. I need not rehearse their banal responses. When, by contrast, we turn to people who surpass and transcend the community, who speak solely for themselves, we hear messages of intense and original interest. Yet these messages turn out, on closer examination, authentically to tell us much about the state of Jewish religion within the larger community, specifically because, to begin with, it is not the intent of the artist, the poet, to testify about anything other than his or her own condition. Muriel Rukeyser is hardly a name renowned among people interested in the Jewish response to the Holocaust. Yet from her poem "To be a Jew in the Twentieth Century" I learn more about American Judaism in the past quarter century than I do from the names one usually contends with:

> To be a Jew in the twentieth century
> Is to be offered a gift. If you refuse,
> Wishing to be invisible, you choose
> Death of the spirit, the stone insanity.

Accepting, take full life, full agonies:
Your evening deep in labyrinthine blood
Of those who resist, fail and resist; and God
Reduced to a hostage among hostages.

The gift is torment. Not alone the still
Torture, isolation; or torture of the flesh.
That may come also. But the accepting wish,
The whole and fertile spirit as guarantee
For every human freedom, suffering to be free,
Daring to live for the impossible.

The theologians hardly explain the observed phenomena of the present age, the renaissance of "Jewish assertion" or "Jewish ethnicity," outside, and despite the best efforts of, the institutional expressions of conventional Jewish religiosity phrased in commonplace terms. The expected end of Jewish distinctiveness in the third and fourth generation, predicted by all the measured facts of the immediate post-war period, has not wholly been fulfilled. For alongside comes something else, something I think we can best begin to study and interpret not through the social sciences but through the words of poets.

Let me generalize. When I wish to study American and modern Judaism generally, I presently have two bodies of information. Yet I wish to introduce for consideration a third, more important one. First, we have, as I said, institutional histories and biographies, which tell us pretty much everything that social scientific positivism finds worth reporting. Second, we have the established concepts of theologians and ideologues.

But the third body of information, the data supplied by creative artists of various kinds, has yet to be introduced into historical discourse. And I contend the evidence of creative minds is going to supply the point of entry into the study of that homogeneous, remarkably coherent corpus of religious expression characteristic of the Jewish people, here and abroad.

To take a European instance with important American ramifications, when we speak of the study of modern Judaism, we normally are understood to refer to the study of modern Jewish thinkers, some European, some American. That is, "modern Judaism" is reduced to those ideas stated by a handful of men (no women known to me) assumed to embody and represent both "modernity" and "Judaism." Who are some of the names? In the nineteenth century, Salomon Formstecher in Europe and S. R. Hirsch in America; in the twentieth, Hermann Cohen, Franz Rosenzweig, and Martin Buber in Europe, Abraham Heschel and Mordecai Kaplan in America. Without meaning to denigrate their intellectual achievements, I say that it is not a very impressive list. Apart from Heschel, none of the list of "modern Jewish thinkers" is characterized by profound knowledge of the Jewish classical tradition. The sum and substance of their ideas hardly constitute an interesting or informed statement either of modernity or of what "Judaism" can consist of in response to modernity. Yet even if we stipulate the opposite, whom and what have we omitted from the testimonies of modernity?

Let me mention, first, our incapacity to cope with the data represented by traditionalism, in Europe or in America. Those data are eliminated, despite their massive presence, because they are not deemed "modern" or a response to "modernity." Immense events, of extraordinary intellectual weight, have taken place in the world of traditionalists, in the *yeshivot* (academies for Torah study) of the nineteenth and twentieth centuries. Some of these events happened even in this country, yet are scarcely taken into account in the study of American Judaism. Our conceptions of what is American and our study of what is modern make no place for traditionalism. Why is that so? Because, we take for granted, traditionalists are somehow outside the scope of America, are premodern, are destined to disappear. Our conception of what is modern and American imposes an extraordinary—yet unarticulated—selectivity. Orthodoxy is not modern, unless we call it so. We admit "modern Orthodoxy" and its Americanized institutions, pretending, for the purposes of our study of Judaism in America, that traditional Orthodoxy is simply not present. Yet it is present, and is considerably more vital than movements whose American-ness is taken for granted. The hermeneutic that sees the modern and American as only the new and different prevents us from examining what is new and different in what seems old and timeless. Therefore we deny ourselves important testimony about America and Judaism. My contention is that when one wants to know what is American about what is happening in Judaism in this country, he or she should turn to those groups that claim to be least in touch with American culture and society. It is through the subtle changes in their perceptions of themselves and the tradition—changes exceedingly difficult to locate and understand—that the most profound traits of the present situation are going to be discerned.

If immigrants deliberately de-Judaized themselves, raised their children with no Jewish education whatever, that supplies an important fact in the study of American Judaism. But are not the facts of traditionalist rejection of the American situation, alongside their unstated, unintended, and unperceived accommodation to the new world, equally important testimonies? I think, indeed, they tell us at least as much about America as we learn from people who, fresh from the boat, assume they know what to do. A striking parallel emerges in the Catholic debates of the last half of the nineteenth century, in which American exceptionalism was the superficial issue. But the changes in Catholic religious life in response to the American situation were more profound than the issues meant to define those changes and allow for their analysis. The unstated reality became clearer in the extraordinary American-ness of the American bishops at Vatican Council II, in their virtually unassimilable character within the world church, than in anything said a half century earlier about whether Catholics should, or should not, fit into American society. The American-ness of the University of Notre Dame is more illuminating, I think, than the articulated reform of the exponents of *aggiornamento*. It speaks more quietly, but also more to the point. On the one side, we have people who make things up as they go along, responding to this and that, calling it "modern" or "American." On the other, we have people who, in stubbornly resisting the new world, testify more surely, and I think more honestly, to what that world consists of.

I asked what we omit from the inquiry into modernity, into American Judaism by our stress on positive facts about institutions, people, and loudly stated ideas, positions, platforms, and the like. A second striking omission, in addition to traditionalism, already broadly alluded to, is the inner spiritual life of the group as a whole. If, as I think, the Jews in America exhibit a remarkable homogeneity of social traits, political behavior, economic characteristics, and the like, then how shall we get at their religious notions? How shall we investigate the corpus of symbols and myths, the ideas in subterranean unarticulated form, which explain for them these effects, these epiphenomena, of reality? For surely people who tend to vote in one way, aspire to raise their children in a single pattern, seek out common sorts of neighborhoods, or, more broadly, people who follow a single pattern of living, from birth to death, a pattern of remarkable cogency and rather simple character, have within their minds surely a single perception of reality. But what is that perception? How is it formed? What does it consist of? How does it relate to the this-worldly behavior of the folk? What does it say in response to birth and death, to the great, common experiences of individual life? How does it understand history, the weighty events surpassing individual life? Where do we come from, where do we go? Who am I? And who are we? These questions and their answers, I offer in definition, are the agenda for the study of American Judaism. How shall we find the answers?

I have already suggested that it is in art, music, and literature, not only or mainly in theology and sociology, that we must seek the answer. And, I hasten to add, it is not primarily in the art, music, and literature coming from artists deliberately expressing what they think Jewish artists should deliberately express that the answers come. I gladly leave to the sociologists the positivist study of the fiction of Chaim Potok, or the scholarship of Max Dimont, or the artists who load their canvases with what they know are immediately recognized "Jewish symbols"—whether they are the Israelis painting for the American market or Americans. To the banal hermeneutic of the sociologists I leave the banal artists, who, if they were not Jewish artists working for a self-consciously Jewish audience, would not enjoy success, because, by the canons and standards and disciplines of the larger world of art, they are not very talented. Kitsch is for sociology, not for aesthetics. I refer rather to the great Jewish novelists who address themselves to their own—therefore, to the human condition, to Meyer Levin, Saul Bellow, Herman Wouk, or Herbert Gold, among novelists; people who can write (if differently) with the genius of a John Updike, and who know and love the English language: I refer to the poets such as Allan Ginzberg or Karl Shapiro. But matters need not remain among the creative artists. What if we turn to the world of politics? There are, again, talented individuals, who—it is true—merely happen to be Jewish. Yet that happenstance supplies extraordinarily interesting information, even insight, about the meaning of public life to the Jews. We learn considerably less from the self-aggrandizing, pretentious postures of a Podhoretz.

Yet we cannot so readily dismiss the Potoks or the Wiesels or the Podhoretzes either, for their popularity is an important fact. What they teach us about the American Jewish imagination—or its poverty—I prefer not to investigate. Rather, let us assess their meaning by contrast to the traits of a different audience. I refer to the vast audience of the Hasidic stories, immensely popular in the nineteenth century. Professor Arnold Band, at the University of California at Los Angeles, presently investigates the aesthetic aspects of Hasidic stories. I report only the generality that those stories rely, he tells me, upon an extraordinarily sophisticated perception of literature, testify to sophistication in matters of form and style not usually associated with East European Yiddish-speaking Jews. We learn, therefore, about a sense of aesthetics, about a feeling for literature; the aesthetics is the outcome of a thousand years of intellectual development, of the form, structure, and other literary-critical aspects of a literature hardly thought of, nowadays, as literature at all. If Band is right, as I believe he is, then what do we learn about the highly educated American Jewish community's response to works which, I think, hardly are to be taken seriously for their literary traits? We may spare ourselves a recital of the specific all-too-obvious lessons.

Thus far I have emphasized the data which, I think, are pertinent to the study of the Jewish religious experience in America. Let me now explain what I should like to learn from those data.

In order to do so, I refer to what is surely the greatest work in the study of religion in America, Sydney Ahlstrom's *Religious History of the American People*, and repeat my fundamental question to him: What does it all mean? What is *American* about the religious history of the American people? What draws together the complex phenomena of religions in this country? What indicates how these discrete phenomena all together suggest that, behind the peoples of America stands an ("the") *American* people, and beyond the religions of America stands a peculiarly American experience of, approach to, *religion*? How, for example, does American Judaism relate to, compare with, other expressions of religions, both historical and contemporary? What can we say about the phenomenon as a whole, about its larger meanings for the analysis of culture and society?

I have two questions that are four. First comes the question, What is Judaic in American Judaism? In what ways have the traditions, beliefs and practices, and the larger conceptions of reality contained within those beliefs and practices responded to the new world? In what ways does the tradition go forward unchanged? Of still greater interest, how has the Judaic tradition so shaped the Jews as to affect their response to America? In what ways does the Judaic tradition persist, enduring in new forms, yet unimpaired? That seems to me a difficult question, but, from the viewpoint of understanding both Judaism and America, an important one.

Second, what is American in American Judaism? How does the religious dimension, the understanding and interpretation of reality on the part of Jews, testify to quintessentially American traits? Clearly, when we ask about America, we want to know about its society and popular culture. But we revert, too, to the classical question, Who is this American, this new man? For it is universally held, within American Jewry, that America is different, and the difference is not solely in economy or politics, but in the Jews themselves. Just as the American, by the second generation, is virtually unassimilable into European culture, so the American requires definition and explanation: What has changed the European, and the European Jew, so rapidly and so completely as to yield, at least in self-perception, this new man, this new woman?

These are the two questions: What is Judaic in American Judaism? What is American in American Judaism? To answer the former, we look backward, a vertical perspective. To answer the latter, we look outward, a horizontal line of vision. Yet what of the interstices, the points at which the lines cross, and the spaces between? For the Jew in America both understands himself or herself and is understood as a kind of American, not merely an amalgam of an enduring Judaic viewpoint (surely not, for few are shaped by the classical viewpoint) and of America, a new and distinctive political and social situation. When we have accounted for, added up the traits (political and social) we see as American and the qualities (cultural and intellectual) we suppose are Judaic, we stand at the beginning, not the end, of the hermeneutic problem.

The issue I propose is hardly the simple dissection of the whole into its components, but rather, the description and interpretation of the whole. The problem is to understand how the whole has become so much more than the sum of its parts. If I turn attention to poetry and literature, to scholarship, and subtle expressions of religiosity, it is because these express the sum of the parts, effect the integration and the wholeness of the whole person.

The two questions, What is Judaic and what is American? yield two more: What is traditional or classic? What is modern? What continues the lines laid out long ago? What crosses those lines or marks a change in their direction? For the American experience is important to humankind as a whole, just as the Jewish experience is suggestive for America as a whole. Specifically, both testify to a larger universal phenomenon: the man and the woman of modernity.

What do we understand by "religion" in the modern age, after the collapse of classical myths and after the end of old modes of believing and acting? That is a question facing much of humankind. Yet the question is too narrow. It leaves no room for the old continuities, not only in, but also in response to, the modern situation. How are we to understand the whole self, the entire worldview, in the presence of so many conflicting testimonies? The answer to that question involves consideration of a still larger one, the question of religion. If we understand by "religion" the fundamental perception by which we both understand and shape reality, understand and shape the private life and public affairs of community and nation, then in studying religion we consider the largest, most inclusive problem in the interpretation of the human condition. Humankind has universally experienced a vast epoch of change, affecting virtually everyone outside the most remote and isolated groups. Change, East and West, has taken villagers and moved them to cities, has utterly revised the inherited means of production and distribution of goods, has completely altered inherited modes of social organization, has made humankind into Americans: uprooted and transplanted people. What has this immense movement, still not fully worked out, done to the mind and imagination, the perception and organization of reality, of humankind? The answer to that question, I believe, will explain much about the discrete events and private lives of communities and individuals alike.

American Judaism, I therefore contend, constitutes something more than the lingering end of olden ways and ancient myths. It is the effort of modern people to make use of archaic ways and myths for the formation of a way of living appropriate to the modern condition. That is why American Judaism is suggestive beyond itself, something more than an ethnic and antiquarian concern. If American Jews have chosen to reconstruct out of the remnants of an evocative but incongruous heritage the materials of a humanly viable community life, they tell us much about the modern condition of humankind, bewildered people who, despite it all, will to endure, to go onward because there is no turning back.

Yet in so phrasing matters, I ask historians to undertake more than their accepted agendum of inquiry. For before us is the work of philosophy and history of religions: the quest for understanding, the task of interpretation. I asked Ahlstrom how he has given us a religious history of the American people, rather than an account of the historical data of various religious groups and institutions and discrete theologies in American society. Merely writing the histories of various religions in different sectors of a diverse population that by chance is located in North America hardly constitutes the history of religions, the account of humankind, in the new world. It not only does not accomplish the *religionsgeschichtlich* or hermeneutical task, it does not even begin it.

It may be fairly argued that that task is irrelevant to the hard data of economics and sociology, politics and manifest culture. But I think not. For in American Judaism one finds not only social stratification and political behavior, but anguish, joy, tragedy, mystery, revealed in social and political behavior. Wilfred C. Smith states, "A religious symbol is successful if men can express in terms of it the highest and deepest vision of which they are capable, and if in terms of it that vision can be nourished and conveyed to others within one's group." Since American Jews uniformly behave as if they possess such symbols, they therefore surely do possess such symbols. That is, they act in such a way as strongly to suggest they profess faith and myth beyond the mundane data of their very worldly and secular life as a group. They respond to, stand within, and express something very like that "Judaism" which is to be discerned in premodern times. True, they seem so committed to rationality, respectability, and worldly culture as to suggest there is no "American Judaism"—a religion worth studying. Yet that judgment seems to me a function of our analysis, not of their condition. For when the sociologists, monopolists of the study of American Judaism, have had their say, they still have not drawn the transcendent thorn from the rational rose. And transcendence, supernaturalism, reference to salvation and the end of time, to things not of this world, and to a New Jerusalem—these seem not solely the perquisites of the religious quest for meaning, but the characteristics of the very "secular" American Jewish community. It is a fact that, while proclaiming their secularity (itself a datum in the study of religions) Jews do understand themselves in mythic terms and respond to the existential challenges of their situation in accord with the classic Judaic response, superficially much revised to be sure.

My contention, therefore, is that America is the model of modernity, and the American Jewish experience of modernity is paradigmatic of that of humankind in confrontation with a modernity. When we want to know what happens to religion beyond the age in which people take ritual for reality and myth for granted, tell as fact the stories meant to convey the structure of being and reveal the truth of life, we turn to the laboratory of modernity: to America. We examine in particular the quintessential modern people, the Jews. We ask about their imaginative life, how they mediate between the claims of contemporaneity and the demands of a vast inheritance of institutions, rituals, myths, theologies, social and cultural patterns derived from the archaic age, a considerable, very present heritage. American Judaism supplies evocative and important materials for a case study of the religious experience of modernity.

PART TWO

THE TORAH: JUDAISM IN HOLY BOOKS AND IN HISTORY

5

The Hebrew Scriptures
of Ancient Israel:
The Crisis Addressed
by the Five Books of Moses

ISRAEL BEFORE JUDAISM:
THE BIBLICAL PRELUDE

The Pentateuch (the Five Books of Moses) refers to events of a long-ago past, beginning with the creation of the world, the making of man and woman, the fall of humanity through disobedience, the flood that wiped out nearly all of humanity except for Noah—progenitor of all humanity—the decline of humanity from Noah to Abraham, then the rise of humanity through Abraham, Isaac, Jacob (also called Israel), and the twelve sons of Jacob, then exile in Egypt, and ultimately Sinai. There, the scriptural narrative continues, God revealed the Torah to Moses, and that revelation contained the terms of the covenant that God made with Israel, the family of Abraham, Isaac, and Jacob. The book of Genesis narrates the story of creation and of the beginnings of the family that Israel would always constitute, the children of Abraham, Isaac, and Jacob. The book of Exodus presents the story of the slavery of the children of Israel in Egypt and how God redeemed them from Egyptian bondage and brought them to Sinai, there to make a covenant with them, by which they would accept the Torah and carry out its rules. The book of Leviticus portrays the founding of the priests' service to God through the sacrifice of the produce of the holy land to which God would bring Israel, and specifies the rules and regulations governing the kingdom of priests and the holy people. The book of Numbers provides an account of the wandering in the wilderness. The book of Deuteronomy then presents a reprise of the story, a long sermon by Moses looking back on the history of Israel from the beginnings through the point of entry into the Promised Land, and a restatement of the rules of the covenant between Israel and God.

Every Judaism, wherever and whenever created, through the Scriptures of ancient Israel[1] traced its beginnings to the creation of the world. Following the biblical record, each system maintained that God created the world and for ten dismal and declining generations, from Adam to Noah, despaired of creation. Then for ten generations, from Noah to Abraham, God waited for humanity to acknowledge the sovereignty of the one God, Creator of heaven and earth. Then came Abraham and Sarah. Abraham obeyed God's commandment to leave his home in Babylonia and to journey to the Promised Land. Israel therefore began with the experience of alienation: "Go from your country and your kindred and your father's house to the land that I will show you" (Gen. 12:1). Through their children, Sarah and Abraham founded Israel, the people of the Lord, to whom God later at Sinai revealed the Torah, the complete record of God's will for humanity, starting with Israel, the Jewish people. The biblical record goes on to speak of David, the king of Israel and founder of the ruling household, from which, at the end of time, the Messiah is destined to come forth. So Judaism tells the story of the world from creation in Adam and Eve, through the revelation of the Torah at Sinai, to the redemption of humanity through the Messiah at the end of time—a picture of the world, beginning, middle, and end. That account of the history of humanity and of all creation derived from a people that traces its origins to the beginnings of time and yet thrives in the world today.

Ancient Israel—tribes of various origins—had entered the land of Canaan, which became the Land of Israel, some time before 1000 B.C.E. We need not rehearse the familiar tale of how these diverse groups all were described as having formed the family of a single man, Abraham, and his wife, Sarah, through their son, Isaac, and his wife, Rebecca, and their grandson, Jacob, and his wives, Leah and Rachel, and their co-wives. Nor do we have to remind ourselves about the story of how the children of this family went down to Egypt on account of a famine, multiplied there, became enslaved, and, led by Moses, under God's orders, escaped to the wilderness of Sinai, there to receive the revelation of God for the founding of their nation and the ordering of their life. We can dispense with a recounting, moreover, of the single account of what was in fact a diverse and various process of conquering the land and settling in it. None of this has any bearing on the history of Judaism, except as a statement in linear and incremental terms of a set of fables, each with its own point of origin, each taken out of its original context and placed into that larger cogent, linear, and incremental setting in which we now receive them all.

In fact, in Scripture we deal with a composite of materials, each with its own viewpoint and traits of mind. It was only after the destruction of the First Temple of Jerusalem in 586 B.C.E. that the Torah, that is, the Five Books of Moses, came into being, a pastiche of received stories, some old, some new, all revised for the purposes of the final authors. It was in the aftermath of the destruction of that Temple and the later restoration of the exiles to the land that those authors wrote of the origins of Israel, the Jewish people. In light of Israel's ultimate destiny, which the authors took to be the loss and restoration of the land, the origins of the people in its land took on their cogent meaning. Israel then began its acquisition of the land through Abraham, and attained its identity as a people through the promise of the land in the covenant of Sinai, and the entry into the land under Joshua. Israel's history then formed the story of how, because of its conduct on the land, Israel lost its land, first in the north, then in the south—despite the prophets' persistent warnings. From the exile in Babylonia in 586 B.C.E., the authors of the Torah recast Israel's history into the story of the conditional existence of the people; their existence was measured in their possession of the land on condition of God's favor. Everything depended on carrying out a contract: Do this, get that, do not do this, do not get that—and nothing formed a given and nothing was unconditional. The task of the authors demanded the interpretation of the conditions of the present, and their message in response to the uncertainty of Israel's life beyond exile and restoration underlined the uncertainty of that life.

The record of the Hebrew Scriptures, called, in Christianity, the Old Testament and, in Judaism, the written (part of the) Torah, came together only after the end of the period of which they speak. Most of the writings in the Hebrew Scriptures describe events of the period before 586 B.C.E., but they were written in the form in which we have them afterward. What made that year (treated as a symbol for its century) important was also what made people look backward for an explanation of events—the destruction of the Temple in Jerusalem. The Temple, a place of sacrifice to God of the natural produce of the land—grain, wine, and meat—on altar fires, had been built four centuries earlier. The writings from pre-586 Israel that were drawn together in the Pentateuch, as well as in important writings of history and prophecy—Joshua, Judges, Samuel, Kings, Isaiah 1–39, Jeremiah, Ezekiel, and some shorter works—all were meant to explain what had ultimately happened: the destruction of the Israelite state, including its Temple, monarchy, and priesthood, in 586 B.C.E.

The pentateuchal formation and explanation of history made two important points. First, the pentateuchal traditions, now drawn together into a single unitary and (more or less) continuous, if repetitive, account, specified that Israel stood in a contractual relationship with God. God had revealed the Torah to Israel, and the Torah contained God's will for Israel. If Israel kept the Torah, God would bless the people, and if not—as Leviticus 26 and Deuteronomy 28 clearly explained—God would exact punishment for violation of the covenant.

Second, the prophetic writings emphasized that God shaped history—those particular events that made a difference—in a pattern that bore deep meaning. Whatever happened carried out God's will, which the prophets conveyed. Put together in the end so that the prophetic writings appeared to foretell the destruction that would come, the prophets' writings therefore contained a message entirely harmonious with the basic message of the pentateuchal ones. Judaism began with the formation of the larger part of the Hebrew Scriptures, the Pentateuch and the main constituents of the prophetic books. We may therefore say that while the (genealogical) Israel of the Torah of Moses traces its origins back to Abraham, Isaac, and Jacob, and while historians tell the story of Israel from remote antiquity, the continuous and unfolding religious tradition we know as Judaism begins with Scripture. Scripture as we have it commences with the destruction of the First Temple by the Babylonians in 586 B.C.E.

If we examine the components of the present composite, we gain our first opportunity to examine whole and complete a single Judaic system. Since all Judaisms begin with the making of the Five Books of Moses as the Torah of God given to Israel in Sinai, we realize that using the word Judaism for a strand of the Pentateuch represents a considerable anachronism. For a single formative experience stood at the beginning of all Judaisms, and each Judaism in its manner recapitulated that experience. The original definitive experience imposed its outlines on every Judaism, framing the questions that characterized them all, but allowing for the diversity of their respective answers. That is why for the materials that came down from the period before 586 B.C.E. we cannot invoke the category Judaism except for purposes of exposition. None of the prior systems in its original statement addressed the urgent question of 586–450, that is, of exile and return, and none of them recapitulated that pattern of human and national experience.

From the seventeenth century, the time of the great Jewish philosopher and scholar of ancient Israel, Baruch Spinoza, scholarship has identified in the Pentateuch a number of distinct strands of narrative, each exhibiting its own indicative marks of language and viewpoint and each addressed to the way of life of a particular Israel. Two are visible to the naked eye: the book of Deuteronomy, which scholars call D, which explicitly announces that it will recapitulate everything that has gone before and then resolutely rewrites the whole— history, law, and theology—and the Priestly Code, recognized as "the Torah of the priests" even by the rabbis of the Talmud (though they understood it to be God's Torah for the priests rather than the Torah in God's name written by the priests, as we now know it to be). The Priestly Code, referred to as P, covers parts of Genesis, Exodus, and the whole of Leviticus and Numbers. Both of these sources, D and P, themselves join together discrete strands of materials.

Another strand among a number of documents now patched together into the Five Books of Moses is called J after the name of the Lord, Yahweh, that is characteristically used in its narratives, and is generally referred to as the Yahwistic account. Another is called E, after the name of God, Elohim, that predominates, and therefore is identified as the Elohist. These two strands are joined together in JE.

The fact that the Pentateuch is made up of strands by itself makes no difference in our understanding of the Torah of Moses as it emerged in the time of Ezra, about 450 B.C.E., and none made a singular impact on any of the Judaisms that flowed from the Torah of Moses. But each in its day made a statement concerning a particular social and political context—an Israel. Each explained the world formed by that Israel—its way of life. And each one also provided a complete picture of the world that came to concrete expression in that way of life—its worldview. So while we cannot call J or D or P a Judaism, each allows us to see a whole and complete system—way of life and worldview, addressed to a particular social group—before the formation of Judaism.

The basis for identifying a strand of the Pentateuch as the writing of the Yahwist—specifically, Genesis 2—11; 12—16; 18—22; 24—34; 38; 49; Exodus 1—24; 32; 34; Numbers 11—12; 14; 20—25; Judges 1—is not only use of the name Yahweh for God. It is also the association of other indications with the appearance of that name. For example, in the Yahwist system Moses' father is called Reuel; the mountain, Sinai; and the Palestinians, Canaanites. Where God is called Elohim, Moses' father-in-law is Jethro; the mountain, Horeb; and the Palestinians, Amorites. For another example, the creation myth of Gen. 1:1 has God/Elohim create the world. Then Gen. 2:5–25 has Yahweh make the world, and this creation myth differs in fundamental ways, in substance and style, from the former. The biblical narrative covers the same ground two or more times. For example, a patriarch fools a foreign king three times about his wife's status (Gen. 12:10–20; 20; 26:1–11), twice with Abraham and Abimelekh. There are two flood stories, with seven animals brought on one ark, but pairs on the other. These and many other indications have persuaded most biblical scholars (outside of circles of believers, who have had no difficulty harmonizing everything into one cogent statement) that there are four strands interwoven in the Pentateuch: (1) the Yahwist, which we consider here; (2) the Elohist; (3) the Deuteronomist; and (4) the Priestly—henceforth J, E, D, and P.[2] We are interested in these materials only as they form systems—complete statements of how things are and why they are the way they are and what "Israel" must do because of that fact. We want to identify the systems—the Yahwist's and the Deuteronomist's and the Priests' in particular—with the circumstances addressed by those systems. That brings us to the Yahwist's account of Israel: who and what Israel is, how Israel should see the world, what Israel should do—J's theory of an Israel, its worldview, and its way of life—J's Judaism.

The way of life of the Judaism that set the norm for the Second Temple period was the holy way of life depicted in the Five Books of Moses. The Pentateuch encompasses these four sources, originally distinct, three—J, E, and D—deriving from the period before 586, and one—P, the Priestly—from the period afterward. But from our perspective, the Judaic system represented by the Pentateuch came into being when the several sources became one—as we now know them. That work was accomplished by priests in the time of Ezra, around 450 B.C.E. The worldview came from the account of heaven and earth and the definition of Israel presented in the Pentateuch. The Israel of that Judaism found its definition in the same Scripture: Israel encompassed the family of an original father, Abraham. Israel now consisted of the genealogical descendants of that original family. Thus the Scripture of the first Judaism was the Five Books of Moses, the setting encompassed Israel after the exile and return to Zion, and the system centered on the explanation of the rules that would keep Israel holy—that is, separate for God alone. Central to the life of holiness was the "tabernacle," conceived as the model for the postexilic Temple.

What Judaism might have been had Israel been spared the crucible of exile and return, alienation and reconciliation, God alone knows. But through the Torah as we know it, God has not told us.

THE YAHWIST'S JUDAISM
FOR AN IMPERIAL ISRAEL, 950 B.C.E.

The Yahwist's Judaism, written in the time of David and Solomon, asked the questions of empire: For what? How long? Why us? These questions in no way intersect with the pentateuchal one in its final formulation: On what condition? For J is a firm and final statement. In the time of King Solomon, people looked backward to account for the great day at hand. The Yahwist's account, produced at the height of the glory of the Davidic monarchy, in the time of Solomon around 950 B.C.E., wanted to tell the story of the federation of the federated tribes, now a single kingdom under Solomon, with a focus on Zion and Jerusalem, the metropolis of the federation. The Yahwist told the history—that is to say the theology—of Israel from its origins. He made the point that the hand of Yahweh directed events. The message he derived from that fact was one of grace. What he wanted to know from the past was the present and future of the empire and monarchy at hand.[3] The Yahwist told the story from the creation of the world to the fulfillment of Israel in the conquest of the land. His purpose was to affirm that what had happened to Israel—its move from a federation of tribes to an empire under David and Solomon—was the work of God, whom he called Yahweh.

W. Lee Humphreys summarizes the Yahwist's Judaism, the world-view explaining an imperial Israel and the way of life of Israel as empire: "The Israel of the empire was Yahweh's creation for which Yahweh had a mission." Humphreys lays great emphasis on how God chose a particular person to carry out the mission: Abraham and Sarah, Isaac, Jacob, and others all appeared weak and unworthy, but God chose them anyway. The message, as Humphreys paraphrases it, is this:

> The Yahwist focused attention on just one man, then on twelve sons, then on a band of slaves in Egypt, then on fugitives in Sinai's wastes. Repeatedly endangered, seemingly about to vanish on many occasions, small, weak, and often unworthy, these ancestors of the Israelite empire of David and Solomon were sustained again and again, even in the land of the god-king pharaoh, because they were a chosen people, elected by a god who upheld and preserved them.

That is the message. What is the place of Moses as lawgiver in this picture? It is minor. The Yahwist's picture reduces the covenant at Sinai to modest propositions; the legal stipulations are few, and are focused in Exodus 34.[4]

> The Lord said, Here and now I make a covenant. . . . You shall not make yourselves gods of cast metal.
> You shall observe the pilgrim feast of unleavened bread. . . .
> For every first birth of the womb belongs to me. . . .
> For six days you shall work but on the seventh day you shall cease work.
> You shall observe the pilgrim feast of Weeks. . . .
> You shall not offer the blood of my sacrifice at the same time as anything leavened. . . .
> You shall bring the choicest first fruits of your soil to the house of the Lord your God.
> You shall not boil a kid in its mother's milk.
>   (Exod. 34:10–26, NEB)

The unconditional quality of the promises of God to Abraham—and later to David—dominates throughout.

At issue are the promises to the patriarchs and their children, not the contract between God and Israel. Israel was destined by divine grace for its glory in Solomon's time. So for the Yahwist Moses was a minor figure relative to the patriarchs. And what was important about Moses was not the giving of law but some of the narratives of his leadership—Exodus 2—24; 32; 34. And these we read as testimonies to the mentality of the Davidic monarchy. So when we hear the tale of the golden calf, the breaking of the tablets, and the forgiveness of God as an act of grace, we listen to sublime narratives told in the age of Solomon and to the world of Solomon: God's grace favored Israel in an age knowing grace, a powerful message to a self-confident empire.

Humphreys provides a systematic statement of this Judaism:

> Adam and Eve are driven from the garden and must thereafter scratch out a living from the ground by hard labor. In time they must die, for they no longer have access to the tree of life. The disorder intensifies as brother turns against brother . . . then man is set against man in a blood feud. . . . The boundary separating the divine and the human is trespassed. . . . Because of human perverseness, nature and the deity destroy humankind in a flood. . . . Finally an attempt by humans to overreach themselves with their tower results in a scattering of nations and confusion of tongues. . . . The human family grows ever more alienated from the deity and from one another until the harmonious order has in every way dissolved. The state of blessing found in the garden has become one of curse. . . . In the Yahwist's epic, death becomes the human fate because of an act of human disobedience, the flood is just punishment by a deity whose creation has turned against him. . . . The range of vision abruptly narrows [with the entry of Abraham]. An alien having only limited contact with the natives and setting but shallow roots, he lives with a promise that alone sustains him. . . . In time the deity's blessing and charge were transferred to his son Isaac, then to Jacob, and through Jacob to the Twelve Tribes. . . . By implication the blessing and charge passed from the Twelve Tribes to the Israel of David and Solomon.[5]

Israel then is given a mission: to serve as a blessing for all the families of earth. Yahweh's promise to Abraham, Humphreys notes, "recalls the promise made through Nathan the prophet to David in 2 Sam. 7:9: "I will make for you a great name, like the name of the great ones of the earth." The promise to Abraham thus came to fulfillment in the empire of David and Solomon. The monarchy fulfilled Yahweh's promise, and in the promise to Abraham God validated the empire building of David and Solomon. Why did God favor Israel? It was, in Humphreys's summary, "to be the vehicle for life, peace, integrity, and harmony in the created order, to reverse the currents set in motion by the first human act of disobedience."

The Yahwist joined the themes of the formation of the tribes into a federation and those of the building of Jerusalem and the monarchy, using the stories to legitimize the empire. What is important in the Yahwist's picture is the unconditional character of the account. The promise to Abraham was not conditional; it was tied to no strings: "The assurances found in Gen. 23:2 and 2 Sam. 7:9–16 carry the force of certainty, of actions already coming into effect."[6]

> I took you from the pastures. . . . I have been with you wherever you have gone. . . . I will make you a great name among the great ones of the earth. I will assign a place for my people Israel; there I will plant them and they shall dwell in their own land. . . . The Lord has told you that he would build up your royal house. When your life ends and you rest with your forefathers, I will set up one of your family, one of your own children, to succeed you and I will establish his kingdom.
>
> (2 Sam. 7:8–13, NEB)

The worldview expressed in this Judaism thus addressed an Israel that "would fill their role in the divine plan. . . . [The Yahwist] reflects the heady days of the empire when briefly under David and especially under Solomon all things seemed possible. For a time Israel would shine forth like a light, revealing Yahweh's concern for all the nations of the earth."[7] What we do not find is more interesting than what we do find: There is no stress on a covenant, the conditional character of Israel's existence, the uncertain right to the land, or the unclear identification of the people. The traits of a heightened reality—in which possession of the land depended upon the character of the society built upon it, and in which the very existence of the people constantly demanded explanation and justification—those recurrent characteristics of the Judaisms after 586 played a slight role in the Yahwist's serene and confident Judaism, in his view of the world from the height of Jerusalem, and in his account of the way of life of a normal people, living securely in its rightful place. No later Judaism would conform to this view.

The Yahwist's picture—with its beginning and middle, but no end—did not impart its attitude on later Judaisms, because the Yahwist's fundamental conception of Israel in the world in no way corresponded to the experience of Israel in the world. This was a Judaism that did not invent, but was invented by, the ordinary reality of the social world—a Judaism that was created by politics. Only later on shall we uncover Judaisms that created their own politics—those world-defining Judaisms that reproduced in diverse settings that original experience of exile and restoration that the Yahwist could not imagine. So the Yahwist gives us a fragment of one Judaism before Judaism. But it is hardly the only one.[8] We move on to another in search of a religion that imparted its own pattern upon the social world.

CRISIS AND RESOLUTION

The small number of Israelite families who remembered the exile, survived in Babylonia, and then toward the end of the sixth and fifth centuries B.C.E. returned to Zion knew things that Israel before 586 could never have imagined. The vast majority of the people did not undergo the experiences of exile and return. One part never left and the other never came back. That fact shows us the true character of the Judaism that would predominate: it began by making a selection of facts it deemed consequential, hence historical, and ignored in that selection the experiences of others who had quite a different perception of what had happened—and for all we know a different appreciation of the message. The fact that the ones who came back and many who were taken away were priests made all the difference, as the books of Ezra and Nehemiah indicate. For to the priests, what mattered in 586 was the destruction of the Temple, and what made a difference "three generations later" was the restoration of Zion and the rebuilding of the Temple. To them the cult was the key, and the Temple was the nexus between heaven and earth.

The nation—as seen and defined by the priests—restored to its land could be compared to a person healed from a life-threatening illness or to a poet. To such as these, nothing loses its astonishing quality. Life cannot be taken for granted. Life becomes a gift, each day an unanticipated surprise. Everything then demands explanation, but uncertainty reigns. The comparison fails when we realize that, while the consciousness of life as a gift of grace changes things for the survivor alone, the return to Zion, cast as it was into the encompassing language of the Five Books of Moses, imposed upon the entire nation's imagination and inner consciousness the unsettling encounter with annihilation avoided, extinction postponed, and life renewed—the Temple restored, as portrayed in P's Leviticus and Numbers.

To explain the power of the priests' tale, we need hardly invoke the conception of a shared national consciousness, a collective myth of nationhood subject to condition and stipulation, forever threatened with desolation, and always requiring renewal. For the Torah taught that one lesson of the human condition of Israel every Sabbath everywhere to everybody. So to Israel the Torah imparted the picture of society subject to judgment. And it was the priests' judgment in particular that prevailed. All Judaisms to come in some way or other found in the priests' pattern the model to which they would have to respond. The priests' Torah, the Pentateuch in its final statement, constituted the first Judaism.

EVENT AND PATTERN

A Judaism asks an urgent question and supplies a self-evident, compelling answer. The issue addressed by Judaic systems from the Pentateuch on was and would remain, Who is Israel? And what are the rules that define Israel as a social and political entity? In one way or another Israel, the Jewish people wherever they lived, sought ways to declare itself distinct from its neighbors. The stress on exclusion of the neighbors from the group, and of the group from the neighbors, ran contrary to the situation of ancient Israel, with the unmarked frontiers of culture and the constant giving and receiving among diverse groups which were generally characteristic of ancient times. The persistent stress on differentiation and the preoccupation with self-definition also contradicted the facts of the matter. In the time of the formation of the Pentateuch, the people Israel was deeply affected by the shifts and changes in social, cultural, and political life and institutions. When, a century and a half after the formation of the Pentateuch under Ezra and Nehemiah, the Greeks under Alexander the Great conquered the entire Middle East (about 320 B.C.E.) and incorporated the Land of Israel into the international Hellenistic culture, the problem of self-definition came to renewed expression. And when the war of independence fought by the Jews under the leadership of the Maccabees (about 160 B.C.E.) produced an independent state for a brief period, that state found itself under the government of a court that accommodated itself to the international style of politics and culture. So what was different? What made Israel separate and secure on its land and in its national identity? In that protracted moment of confusion and change, the heritage of the Five Books of Moses came to completion. The same situation persisted that had marked the age in which the Pentateuch had delivered its message, answering with compelling responses the urgent question of the nation's existence. That constituted the formative chapter in the history of all Judaisms: exile and return as the history of Judaism. Let us begin from the beginning, with the pentateuchal reading of events and their meanings framed after 586.

The principles of the pentateuchal Torah and the historical and prophetic writings of the century after 586, namely, Israel's heightened sense of its own social reality, its status as an elected people standing in a covenantal relationship with God, in fact spoke out of the inner structure of the system. They expressed its logic, not a logic intrinsic in events, even in events selected and reworked. They applied its premises, not the data of Israel's common life in either Babylonia or the Land of Israel. For the system not only selected the events it deemed consequential, but also spoke of events that had simply never happened. Consider the Jews who remained in the land after 586, or those who remained in Babylonia after Cyrus's decree permitting the return to Zion. For both groups, for different reasons, there was no alienation, also, consequently, no reconciliation, and their lives corresponded to the merely normal, as in any other nation. Treating exile and return as normative imparted to the exile a critical and definitive position. It marked Israel as special, elect, and subject to the rules of the covenant and its stipulations. But to those who stayed put, the urgent question of exile and return, and the response of election and covenant, bore slight relevance. If we want an example of a religious system creating a society, we can find few better instances than the power of the conception of Israel expressed by the Pentateuch and associated writings, of the period after 586 B.C.E., to tell people not only the meaning of what had happened but also what had happened: to create for Israelite society a picture of what it must be and therefore what it had been. That sense of heightened reality and that intense focus on the identification of the nation as extraordinary represented only one possible meaning of the events from 586 onward. But the system of the Torah and the prophetic and historical writings as framed by the priests and given definitive statement under the auspices of the Iranians' Jewish viceroy in Jerusalem, Nehemiah, with Ezra as counselor is the only one to have prevailed for all the succeeding centuries.

What happened in 586 and after does not correspond to the myth fabricated out of what happened. In both the Torah and the prophetic-historical books, Scripture said that Israel had suffered through exile, atoned, and attained reconciliation, and had renewed the covenant with God, as signified by the return to Zion and the rebuilding of the Temple. Although only a part of Israel in fact had undergone those experiences, the Judaic system of the Torah made normative that experience of alienation and reconciliation. In this case, religion did more than merely recapitulate resentment; it precipitated it by selecting as events only a narrow sample of what had happened, and by imparting to that selection of events meanings pertinent to only a few.

Thus the paradigm began as a paradigm, not as actual events transformed into a pattern. The conclusions derived from the pattern came not from reflection on events but from the logic of the paradigm itself. The paradigm created expectations that could not be met, and so renewed the resentment captured by the myth of exile. At the same time it resolved the crisis of exile with the promise of return. This self-renewing pattern formed the self-fulfilling prophecy that all Judaisms have offered as the generative tension and critical symbolic structure of their systems.

Since chief among the propositions of the Torah of Moses is the notion of the election of Israel effected in the covenant, we may say that, systemically speaking, Israel—the Israel of the Torah and the historical-prophetic books of the sixth and fifth centuries—selected itself. The system created the paradigm of the society that had gone into exile and come back home and also the covenant that certified not election but self-selection.

At the very foundations of the original Judaic system, the account of the sequence of events from 586 when the Israelites were exiled to Babylonia to about 450 when they returned to Zion and rebuilt the Temple, we find history systemically selected and, therefore, by definition invented. The same is so for a long list of systemic givens, none of them actually matters of self-evidence. It follows that it is Scripture—and Scripture alone—that says that what happened was that Israel died and was reborn, was punished through exile and then forgiven, and therefore—and this is critical—to be Israel in a genealogical sense is to have gone into exile and returned to Zion.

THE MODEL JUDAISM: THE PRIESTS' SYSTEM FOR ISRAEL AFTER EXILE AND RETURN

While the Judaism represented by the Pentateuch of about 450 B.C.E. drew abundant materials from the period before 586 (which is why we have such components of Scripture as the Yahwist's and Deuteronomist's writings), the statement at the end derived from and expressed the viewpoint of the priesthood. That is why a large portion of the Pentateuch devotes time and attention to the matter of the cult—the centrality of sacrifice, the founding of the priesthood and its rules, and the importance of the Temple in Jerusalem. That is why many of the stories of Genesis are aimed at explaining the origin, in the lives and deeds of the patriarchs, of the locations of various cultic centers prior to the centralization of the cult in Jerusalem. They explain the beginnings of the priesthood, the care and feeding of priests, the beginnings and rules of the sacrificial system, the contention between priestly castes—Levites and priests—and diverse other matters. The Pentateuch in these ways laid emphasis upon serving God through sacrifice in the Temple, conducted by the priests, and upon Israel's living a holy way of life as a "kingdom of priests and a holy people,"—all in accord with God's message to Moses at Sinai.

But of course "Sinai" stood for Babylonia. In Babylonia the priests drew together the elements of the received picture and reshaped them into the fairly coherent set of rules and narratives we now know as the Pentateuch.

While making ample use of ancient tales, the framers of the Pentateuch as we now have it flourished in Babylonia after 586 and conceived as their systemic teleology the return to Zion and the rebuilding of the Temple—hence the centrality in the wilderness narratives of the tabernacle and its cult. So the setting of the Judaism of the priests imparted to the Scripture of that first setting its ultimate meaning: response to historical disaster followed by unprecedented triumph. Their vision is characterized as follows:

> In the priests' narrative the chosen people are last seen as pilgrims moving through alien land toward a goal to be fulfilled in another time and place, and this is the vision, drawn from the ancient story of their past, that the priests now hold out to the scattered sons and daughters of old Israel. They too are exiles encamped for a time in an alien land, and they too must focus their hopes on the promise ahead. Like the Israelites in the Sinai wilderness, they must avoid setting roots in the land through which they pass, for diaspora is not to become their permanent condition, and regulations must be adopted to facilitate this. They must resist assimilation into the world into which they are now dispersed, because hope and heart and fundamental identity lay in the future. Thus, the priestly document not only affirms Yahweh's continuing authority and action in the lives of his people but offers them a pattern for life that will ensure them a distinct identity.[9]

The net effect of the pentateuchal vision of Israel, that is, its world-view seen in the aggregate, was to lay stress on the separateness and the holiness of Israel while pointing to dangers of pollution by the outsider. The way of life corresponded with its stress on the distinguishing traits of an Israel threatened by the outsider. The fate of the nation depended upon the loyalty of the people in their everyday life and to the requirements of the covenant with God. So history formed the barometer of the health of the nation. In these ways the several segments of the earlier traditions of Israel were so drawn together as to make the point peculiarly pertinent to Israel in exile. The center of the system lay in the covenant that told Israel: Keep these rules and you will not again suffer as you have suffered. Violate them and you will. At the heart of the covenant was the call for Israel to form a kingdom of priests and a holy people.

If we ask for a single passage to express the priests' Judaism, we look to the book of Leviticus, which concerns the priesthood above all, and its version of the covenant:

> And the Lord said to Moses, "Say to all the congregation of the people of Israel, You shall be holy, for I the Lord your God am holy.
>
> "Every one of you shall revere his mother and father and you shall keep my sabbaths, I am the Lord your God.
>
> "Do not turn to idols or make for yourselves molten gods; I am the Lord your God.
>
> "When you offer a sacrifice of peace offerings to the Lord, you shall offer it so that you may be accepted. It shall be eaten the same day you offer it or on the morrow, and anything left over until the third day shall be burned with fire. If it is eaten at all on the third day, it is an abomination, it will not be accepted, and every one who eats it shall bear his iniquity, because he has profaned a holy thing of the Lord; and that person shall be cut off from his people.
>
> "When you reap the harvest of your land, you shall not reap your field to its very border, neither shall you gather the gleanings after your harvest. And you shall not strip your vineyard bare, neither shall you gather the fallen grapes of your vineyard; you shall leave them for the poor and for the sojourner. I am the Lord your God.
>
> "You shall not steal, nor deal falsely, nor lie to one another. And you shall not swear by my name falsely and so profane the name of your God; I am the Lord.
>
> "You shall not oppress your neighbor or rob him. The wages of a hired servant shall not remain with you all night until the morning. You shall not curse the deaf or put a stumbling block before the blind, but you shall fear your God; I am the Lord.
>
> "You shall do no injustice in judgment; you shall not be partial to the poor or defer to the great, but in righteousness shall

you judge your neighbor. You shall not go up and down as a
slanderer among your people, and you shall not stand forth
against the life of your neighbor; I am the Lord.

"You shall not hate your brother in your heart, but you shall
reason with your neighbor, lest you bear sin because of him.
You shall not take vengeance or bear any grudge against the
sons of your own people, but you shall love your neighbor as
yourself; I am the Lord." (Lev. 19:1–18, RSV)

The children of Abraham, Isaac, and Jacob would form an extended
family, genealogically the people of God, keeping the covenant God
sets forth. This mixture of rules we should regard as cultic as to
sacrifice, moral as to support of the poor, ethical as to right dealing,
and above all religious as to "being holy for I the Lord your God am
holy." All together the mixture of rules portrays a complete and whole
society: its worldview holiness in the likeness of God, its way of life
an everyday life of sanctification through the making of distinctions,
and its Israel, Israel. But as we know from other writings of the time,
it was a very special Israel, an Israel characterized by genealogical
purity, meaning, in this context, separation not only from the nations
but also from those Israelites who had not undergone the experience
of exile and return to Zion. For along with the revelation of the Torah
of Moses, Ezra insisted that the Israelites divorce the wives they had
taken from the "peoples of the land," who were none other than
the descendants of those Jews who had not gone off into exile in
Babylonia. The definition of who is Israel lay at the foundation of the
system.

Elsewhere the book of Leviticus contains a clear statement of
the consequence geared to the events of the recent past:

> If you walk in my statutes and observe my commandments
> and do them, then I will give you your rains in their season.
> (Lev. 26:3)
>
> But if you will not hearken to me and will not do all these
> commandments, . . . I will do this to you: I will appoint over you
> sudden terror . . . and you shall sow your seed in vain for your
> enemies shall eat it. . . . Then the land shall enjoy its sabbaths as
> long as it lies desolate while you are in your enemies' land. (Lev.
> 26:34)

The Judaism of the priests answered the question of how to prevent the events of the recent past from ever happening again. It gave as its answer the formation of a separate and holy society, an Israel. Israel must obey the rules of holiness. If it does, then by keeping its half of the covenant it could make certain God would honor the other half: "And I will give peace in the land, and you shall lie down and none shall make you afraid" (Lev. 26:6). For the next five hundred years the Judaic system of the Pentateuch predominated. And this brings us back to the proposition that, in the case of Judaism, religion imparted its pattern upon the social world and polity of Jews.

Why has the original paradigm survived? For it is one thing to explain how a system took shape, but another to account for its long-term effect. One reason covers the near term. Another explains its long-term power of self-evidence.

As to the power of the pentateuchal system in its original fifth-century context, the Judaism that obtained through the Second Temple period—the priests' system of sanctification, the way of life conforming in its fundamental structure to the priests' points of concern, the worldview repeating in mythic-historic language the priests' perspective on what counted—flourished because the priests had the power to make it stick. The reasons are clear. First, framing matters in their terms, the priests were the ones who organized and set forth the Torah as the Jews would receive and revere it. Furthermore, they controlled the political institutions of the country as the Persian government established them. Consequently their perspective—with its emphasis on the Temple and its holiness, and the cult and its critical role in sustaining the life of the land and the nation—predominated in defining public policy. And the Temple government had the necessary political support to sustain its authority. It laid forth the Torah as its political myth, and did not have to resort to force at all. Since the Torah of Moses at Sinai defined the faith, explained what had happened, and set forth the rules to ensure God's continuing favor to Israel, the final shape and system of the Torah made a deep impact on the consciousness and attitude of the people as a whole.

But why did this particular Judaic system prove definitive long after the political facts had changed? The original Judaism answered the question of exile and restoration. With the continuing authority of the Torah in Israel, the experience to which it was originally a response was recapitulated, in age after age, through the reading and authoritative exegesis of the original Scripture that had preserved and portrayed it:

> Your descendants will be aliens living in a land that is not theirs . . . but I will punish that nation whose slaves they are, and after that they shall come out with great possessions. (Gen. 15:13–14)

The priests' Judaism persisted because the Scriptures themselves retained their authority. More important was the fact that the Judaic system devised by the priests in the Pentateuch addressed and also created a continuing and chronic social fact of Israel's life.

So long as the people perceived the world in a way that made urgent the question that Scripture framed and answered, Scripture enjoyed the power of persuasion that imparted to it the self-evident status of God's will revealed to Israel. The priests' system therefore imposed itself even in situations in which its fundamental premises hardly pertained. When the world imposed upon Jewry questions of a different order, then Jews went in search of more answers—an additional Torah (hence the formation of the Judaism of the dual Torah)—and even different answers (hence the formation, in modern times, of Judaic systems of a different character altogether). But even then a great many Jews continued to view the world through that original perspective created in the aftermath of destruction and restoration, that is, to see the world as a gift instead of a given, and to see themselves as chosen for a life of special suffering but also special reward.

There were two reasons for the perennial power of the Judaic system of the priests to shape the worldview and way of life of the Israel addressed by that Judaism. The first reason is that the tension precipitated by the interpretation of the life of the Jews as exile and return persisted; it persisted and kept renewing the resentment, since the memory of loss and restoration joined with the danger of further loss.

The second reason is more important: the question answered by the Five Books of Moses persisted at the center of national life and remained urgent. It is true that the question persisted because Scripture kept reminding people to ask it. But we have to ask what was at stake and so penetrate into the deepest layers of the structure. For the sacred persistence in the end rested on judgments found valid in circumstances remote from the original world subject to those judgments.

SACRED PERSEVERANCE AND THE
EXEGESIS OF THE EVERYDAY:
WHY THE PRIESTS' JUDAIC SYSTEM OF
SANCTIFICATION PERSISTED

The Temple and its rites formed the centerpiece of the national life of Israel. Large numbers of people came to Jerusalem for the pilgrim festivals of the autumn and spring: Tabernacles in the autumn, Passover and Pentecost in the spring. So it was not only the minor sects or the writings of a small political-theological elite that testified to the centrality of the priests' vision in the life of Israel. The very critical role played by Jerusalem, with stress on the holiness of the Temple and the supernatural importance of its cult, makes us realize the importance of that original Judaism, the Judaism of the Five Books of Moses that took shape after 586. Accordingly we have to wonder why the priestly themes and repertoire of concerns should have so occupied the imagination and fantasy of the people as a whole. What requires explanation is the continuity from the Priestly Code of the sixth century B.C.E. to the beginnings of the mishnaic code of the second century C.E.—a period of seven hundred years, longer than the span of time that separates us from Edward the Confessor and an independent Wales, or from the West's Fourth Crusade to the Land of Israel. For as we shall see, the Mishnah—and therefore the Judaism that flowed from that central document—represents the fundamental structure generated by the priestly perspective on the condition of Israel.

The grammar of the sacred belonged to the priesthood from olden times. That is why it becomes urgent to dwell on why the Priestly Code should have exercised so profound and formative an influence upon the life of the Second Temple and beyond. The Priestly Code of the Five Books of Moses, which expressed the priestly emphasis on sanctification, exercised the formative power it did for the following reason:

The problems addressed and solved by the Judaism of the Five Books of Moses remained chronic long after the period of its formation, from the seventh century down to its closure in the time of Ezra and Nehemiah. The Priestly Code states a powerful answer to a pressing and urgent question. Since that question would remain a perplexity continuing to trouble Israelites for a long time, it is not surprising that the categorical structure of the priestly answer, so profound and fundamental in its character, should for its part have continued to define systems that would attract and impress people.

Once more we have to locate ourselves in the time of the completion of the Mosaic Scriptures, that is, in the late sixth and fifth centuries B.C.E., to identify the critical tensions of that period. The same tensions persisted and confronted the thinkers whose reflection led to the conclusion—in resolution of those ongoing points of dissonance—that the Temple's holiness enveloped and surrounded Israel's land and demarcated its people too. What marked ancient Israel as distinctive was preoccupation with defining itself.

The reason for the persistence of the exegesis of the everyday as a sequence of acts of sanctification—was the Torah's encapsulation, as normative and recurrent, of the experience of the loss and recovery of the land and of political sovereignty. Israel because of its own perception of its amazing experience had attained a self-consciousness that continuous existence in a single place under a long-term government had denied others (and had denied Israel before 586, as the Yahwist and the Deuteronomist testify). There was nothing given, nothing to be merely celebrated (as the Yahwist thought) or taken for granted (as the Deuteronomist thought) in the life of a nation that had ceased to be a nation on its own land and had then once more regained that (once normal, now abnormal) condition. Judaism took shape as the system that accounted for the death and resurrection of Israel, the Jewish people, and pointed for the source of renewed life toward sanctification now and salvation at the end of time.

The result of the codification and closure of the law under Ezra and Nehemiah was to produce the Torah as a law code that laid heavy emphasis on the exclusive character of the Israelite God and cult. "Judaism"—the priestly Judaism of the pentateuchal composite—gained the character of a cultically centered way of life and worldview. Both rite and myth aimed at the continuing self-definition of Israel by separation from the rest of the world and exclusion of the rest of the world. Order against chaos meant holiness over uncleanness and life over death. The purpose was to define Israel against the background of the other peoples of the Near and Middle East, with whom Israel had much in common, and especially to differentiate Israel from its near relations and neighbors—for example, Samaritans—in the same country. The issue of who the other is persisted, extending the definition of the other: the woman, the slave, the minor, the near-Israelite, the Gentile; later on the Christian (sharing common Scriptures) was a special kind of not-Gentile Gentile.

Acute differentiation was required because the social and cultural facts were precisely to the contrary: common traits hardly bespoke clear-cut points of difference, except of idiom. The mode of differentiation taken by the Torah literature in general and the priestly sector of that literature in particular was cultic. The meaning, however, was also social. The power of the Torah composed in this time lay in its control of the Temple. The Torah made the Temple the pivot and focus of all life. The Torah literature, with its concerned God, who cares what people do about rather curious matters, and the Temple cult, with its total exclusion of the non-Israelite from participation and (even more so) from cultic commensality—these raised high the walls of separation and underlined such distinctiveness as already existed. The life of Israel flowed from the altar; what made Israel itself was the altar.

The differentiation contrasted with the life of Israel before 586. So long as Israel remained essentially within its own land and frame of social reference, the issue of separation from neighbors could be treated casually. When the very heart of what made Israel was penetrated by the doubly desolating and disorienting experiences of both losing the Land and then coming back, the issue of who was Israel came to the fore. Confusion in economic and social relationships, and the fact that the land to which Israelites returned in no way permitted distinct Israelite settlement, made the issue of self-definition pressing. The issue has persisted for the rest of Israelite history, from the return to Zion and the formation of the Torah literature even down to our own day. The reason for this persistence? It is that the social forces that lent urgency to the issue of who is Israel would remain. So long as memory remained, the conflicting claims of exclusivist Torah literature and universalist prophecy, of a people living in utopia, in no particular place, while framing its vision of itself in the deeply locative symbols of cult and center—these conflicting claims would make vivid the abiding issue of self-definition. At issue was life—its source and its sustenance. For if we ask why the Temple with its cult proved enduringly central in the imagination of the Israelites in the country, we have only to repeat the statements that the priests of the Temple and their imitators in the sects were prepared to make. These explain the critical importance of cult and rite. If we reread the priestly viewpoint as it is contained in the books of Leviticus and Numbers, as well as in priestly passages of Genesis and Exodus, this is the picture we derive.

The altar was the center of life, the conduit of life from heaven to earth and from earth to heaven. All things were to be arrayed in relationship to the altar. The movement of the heavens demarcated and celebrated at the cult marked out the divisions of time in relationship to the altar. The spatial dimension of the land was likewise demarcated and celebrated in relationship to the altar. The natural life of Israel's fields and corrals, the social life of its hierarchical caste system, and its political life (not only in theory) centered on the Temple as the locus of ongoing government—all things in order and in place. The natural order of the world corresponded to, reinforced, and was reinforced by the social order of Israel. Both were fully realized in the cult—the nexus between the opposite and corresponding forces, the heavens and the earth.

The lines of social and political structure emanated from the altar. And it was these lines of structure that constituted high and impenetrable frontiers to separate Israel from the Gentiles. Israel, which was holy, ate holy food, reproduced itself in accord with the laws of holiness, and conducted all of its affairs, both affairs of state and the business of the table and the bed, in accord with the demands of holiness. So the cult defined holiness. Holiness meant separateness. Separateness meant life. Why? Because outside the land—the realm of the holy—lay the domain of death. The lands were unclean. The land was holy. In the scriptural vocabulary, one antonym for *holy* is *unclean*, and one opposite of unclean is holy. The synonym of holy is life. The primary symbol of uncleanness and its highest expression is death. So the Torah stood for life, the covenant with the Lord would guarantee life, and the way of life required sanctification in the here and now of the natural world.

NOTES

1. In Christianity, the Old Testament; in Judaism, Tanakh, that is, Torah, referring to the Five Books of Moses, Nebiim (the Hebrew for the prophets, inclusive of the historical books of Joshua through Kings), and Ketuvim (the Hebrew for writings, referring to Psalms, Prophets, Job, and other books). In general I shall refer to the ancient Israelite Scriptures as "the Hebrew Scriptures" as an inclusive term.

2. W. Lee Humphreys, *Crisis and Story: Introduction to the Old Testament* (Palo Alto, Calif.: Mayfield Publishing, 1979), pp. 65–69.

3. I follow the excellent and clear account of Humphreys, *Crisis and Story*. I take Humphreys, rather than a broader selection of scholarly writings, simply because he seems to me to provide a clear and simple statement of the consensus view.

4. Humphreys, *Crisis and Story*, p. 76.

5. Ibid., p. 9.

6. Ibid., p. 76.

7. Ibid., p. 77.

8. How should we ignore the fact that the Yahwist's and the Elohist's strands were woven together? That too testifies to its own setting, one not defined by the experience of exile and return. It is not pertinent to my argument, merely a further exemplification of it.

9. Humphreys, *Crisis and Story*, p. 217.

6

The Beginning
of Rabbinic Judaism:
The Crisis Addressed by the
Mishnah in 70 C.E.

PHARISAISM BEFORE, AND
JUDAISM AFTER, 70 C.E.

When, exactly, did the Judaism of the two Torahs originate? While drawing on much older materials, beginning with the Scriptures themselves, the Judaism of the dual Torah began to take shape as we now know it only in the first century. What groups contributed to this Judaism? The scribes, a profession, and the Pharisees, a sect, contributed the contents and the method of Judaism, respectively. Under what circumstances was this union of established elements in a striking new way accomplished? In the aftermath of the destruction of the Second Temple in Jerusalem in 70, the two groups coalesced and began the process that in the next six centuries yielded Judaism in the form in which we now know it.

In 66 C.E. a Jewish rebellion broke out in Jerusalem against Rome's rule of the country. Initially successful, the rebels in the end were pushed back into the holy city, which fell in August, 70 C.E. The Temple, destroyed in 586 B.C.E. and rebuilt three generations later, by the time of its second destruction had stood for five hundred years, as long a time as separates us from Columbus. And because of the message of the Judaism of the Torah of Moses, people regarded the fate of the Temple as the barometer of their nation's relationship to God. With the Temple's destruction by the Romans, the foundations of national and social life in the Land of Israel were shaken. People related the movement of the seasons and the sun in heaven to the cult in the Temple. They associated the first full moon after the vernal equinox with the rite of the Passover, and the first full moon after the autumnal equinox with that of Tabernacles. They attained personal atonement for their sins of inadvertence by minor offerings, and they believed that in the rite of the Day of Atonement, they reconciled themselves with God. The Temple had served as the basis for the many elements of autonomous self-government and political life left in the Jews' hands by the Romans. The government of the country appealed for legitimacy to the Temple and the priesthood, with which it associated itself. The structure not only of political life and of society, but also of the imaginative life of the country, depended upon the Temple and its worship and cult. It was there that people believed they served God. At the Temple the lines of structure—both cosmic and social—converged. The altar was the point at which the transfer of life from heaven to earth took place: the transaction that sustained the world. Consequently the destruction of the Temple meant not merely a significant alteration in the cultic or ritual life of the Jewish people, but also a profound and far-reaching crisis in their inner and spiritual existence.

When the Temple was destroyed, two distinct groups survived: the scribes with their learning, and the priests with their memories, their sense of what God required for service, and their notion that every Jew stood in relationship to all others within the grid of holiness. Over the next half century or so these two groups began to forge the system that—through and beyond the Mishnah—would become the Judaism of the dual Torah. The period from 70 to the Bar Kokhba war (ca. 132–135) yielded the foundations of the mishnaic system, a system derived from the combination of three distinct political forces: Roman rule; a local Jewish authority called the patriarch, recognized by Rome as the legitimate Jewish administrator of Israel's affairs; and the administration of the patriarch, staffed by knowledgeable clerks, called sages. The system that took shape from 70 on originally appeared in Yavneh, a coastal town.

We recall that the Persians, ruling a diverse empire, under Cyrus adopted the policy of identifying local groups and ruling through them, a standard imperial procedure followed when the ruling empire did not choose to settle its own population in a conquered area. Fortunately for Israel the several successor empires—from the Persians, through the Macedonians under Alexander and then the inheritor states of Ptolemies and Seleucids, and, finally the Romans—

decided to leave the Land of Israel in the hands of loyal regents. The Romans first supported the Maccabees, and then Herod and his family. That policy remained in effect even after the Jewish wars against Rome in 66 and 132. Roman policy involved finding in native populations trustworthy leaders who would keep the peace and execute Roman policy.

After 70 the Romans gave up on the policy of depending on the family of Herod, which had manifestly failed. They accorded some sort of limited recognition to a Jewish ruler of a different family, a Pharisaic one. Our knowledge of the new ruling figure scarcely extends beyond his name, Gamaliel, though we know that his heirs later sustained the institution of Jewish rule that he began. How and why the Romans turned to Gamaliel we can only guess. He was the son of Simeon b. Gamaliel, a leading figure among the Pharisees before 70 and grandson of yet another such figure. That means that Gamaliel got Roman recognition as a promising local authority of a distinguished family prepared to cooperate with the government. Called the patriarch—in Hebrew *nasi*,—Gamaliel associated with himself two sorts of survivors of the war. One represented the pre-70 Pharisees, of which he was probably an adherent. The other derived from the important state officials of the period before 70, who, in the aggregate, are known as scribes: people who knew and administered the laws. The sages that associated themselves with the patriarchal regime contributed the know-how of government, and such administration, on a local basis, as the Jews of the Land of Israel knew, derived from that group. The patriarchal government with its scribal staff from the Roman perspective enjoyed only modest success, because they could not prevent the war of Bar Kokhba from breaking out. But once more the Romans after Bar Kokhba's defeat turned back to the system of ethnarchies and restored the ruling regime, this time with complete success. It endured into the fifth century, at which time the Christian government of Rome determined not to accord it further recognition. An equivalent system employed by the Parthian and then the Sassanian rulers of Iran, across the eastern frontier from Rome, led to the development there of a Jewish ethnarchy, called the exilarchate. Both regimes adopted as their constitution and law the Mishnah produced by Judah the Patriarch, on account of which the document enjoyed immediate acceptance as the Jews' law code after Scripture. Thus the first and most important reason for the development of Judaism was the political choices made by outsiders. Later we shall observe that Judaism in the same form endured in part for the same reason: Christendom and Islam tolerated it. But the other reason matters far more: the Jews wanted to form their world within the structure of that Judaism—in that form. That was the Judaism that asked the questions they found urgent and provided the answers they deemed valid.

In the world beyond Yavneh—the site of the sages' meeting place where Pharisaism and scribism were joined into a new Jewish regime under Roman rule—people looked for a coming cataclysm. The Judaism of the Torah had after all accounted for such a calamity as had just taken place. The pattern of sin, suffering, atonement, reconciliation, and restoration certainly predominated in peoples' minds. After three generations had passed, a second war against Rome broke out, the Bar Kokhba rebellion of 132–135. But the old pattern failed to be realized. Bar Kokhba's armies, successful for a brief time, confronted Rome at the height of its power, and lost, despite the bravery of the Jewish soldiers. For a time the Romans engaged in a policy of repression of Judaism—which they saw as the source of sedition—but they soon reverted to their established politics. After the Romans had once more succeeded in pacifying the country, they again turned to the native regime and reestablished its authority. The sages—disciples of the masters of Yavneh and now heirs of a tradition half a century in the making—thus regained recognition and took over such political power as Rome allowed the Jews. This time they derived considerably greater satisfaction from the result, since the patriarchal government administered the Jewish affairs of the Land of Israel down to its dissolution in 429 in the aftermath of the Christianization of the Roman Empire.

From the political foundations of the system we turn to its method and doctrine—its worldview and way of life. The character of Pharisaic Judaism before 70 helped ensure the success of the Judaism that the Pharisees helped to shape. When the Temple was destroyed, it turned out that the Pharisees had prepared for that tremendous change in the sacred economy. Even after the destruction of the Temple to which their laws had applied, lay people pretending to be priests could continue in the paths of holiness that the Temple had shown for centuries by keeping the laws of purity at home. Israel the people was holy, not only the place of the Temple and Jerusalem, and not only the rite of the cult in the Temple. The Pharisees (like the Essenes) had a doctrine of Israel as the holy people living the holy life that proved remarkably congruent to the urgent issue posed by the destruction of the Temple. The answer to the questions of the destruction—Who is Israel now? Is Israel yet holy now?—was that Israel is the bearer of the holy, Israel as a whole and not solely the priesthood, Israel in its everyday life and not only the priests in the Temple. The destruction of the Temple as a real place found compensation in the pretense that the Pharisees had maintained before 70. True, the buildings were gone, but the critical issue was holiness, and holiness endured; this was a powerful and acutely pertinent answer to the question of the day. The remarkable congruity between the Pharisaic view of Israelite life and the circumstances prevailing after the destruction of the Temple in 70 accounts for the success of the Judaism to which the Pharisees made a major contribution. The political advantages accorded to the Pharisees through Gamaliel after 70 should not obscure the doctrinal ones they enjoyed.

The Mishnah's system inherited important components from the Pharisaism of the period before 70 and therefore could maintain the holiness of the life of Israel after the physical destruction of the building and the cessation of sacrifices. Israel the people was holy, the medium and instrument of God's sanctification. The system instructed Israel to act as if there were a new Temple formed of Israel, the Jewish people. Joined to the Pharisaic mode of looking at life, now centered in the doctrine of the holiness of Israel the people, was the substance of the scribal ideal—the emphasis on learning the Torah and carrying out its teachings. The emerging system claimed, as did the scribes of old, that it was possible to serve God not only through sacrifice but also through the study of Torah.

The union of the scribe and the priest yielded the sage who bore the honorific title Rabbi. A priest is in charge of the life of the community, just as the priests had said. But the new priest was qualified not by birth in the priestly caste. Rather, his validation derived from his learning in the Torah: the new priest was a sage. The old sin offerings could still be carried out. But now it was the sacrifice of deeds of loving-kindness in the tradition of wisdom that the sage, the rabbi, taught. Like the prophets and historians in the time of the first destruction, in 586 B.C.E., the sages or rabbis claimed that it was because the people had sinned and had not kept the Torah that the

Temple had been destroyed. The disaster was made to vindicate the rabbinic teaching and to verify its truth. When the people lived up to the teachings of the Torah as the rabbis expressed them, the Temple would be restored in response to the people's repentance and renewal.

The professional ideal of the scribes stressed the study of the Torah and the centrality of the learned person in the religious system. But there was something more. It was the doctrine of Israel that made all the difference. If the worldview came from the scribes and the way of life from the Pharisees, the doctrine of who was Israel—and the social reality beyond the doctrine—was fresh and unpredictable. It was Israel surviving, the Jewish people beyond the break marked by the destruction of the Temple. What made the Judaic system after 70 C.E. more than the sum of its parts, Pharisaism and scribism, was the very doctrine that neither Pharisaism nor scribism contributed. The crisis of the destruction centered attention on what had endured, persisting beyond the end—the people itself. The most typical fundamental characteristic of the original paradigm was recapitulated. Israel because of its amazing experience of loss and restoration, death and resurrection, had become remarkably self-conscious. For a nation that had ceased to be a nation on its own land and then had once more regained that condition, the new calamity represented for it once more the paradigm of death and resurrection. Consequently the truly fresh and definitive component of the new system, after 70, in fact restated in contemporary terms the fixed and established doctrine with which the first Judaism, the Judaism of the Torah of Moses after 450 B.C.E., had begun.

The genius of the Judaic system of sanctification that took shape after 70 and reached its full expression in the Mishnah was to recognize that the holy people might reconstitute the Temple in the sanctity of its own community life. Therefore the people had to be made holy, as the Temple had been holy. The people's social life had to be sanctified as the surrogate for what had been lost. That is why the rabbinic ideal for Judaism maintained that the rabbi served as the new priest, the study of the Torah substituted for Temple sacrifices, and deeds of loving-kindness were the social surrogate for the sin offering—personal sacrifice instead of animal sacrifice. All things fitted together to construct out of the old Judaisms the worldview and the way of life of the new and enduring system that ultimately became the Judaism of the dual Torah. But not just yet. Before proceeding to the second stage in the formation of Judaism, we have to describe the first stage in its full literary statement. And that brings us to the Mishnah—its contents, character, and system.

THE MISHNAH:
HISTORY OF ITS SYSTEM

What defined the Mishnah's system was the questions the framers addressed to the facts upon which the document drew. To appreciate the work of the authors of the Mishnah, we must recognize the antiquity of many of the facts upon which they drew— beginning with Scripture itself.

Three points of ordinary life formed the focus for social differentiation in the Mishnah's system: food, sex, and marriage. What people ate, how they conducted their sexual lives, and whom they married or to whom they gave their children in marriage defined the social parameters of their group. These factors indicated who was kept within the bounds and who was excluded and systematically kept at a distance. The people behind the laws could not tell people other than their associates what to eat or whom to marry, but they could make their own decisions on these important, but humble, matters. Moreover by making those decisions, they could keep outsiders at a distance and could keep those who adhered to the group within bounds. Without political control they could not govern the transfer of property or other matters of public interest, but they could govern the transfer of their women. It was in that intimate aspect of life that the Israelites firmly established the outer boundary of their collective existence. It therefore seems no accident at all that the strata of mishnaic law which appear to go back to the period before the wars, well before 70, deal specifically with the special laws of marriage (in Yebamot), distinctive rules on when sexual relations may and may not take place (in Niddah), and the laws covering the definition of sources of uncleanness and the attainment of cleanness, with specific reference to domestic meals (in certain parts of Oholot, Zabim, Kelim, and Miqvaot). Nor is it surprising that for the conduct of the cult and the sacrificial system—about which the group may have had its own doctrines but over which it neither exercised control nor even aspired to—there appears to be no systemic content or development whatsoever.

THE TOPICAL PROGRAM OF
THE MISHNAH

The Mishnah is a six-part code of prescriptive rules. The six divisions (or orders) of the Mishnah are (1) agricultural rules; (2) laws governing appointed seasons, for example, Sabbaths and festivals; (3) laws on the transfer of women and property along with women from one man (father) to another (husband); (4) the system of civil and criminal law, corresponding to what we today should regard as "the legal system"; (5) laws for the conduct of the cult and the Temple; and (6) laws on the preservation of cultic purity both in the Temple and under certain domestic circumstances, with special reference to the table and bed.

The critical issue of economic life—farming—is treated in two parts, revealed in the first division. First, Israel as tenant on God's Holy Land maintains the property in the ways God requires, keeping the rules that mark the Land and its crops as holy. Second, the time at which the sanctification of the Land reaches a critical mass, namely, in the ripened crops, is a moment ponderous with danger and heightened holiness. Israel's will so affects the crops as to mark a part of them as holy, the rest of them as available for common use. The human will is determinative in the process of sanctification.

In the second mishnaic division, what happens in the Land at certain times—at "appointed times"—marks off spaces of the Land as holy in yet another way. The center of the Land and the focus of its sanctification is the Temple. There the produce of the Land is received and given back to God, the one who created and sanctified the Land. At these unusual moments of sanctification, the inhabitants of the Land in their social units in villages enter a state of spatial sanctification. That is to say, village boundaries mark off holy space, within which one must remain during the holy time. This is expressed in two ways. First, the Temple itself observes and expresses the special, recurring holy time. Second, the villages of the Land are brought into alignment with the Temple, forming a complement and completion to the Temple's sacred being. The advent of the appointed times precipitates a spatial reordering of the Land, so that the boundaries of the sacred are matched and mirrored in village and Temple. At the times of heightened holiness marked by these moments, therefore, the occasion for an affective sanctification is worked out. Like the harvest, the advent of an appointed time in Israel—a pilgrim festival, also a sacred season—is made to express that regular, orderly, and predictable sort of sanctification that the system as a whole seeks.

If for a moment we skip the next two divisions, the third and fourth, we come to the counterparts of the divisions on agriculture and appointed times. These are the fifth and sixth divisions on holy things and purities; they deal with the everyday and the ordinary, as against the special moments of harvest and special times or seasons. The fifth division, holy things, is about the Temple on ordinary days. The affairs of Temple, the locus of sanctification, are conducted in a wholly routine, trustworthy, and punctilious manner. The one thing that may unsettle matters is the intention and will of the human actor. This is subjected to carefully prescribed limitations and remedies. The division of holy things generates its companion, the sixth division, purities, or cultic cleanness. The relationship between the two is like that between agriculture and appointed times, the former locative, the latter utopian, the former dealing with the fields, the latter with the interplay between fields and altar.

In the sixth division, too, once we speak of the one place, the Temple, we also address the cleanness that pertains to every place. A system of cleanness, taking into account what imparts uncleanness and how this is done, what is subject to uncleanness, and how that state is overcome—that system is fully expressed, once more, in response to the participation of the human will. Without the wish and act of a human being, the system does not function. It is inert. Sources of uncleanness, which come naturally and not by volition, and modes of purification, which work naturally and not by human intervention, remain inert until human will has imparted susceptibility to uncleanness, that is, until people have introduced into the system that food and drink, bed, pot, chair, and pan which form the focus of the system in the first place. The movement from sanctification to uncleanness takes place when human will and work precipitate it.

This now brings us back to the middle divisions, the third and fourth, on women and damages. They take their place in the structure of the whole by showing the congruence, within the larger framework of regularity and order, of such human concerns as family and farm, politics and workaday transactions among ordinary people. For without attending to these matters, the Mishnah's system does not encompass what, at its foundations, it is meant to comprehend and order. So what is at issue is fully consistent with the rest. In the case of the third division, on women, attention focuses upon the point of disorder marked by the transfer of that disordering anomaly, woman, from the regular status provided by one man to the equally trustworthy status provided by another. That is the point at which the Mishnah's interests are aroused: once more, predictably, the moment of disorder. In the case of damages, the fourth division, there are two important concerns. First, there is the paramount interest in preventing, so far as possible, the disorderly rise of one person and fall of another, and in sustaining the status quo of the economy, the house and household, of Israel, keeping the holy society in eternal stasis. Second, there is the necessary concomitant in the provision of a system of political institutions to carry out the laws that preserve the balance and steady state of persons.

The sages of the late first and second centuries produced a document to contain the most important things they could specify; they chose as their subjects six matters of which, I am inclined to think, for the same purpose we would probably reject at least four, and possibly all six. That is, four of the divisions of the Mishnah are devoted to purity laws, tithing, laws for the conduct of sacrifice in the Temple cult, and the way in which the sacrifices are carried out at festivals—four areas of reality which, I suspect, would not find a high place on a list of our own most fundamental concerns. The other two divisions, which deal with the transfer of women from one man to another and with matters of civil law—including the organization of the government, civil claims, torts, damages, real estate, and the like—complete the list. When we attempt to interpret the sort of world the rabbis of the Mishnah proposed to create, therefore, at the very outset we realize that that world in no way conforms, in its most profound and definitive categories of organization, to our own. It follows that the critical work of making sense and use of the Mishnah is to learn how to hear what the Mishnah wishes to say in its own setting and to the people addressed by those who composed it. For that purpose it is altogether too easy to raise our questions and take for granted that, when the sages seem to say something relevant to our questions, they therefore propose to speak to us. Anachronism takes many forms. The most dangerous comes when an ancient text seems readily accessible and immediately clear.

THE MISHNAH'S SYSTEM
AS A WHOLE

Overall, the system emphasizes sanctification, understood as the correct arrangement of all things, each in its proper category, each called by its rightful name, just as at the creation. Everything having been given its proper name, God called the natural world very good and God sanctified it. The Mishnah makes a statement of philosophy, concerning the order of the natural world in its correspondence with the supernatural world. Later on, the Midrash-compilations and the Talmud of the Land of Israel would make a statement of theology, concerning the historical order of society in its progression from creation through salvation at the end of time. Judaism in the dual Torah constituted a complete statement about philosophy and nature, theology and history, the one in the oral, the other in the written Torah. Together the two components constituted that one whole Torah of Moses, our rabbi.

The system of philosophy expressed through concrete and detailed law presented by the Mishnah, consisted of a coherent logic and topic, a cogent worldview and a comprehensive way of living. It was a worldview that spoke of transcendent things, a way of life responding to the supernatural meaning of what was done, a heightened and deepened perception of the sanctification of Israel in deed and in deliberation. Sanctification thus meant two things: first, distinguishing Israel in all its dimensions from the world in all its ways; second, establishing the stability, order, regularity, predictability, and reliability of Israel in the world of nature and supernature especially in moments and in contexts of danger. Danger meant instability, disorder, irregularity, uncertainty, and betrayal. Each topic of the system as a whole took up a critical and indispensable moment or context of social being. Through what was said in regard to each of the Mishnah's principal topics, what the halakhic system as a whole wished to declare was fully expressed. Yet if the parts severally and jointly gave the message of the whole, the whole could not exist without all of the parts, so well joined and carefully crafted are they all.

If then we turn to the contents of the document, we are helped not at all in determining the place of the Mishnah's origin, the purpose of its formation, or the reasons for its anonymous and collective plane of discourse and monotonous tone of voice. For the Mishnah covers a carefully defined program of topics. But the Mishnah never tells us why one topic is introduced and another is omitted, or what the combining of these particular topics is meant to accomplish in the formation of a system or imaginative construction. Nor is there any way to predict how a given topic will be treated, or why a given set of issues will be explored in close detail and another set of possible issues ignored. Discourse on a theme begins and ends as if all things are self-evident—including the reason for beginning at one point and ending at another. This strange and curious book looks like a rule-book. It appears on the surface to be a book lacking all traces of eloquence and style, revealing no evidence of system and reflection, and serving no important purpose. Who would want to have made such a thing? Who would now want to refer to it?

The answer to that question is deceptively straightforward: the Mishnah is important because it is a principal component of the canon of Judaism. But that answer begs the question: Why should some of the ancient Jews of the holy land have brought together these particular facts and rules into a book and set them forth for the Israelite people? Why should the Mishnah have been received, as it certainly was received much later on, as a half of the "whole Torah of Moses at Sinai"? After it was compiled, the Mishnah was represented as the part of the whole Torah of Moses, our rabbi, that had been formulated and transmitted orally, so it bore the status of divine revelation along with the Pentateuch. But little in the actual contents of the document evoked the character or the moral authority of the written Torah of Moses. None pretended otherwise.

Indeed, most of the authorities named in the Mishnah lived in the century and a half prior to the promulgation of the document so the claim that things said by men known to the very framers of the document in fact derived from Moses at Sinai through a long chain of oral tradition contradicted the well-known facts of the matter. So this claim presents a paradox even on the surface: How can the Mishnah be deemed a book of religion, a program for consecration, and a mode of sanctification? Why should Jews from the end of the second century to our own day have deemed the study of the Mishnah to be a holy act—a deed of service to God through the study of an important constituent of God's Torah, God's will for Israel, the Jewish people?

We can derive no answers from the world in which the document emerged. The world addressed by the Mishnah was hardly congruent to the worldview presented within the Mishnah. In the aftermath of the war against Rome in 132–135, the Temple was declared permanently prohibited to Jews, and Jerusalem was closed off to them as well. Thus there was no cult, no Temple, no holy city to which at this time the description of the mishnaic laws applied. Therefore a sizable proportion of the Mishnah deals with matters to which the sages had no material access or practical knowledge at the time of their work. The Mishnah contains a division on the conduct of the cult—the fifth—as well as one on the conduct of matters so as to preserve the cultic purity of the sacrificial system along the lines laid out in the book of Leviticus—the sixth division. The fourth division—on civil law—presents an elaborate account of a political structure and system of Israelite self-government, in tractates Sanhedrin and Makkot, not to mention Shebuot and Horayot. This system speaks of king, priest, Temple, and court. It was not, however, the Jews—their kings, priests, and judges—but the Romans who conducted the government of Israel in the Land of Israel in the time in which the second-century authorities did their work. Well over half of the document speaks of cult, Temple, government, and priesthood. And the Mishnah takes a profoundly priestly and Levitical conception of sanctification. When we consider that, in the very time in which the authorities before us did their work, the Temple lay in ruins, the city of Jerusalem was prohibited to all Israelites, and the Jewish government and administration that had centered on the Temple and based its authority on the holy life lived there were in ruins, the fantastic character of the Mishnah's address to its own catastrophic day becomes clear. Much of the Mishnah speaks of matters not in existence in the time in which the Mishnah was created, because the Mishnah wishes to make its statement on what really matters.

THE MISHNAH AND JUDAISM

The Mishnah did not encompass everything that its authorship held important, but it does present a Judaic system, for it describes a whole world and tells us the framers' principal concerns. This generative concern involved the ongoing sanctification of Israel. An authorship that had seen the holiness of the life of Israel, the people, as centered on the Temple, and had endured and transcended the destruction of the building and the cessation of sacrifices, found urgent the question of sanctification after the destruction. The Mishnah's system had one fundamental premise: Israel the people was the medium and instrument of God's sanctification. What required sanctification were the modalities of life lived in community (and none conceived of a holy life in any other mode). The system then instructed Israel to act as if it formed a utensil of the sacred.

So far as the Mishnah is a document about the holiness of Israel in its land, it expresses the conception of sanctification and the theory of its modes that were shaped among the caste of the priests. To them the Temple and its technology of joining heaven and holy land through the sacred place defined the core of being. So far as the Mishnah takes up the way in which transactions are conducted among ordinary folk and takes the position that it is through documents that transactions are embodied and expressed, the Mishnah expresses what was self-evident to scribes. Just as to the priest there was a correspondence between the table of the Lord in the Temple and the locus of the divinity in the heavens, so to the scribe there was a correspondence between the documentary expression of the human will on earth—in writs of all sorts and in the orderly provision of courts for the predictable and just disposition of exchanges of persons and property—and heaven's judgment of these same matters. So there are scribal divisions—the third and fourth—and priestly divisions—the first, fifth, and sixth; the second is shared between the two groups. These two social groups—the priestly caste and the scribal profession—were not categorically symmetrical with one another. But for both groups the Mishnah made self-evident statements. The scribal profession later became a focus of sanctification. The scribe was transformed into the rabbi, honored man and locus of the holy through what he knew, just as the priest had been and would remain locus of the holy through what he could claim by genealogy. The divisions of special interest to scribes-become-rabbis and to their governance of Israelite society—those of women and damages, together with certain others particularly relevant to utopian Israel beyond the system of the Land—those tractates grew and grew. Many, though not all, of the others remained essentially as they were at the completion of the Mishnah. So we must notice that the Mishnah spoke for the program of topics important to the priests. It took up the persona of the scribes, speaking through their voice and in their manner.

The crisis precipitated by the destruction of the Second Temple affected both the nation and the individual, since, in the nature of things, what happened in the metropolis of the country inevitably touched affairs of home and family. What connected the individual fate to the national destiny was the long-established Israelite conviction that the fate of the individual and the destiny of the Jewish nation depended upon the moral character of both. Disaster came about because of the people's sin, so went the message of biblical history and prophecy. The sins of individuals and of nation alike ran against the revealed will of God, the Torah. So reflection upon the meaning of the recent catastrophe inexorably followed paths laid out long ago, trod from one generation to the next. But there were two factors which at just this time made reflection on the question of sin and history, atonement and salvation, particularly urgent.

First, although there was a deep conviction of having sinned and a profound sense of guilt affecting community and individual alike, the established mode of expiation and atonement for sin proved to be unavailable. The sacrificial system—which the priestly Torah describes as the means by which the sinner attains forgiveness for sin—lay in ruins. So when sacrifice was acutely needed for the restoration of psychological stability in the community at large, sacrifice was no longer possible.

Second, in August 70 C.E., minds naturally turned to August 586 B.C.E. From the biblical histories and prophecies emerged the vivid expectation that sin would be atoned and expiation attained through the suffering of the day. So, people supposed that just as before, whatever guilt had weighed down the current generation and led to the catastrophe would be worked out in three generations through the sacrifice consisting of the anguish of a troubled time. It must follow that somewhere down the road lay renewal. The ruined Temple would yet be rebuilt, the lapsed cult restored, and the Levites' silent song sung once more.

Now these several interrelated themes—suffering, sin, atonement, and salvation—had long been paramount in the frame of the Israelite consciousness. A famous, widely known ancient literature of apocalyptic prophecy had for a long time explored them. The convictions that events carry preponderant meaning, that Israelites could control what happened by keeping or not keeping the Torah, and that in the course of time matters would come to a resolution—these commonplaces were given mythic reality in the apocalyptic literature. Over many centuries in that vast sweep of apocalyptic-prophetic writings all of the changes had been rung for every possible variation on the theme of redemption in history. So it is hardly surprising that, in the aftermath of the burning of the Temple and the cessation of the cult, people reflected upon familiar themes in established modes of thought. They had no choice, given the history of the country's consciousness and its scriptural frame of reference, but to think of the beginning, middle, and coming end of time.

The second stage in the formation of the earlier phases of rabbinic Judaism coincided with the flowering, in the second century, of that general movement both within Christianity and outside it called Gnosticism. It is as important as was the apocalyptic movement in establishing a base for comparison and interpretation of earlier rabbinic Judaism. One principal theme of the Mishnah and of Judaism involved the affirmation of God's beneficence in creating the world and revealing the Torah. Principal motifs of diverse Gnostic systems were God's malevolence in creating the world, or the malicious character of the creator-god, and the rejection of the Torah. In the Judaism of the sages represented in the Mishnah and later writings we see a direct confrontation on paramount issues of the day between rabbinic Judaism and the family of systems we call Gnosticism.

The thinkers of the Mishnah addressed two principal issues also important to Gnostic thought—the worth of the creation and the value of the Torah. They took the opposite position on both matters. The Mishnah's profoundly priestly celebration of creation and its slavishly literal repetition of what is clearly said in Scripture gain significance specifically in that very context in which, to others, these were subjected to a different and deeply negative valuation.

At the time of the formation of the Mishnah, Christian communities from France to Egypt were taking a position sharply at variance with that of the Hebrew Scriptures on the questions of creation, revelation, and redemption that confronted the Israelite world of the second century. Among the many positions taken up in the systems reported by Christian writers or documented through Gnostic-Christian writings found at Nag Hammadi, three are remarkably pertinent. First, the creator-god is evil, because, second, creation is deeply flawed, and third, revelation as Torah is a lie. For one Gnostic-Christian thinker after another these conclusions yielded the simple proposition that redemption is gained in escape; the world is to be abandoned, not constructed, affirmed, and faithfully tended in painstaking detail. It is in the context of this widespread negative judgment on the very matters on which Mishnah's sages registered a highly affirmative opinion that the choices made by the framers of the Mishnah become fully accessible.

Characterizing the Mishnah's ultimate system as a whole, we may call it both locative and utopian, in that it focuses upon Temple but is serviceable anywhere. In comparison to the Gnostic systems, it was profoundly scriptural; but it was also deeply indifferent to Scripture. It drew heavily upon the information supplied by Scripture for the construction and expression of its own systemic construction, which in form and language was wholly independent of any earlier Israelite document. It was finally a statement of affirmation of this world, of the realm of society, state, and commerce, and at the same time a vigorous denial that things were how they had to be. For the mishnaic system speaks of the building of a state, government, civil, and criminal system; of the conduct of transactions of property, commerce, and trade; of forming the economic unit of a family through transfer of women and property and the ending of such a family-economic unit; and similar matters, touching all manner of dull details of everyday life.

The Mishnah's principal message, which makes the Judaism of this document and of its social components distinctive and cogent, is that man is at the center of creation, the head of all creatures upon earth, corresponding to God in heaven in whose image man is made. The way in which the Mishnah makes this simple and fundamental statement is to impute power to man to inaugurate and initiate those corresponding processes, sanctification and uncleanness, which play so critical a role in the Mishnah's account of reality. The will of man, expressed through the deed of man, is the active power in the world. Will and deed constitute those actors of creation which work upon neutral realms, subject to either sanctification or uncleanness: the Temple and the table, the field and the family, the altar and the hearth, woman, time, space, and transactions in the material world and in the world above. Just as the entire system of uncleanness and holiness awaits the intervention of man, which imparts the capacity to become unclean upon what was formerly inert, or which removes the capacity to impart cleanness from what was formerly in its natural and puissant condition, so in the other ranges of reality man is at the center on earth just as God is in heaven. Man is counterpart and partner and creation, in that like God he has power over the status and condition of creation, by putting everything in its proper place and calling everything by its rightful name.

7

The Mishnah

HUMANITY IN CRISIS: WHAT CAN ISRAEL DO?

The Mishnah's framers were addressing an age of defeat and despair, in consequence of the permanent closure of the Temple in Jerusalem. Their principal message, which makes the Judaism of this document and of its social components distinctive and cogent, is that the human being is at the center of creation, the head of all creatures upon earth, corresponding to God in heaven, in whose image the human being is made. The way in which the Mishnah makes this simple and fundamental statement is illustrated on nearly every page of the document. It is to impute to the human being the power, effected through an act of sheer human will or intentionality, to inaugurate and initiate those corresponding processes—sanctification and uncleanness—which play so critical a role in the Mishnah's account of reality. The will of the human being, expressed through the deed of the human being, is the active power in the world. As matters would be phrased in later writings, "Nothing whatsoever impedes the human will." But, of course, looking back on that age, we know that everything did. The "Israel" of the Mishnah never achieved its stated goals, for example, in once more setting up a government of priests and kings, in once more regaining that order and stasis that people imagined had once prevailed. But of course, the key is in the "once more," for these were things that, in point of fact, had not been at all. The will for "once more" encompassed nowhere and never.

So, stated briefly, the question taken up by the Mishnah and answered by Judaism is: What can a person do? And the answer laid down by the Mishnah is: the human being, through will and deed, is master of this world, the measure of all things. But that world of all things, of which the human being is the measure, is *within*: in intellect, imagination, sentient reality. Since, when the Mishnah thinks of a human being, it means the Israelite, who is the subject and actor of its system, the statement is clear. This is the Judaism that identifies at the center of things Israel, the Israelite person, who can do what he or she wills. In the aftermath of two wars and defeats of millennial proportions, the message of the Mishnah cannot have proved more pertinent—or more poignant and tragic. Yet the power of the message shaped the entire history of Israel, the Jewish people, and of Judaism, from then to now. For Israel, the Jewish people, understood as the answer to the ineluctable questions of frailty and defeat in society, and death for everyone who walked on earth, the self-evident truth that *everything that matters depends upon the human will and intention*: we are what, in mind, imagination, sentiment, and heart, we hope, believe, and insist we are, and above all, by act of will, persist in being.

WOMEN IN THE MISHNAH

The social vision of mishnaic Judaism says the same thing about everything. Accordingly, knowing the urgent question and the system's self-evidently valid answer, we can predict what the system has to say about any topic it chooses to treat. The social vision of the Mishnah's Judaism encompasses issues of gender, social structure, wealth and transactions in property, and the organization of the castes of society. In all these matters the system seeks the principles of order and proper classification, identifying as problems the occasions for disorder and improper disposition of persons or resources. The fact that we can find our document saying one thing about many things tells us that the document stands for a well-considered view of the whole, and, when we come to the theological and philosophical program of the same writing, that consistent viewpoint will guide us to what matters and what is to be said about what matters.

The principal focus of a social vision framed by men, such as that of the Mishnah, not only encompasses, but focuses upon, women, who are perceived as the indicative abnormality in a world in which men are the norm. But to place the Mishnah's vision of woman in

perspective, we have to locate woman within the larger structure
defined by the household. This is for two reasons. First of all, as a
matter of definition, woman forms the other half of the whole that is
the householder. Second, since the household forms the building block
of the social construction envisioned by the Mishnah's framers, it is in
that setting that every other component of the social world of the
system must situate itself.

In the conception at hand, which sees earthly Israel as made up
of households and villages, the economic unit also frames the social
one, and the two together, in conglomerates, compose the political
one; hence we have a political economy (Gr. *polis, oikos*) initiated
within an economic definition formed out of the elements of production. That explains why women cannot be addressed outside of the
framework of the economic unit of production defined by the household. For the Mishnah throughout makes a single cogent statement,
that the organizing unit of society and politics finds its definition in
the irreducible unit of economic production. The Mishnah conceives
no other economic unit of production than the household, though it
recognizes that such existed; its authorship perceives no other social
unit of organization than the household and the conglomeration of
households, even though that limited vision omits all reference to
substantial parts of the population perceived to be present, for example, craftsmen, the unemployed, the landless, and the like. But what
about women in particular?

The framers of the Mishnah do not imagine a household headed
by a woman; a divorced woman is assumed to return to her father's
household. The framers make no provision for the economic activity
of isolated individuals, out of synchronic relationship with a household or a village made up of householders. Accordingly, craftsmen
and day laborers or other workers, skilled and otherwise, enter the
world of social and economic transactions only in relationship to
the householder. The upshot, therefore, is that the social world is
made up of households, and since households may be made up of
many families (husbands, wives, children, all of them dependent upon
the householder), households are in no way to be confused with the
family. The indicator of the family is kinship, that of the household,
"propinquity" or "residence." And yet, even residence is not always a
criterion for membership in the household unit, since craftsmen and
day laborers are not assumed to live in the household compound at

all. Accordingly, the household forms an economic unit, with secondary criteria deriving from that primary fact.

The mishnaic law of women defines the position of women in the social economy of Israel's supernatural and natural reality. That position acquires definition in relationship to men, who give form to the Israelite social economy. It is effected through both supernatural and natural (this-worldly) action. What man and woman do on earth provokes a response in heaven, and the correspondences are perfect. So the position of women is defined and secured both in heaven and here on earth, and that position, always and invariably relative to men, is what comes into consideration. The principal point of interest on the Mishnah's part is the time at which a woman changes hands. That is, she becomes, and ceases to be, holy to a particular man, enters and leaves the marital union. These are the dangerous and disorderly points in the relationship of woman to man, and therefore to society.

Five of the seven tractates that pertain to women and family are devoted to the transfer of women, the formation and dissolution of the marital bond. Three—Qiddushin, Ketubot, and Gittin—treat what is done by man here on earth, formation of a marital bond through betrothal and marriage-contract, and dissolution through divorce and its consequences. One (Sotah) is devoted to what is done by woman here on earth. Yebamot, greatest of the seven in size and in formal and substantive brilliance, deals with the corresponding heavenly intervention into the formation and dissolution of marriage: the dissolution of that bond through death. The other two tractates, Nedarim and Nazir, draw into one the two realms of reality, heaven and earth, as they work out the effects of vows—generally taken by married women and subject to the confirmation or abrogation of the husband—to heaven. These vows make a deep impact upon the marital relationship of the woman. So, in all, we consider the natural and supernatural character of the woman's relationship to the social economy framed by man from its beginning to its end.

WOMEN: YEBAMOT, CHAPTER 10
(M. YEB. 10:1–5)

For our sample of the Mishnah's treatment of women, we take up the disposition of matters of doubt in marital ties. In Mishnah tractate Yebamot 10:1–5, we consider the results of an erroneous union. Let us examine the composition of the sustained passage. M. Yebamot 10:1 is the keystone of the first unit. There we discover that a woman's husband has gone abroad and been reported dead. The woman remarries, but the husband turns out not to have died. At first glance, the consequences are unambiguous. The woman is put aside by both men and receives financial compensation from neither. These penalties are worked out so as to treat the woman like an adulterer. But there are some complications. First, several second-century authorities protest that, in certain property matters, the woman does have a valid claim. Second, M. Yebamot 10:1S makes explicit that these rules are invoked only if the woman marries with a court's permission. In this case she has deliberately violated the sanctity of her first marriage. But if she does not have permission to remarry, she may return to the first husband and the second marriage is null. M. Yebamot 10:2 contradicts this view by saying that even if the woman remarried with a court's permission, she nonetheless is put aside, but she owes no sin-offering. If she did not have a court's permission, she also is put aside, but now she does owe an offering. The harmonization of these rules at M. Yebamot 10:1S and M. Yebamot 10:2A need not detain us.

At M. Yebamot 10:3–4 we have a series of cases in which a man or a woman enters into a marriage and finds it was not valid. For instance, if a man goes abroad with his son, and his wife is told that the man has died, and then the son also died, she is exempt from levirate marriage, that is, with the brother of the deceased. If she finds that she is not exempt—the son having died first—she must be divorced from her second husband. Children by that husband are *mamzerim* ("bastards"). The principle here is that the children of unions formed in violation of a negative commandment are mamzerim. Sages hold that violation of levirate rules—negative commandments—does not produce mamzerim. There are several other cases in which marriage has taken place because of incorrect information, with the result that the woman must go hence and the children are mamzerim. At M. Yebamot 10:4 we have a man who marries his wife's sister, falsely assuming his wife has died. Such a marriage is null. If a man is told that his wife has died and he marries her sister and discovers that at the time of the remarriage the wife had not died, but she subsequently did die, then children born before the actual death are deemed mamzerim, those afterward are not. M. Yebamot 10:5 concludes this construction with a sequence of marriages, which present a rather simple conundrum for solution.

M. Yebamot 10:1

A. The woman whose husband went overseas,

B. and whom they came and told, "Your husband has died,"

C. and who remarried,

D. and whose husband afterward returned,

E. (1) goes forth from this one [the second husband] and from that one [the first].

F. And (2) she requires a writ of divorce from this one and from that.

G. And she has no claim to (3) [payment of her] marriage contract, (4) usufruct, (5) alimony, or (6) indemnification, either on this one or on that.

H. (7) If she had collected anything [of G] from this one or from that, she must return it.

I. (8) And the offspring is deemed a *mamzer*, whether born of the one marriage or the other.

J. And (9) neither one of them [if he is a priest] becomes unclean for her [if she should die and require burial].

K. And neither one of them has the right either (10) to what she finds or (11) to the fruit of her labor, or (12) to annul her vows.

L. [If] (13) she was an Israelite girl, she is rendered invalid for marriage into the priesthood; a Levite, from eating tithe; and a priest-girl, from eating heave-offering.

M. And the heirs of either one of the husbands do not inherit her ketubah.

N. And if they died, a brother of this one and a brother of that perform the rite of *halisah* but do not enter into levirate marriage.

O. R. Yosé says, "Her marriage contract is [a lien] on the property of her first husband."

P. R. Eleazar says, "The first husband has a right to what she finds and to the fruit of her labor and to annul her vows."

Q. R. Simeon says, "Having sexual relations with her or performing a rite of halisah with her on the part of the

brother of the first husband exempts her co-wife [from
levirate connection].

R. "And offspring from him is not a mamzer."

S. But if she should remarry without permission, [since the
remarriage was an inadvertent transgression and null], she is
permitted to return to him.

This is a slightly complicated pericope, formally and substan-
tively. What makes it formally difficult is the succession of unformu-
lated disputes, that is, O contradicts G3, P rejects K, Q–R differ from
I—three points at which named authorities would have stated matters
in their own way. Furthermore, S presupposes a contrary statement
at C ("who remarried *with permission*"). The omission is noteworthy
because M. Yebamot 10:2 sets up precisely the contrast expected at
10:1 (and, it goes without saying, routinely read into 10:1).

Let us turn to the problems of substance. If we read our case,
A–D, without the qualification at S, then we have a clear-cut incident
of deliberate remarriage in error. The husband has not died; the second marriage is null. There are, as I count them, thirteen specific
consequences of that fact, all of them based on the conception that
the deliberate remarriage was valid and the woman is penalized on its
account. The woman is prohibited to remain wed to either man (E).
She must be properly divorced by each (F). She has no material claim
on either man (G–H). That is, she loses her payment of a marriage
contract. The husband does not have to compensate her for the usufruct of *melog*-property. He does not have to provide support for her.
He does not have to compensate her for the wear and tear on property
belonging to her. If the woman has collected any of the items of G,
she must restore the goods. If she produced offspring with the second
husband, the child is a mamzer; if she went back to the first man and
produced offspring with him, that child is a mamzer also (I). Neither
one is deemed her husband as regards burial (J) or any other aspect
of marriage (K). L is clear as stated. The marriage contract is not
inherited by the heirs (M). The reference is to male heirs of the
woman, who ordinarily would have a claim on the payment of
the marriage contract. If the woman and the two men die, the male
children do not inherit the payment. N is consistent with F. Just as
the second man must give a writ of divorce, so his surviving brother
must perform the rite of halisah. R. Yosé, as we saw, differs from G3,

and contends that the first husband does owe the marriage contract. R. Eleazar concurs with Yosé's general conception, but, at K, R. Simeon turns to N and regards the brother of the first husband as *levir* in all regards; therefore the second man's brother need not perform the rite of halisah. R differs from I(8), stating that offspring from the first husband are legitimate. It follows that, in the specified details, authorities for O–R will not concur that the first husband's relationship has been totally severed by the unfortunate mistake of his wife.

S is a separate conception. It interprets the most fundamental supposition of the whole. It holds that we invoke these thirteen penalties specifically when the woman goes to court for permission to remarry, implying that she does so deliberately. But if she did not go to court and simply assumed her husband dead, her action is in error, the second marriage never was valid, as it would have been had she enjoyed a court's protection. It follows that, in the conception of S, we invoke none of the penalties and the woman simply reverts to her original status.

M. Yebamot 10:2

A. [If] she was remarried at the instruction of a court,

B. she is to go forth,

C. but she is exempt from the requirement of bringing an offering.

D. [If] she did not remarry at the instruction of a court, she goes forth,

E. and she is liable to the requirement of bringing an offering.

F. The authority of the court is strong enough to exempt.

G. [If] the court instructed her to remarry, and she went and entered an unsuitable union,

H. she is liable for the requirement of bringing an offering.

I. For the court permitted her only to marry [properly].

M. Yebamot 10:2 augments M. Yebamot 10:1A–D, on which the pericope depends for context and meaning. A–C are balanced against D–E, then F comments on the whole. G–I form an integral, additional gloss. The point is that, if the court approved her remarriage, she does not owe a sin-offering; otherwise she does. G–I then clarify the obvious: If as a widow she married a high priest or as a divorcee an ordinary priest, the court's instruction has been carried out and its leniency no longer pertains. The real question is whether M. Yebamot 10:1S and M. Yebamot 10:2A–B are in accord with one another. If we understand correctly, M. Yebamot 10:1S allows the woman to return to the first husband, while M. Yebamot 10:2B has her leave both men.

M. Yebamot 10:3–4

[10:3]

A. The woman whose husband and son went overseas,
B. and whom they came and told, "Your husband died, and then your son died,"
C. and who remarried,
D. and whom they afterward told, "Matters were reversed"—
E. goes forth [from the second marriage].
F. And earlier and later offspring are in the status of mamzer.
G. [If] they told her, "Your son died and afterward your husband died," and she entered into levirate marriage, and afterward they told her, "Matters were reversed,"
H. she goes forth [from the levirate marriage].
I. And the earlier and later offspring are in the status of mamzer.
J. [If] they told her, "Your husband died," and she married, and afterward they told her, "He was alive, but then he died,"
K. she goes forth [from the second marriage].
L. And the earlier offspring is a mamzer, but the later is not a mamzer.
M. [If] they told her, "Your husband died," and she became betrothed, and afterward her husband came home,
N. she is permitted to return to him.
O. Even though the second man gave her a writ of divorce, he has not rendered her invalid from marrying into the priesthood.
P. This did R. Eleazar b. Matya expound, *"And a woman divorced from her husband* (Lev. 21:7)—and not from a man who is not her husband."

[10:4]

A. He whose wife went overseas, and whom they came and told, "Your wife has died,"

B. and who married her sister,

C. and whose wife thereafter came back—

D. she is permitted to come back to him.

E. He is permitted to marry the kinswomen of the second, and the second woman is permitted to marry his kinsmen.

F. And if the first died, he is permitted to marry the second woman.

G. [If] they said to him, "She was alive, but then she died"—

H. the former offspring is a mamzer [born before the wife died], and the latter is not a mamzer.

I. R. Yosé says, "Anyone who invalidates [his wife] for [marriage] with others invalidates her for marriage with himself, and whoever does not invalidate his wife for marriage with others does not invalidate her for himself."

At M. Yebamot 10:3 we have three parallel cases (A–L). The opening unit is in the expected abbreviated form, and the rest in declarative sentences, as indicated. The important point throughout is the status of the offspring. The woman has a child before she hears that matters are not as she had supposed, then she has one after she receives the report. In the first case, the woman assumes (A–C) that since her husband did not die childless, she may remarry without levirate rites. If matters are reversed (D), then her remarriage is null. The second marriage is now invalid. All offspring produced in the second marriage are in the status of mamzer (in Akiva's view [m. Yebamot 4:13]), since the woman has remarried without the rite of halisah. The same rule applies in the contrary situation of G–I, in which the woman realizes that she has married her brother-in-law, but not in a levirate connection, and this is prohibited. In the third case, the earlier offspring are produced before the husband died, the later ones, after his death. There is no reason for the latter to be deemed mamzer. The application of *earlier . . . later . . .* at F and I is meaningless, but at L is not (compare B. T. Yebamot 92a [= Babylonian Talmud, Tractate Yebamot, p. 92, the front side of the page]). M–P are distinct from the foregoing, although the basic problem is parallel. The betrothal is null and produces no effect, even though a writ of divorce is given.

M. Yebamot 10:4 gives us two cases parallel to M. Yebamot 10:3G–I and J–L. In the former case, we have marriage to the woman's sister, which turns out to be illegal. It is treated (E) as entirely null, I assume, along the lines of M. Yebamot 10:1A. In the final case, we have a problem of offspring, resulting from the foregoing situation. The rule is the same as at M. Yebamot 10:3J–L. An offspring produced while the former wife was alive is a mamzer, but one produced after her death is not.

The interpretation of R. Yosé's saying (I) is not self-evident, since there is no clear connection to the context established at A–H. The Babylonian Talmud, Tractate Yebamot, p. 95b wishes to read I in the setting of A–D. There we have a man's wife and her brother-in-law who had gone abroad; the man believes they have died and he married his wife's sister, who had been married to his brother. The two then came home. May he then go back to his wife? Yes, he may. And, it follows, the brother-in-law also may return to his original wife. Since the man's wife is permitted to him, so is the brother-in-law's. This view is rejected, since the necessary language should be, "Whoever does not invalidate for himself does not invalidate for others." In another view, commentators posit a man's wife going abroad with her brother-in-law (her sister's husband). They are reported dead. The man marries his wife's sister. The wife and brother-in-law come home. Since the man prohibits his wife's sister from remarrying her husband—in line with M. Yebamot 10:1—he also prohibits his own wife from returning to him. If, on the other hand, his wife's sister has been married without permission and may return to her husband, he does not prohibit his wife from returning to him. But the other proposed interpretations of R. Yosé's saying require that we read into it considerations and conditions by no means contained at M. Yebamot 10:4A–H, so we must concede that we cannot interpret the saying solely within the limits of information provided by the Mishnah itself. Then, for this passage, we cannot explain the passage at all. It happens.

THE SOCIAL VISION OF
THE MISHNAH

Critical to the social system of the Mishnah is its principal social entity, the village, imagined as a society that never changes in any important way, comprising households. The model comprising household, village, and "all Israel" comprehensively covers whatever of

"Israel" the authorship has chosen to describe. We must then identify the centrality of political economy as systemically indicative—"community, self-sufficiency, and justice"—within the system of the Mishnah. It is no surprise, either, that the originality of the mishnaic system's political economy resides in its focus upon a society organized in relationship to the control of the means of production—the farm, for the household is always the agricultural unit. I cannot point to any other systemic statement among the Judaisms of antiquity, to any other form of Judaism, that takes as its point of departure, in the pattern of the Mishnah, the definition of an "Israel" as a political economy, that is, as an aggregation of villages made up of households. We realize, in the context of the social thought of ancient times, that this systemic focus upon political economy also identifies the Mishnah's authorship with the prevailing conventions of a faraway land and a long-ago age, namely, Greece in the time of Aristotle. Thinkers, represented by Aristotle, took for granted that society was formed of self-sufficient villages, made up of self-sufficient farms: households run by householders. But, as we know, in general nothing can have been further from the facts of the world of "Israel," that is, the community of Jews in the Land of Israel, made up as it was not only of villages but cities, not only of small but larger landholders, and, most of all, of people who held no land at all and never would.

In the context of a world of pervasive diversity, the Mishnah's authorship sets forth a fantastic conception of a simple world of little blocks formed into big ones: households into villages, no empty spaces, but also no vast cities. In the conception of the authorship of the Mishnah, community or village (Gr. *polis*) is made up of households, and the household (Heb. *bayit*; Gr. *oikos*) constituted the building block of both society and economy. It follows that the household forms the fundamental, irreducible, and of course representative unit of the economy, the locus and the unit of production. We should not confuse the household with class-status, for example, thinking of the householder as identical with the wealthy. The opposite is suggested on every page of the Mishnah, in which householders vie with craftsmen for the leavings of the loom and the chips left behind by the adze. The household, rather, forms an economic and social classification, defined by function, specifically economic function. A poor household was a household, and (in theory, though the Mishnah's authorship knows none such in practice) a rich landholding that did not function as the center of a social and economic unit, for example, a rural "industrial" farm, was not a household. The household constituted the center of the productive economic activities we now handle through the market. Within the household all local (as distinct from cultic), economic, therefore social, activities and functions were held together. For the unit of production comprised also the unit of social organization and, of greater import still, the building block of all larger social and also political units, with special reference to the village.

In its identification of the householder as the building block, to the neglect of the vast panoply of "others," "non-householders," including, after all, that half of Israelite society comprising women, the Mishnah's authorship reduced the dimensions of society to one component: the male landowner engaged in agriculture. But that is the sole option open to a system that, for reasons of its own, wished to identify productivity with agriculture, individuality in God's image with ownership of land, and social standing and status, consequently, with ownership and control of the land. Now, if we were to list all of the persons and professions who had no role in the system, or who are treated as ancillary to the system, we would have to encompass not only workers—the entire landless working class!—but also craftsmen and artisans, teachers and physicians, clerks and officials, traders and merchants, the whole of the commercial establishment, not to mention women as a caste. Such an economics, disengaged from so large a sector of the economy of which it claimed (even if only in theory) to speak, can hardly be called an economics at all. And yet, as we have seen and shall realize still more keenly in the coming chapters, that economics bore an enormous burden of the systemic message and statement of the Judaism set forth by the authorship of the Mishnah.

Fair and just to all parties, the authorship of the Mishnah nonetheless speaks in particular for the Israelite landholding, proprietary person. The Mishnah's problems are the problems of the householder, its perspectives are his. Its sense of what is just and fair expresses his sense of the givenness and cosmic rightness of the present condition of society. These are men of substance and of means, however modest, aching for a stable and predictable world in which to tend their crops and herds, feed their families and dependents, keep to the natural rhythms of the seasons and lunar cycles, and, in all, live out their lives within strong and secure boundaries on earth and in heaven. This is why the sense of landed place and its limits, the sharp line drawn between village and world, in the first place, Israelite and Gentile, in the second, Temple and world, in the third, evoke metaphysical correspondences. Householder (which is "Israel") in the village, and Temple beyond, form a correspondence. Only when we understand the systemic principle concerning God in relationship to Israel on its land shall we come to the fundamental and generative conception that reaches concrete expression in the here-and-now of the householder as the centerpiece of society.

In this regard, therefore, the Mishnah's social vision finds within its encompassing conception of who forms the polis, and who merely occupies space within the polis, its definition of the realm to which "economics" applies. In the Mishnah's social vision, the householder is systemically the active force, and all other components of the actual economy (as distinct from the economics) prove systemically inert. As such, of course, the Mishnah's social vision ignores most of the Jewish people in the Land of Israel in the first and second centuries C.E. But then, what of the economically active members of the polis, those who had capital and knew how to use it? If they wished to enter that elevated "Israel" which formed the social center and substance of the Mishnah's Israel, they had to purchase land. The Mishnah's social vision thus describes a steady-state society.

No wonder that the framers of the Mishnah conceived of the economy as self-sufficient, made up as it was (in their minds, at least) of mostly self-sufficient households joined in essentially self-sufficient villages. They further carry forward the odd conception of the priestly authorship of Leviticus that the ownership of land is supposed to be stable, indeed inalienable from the family, if not from the individual, as at Leviticus 27, so that, if a family has inalienable rights to inherited property, it reverts to that family's ownership after a span of time. The conception of the steady-state economy therefore dominated, so that no one would rise above his natural or inherent standing, and no one would fall either. And that is the economy they portray and claim to regulate through their legislation. In such an economy, the market did not form the medium of rationing and had no role to play, except one: to ensure equal exchange in all transactions, so that the market formed an arena for transactions of equal value and worth among households each possessed of a steady-state worth.

To place the social vision of the Mishnah's authorship into context, we must now ask a final question: For whom and to whom does the Mishnah speak?

The priesthood. Insofar as the Mishnah is a document about the holiness of Israel in its Land, it expresses that conception of sanctification and theory of its modes which will have been shaped among those to whom the Temple and its technology of joining heaven and holy land through the sacred place defined the core of being; that is, the caste of the priests.

The scribes. Insofar as the Mishnah takes up the way in which transactions are conducted among ordinary folk and takes the position that it is through documents with a supernatural consequence that transactions are embodied and expressed, the Mishnah expresses what is self-evident to scribes.

Just as to the priest there is a correspondence between the table of the Lord in the Temple and the locus of the Divinity in the heavens, so to the scribe there is a correspondence between the documentary expression of the human will on earth—in writs of all sorts, in the orderly provision of courts for the predictable and just disposition of exchanges of persons and property—and heaven's judgment of these same matters. When a woman becomes sanctified to a particular man on earth through the appropriate document governing the transfer of her person and property, the woman is deemed truly sanctified to that man in heaven, as well. A violation of the writ therefore is not merely a crime, it is a sin. That is why the Temple rite involving the wife accused of adultery is integral to the system laid out in the Mishnah's division on women.

So there are these two social groups, not categorically symmetrical with one another, the priestly caste and the scribal profession, for whom the Mishnah makes self-evident statements. We know, moreover, that in time to come, the scribal profession would become a focus of sanctification too. The scribe would be transformed into the rabbi, locus of the holy through what he knew, just as the priest had been (and would remain) locus of the holy through what he could claim genealogically. The tractates of special interest to scribes-become-rabbis and to their governance of Israelite society—those on women and damages, together with certain others particularly relevant to utopian Israel beyond the system of the Land—would grow. Others would remain essentially as they were with the closure of the

Mishnah. So we must note that the Mishnah speaks for the program of topics important to the priests, and takes up the personae of the scribes, speaking through their voice and in their manner.

What we do not find, which is astonishing in the light of these observations, is sustained and serious attention to the caste of priests and the profession of scribe. True, scattered through the tractates are exercises, occasionally sustained and important, on the genealogy of the priestly caste, on their marital obligations and duties, as well as on the things priests do and do not do in the cult, in collecting and eating their sanctified food, and in other topics of keen interest to priests. Indeed, it would be no exaggeration to say that the Mishnah's system seen whole is not a great deal more than a handbook of how the priestly caste wished to design its life in Israel and the world. And yet in the fundamental structure of the document, its organization into divisions (orders) and tractates, there is no place for a division of the priesthood, no room even for a complete tractate on the rules of the priesthood, except, as we have seen, for the pervasive way of life of the priestly caste, which is everywhere. This absence of sustained attention to the priesthood is striking, when we compare the way in which the priestly code at Leviticus 1—15 spells out its concerns: the priesthood, the cult, the matter of cultic cleanness. Since we do have divisions for the cult (the fifth) and for cleanness (the sixth) at holy things and purities, it is remarkable that we do not have a division for the priesthood.

So the components of the system at the very basis of things are the social groups to which the system refers. These groups obviously are not comparable to one another. They are not three species of the same social genus. One is a class; the second, a caste; the third, a profession. What they have in common is (1) they do form groups, and (2) the groups are social in foundation and collective in expression. That is not a sizable claim. The priesthood is a social group; it coalesces. Priests see one another as part of a single caste, with whom, for example, they will want to intermarry. The scribes are a social group, because they practice a single profession, following a uniform set of rules. They coalesce in the methods by which they do their work. The householders are a social group, the basic productive unit of society, around which other economic activity is perceived to function. In an essentially agricultural economy, it is quite reasonable to regard the householder, the head of a basic unit of production, as part of a single class.

This brings us back to the point at which we began: the social vision of the Mishnah, part of the encompassing worldview that the Mishnah's authorship sets forth, in the excruciating detail of the way of life that that same authorship prescribes for the social entity, holy Israel, which the authorship addresses. The Mishnah through its six divisions sets forth a coherent worldview and comprehensive way of living for holy Israel. It is a worldview that speaks of transcendent things, a way of life in response to the supernatural meaning of what is done, a heightened and deepened perception of the sanctification of Israel in deed and in deliberation. Sanctification means two things: first, distinguishing Israel in all its dimensions from the world in all its ways; second, establishing the stability, order, regularity, predictability, and reliability of Israel at moments and in contexts of danger. Danger means instability, disorder, irregularity, uncertainty, and betrayal. Each topic of the system as a whole takes up a critical and indispensable moment or context of social being. Each orders what is disorderly and dangerous. Through what is said in regard to each of the Mishnah's principal topics, what the system as a whole wishes to declare is fully expressed. These writers are obsessed with order and compelled by a vision of a world in which all things are in their right place, each bearing its own name, awaiting the blessing that comes when, everything in order, God pronounces the benediction and brings about the sanctification of the whole.

8

The Formation
of Rabbinic Judaism:
The Crisis Addressed by
the Talmuds and the Midrash

THE UNFOLDING OF
THE MISHNAH'S TRADITION

The Judaism of the dual Torah, which emerged at the end of late antiquity and reached its final statement in the Talmud of Babylonia, took shape in response to both internal and external stimuli. The internal questions derived from the character of the Mishnah itself and the external questions from the catastrophic political change brought on by the conversion of the Roman emperor to Christianity and the establishment of the Christian religion as the religion of the state. We begin with the reception of the Mishnah, the issue that dominated in the third and early fourth centuries. Then we move on to the decisive political events of the later fourth and fifth centuries, the challenge of Christianity as the religion of the Roman state.

As soon as the Mishnah made its appearance, the vast labor of explaining its meaning and justifying its authority got under way. The Mishnah presented one striking problem in particular. It rarely cited scriptural authority for its rules. By omitting scriptural proof, texts bore the implicit claim to an authority independent of Scripture, and in that striking fact the document set a new course for itself and raised problems for those who wanted to apply its law to Israel's life. For from the formation of ancient Israelite Scripture into a holy book in Judaism in the aftermath of the return to Zion, and the creation of the Torah book in Ezra's time (about 450 B.C.E.) as the established canon of revelation, coming generations routinely set their ideas into relationship with Scripture. They did this by citing proof-texts alongside their own rules. Otherwise the new writings could find no ready hearing in the setting of Israelite culture.

Over the six hundred years beginning with the formation of the Torah of Moses in the time of Ezra, from about 450 B.C.E. to about 200 C.E., four conventional ways to accommodate new writings—new "tradition"—to the established canon of received Scripture had come to the fore. First and simplest, a writer would sign a famous name to his book, attributing his ideas to Enoch, Adam, Jacob's sons, Jeremiah, Baruch, or any number of others, down to Ezra. But the Mishnah bore no such attribution. Implicitly, to be sure, the statement of M. Abot 1:1, "Moses received Torah from Sinai," carried the further notion that sayings of people on the list of authorities from Moses to nearly their own day derived from God's revelation at Sinai. But no one made that premise explicit before the time of the Talmud of the Land of Israel. Second, an author might also imitate the style of biblical Hebrew and so try to creep into the canon by adopting the cloak of Scripture. But the Mishnah's authorship does not use biblical syntax or style. Third, an author would surely claim that his work was inspired by God, a new revelation for an open canon. But that claim had no explicit impact on the Mishnah, which contains nothing attributed to God through prophecy, for instance. Fourth, at the very least, someone would link his opinions to biblical verses so Scripture would validate his views. The authorship of the Mishnah did so occasionally, but far more commonly stated on its own authority whatever rules it proposed to lay down.

The solution to the problem of the authority of the Mishnah, that is, its relationship to Scripture, was worked out in the period after the completion of the Mishnah. Since no one could now credibly claim to sign the name of Ezra or Adam to a book of this kind, the only options lay elsewhere. These were first, to provide a myth of the origin of the contents of the Mishnah, and second, to link each allegation of the Mishnah, through processes of biblical (not mishnaic) exegesis, to verses of the Scriptures. These two procedures together established for the Mishnah the standing that the uses to which the document was to be put demanded for it: a place in the canon of Israel, and a legitimate relationship to the Torah of Moses. There were several ways in which the work went forward. These are represented by diverse documents that succeeded and dealt with the Mishnah. Let me now state the three principal possibilities:

(1) the Mishnah required no systematic support through exegesis of Scripture in light of mishnaic laws; (2) the Mishnah by itself provided no reliable information and all of its propositions demanded linkage to Scripture, to which the Mishnah must be shown to be subordinate and secondary; (3) the Mishnah is an autonomous document, but closely correlated with Scripture.

The first extreme is represented by the Abot, about 250 C.E., which represents the authority of the sages cited in Abot as autonomous of Scripture. The authorities in Abot do not cite verses of Scripture, but what they say constitutes a statement of the Torah. There can be no clearer way of saying that what these authorities present in and of itself falls into the classification of the Torah. The authorship of the Tosefta, about 400 C.E., takes the middle position. It very commonly cites a passage of the Mishnah and then adds to that passage an appropriate proof-text. That is a quite common mode of supplementing the Mishnah. The mediating view is also taken by the Talmud of the Land of Israel, about 400 C.E., among the various documents produced by the Jewish sages of the Land of Israel between the end of the second century and the sixth. The Talmud of the Land of Israel (also called the Palestinian Talmud of the Land of Israel, or Yerushalmi; I use these terms interchangeably) like the Talmud of Babylonia (Bavli), composed in the same period—the third and fourth centuries—was organized around the Mishnah. It provided a line-by-line or paragraph-by-paragraph exegesis and amplification of the Mishnah. Produced by schools in Tiberias, Sepphoris, Lud (Lydda), and Caesarea, the Talmud of the Land of Israel developed a well-crafted theory of the Mishnah and its relationship to Scripture. The far extreme—that everything in the Mishnah makes sense only as a (re)statement of Scripture or upon Scripture's authority—is taken by the Sifra, a post-mishnaic compilation of exegeses on Leviticus, redacted at an indeterminate point, perhaps about 300 C.E. The Sifra systematically challenges reason (the Mishnah) unaided by revelation (that is, exegesis of Scripture) to sustain positions taken by the Mishnah, which is cited verbatim, and everywhere proves that it cannot be done.

The final and normative solution to the problem of the authority of the Mishnah, worked out in the third and fourth centuries, produced the myth of the dual Torah, oral and written, which formed the indicative and definitive trait of the Judaism that emerged from late antiquity. Tracing the unfolding of that myth leads us deep into the processes by which that Judaism took shape. The Yerushalmi knows the theory that there is a tradition separate from, and in addition to, the written Torah. This tradition it knows as "the teachings of scribes." The Mishnah is not identified as the collection of those teachings. An ample instantiation of the Yerushalmi's recognition of this other, separate tradition is contained in the following discourse from Yerushalmi tractate Zarah. What is interesting is that, if these discussions take for granted the availability to Israel of authoritative teachings in addition to those of Scripture, they do not also claim that those teachings are contained uniquely or even partially in the Mishnah in particular. Indeed, the discussion is remarkable in its supposition that extrascriptural teachings are associated with the views of scribes, perhaps legitimately called sages, but are not in a book to be venerated or memorized as a deed of ritual learning.

Y. Abodah Zarah 2:7

III.

A. Associates in the name of R. Yohanan: "The words of scribes are more beloved than the words of Torah and more cherished than words of Torah: 'Your palate is like the best wine'" (Song of Songs 7:9).

B. Simeon bar Ba in the name of R. Yohanan: "The words of scribes are more beloved than the words of Torah and more cherished than words of Torah: 'For your love is better than wine'" (Song of Songs 1:2). . . .

D. R. Ishmael repeated the following: "The words of Torah are subject to prohibition, and they are subject to remission; they are subject to lenient rulings, and they are subject to strict rulings. But words of scribes all are subject only to strict interpretation, for we have learned there: He who rules, 'There is no requirement to wear phylacteries,' in order to transgress the teachings of the Torah, is exempt. But if he said, 'There are five partitions in the phylactery, instead of four,' in order to add to what the scribes have taught, he is liable" [M. San. 11:3].

E. R. Haninah is the name of R. Idi in the name of R. Tanhum b. R. Hiyya: "More stringent are the words of the elders than the words of the prophets. For it is written, 'Do not preach'—

thus they preach—'one should not preach of such things'
(Micah 2:6). And it is written, '[If a man should go about
and utter wind and lies, saying,] "I will preach to you of
wine and strong drink," he would be the preacher for this
people!' (Micah 2:11).

F. "A prophet and an elder—to what are they comparable? To a
king who sent two senators of his to a certain province.
Concerning one of them he wrote, 'If he does not show you
my seal and signet, do not believe him.' But concerning the
other one he wrote, 'Even though he does not show you my
seal and signet, believe him.' So in the case of the prophet,
he has had to write, 'If a prophet arises among you . . . and
gives you a sign or a wonder . . .' (Deut. 13:1). But here
[with regard to an elder:] '. . . according to the instructions
which they give you . . .' (Deut. 17:11) [without a sign or a
wonder]."

What is important in the foregoing anthology is the distinction
between teachings contained in the Torah and teachings in the name
or authority of scribes. These latter teachings are associated with quite
specific details of the law and are indicated in the Mishnah's rule
itself. Further, at E we have "elders" (that is, sages) as against
prophets.

What conclusion is to be drawn from this mixture of word
choices that all together clearly refer to a law or tradition in addition
to that of Scripture? The commonplace view, maintained in diverse
forms of ancient Judaism, that Israel had access to a tradition beyond
Scripture, clearly was well known to the framers of the Yerushalmi.
The question of how, in that context, these framers viewed the Mishnah is not to be settled by that fact. I cannot point to a single passage
in which explicit judgment upon the character and status of the Mishnah as a complete document is laid down. Nor is the Mishnah treated
as a symbol or called "the oral Torah." But there is ample evidence,
once again implicit in what happens to the Mishnah in the Talmud of
the Land of Israel, or Yerushalmi, to allow a reliable description
of how the founders of the Yerushalmi viewed the Mishnah. The
Mishnah rarely cites verses of Scripture in support of its propositions.
The Yerushalmi routinely adduces scriptural bases for the Mishnah's
laws. The Mishnah seldom undertakes the exegesis of verses of Scrip-

ture for any purpose. The Yerushalmi consistently investigates the meaning of verses of Scripture, and does so for a variety of purposes. Accordingly, the Yerushalmi, subordinate as it is to the Mishnah, regards the Mishnah as subordinate to, and contingent upon, Scripture. That is why, in the view of the Talmud of the Land of Israel, the Mishnah requires the support of proof-texts of Scripture. That fact can mean only that, by itself, the Mishnah exercises no autonomous authority and enjoys no independent standing.

What is important in the following abstract is that the search for proof-texts in Scripture sustains not only propositions of the Mishnah, but also those of the Tosefta as well as those of the Yerushalmi's own sages. This is a stunning fact. It indicates that the search of Scriptures is primary, and the source of propositions or texts to be supported by those Scriptures, secondary. There is no limit, indeed, to the purposes for which scriptural texts will be found relevant.

Y. Sanhedrin 10:4

II.

A. The party of Korach has no portion in the world to come and will not live in the world to come [M. San. 10:4].

B. What is the Scriptural basis for this view?

C. "[So they and all that belonged to them went down alive into Sheol;] and the earth closed over them, and they perished from the midst of the assembly" (Num. 16:33).

D. "The earth closed over them"—in this world.

E. "And they perished from the midst of the assembly"—in the world to come [M. San. 10:4D–F].

F. It was taught: R. Judah b. Batera says, "[The contrary view] is to be derived from the implication of the following verse:

G. "I have gone astray like a lost sheep: seek thy servant [and do not forget thy commandments]" (Ps. 119:176).

H. "Just as the lost object which is mentioned later on in the end is going to be searched for, so the lost object which is stated herein is destined to be searched for" [T. San. 13:9].

I. Who will pray for them?

J. R. Samuel bar Nahman said, "Moses will pray for them:

K. 'Let Reuben live, and not die, [nor let his men be few]'" (Deut. 33:6).

L. R. Joshua b. Levi said, "Hannah will pray for them."

> M. This is the view of R. Joshua b. Levi, for R. Joshua b. Levi said, "Thus did the party of Korach sink ever downward, until Hannah went and prayed for them and said, 'The Lord kills and brings to life; he brings down to Sheol and raises up'" (1 Sam. 2:6).

We have a striking sequence of proof-texts, serving, one by one, the cited statement of the Mishnah, A–C, then an opinion of a rabbi in the Tosefta, F–H, and then the position of a talmudic rabbi, J–K, L–M. The process of providing the proof-texts is therefore central, and the differentiation among the passages requiring the proof-texts, a matter of indifference. The search for appropriate verses of Scripture vastly transcended the purpose of the study of the Mishnah, the exegesis of its rules, and the provision of adequate authority for the document and its laws. In fact, any proposition to be taken seriously elicited interest in scriptural support, whether in the Mishnah, in the Tosefta, or in the mouth of a talmudic sage. So the main thing is that the Scripture was at the center and focus. A verse of Scripture settled all pertinent questions, wherever they were located, whatever their source. That was the Yerushalmi's position. We know full well that it was not the Mishnah's position.

This fact shows us in a detail a part of a broad shift that took place in the generations that received the Mishnah, that is, over the third and fourth centuries. If the sages of the second century, who made the Mishnah as we know it, spoke in their own name and in the name of the logic of their own minds, those who followed, certainly the ones who flourished in the later fourth century, took a quite different view. Reverting to ancient authority like others of the age, they turned back to Scripture, deeming it the source of certainty about truth. Unlike their masters in the Mishnah, theirs was a quest for a higher authority than the logic of their own minds. The shift from age to age is clear. The second-century masters took commonplaces of Scripture, well-known facts, and stated them wholly in their own language and context. Fourth-century masters phrased commonplaces of the Mishnah or banalities of worldly wisdom so far as they could in the language of Scripture and its context.

The real issue was not the Mishnah at all, not even its diverse sayings vindicated one by one. Once what a sage said was made to refer to Scripture for proof, it followed that a rule of the Mishnah and of the Tosefta likewise were asked to refer to Scripture. The fact that the living sage validated what he said through Scripture explains why the sage also validated through verses of Scripture what the ancient sages of the Mishnah and Tosefta said. It was one undivided phenomenon. The reception of the Mishnah constituted testimony to a prevalent attitude of mind, important for the age of the Talmud of the Land of Israel and not solely for the Mishnah. The stated issue was the standing of the Mishnah. But the heart of the matter was the authority of the sage himself, who identified with the authors of the Mishnah and claimed authoritatively to interpret the Mishnah and much else, including Scripture. So the appeal to Scripture in behalf of the Mishnah represented simply one more expression of what proved critical in the formative age of Judaism: the person of the holy man himself. When revelation—Torah—became flesh, Judaism was born.

SYSTEMIC CHANGES
IN THE FOURTH CENTURY:
CANON, SYMBOL, TELEOLOGY

The documents that carried forward and continued the Mishnah exhibited striking changes, in particular those writings completed at the end of the fourth century. Fundamental in character, those changes marked dramatic shifts in the modes of symbolization of the canon, of the system as a whole, and of the purpose and goal of the system. We shall see that each of the important changes in the documents first redacted at the end of the fourth century responded to a powerful challenge presented by the triumph of Christianity in the age of Constantine. On that basis I maintain that the Judaism of the dual Torah took as its set of urgent questions the issue defined by Christianity as it assumed control of the Roman Empire, and that it provided as valid answers a system deriving its power from the Torah, read by sages, embodied by sages, and exemplified by sages.

Canon

The first change revealed in the unfolding of the sages' canon pertained to the use of Scripture. The change at hand was specifically to make books out of the collection of exegeses of Scripture. That represented an innovation because the Mishnah, and the exegetical literature that served the Mishnah, did not take shape around the explanation of verses of Scripture. The authorship of the Mishnah and its principal heirs followed their own program, which was a topical one. They arranged ideas by subject matter. But in the third and later fourth centuries, other writings entering the canon took shape around the explanation of verses of Scripture rather than a set of topics. What this meant was that a second mode of organizing ideas now developed.

Let me make the question clear by framing it in negative terms. The problem is not why Jews in general began to undertake exegesis of the Hebrew Scriptures. Judaism in all forms had always done that. Nor was there anything new even in collecting exegeses and framing them for a particular polemical purpose, that is, creating a book out of comments on the Scripture and in the form of a commentary. The Essene library at Qumran presents us with compositions of biblical commentary and exegesis. The school of Matthew provides an ample picture of another sort of exercise in systematic composition based on the amplification and application of Israel's ancient Scriptures.

But within the formation of the holy literature of rabbinic Judaism in particular, so far as we know, no one before the fourth century had produced a composition of biblical exegeses formed into holy books. Why then? Why do it at all? My answer is in two parts. First, making such collections defined the natural next step in the process precipitated by the appearance of the Mishnah and the task of exegesis of the Mishnah. Second, equally pressing in the confrontion with Christianity was the task of showing in a systematic and orderly way how Scripture was to be read in Israel.

With Christianity addressing the world with a systematic exegetical apologetic, beginning of course with the Gospels' demonstration of how events in the life of Jesus fulfilled the prophecies of the shared Scripture, a Judaic response took the form of a counterpart exegesis. When in the Mishnah sages found a systematic exegesis of Scripture unnecessary, it was because they saw no need, since there was no reading contrary to theirs that presented a challenge to them. But the Christians composed a powerful apologetic out of the systematic exegesis of the shared Scripture, and when Christianity made further indifference impolitic and impossible, sages replied with their compositions.

By the fourth century the church had reached a consensus on the bulk of the New Testament canon, having earlier accepted the Hebrew Scriptures as its own Old Testament. Accordingly, the issue of Scripture had come to the fore, and in framing the question of Scripture, the church focused sages' attention on the larger matter of systematic exegesis. When, for example, Jerome referred to the Jews' having a "second" Torah, one that was not authoritative, and when a sequence of important church fathers produced exegeses of Scripture in profoundly christological terms, the issue was raised. It would be joined when sages speaking on their own and to their chosen audience went through pretty much the same processes. This they did by explaining the standing of that "second Torah," and by producing not merely counterpart exegeses to those of the Christians but counterpart compilations of such exegeses.

Symbol

The generative symbol of the literary culture of the sages, the Torah, stands for the system as a whole. From the Yerushalmi onward, the symbol of the Torah took on the meaning that would prove indicative when Judaism had reached its final form at the end of this period. It was the doctrine that, when Moses received the Torah at Mount Sinai, had come down with him in two media, written and oral. The written Torah was transmitted, as its name says, through writing and is now contained in the canon of Scripture. The oral Torah was transmitted through the process of formulation for ease in memorization and then through the memories of sages and their disciples, from Moses and Joshua to the most current generation. That doctrine of the dual Torah—the Torah in two media—came about in response to the problem of explaining the standing and authority of the Mishnah. But the broadening of the symbol of the Torah first took shape around the figure of the sage. That symbolism accounted for the sages' authority. Only later on, in the fourth century, in the pages of the Yerushalmi, did the doctrine of the dual Torah reach expression. So in the unfolding of the documents of the canon of Judaism the symbol of Torah revealed a striking change. Beginning as a rather generalized account of how sages' teachings relate to God's will, the symbol of Torah gained concrete form in its application to the dual Torah, written and oral, Scripture and Mishnah. Within the unfolding of the canonical writings, such a shift represented a symbolic change of fundamental character.

When we speak of Torah in the rabbinical literature of late antiquity, we no longer denote a particular book, or the contents of such a book. Instead we connote a broad range of clearly distinct categories of noun and verb, concrete fact and abstract relationship. Torah stood for a kind of human being, a social status, social group, social relationship, or legal status. The main points of the whole of Israel's life and history came to full symbolic expression in that single word. The Torah symbolized the whole.

After the appearance of the Mishnah, the movement of the Torah from standing for a concrete, material object—a scroll—to symbolizing a broad range of relationships, proceeded in two significant stages. The first was marked off by tractate Abot, the second by the Yerushalmi. Abot regards study of Torah as what a sage does. The substance of Torah is what a sage says. That is so whether or not the saying relates to scriptural revelation. The content of the sayings attributed to sages endows those sayings with self-validating status. The sages usually do not quote verses of Scripture and explain them, nor do they speak in God's name. Yet, it is clear, sages talk Torah. What follows? It is this: if a sage says something, what he says is Torah. More accurately, what he says falls into the classification of Torah. Accordingly, Abot treats Torah learning as symptomatic, an indicator of the status of the sage, hence as merely instrumental. At issue in Abot is not Torah, but the authority of the sage. It is that standing that transforms a saying into a Torah saying, or that places a saying into the classification of Torah. Abot then stands as the first document of incipient rabbinism—the doctrine that the sage embodies the Torah and is a holy man, like Moses "our rabbi," in the likeness and image of God. First came the claim that a saying falls into the category of Torah if a sage says it as Torah. Then came the view that the sage himself was Torah incarnate.

To the rabbis the principal salvific deed was to study Torah, by which they meant memorizing Torah sayings by constant repetition. For some sages it meant profound analytic inquiry into the meanings of those sayings. The innovation now was that the study of Torah imparted supernatural power. For example, by repeating words of Torah, the sage could ward off the angel of death and accomplish other kinds of miracles as well. So Torah formulas served as incantations. Mastery of Torah transformed the man engaged in Torah-learning into a supernatural figure who could do things ordinary folk could not do. The category of Torah had already vastly expanded so that, through transformation of the Torah from a concrete thing to a symbol, a Torah scroll could be compared to a man of Torah, namely, a rabbi. Now, the principle had been established that salvation would come from keeping God's will in general, as Israelite holy men had insisted for so many centuries. So it was a small step for rabbis to identify their particular corpus of learning—the Mishnah and associated sayings—with God's will expressed in Scripture, the universally acknowledged medium of revelation.

The history of the symbolization of the Torah proceeded to its transformation into something quite different and abstract, quite distinct from the document and its teachings. In the history of the word Torah as abstract symbol, a metaphor serving to sort out one abstract status from another gained concrete and material reality of a new order. The message of Abot was that the Torah served the sage. How so? The Torah indicated who was a sage and who was not. Accordingly, the apology of Abot for the Mishnah was that the Mishnah contained things sages had said. What the sages said formed a chain of tradition extending back to Sinai. Hence it was equivalent to the Torah. The outcome was that words of sages enjoyed the status of the Torah. The small additional step was to claim that what sages said was Torah, as much as what Scripture said was Torah.

A further small step moved matters to the position that there were two media in which the Torah reached Israel: one in writing, the other handed on orally, that is, in memory. This final step, fully revealed in the Yerushalmi, brought the conception of Torah to its logical conclusion. Torah came in several media, written, oral, incarnate. So what the sage said was in the status of the Torah, was Torah, because the sage was Torah incarnate. The abstract symbol now had become concrete and material once again.

The Yerushalmi's theory of the Torah thus carries us through several stages in the symbolization of the word *Torah*. First transformed from something material and concrete into something abstract and beyond all metaphor, the word *Torah* finally emerged once more in a concrete aspect—now as the encompassing and universal mode of stating the whole doctrine, all at once, of Judaism in its formative age.

Teleology

The teleology of a system answers the question of purpose and goal. It explains why someone should do what the system requires. It may also spell out what will happen if someone does not do what the system demands. The Mishnah and its successor documents, Abot and the Tosefta in particular, present one picture of the purpose of the system as a whole, a teleology without eschatological focus. The two Talmuds—along with some intermediate documents—later laid forth an eschatological teleology. The documents do cohere. The Talmuds, beginning with the former of the two, carried forward not only the exegesis of the Mishnah but also the basic values of the Mishnah's system. But they presented substantial changes too. While what people said about the affective life remained constant, what they said about teleology shifted in substantial ways. The philosophers of the Mishnah did not make use of the Messiah myth in the construction of a teleology for their system. The appearance in the Talmuds of a messianic eschatology fully consonant with the larger characteristic of the rabbinic system indicated that the encompassing rabbinic system stood essentially autonomous of the prior, mishnaic system. True, what had gone before was absorbed and fully assimilated. But the talmudic system—expressed in part in each of the non-mishnaic segments of the canon and fully spelled out in all of them—was different in the aggregate from the mishnaic system.

The Mishnah and its closely related documents, Abot and the Tosefta, did not appeal to eschatology in their framing of their theory of teleology. They spoke more commonly about preparing in this world for life in the world to come, and the focus was on the individual and his or her personal salvation, rather than on the nation and its destiny at the end of time. So the Mishnah presented an ahistorical teleology, and did not make use of the Messiah theme to express its teleology. By contrast, the Talmuds provide an eschatological and therefore a Messiah-centered teleology for their system. Theirs is the more familiar teleology of Judaism, which, from the Yerushalmi on, commonly explains the end and meaning of the system by referring to the end of time and the coming of the Messiah. The Judaism that emerged from late antiquity therefore took shape as a profoundly eschatological and messianic statement.

The Mishnah's authorship constructed a system of Judaism in which the entire teleological dimension reached full exposure while hardly invoking the person or functions of a messianic figure of any kind. The Mishnah's noneschatological teleology presented a striking contrast to that of the Yerushalmi, which framed the teleological doctrine around the person of the Messiah. If, as in the Mishnah, what was important in Israel's existence was sanctification, an ongoing process, and not salvation, understood as a one-time event at the end, then no one would find reason to narrate history. Few then would form the obsession about the Messiah so characteristic of Judaism in its later, rabbinic mode.

Since the Mishnah does speak of a goal and end, we ask, where, if not in the end of time, do things end? The answer once more is provided by Abot. Death is the destination. In life we prepare for the voyage. Israel must keep the law in order to make the move required of us all. Abot constructed a teleology beyond time, providing a purposeful goal for every individual. Life is the antechamber, death the destination; what we do is weighed and measured. When we die, we stand on one side of the balance, while our life and deeds stand on the other.

In the Yerushalmi (and afterward in the Talmud of Babylonia, the Bavli), the situation changed radically. The figure of the Messiah loomed large in both documents. The teleology of the system portrayed in them rested upon the premise of the coming of the Messiah. If one does so and so, the Messiah will come, and if not, the Messiah will tarry. So the compilers and authors of the two Talmuds laid enormous emphasis upon the sin of Israel and the capacity of Israel through repentance both to overcome sin and to bring the Messiah. "The attribute of justice" delays the Messiah's coming. The Messiah will come this very day, if Israel deserves. The Messiah will come when there are no more arrogant (conceited) Israelites, when judges and officers disappear, when the haughty and judges cease to exist, "Today, if you will obey" (Ps. 95:7).

In the hands of the framers of the late canonical literature of Judaism, the Messiah served to keep things pretty much as they were, while at the same time promising dramatic change. The condition of that dramatic change was not richly instantiated. It was given in the most general terms. But it is not difficult to define. Israel had to keep God's will, expressed in the Torah and the observance of the rites described therein. So Israel would demonstrate its acceptance of God's rule. The net effect was to reinforce the larger system of the Judaism of Torah study and the doing of religious duties expressed partially in the Talmuds of the Land of Israel and of Babylonia, with their exegesis of the Mishnah, and partially in the various exegetical compositions organized around the order and program of some of the books of Scripture. It was first in the Yerushalmi that Judaism drew into its sphere the weighty conception embodied in the Messiah myth. The matter of the Messiah remained subordinated: "If you do this or that, the Messiah will come." So the Messiah myth supplied the fixed teleology for the variety of unavoidable demands of the system as a whole. But the symbolic expression of the system's teleology underwent remarkable revision, first surfacing in a late fourth-century composition.

What happened was that the rabbinic system of the Talmuds transformed the Messiah myth in its totality into an essentially ahistorical force. If people wanted to reach the end of time, they had to rise above time and stand off at the side of great ephemeral political and military movements. That was the message of the Messiah myth as it reached full exposure in the rabbinic system of the two Talmuds. At its foundation it was precisely the message of the teleology without eschatology expressed by the Mishnah and its associated documents. We cannot claim that the talmudic system constituted a reaction against the mishnaic one. To the contrary, we must conclude that in the Talmuds and their associated documents was the restatement, in classical-mythic form, of the ontological convictions that had informed the minds of the second-century philosophers of the Mishnah. The new medium contained the old, enduring message: Israel must turn away from time and change, submit to whatever happens, so as to win for itself the only government worth having—God's rule, accomplished through God's anointed agent, the Messiah.

THE CRISIS OF
THE FOURTH CENTURY

The fourth century marked the first century of Christian rule: the Judaism of the dual Torah would flourish in the West (as well as in the Islamic world), and Christianity in its political formulation would define and govern the civilization of the West. When, in the aftermath of Constantine's legalization of Christianity in 312 C.E., Christianity became first the most favored religion, then the established one, and finally, by the end of the fourth century, triumphant, the condition of Israel changed in some ways but not in others. What remained the same was the politics and social circumstance of a defeated nation. What changed was the context of the religious system of Judaism. The worldly situation of Israel did not change, but the setting of Judaism did. For while Israelites in the Land of Israel persisted as a subject people, Judaism confronted a world in which its principal components—interpretation, teleology, symbol—met an effective challenge in the corresponding components of the now-triumphant faith in Christ. Specifically, Christianity now demanded that the Hebrew Scriptures—the written Torah—be read as the Old Testament predicting the New. In the Christian view, the reason was that history proved that Scripture's prophetic promises of a king-Messiah pointed toward Jesus, now Christ enthroned. Concomitantly, in the Christians' mind the teleology of the Israelite system of old, focused as it was on the coming of the Messiah, found confirmation and realization in the rule of Jesus, Christ enthroned. And the symbol of the whole—interpretation and teleology alike—rose in heaven's heights: the cross that had triumphed at the Milvian Bridge.

Why did the conversion of the empire to Christianity make a difference to Israel's sages, although they had paid slight heed to Christianity in its prior apolitical condition? A move of the empire from reverence for Zeus to adoration of Mithra had meant nothing; paganism was what it was, lacking all differentiation in the Jewish eye. Christianity was something else. It was like Judaism. Christians read the Torah and claimed to declare its meaning. Accordingly, the trend of sages' speculation could not avoid the issue of the place, within the Torah's messianic pattern, of the remarkable turn in world history represented by the triumph of Christianity.

What in fact sages did at that time is clear. They composed the Yerushalmi (Talmud of the Land of Israel) as we know it. They collected exegeses of Scripture and made them into a systematic and sustained account, initially of the meaning of the Pentateuch.

In the fourth century the sages compiled exegeses of Scripture, as part of a Jewish apologetic response to what Christians had to say to Israel. For one Christian message had been that Israel "after the flesh" had distorted and continually misunderstood the meaning of what had been its own Scripture. Failing to read the Hebrew Scriptures in the light of the Christian New Testament, failing to read the prophetic promises in the perspective of Christ's fulfillment of those promises, Israel after the flesh had lost access to God's revelation to Moses at Sinai. If we were to propose a suitably powerful yet appropriately proud response, it would have two qualities. First, it would supply a complete account of what Scripture had meant and must always mean, as Israel read it. Second, it would do so in such a way as not to dignify the position of the other side with the grace of an explicit reply at all. The compilations of exegeses and the Yerushalmi that were accomplished at this time assuredly took up the challenge of restating the meaning of the Torah revealed by God to Moses at Mount Sinai. This the sages did in a systematic and thorough way. At the same time, if the charges of the other side had precipitated the work of compilation and composition, the consequent collections in no way suggest it. The issues of the documents were made always to emerge from the inner life not even of Israel in general but of the sages' estate in particular. Scripture was thoroughly rabbinized, as earlier it had been Christianized. None of this suggests that the other side had won a response for itself. Only the net effect—a complete picture of the whole, as Israel must perceive the whole of revelation—suggests the extraordinary utility for apologetics, outside as much as inside the faith, that was served by these compilations.

The changes at the surface, in articulated doctrines of teleology, interpretation, and symbolism, responded to changes in the political condition of Israel as well as in the religious foundations of the politics of the day. Paganism had presented a different and simpler problem to the sages. Christianity's explicit claims, validated in world-shaking events of the age, demanded a reply. The sages of the Talmud of the Land of Israel provided it. So it is at the very specific points at which the Christian challenge met head on old Israel's worldview that the sages' doctrines changed. What did Israel have to present to the cross? The Torah, in the doctrine of the status of the Mishnah as oral and memorized revelation and, by implication, of other rabbinical writings. The Torah in the encompassing symbol of Israel's salvation. The Torah, finally, in the person of the Messiah, who would of course be a rabbi. The Torah in all three modes confronted the cross, with its doctrine of the triumphant Christ, Messiah and King, ruler now of earth as of heaven.

9

The Talmud of the
Land of Israel, the Midrash,
and the Talmud of Babylonia

THE TALMUD OF THE
LAND OF ISRAEL

The Judaism of the dual Torah so successfully addressed the condition of Israel, the holy people, that its Judaism has predominated from late antiquity to our own day. The reason lay in its success in answering the two urgent questions made critical by the political changes in the Jews' condition: their loss of standing as a political entity, on the one side, and the triumph of Christianity in the Roman Empire, on the other. The Jews' condition, defined by Christianity and affirmed later by Islam, was subordination and, at best, toleration. For long centuries afterward, the Jews' Judaism drew upon the writings of the period at hand to address the now-chronic issues of political subordination and religious disappointment and resentment. Only when the world in which Jews lived found its definitions other than in Christianity, and the Jews' political circumstances were vastly changed from the ones that prevailed until the formation of the nation-state within the capitalist world, did new Judaisms emerge, each asking its urgent question and offering its self-evidently valid answer.

That explains the importance of the Talmud of the Land of Israel (Yerushalmi) as a commentary to and successor and heir of the Mishnah. The urgent question that predominates in that enormous document, which is given the form of an extended elaboration of the Mishnah, is the issue of salvation: When, why, and, above all, how long postponed? In answering these questions, the authors of the

Talmud of the Land of Israel completed the forming of the symbolic system of the Judaism of the dual Torah. For it is only in the Talmud of the Land of Israel and its closely allied documents, Genesis Rabbah and Leviticus Rabbah, ca. 400—450 C.E., that that Judaism's principal and indicative doctrines, symbols, and beliefs came to full and complete expression.

To understand how the Yerushalmi develops a conception of history and salvation at the end of time, we have to recall the Mishnah's theory of the same matter. Only in that context can we understand the full weight and meaning of the Yerushalmi's authors' rethinking of the basic categories of events and their meanings. To begin with, the framers of the Mishnah present us with a kind of historical thinking quite different from the one they, along with all Israel, had inherited in Scripture. The legacy of prophecy, apocalypse, and mythic history (*Heilsgeschichte*) handed on by the writers of the books of the Hebrew Scriptures exhibits a single and quite familiar conception of history seen whole. Events bear meaning, God's message, and judgment. What happens is singular, therefore, an event to be noted, and points toward lessons to be drawn concerning where things are heading and why. Although events do not happen randomly, neither do they form indifferent patterns of merely secular, social facts. Events are important because of their meaning. That meaning is to be discovered and revealed through the narrative of what has happened. So for all forms of Judaism until the Mishnah, the writing of history served as a form of prophecy. Just as prophecy takes up the interpretation of historical events, so historians retell these events in the frame of prophetic theses. And out of the two— historiography as a mode of mythic reflection, prophecy as a means of mythic construction—emerges a picture of future history, that is, a picture of what is going to happen. That picture, framed in terms of visions and supernatural symbols, in the end focuses upon the here and now, as much as do prophecy and history-writing.

By contrast, the Mishnah contains no sustained narrative whatsoever, only a very few tales, and no large-scale conception of history. It organizes its system in non-historical and socially unspecific terms, lacking all precedent in prior systems of Judaism or in prior kinds of Judaic literature. Instead of narrative, it gives description of how things are done, that is, descriptive laws. Instead of reflecting on the meaning and end of history, it constructs a world in which history

plays little part. Instead of narratives full of didactic meaning, it provides lists of events so as to expose the traits that they share and thus
the rules to which they conform. The definitive components of a
historical-eschatological system of Judaism—description of events as
one-time happenings, analysis of the meaning and end of events, and
interpretation of the end and future of singular events—were all commonplace constituents of all other systems of Judaism (including
nascent Christianity) in ancient times. But none of these components
finds a place in the Mishnah's system of Judaism.

Coming to the Talmud of the Land of Israel, let us first survey
what is new and striking. From the viewpoint of the Mishnah, as I
have suggested, the single most unlikely development is interest in
the history of a nation other than Israel. For the Mishnah views the
world beyond the sacred Land as unclean, tainted in particular with
corpse-uncleanness. Outside the holy lies the realm of death. The
faces of that world are painted in the monotonous white of the grave.
Only within the range of the sacred do things happen. There, events
may be classified and arranged, all in relationship to the Temple and
its cult. But, standing majestically unchanged by the vicissitudes of
time, the cult rises above history. Now the ancient Israelite interest in
the history of the great empires of the world—perceived, to be sure,
in relationship to the history of Israel—reemerges within the framework of the Yerushalmi, among all of the documents that succeeded
the Mishnah. Naturally, in the Land of Israel only one empire mattered—Rome, which in the Yerushalmi is viewed solely as the counterpart to Israel. The world then consists of two nations: Israel, the
weaker; Rome, the stronger. Jews enjoy a sense of vastly enhanced
importance when they contemplate such a world, containing as it
does only two peoples that matter, one of whom is Israel. But from
our perspective, the morale-building aspect for this defeated people
holds no interest. Rather, what strikes us is the evidence of the formation of a second and separate system of historical interpretation,
beyond the Mishnah's.

In the Yerushalmi, history and doctrine merge, with history
made to yield doctrine. What is stunning is the perception of Rome as
an autonomous actor, that is, as an entity with a point of origin, just
as Israel has a point of origin, and a tradition of wisdom, just as Israel
has such a tradition. These are the two points at which the large-scale
conception of historical Israel finds a counterpart in the present liter-

ary composition. This sense of poised opposites, Israel and Rome, comes to expression in two ways.

First, as we shall now see, it is Israel's own history that calls into being its counterpoint, the anti-history of Rome. Without Israel, there would be no Rome—a wonderful consolation to the defeated nation. For if Israel's sin created Rome's power, then Israel's repentance will bring Rome's downfall.

According to the Yerushalmi, Solomon's sin in marrying the daughter of the Egyptian pharaoh (1 Kings 3:1) provoked heaven's founding of Rome, thus history, lived by Israel, and provoking anti-history, lived by Rome.

Quite naturally, the conception of history and anti-history will assign to the actors in the anti-history—the Romans—motives explicable in terms of history, that is, the history of Israel. The entire world and what happens in it enter into the framework of meaning established by Israel's Torah. So what the Romans do, their historical actions, can be explained in terms of Israel's conception of the world. A striking example of the tendency to explain Romans' deeds through Israel's logic is the reason given for Trajan's war against the Jews:

Y. Sukkah 5:1

VII.

A. In the time of Tronianus, the evil one, a son was born to him on the ninth of Ab, and the Israelites were fasting.

B. His daughter died on Hanukkah, and the Israelites lit candles.

C. His wife sent a message to him, saying, "Instead of going out to conquer the barbarians, come and conquer the Jews, who have rebelled against you."

D. He thought that the trip would take ten days, but he arrived in five.

E. He came and found the Israelites occupied in study of the Light of Torah, with the following verse: "The Lord will bring a nation against you from afar, from the end of the earth, as swift as the eagle flies, a nation whose language you do not understand" (Deut. 28:49).

F. He said to them, "With what are you occupied?"

G. They said to him, "With thus-and-so."

H. He said to them, "That man [I] thought that it would take ten days to make the trip, but arrived in five days." His legions surrounded them and killed them.

I. He said to the women, "Obey my legions, and I shall not kill you."

J. They said to him, "What you did to the ones who have fallen do also to us who are yet standing."

K. He mingled their blood with the blood of their men, until the blood flowed into the ocean as far as Cyprus.

L. At that moment the horn of Israel was cut off, and it is not destined to return to its place until the son of David will come.

The source of what we might call "historical explanation" is important here, deriving, as it does, from the larger framework of sages' conviction. Trajan had done nothing except with God's help and by God's design. Here is another example:

Y. Gittin 5:7

I.

A. In the beginning the Romans decreed oppression against Judah, for they had a tradition in their hands from their forefathers that Judah had slain Esau, for it is written, "Your hand shall be on the neck of your enemies" (Gen. 49:8).

This means, again, that things make sense wholly in the categories of Torah. The world retains its logic, and Israel knows (and can manipulate) that logic.

At the foundations is the tension between Israel's God and pagan gods. That is, historical explanation here invokes the familiar polemic of Scripture. Accordingly, the development of an interest in Roman history—of a willingness to take as important the events in the history of some nation other than Israel—flows from an established (and rather wooden) notion of the world in which God and gods (idols) compete. Israel's history of subjugation testifies not to the weakness but to the strength of Israel's God. The present prosperity of idolaters, involving the subjugation of Israel, attests only to God's remarkable patience, God's love for the world he made.

The concept of two histories balanced opposite one another comes to particular expression, with the Yerushalmi, in the balance of Israelite sage and Roman emperor. Just as Israel and Rome, God and no-gods, compete, with a foreordained conclusion, so do sage and emperor. In this age, it appears that the emperor has the power, as does Rome, as do the pagan gods with their temples in full glory. God's Temple, by contrast, lies in ruins. But just as sages overcome the emperor through their inherent supernatural power, so, too, will Israel and Israel's God control the course of events in the coming age.

The Mishnah finds ample place for debates between "philosophers" and rabbis. But in the Mishnah the high priest in the Temple and the king upon his throne do not weigh in the balance or stand poised against the equal and opposite powers of the pagan priest in his temple and the Roman emperor on his throne. The very conception is inconceivable within the context of the Mishnah. In the Yerushalmi, by contrast, two stunning innovations appear: (1) the notion of emperor and sage in mortal struggle; and (2) the idea of an age of idolatry and an age beyond idolatry. The world had to move into a new orbit indeed for Rome to enter into the historical context formerly defined wholly by what happened to Israel.

To our secular eyes these developments seem perfectly natural. After all, the Jews really had been conquered. Their Temple really had been destroyed. So why should they not have taken an interest in the history of the conqueror and tried to place the things that happened to him into relationship with their own history? We find self-evident, moreover, the comfort to be derived from the explanations consequent upon the inclusion of Roman history in the Yerushalmi's doctrine of the world. But Israel had been defeated many times before the composition of the Mishnah, and the Temple had lain in ruins for nearly a century and a half when Judah the Patriarch promulgated the Mishnah as Israel's code of law. So the circumstances in which the Yerushalmi's materials were composed hardly differed materially from the condition in which, from Bar Kokhba onward, sages selected from what was available and composed the Mishnah.

The Scriptures that, after all, also lay to hand offered testimony to the centrality of history as a sequence of meaningful events. To the message and uses of history as a source of teleology for an Israelite system, biblical writings amply testified. Prophecy and apocalyptic had long coped quite well with defeat and dislocation. Yet, in the Mishnah, Israel's deeds found no counterpart in Roman history, while in the Yerushalmi they did. In the Mishnah, time is differentiated entirely in other than national-historical categories. For, as in Abot, "this world" is when one is alive; "the world to come" is when a person dies. True, we also find "this world" and "the time of the Messiah." But detailed differentiation among the ages of "this world" or "this age" hardly generates problems in mishnaic thought. Indeed, no such differentiation appears. Accordingly, the developments briefly outlined up to this point constitute a significant shift in the course of intellectual events to which the sources at hand—the Mishnah, Tosefta, and Yerushalmi of the Land of Israel—amply testify.

The most important change is the shift in historical thinking suggested in the pages of the Yerushalmi, a shift from focusing on the Temple and its supernatural history to focusing on the people, Israel, and its natural, this-worldly history. Once Israel, holy Israel, had come to form the counterpart to the Temple and its supernatural life, that other history—Israel's—would stand at the center of things. Accordingly, a new sort of memorable event came to the fore in the Yerushalmi. Let me give this new history appropriate emphasis: it was the story of the suffering of Israel, the remembrance of that suffering, on the one side, and the effort to explain events of that tragic kind, on the other. So a composite "history" constructed out of the Yerushalmi's units of discourse pertinent to consequential events would contain long chapters on what happened to Israel, the Jewish people, and not only, or mainly, what had earlier occurred in the Temple.

This expansion in the range of historical interest and theme forms the counterpart to the emphasis throughout the law on the enduring sanctity of Israel, the people, which paralleled the sanctity of the Temple in its time. What is striking in the Yerushalmi's materials on Israel's suffering is the sages' interest in finding a motive for the Romans' actions. That motive derived specifically from the repertoire of explanations already available in Israelite thought. In adducing scriptural reasons for the Roman policy, as we saw, sages extended to the world at large that same principle of intelligibility, in terms of Israel's own Scripture and logic that, in the law itself, made everything sensible and reliable. So the labor of history-writing (or at least, telling stories about historical events) went together with the work of law-making. The whole formed a single exercise in explanation of things that had happened—that is, historical explanation. True, one enterprise involved historical events, the other legal constructions. But the outcome was one and the same.

The components of the historical theory of Israel's sufferings were manifold. First and foremost, history taught moral lessons. Historical events entered into the construction of a teleology for the Yerushalmi's system of Judaism as a whole. What the law demanded reflected the consequences of wrongful action on the part of Israel. So, again, Israel's own deeds defined the events of history. Rome's role, like Assyria's and Babylonia's, depended upon Israel's provoking divine wrath, executed by the great empire.

The paradox of the Yerushalmi's system lies in the fact that Israel frees itself from control by other nations only by humbly agreeing to accept God's rule instead. The nations—Rome, in the present instance—rest in one pan of the balance, while God rests, as it were, in the other. Israel must then choose between them. There is no such thing, for Israel, as freedom from both God and the nations, total autonomy and independence. There is only a choice of masters, a ruler on earth or a ruler in heaven.

With propositions such as these, the framers of the Mishnah will assuredly have concurred. And why not? For the fundamental affirmations of the Mishnah about the centrality of Israel's perfection in stasis—sanctification—readily prove congruent to the attitudes at hand. Once the Messiah's coming had become conditional upon Israel's condition, not upon Israel's actions in historical time, then the Mishnah's system will have imposed its fundamental and definitive character upon the Messiah myth. An eschatological teleology framed through that myth then will prove wholly appropriate to the method of the larger system of the Mishnah.

What, after all, makes a messiah a false messiah? In this Yerushalmi, it is not his claim to save Israel, but his claim to save Israel without the help of God. The meaning of the true Messiah is Israel's total submission, through the Messiah's gentle rule, to God's yoke and service. So God is not be manipulated through Israel's humoring heaven in rite and cult. The notion of keeping the commandments so as to please heaven and get God to do what Israel wants is a nakedly manipulative system that is totally incongruent to the text at hand. Keeping the commandments as a mark of submission, loyalty, and humility before God is what marks the rabbinic system of salvation. So Israel does not "save itself." Israel never controls its own destiny, either on earth or in heaven. The only choice is whether to cast one's fate into the hands of cruel, deceitful men, or to trust in the living God of mercy and love. We shall now see how this critical position is spelled out in the setting of discourse about the Messiah in the Yerushalmi of the Land of Israel.

Bar Kokhba exemplifies, above all, arrogance against God. He lost the war because of that arrogance. In particular, he ignored the authority of sages:

Y. Taanit 4:5

X.

J.   Said R. Yohanan, "Upon orders of Caesar Hadrian, in Betar they killed eight hundred thousand."

K.   Said R. Yohanan, "There were eighty thousand pairs of trumpeteers surrounding Betar. Each one was in charge of a number of troops. Ben Kozeba was there, and he had two hundred thousand troops who, as a sign of loyalty, had cut off their little fingers.

L.   "Sages sent word to him, 'How long are you going to turn Israel into a maimed people?'

M.   "He said to them, 'How otherwise is it possible to test them?'

N.   "They replied to him, 'Whoever cannot uproot a cedar of Lebanon while riding on his horse will not be inscribed on your military rolls.'

O.   "So there were two hundred thousand who qualified in one way, and another two hundred thousand who qualified in another way."

P.   When he would go forth to battle, he would say, "Lord of the world! Do not help and do not hinder us! 'Hast thou not rejected us, O God? Thou dost not go forth, O God, with our armies' " (Ps. 60:10).

Q.   Three and a half years did Hadrian besiege Betar.

R.   R. Eleazar of Modiin would sit on sackcloth and ashes and pray every day, saying "Lord of the ages! Do not judge in accord with strict judgment this day!"

S.   Hadrian wanted to go to him. A Samaritan said to him, "Do not go to him, until I see what he is doing, and so hand over the city [of Betar] to you. ['Make peace . . . for you.']"

T.   He got into the city through a drain pipe. He went and found R. Eleazar of Modiin standing and praying. He pretended to whisper something into his ear.

U.   The townspeople saw [the Samaritan] do this and brought him to Ben Kozeba. They told him, "We saw this man having dealings with your friend."

V.   [Bar Kokhba] said to him, "What did you say to him, and what did he say to you?"

W.   He said to [the Samaritan], "If I tell you, then the king will kill me, and if I do not tell you, then you will kill me. It is better that the king kill me, and not you.

X.   "[Eleazar] said to me, 'I should hand over my city.' ['I shall make peace . . .']."

Y.   He turned to R. Eleazar of Modiin. He said to him, "What did this Samaritan say to you?"

Z.   He replied, "Nothing."

AA. He said to him, "What did you say to him?"

BB. He said to him, "Nothing."

CC. [Ben Kozeba] gave [Eleazar] one good kick and killed him.

DD. Forthwith an echo came forth and proclaimed the following verse:

EE. "Woe to my worthless shepherd, who deserts the flock! May the sword smite his arm and his right eye! Let his arm be wholly withered, his right eye utterly blinded!" (Zech. 11:17).

FF. "You have murdered R. Eleazar of Modiin, the right arm of all Israel, and their right eye. Therefore may the right arm of that man wither, may his right eye be utterly blinded!"

GG. Forthwith Betar was taken, and Ben Kozeba was killed.

We notice two complementary themes. First, Bar Kokhba treats heaven with arrogance, asking God merely to keep out of the way. Second, he treats an especially revered sage with a similar arrogance. The sage had the power to preserve Israel. Bar Kokhba destroyed Israel's one protection. The result was inevitable.

Now in noticing the remarkable polemic in the story, in favor of sages' rule over that of Israelite strong men, we should not lose sight of the importance of the tale for our present argument about the Messiah and history.

First, the passage quite simply demonstrates an interest in narrating events other than those involving the Temple, on the one side, and the sages in court, on the other. This story and numerous others not quoted here testify to the emergence of a new category of history (or reemergence of an old one), namely, the history not of the supernatural cult but of Israel the people. It indicates that, for the framers of those units of the Yerushalmi that are not concerned with Mishnah-exegesis, and for the editors who selected materials for the final document, the history of Israel the people had now attained importance and demanded its rightful place. Once Israel's history thus reached center stage, a rich heritage of historical thought would be invoked.

Second, at that point the Messiah, centerpiece of the history of salvation and hero of the tale, would emerge as a critical figure. The historical theory of the framers of this Yerushalmi passage is stated very simply. In their view Israel had to choose between the war fought by Bar Kokhba and the "war for Torah." "Why had they been punished? It was because of the weight of the war, for they had not wanted to engage in the struggles over the meaning of the Torah" (Y. Taan. 3:9 XVI.I). Those struggles, that is, ritual arguments about ritual matters, promised the one victory worth winning. Israel's history then would be written in terms of wars over the meaning of the Torah and the decision of the law.

True, the skins are new. But the wine is very old. For while we speak of sages and learning, the message is the familiar one. It is Israel's history that works out and expresses Israel's relationship with God. The critical dimension of Israel's life, therefore, is salvation, the definitive trait, movement in time from now to then. It follows that the paramount and organizing category is history and its lessons. As I suggested at the outset, in the Yerushalmi we witness, among the Mishnah's heirs, a striking reversion to biblical convictions about the centrality of history in the definition of Israel's reality. The heavy weight of prophecy, apocalyptic, and biblical historiography, with their emphasis upon salvation and on history as the indicator of Israel's salvation, stood against the Mishnah's quite separate thesis of what truly mattered. What, from their viewpoint, demanded description and analysis and required interpretation? It was the category of sanctification for eternity. The true issue framed by history and apocalypse was how to move toward the foreordained end of salvation, how to act in time so as to reach salvation at the end of time. The Mishnah's teleology beyond time, its capacity to posit an eschatology lacking all place for a historical Messiah take a position beyond the imagination of the entire antecedent sacred literature of Israel. Only one strand, the priestly one, had ever taken so extreme a position on the centrality of sanctification and the peripherality of salvation. Wisdom had stood in between with its own concerns, drawing attention both to what happened and to what endured. To wisdom, however, what finally mattered was not nature or supernature but abiding relationships in historical time.

This reversion by the authors of the Yerushalmi to Scripture's paramount motifs, with Israel's history and destiny foremost among them, forms a complement to the Yerushalmi's principal judgment upon the Mishnah itself. This is because an important exegetical initiative of the Yerushalmi was to provide, for statements of the Mishnah, proof-texts deriving from Scripture. Whereas the framers of the Mishnah did not think their statements required evidentiary support, the authors of the Yerushalmi's Mishnah-exegetical units of discourse took proof-texts drawn from Scripture to be the prime necessity. Accordingly, at hand is yet another testimony to the effort among third- and fourth-century heirs of the Mishnah to draw that document back within the orbit of Scripture, to "biblicize" what the Mishnah's authors had sent forth as a free-standing and "nonbiblical" Torah.

The framers of the Mishnah had found it possible to construct a complete and encompassing teleology for their system with scarcely a single word said about the Messiah's coming, the time when the system would be perfectly achieved. So with their interest in explaining events and accounting for history, third- and fourth-century sages represented in the units of discourse at hand invoked what their predecessors had at best found of peripheral consequence to their system. The following contains the most striking expression of the viewpoint at hand.

Y. Taanit 1:1

X.

J. "The oracle concerning Dumah. One is calling to me from Seir, 'Watchman, what of the night? Watchman, what of the night?' " (Isa. 21:11).

K. The Israelites said to Isaiah, "O our Rabbi, Isaiah, What will come for us out of this night?"

L. He said to them, "Wait for me, until I can present the question."

M. Once he had asked the question, he came back to them.

N. They said to him, "Watchman, what of the night? What did the Guardian of the ages tell you?"

O. He said to them, "The watchman says 'Morning comes; and also the night. If you will inquire, inquire; come back again' " (Isa. 21:12).

P. They said to him, "Also the night?"

Q. He said to them, "It is not what you are thinking. But there will be morning for the righteous, and night for the wicked, morning for Israel, and night for idolaters."

R. They said to him, "When?"

S. He said to them, "Whenever you want, he too wants [it to be]—if you want it, he wants it."

T. They said to him, "What is standing in the way?"

U. He said to them, "Repentance: 'Come back again' " (Isa. 21:12).

V. R. Aha in the name of R. Tanhum b. R. Hiyya, "If Israel repents for one day, forthwith the son of David will come.

W. "What is the scriptural basis? 'O that today you would hearken to his voice!' " (Ps. 95:7).

X. Said R. Levi, "If Israel would keep a single Sabbath in the proper way, forthwith the son of David will come.

Y. "What is the scriptural basis for this view? 'Moses said, Eat it today, for today is a sabbath to the Lord; today you will not find it in the field' (Exod. 16:25).

Z. "And it says, 'For thus said the Lord God, the Holy One of Israel, "In returning and rest you shall be saved; in quietness and in trust shall be your strength." And you would not' " (Isa. 30:15).

The discussion of the power of repentance would hardly have surprised a Mishnah sage. What is new is at V–Z, the explicit linkage of keeping the law with achieving the end of time and the coming of the Messiah. That motif stands separate from the notions of righteousness and repentance, which surely do not require it. So the condition of "all Israel," a social category in historical time, comes under consideration, and not only the status of individual Israelites in life and in death. The latter had formed the arena for Abot's account of the Mishnah's system's meaning. Now history as an operative category, drawing in its wake Israel as a social entity, comes once more on the scene. But, except for the Mishnah's sages, it had never left the stage.

We must not lose sight of the importance of this passage, with its emphasis on repentance, on the one side, and the power of Israel to reform itself, on the other. The Messiah will come any day that Israel makes it possible. If all Israel will keep a single Sabbath in the proper (rabbinic) way, the Messiah will come. If all Israel will repent for one day, the Messiah will come. "Whenever you want," the Messiah will come. Two things are happening here. First, the system of religious observance, including study of Torah, is explicitly invoked as having salvific power. Second, the persistent hope of the people for the coming of the Messiah is linked to the system of rabbinic observance and belief. In this way, the austere program of the Mishnah, with no trace of a promise that the Messiah will come if and when the system is fully realized, undergoes a new development. A teleology lacking all eschatological dimension here gives way to an explicitly messianic statement that the purpose of the law is to attain Israel's salvation: "If you want it, God wants it, too." The one thing Israel commands is its own heart; the power it yet exercises is the power to repent. These suffice. The entire history of humanity will respond to Israel's will, to what happens in Israel's heart and soul. And, with the Temple in ruins, repentance can take place only within the heart and mind.

The framers of the Yerushalmi took over a document that portrayed a system centered upon sanctifying Israel through the creation of a world in stasis, wholly perfect within itself. They left behind them a document in which that original goal of sanctification in stasis competed with another. For within the pages of the Yerushalmi of the Land of Israel we find a second theory of what matters in Israel's life.

A system centered on the salvation of Israel in a world moving toward a goal, a world to be perfected only at the conclusion of the journey through time, now came to full expression. So the bridge formed by the Yerushalmi of the Land of Israel leads from a world in which nothing happens but sanctification is, to one in which everything happens en route to salvation at the end.

THE MIDRASH: GENESIS RABBAH
AND LEVITICUS RABBAH

Genesis Rabbah

Genesis Rabbah in the aggregate responds to the question of the meaning of history, in particular, the history of Israel confronted by the triumph of its sibling-enemy. To find that meaning at the end, sages turned to the picture of creation in the beginning. That is why, in the book of Genesis, as the sages who composed Genesis Rabbah saw things, God set forth to Moses the entire scope and meaning of Israel's history among the nations and salvation at the end of days. They read Genesis not as a set of individual verses, one by one, but as a single and coherent statement, whole and complete. In a few words let me restate the conviction of the framers of Genesis Rabbah about the message and meaning of the book of Genesis:

We now know what will be in the future. How do we know it? Just as Jacob had told his sons what would happen in time to come, just as Moses told the tribes their future, so we may understand the laws of history if we study the Torah. And in the Torah, we turn to beginnings: the rules as they were laid out at the very start of human history. These we find in the book of Genesis, the story of the origins of the world and of Israel.

The Torah tells us not only what happened but why. The Torah permits us to discover the laws of history. Once we know those laws, we may also peer into the future and come to an assessment of what is going to happen to us—and, especially, of how we shall be saved from our present existence. Because everything exists under the aspect of a timeless will, God's will, and all things express one thing, God's program and plan, in the Torah we uncover the workings of God's will. Our task as Israel is to accept, endure, submit, and celebrate.

To the rabbis who created Genesis Rabbah, the book of Genesis told the story of Israel, the Jewish people, in the here and now. The principle was that what happened to the patriarchs and matriarchs signaled what would happen to their descendants: the model of the ancestors sent a message for the children. So the importance of Genesis, as the sages of Genesis Rabbah read the book, derived not from its lessons about the past but its message for Israel's present and, especially, its future. Their conviction was that what Abraham, Isaac, and Jacob did shaped the future history of Israel. In line with the Mishnah's view, sages maintained that the world reveals not chaos but order, and God's will works itself out not once but again and again. Bringing to the stories of Genesis the conviction that the book of Genesis told not only the story of yesterday but also the tale of tomorrow, the sages transformed a picture of the past into a prophecy for a near tomorrow.

At the beginning of the fifth century, sages entertained deep forebodings about Israel's prospects. In Genesis Rabbah every word of Genesis was read against the background of the world-historical change that had taken place in the time of the formation of the document. The people who compiled the materials made a statement through what they selected and arranged. Let me give one concrete example of how sages responded in Genesis Rabbah. Rome now claimed to be Israel, that is, Christian and heir to the testament of the founders. Sages of Genesis Rabbah did not deny it, they affirmed it: Rome is Esau, or Moab, or Ishmael. "We are Israel." To them Genesis talked about the here and now, "about us, Israel, and about our sibling, Rome." That concession—Rome is a sibling, a close relative of Israel—represented an implicit recognition of Christianity's claim to share the patrimony of Judaism, to be descended from Abraham and Isaac. To deal with the glory and the power of our brother, Esau, and to assess today the future history of Israel, the salvation of God's first, best love, sages took the simple tack of restating matters already clear in Scripture. That is, it was not by denying Rome's claim but by evaluating it.

In Genesis Rabbah sages represented Rome as Israel's brother, counterpart, and nemesis. Rome was the one thing standing in the way of Israel's ultimate salvation and the world's. It was not a political Rome but a messianic Rome that was at issue: Rome as surrogate for Israel, Rome as obstacle to Israel. The reason of course was that Rome now confronted Israel with a crisis, and Genesis Rabbah constituted a response to that crisis. In the fourth century Rome became Christian. Sages responded by facing that fact quite squarely and saying, "Indeed, it is as you say, a kind of Israel, an heir of Abraham as your texts explicitly claim. But we remain the sole legitimate Israel, the bearer of the birthright—we and not you. So you are our brother: Esau, Ishmael, Edom." By rereading the story of the beginnings, sages discovered the answer and the secret of the end. Rome claimed to be Israel, and indeed, sages conceded, Rome shared the patrimony of Israel. That claim took the form of the Christians' appropriation of the Torah as their Old Testament, so sages acknowledged a simple fact in acceding to the notion that, in some way, Rome, too, formed part of Israel. But it was the rejected part, the Ishmael, the Esau, not the Isaac, not the Jacob. The advent of Christian Rome precipitated the sustained, polemical, and rigorous, and well-argued rereading of beginnings in light of the end. Rome then marked the conclusion of human history as Israel had known it. Beyond lay the coming of the true Messiah, the redemption of Israel, the salvation of the world, and the end of time.

Let us consider a simple example of how ubiquitous the shadow of Ishmael/Esau/Edom/Rome was. Wherever sages reflected on future history, their minds turned to their own day. They found the hour difficult, because Rome, now Christian, claimed the very birthright and blessing that they understood to be theirs alone. Christian Rome posed a threat without precedent. Now another dominion besides Israel's claimed the rights and blessings that sustained Israel. Wherever in Scripture they turned, sages found comfort in the message that the birthright, the blessing, the Torah, and the hope all belonged to them and to none other. Here is a striking statement of that constant proposition.

Genesis Rabbah LIII:XII.

1.

A. "[So she said to Abraham, 'Cast out this slave woman with her son, for the son of this slave woman shall not be heir with my son Isaac.'] And the thing was very displeasing to Abraham on account of his son" (Gen. 21:11).

B. That is in line with this verse: "And shuts his eyes from looking upon evil" (Isa. 33:15). [Freedman, p. 471 n. 1: He shut his eyes from Ishmael's evil ways and was reluctant to send him away.]

2.

A. "But God said to Abraham, 'Be not displeased because of the lad and because of your slave woman; whatever Sarah says to you, do as she tells you, for through Isaac shall your descendants be named' " (Gen. 21:12).

B. Said R. Yudan bar Shillum, "What is written is not 'Isaac' but 'through Isaac.' [The matter is limited, not through all of Isaac's descendants but only through some of them, thus excluding Esau.]"

Among the descendants of Isaac will be found Abraham's heirs, but not all the descendants of Isaac will be heirs of Abraham. Number 2, above, explicitly excludes Esau, that is, Rome. As the several antagonists of Israel stood for Rome in particular, so the traits of Rome, as sages perceived them, characterized the biblical heroes. Esau provided a favorite target. Israel and Rome contended from the womb. Specifically, Esau hated Israel even while he was still in the womb. Jacob, for his part, revealed from the womb those virtues that would characterize him later on. He was as eager to serve God as Esau was eager to worship idols. The ambiguous status of Rome as Christian brought sages to compare Rome to the swine, which in one trait appeared to be acceptable but in reality was unacceptable.

Genesis Rabbah LXV:I

1.

A. "When Esau was forty years old, he took to wife Judith, the daughter of Beeri, the Hittite, and Basemath the daughter of Elon the Hittite; and they made life bitter for Isaac and Rebecca" (Gen. 26:34–35).

B. "The swine out of the wood ravages it, that which moves in the field feeds on it" (Ps. 80:14).

C. R. Phineas and R. Hilqiah in the name of R. Simon: "Among all of the prophets, only two of them spelled out in public [the true character of Rome, represented by the swine], Asaf and Moses.

D. "Asaf: 'The swine out of the wood ravages it.'

E. "Moses: 'And the swine, because he parts the hoof' (Deut. 14:8).

F. "Why does Moses compare Rome to the swine? Just as the swine, when it crouches, puts forth its hoofs as if to say, 'I am clean,' so the wicked kingdom steals and grabs, while pretending to be setting up courts of justice.

G. "So Esau, for all forty years, hunted married women, ravished them, and when he reached the age of forty, he presented himself to his father, saying, 'Just as father got married at the age of forty, so I shall marry a wife at the age of forty.'

H. " 'When Esau was forty years old, he took to wife Judith, the daughter of Beeri, the Hittite, and Basemath the daughter of Elon the Hittite.' "

The exegesis of course once more identified Esau with Rome. The roundabout route linked Esau's taking a wife with Roman duplicity. Whatever the government did it claimed to do in the general interest. But it really had no public interest at all. Esau for his part spent all forty years pillaging women and then, at the age of forty, pretended to his father to be upright. That, at any rate, was the parallel clearly intended by this obviously unitary composition. The issue of the selection of the intersecting verse does not present an obvious solution to me; it seems to me that only the identification of Rome with the swine accounts for the choice.

Identifying Rome as Esau was a fresh idea. In the Mishnah, two hundred years earlier, Rome appeared as a place, not as a symbol. But in Genesis Rabbah, Rome was symbolized by Esau. Why Esau in particular? Because Esau was sibling: relation, competitor, enemy, brother. In choosing Rome as the counterpart to Israel, sages simply opened Genesis and found there Israel, that is, Jacob, and his brother, his enemy Esau. So why not understand the obvious: Esau stood for Rome, Jacob for Israel, and their relationship represented what Israel and Rome would work out even then, in the fourth century, the first century of Christian rule. So Esau ruled now, but Jacob possessed the birthright. Esau/Rome was the last of the four great empires (Persia,

Media, Greece, Rome). On the other side of Rome? Israel's age of glory. And why was Rome now brother? Because, after all, the Christians did claim a common patrimony in the Hebrew Scriptures and did claim to form part of Israel. The claim was not ignored; it was answered: yes, part of Israel, the rejected part. Jacob bore the blessing and transmitted the blessing to humanity, Esau did not. Such a message bore meaning only in its context. So in a concrete way Genesis talked about "us," Israel, and about "our sibling," Rome. That concession—Rome was a sibling, a close relative of Israel—represented an implicit recognition of Christianity's claim to share the patrimony of Judaism, to be descended from Abraham and Isaac. So how to deal with the glory and the power of our brother, Esau? And what were they to say about the claim of Esau to enthrone Christ? And how to assess the future history of Israel, the salvation of God's first, best love? It was not by denying Rome's claim but by evaluating it, not by turning a back to the critical events of the hour but by confronting those events forcefully and authoritatively.

Leviticus Rabbah

Leviticus Rabbah deals with a biblical book, not a Mishnah tractate. But it approaches that book with a fresh plan, one in which exegesis does not dictate rhetoric, and in which amplification of an established text (whether Scripture or Mishnah) does not supply the underlying logic by which sentences are made to compose paragraphs, or completed thoughts. The framers of Leviticus Rabbah treated topics, not particular verses. They made generalizations that were freestanding. They expressed cogent propositions through extended compositions, not episodic ideas. Earlier, things people wished to say were attached to predefined statements based on an existing text and constructed in accord with an organizing logic independent of the systematic expression of a single, well-framed idea. Now the authors collected and arranged their materials so that an abstract proposition emerged. The proposition was not expressed only or mainly through episodic restatements assigned to an order established by a basetext. Rather it emerged through a logic of its own. The framers of the composition undertook to offer propositions in which they said what they had in mind through the exegesis of verses of Scripture not in the order of Scripture, but through an order dictated by their own sense of the logic of syllogistic composition. To begin with, they laid down their own topical program, related to but essentially autonomous of that of the book of Leviticus. Second, in expressing their ideas on these topics, they never undertook simply to cite a verse of Scripture and then to claim that the verse stated precisely what they had in mind to begin with. The framers said what they wished to say in their own way—just as had the authors of the Mishnah itself. In so doing, the composers of Leviticus Rabbah treated Scripture as had their predecessors; to them as to those who had gone before, Scripture provided a rich treasury of facts.

Statements in the Leviticus Rabbah became intelligible not on the strength of an established text, but on the basis of a deeper logic of meaning. Leviticus Rabbah is topical, not exegetical. Each of its thirty-seven parashiyyot (chapters) pursues its given topic and develops points relevant to that topic. In Leviticus Rabbah, rabbis took up the problem of saying what they wished to say not in an exegetical, but in a syllogistic and freely discursive logic and rhetoric. Just as the Mishnah marked a radical break from all prior literature produced by Jews, so Leviticus Rabbah marked a stunning departure from all prior literature produced by rabbis. Since these rabbis defined Judaism as we have known it from their time to ours, we rightly turn to the book at hand for evidence about how the Scripture entered into, was absorbed by, and reached full status as the foundation document of the Judaism taking shape at this time.

The dominant exegetical construction in Leviticus Rabbah was the base–verse/intersecting–verse exegesis. In this construction, a verse of Leviticus was cited (hence, base verse), and then another verse from such books as Job, Proverbs, Qohelet, or Psalms was cited. The latter, not the former, was subjected to detailed and systematic exegesis. But the exegetical exercise ended up by leading the intersecting verse back to the base verse and reading the latter in terms of the former. In such an exercise, what in fact do we do? We read one thing in terms of something else. To begin with, it is the base verse in terms of the intersecting verse. But it also is the intersecting verse in other terms as well—a multiple-layered construction of analogy and parable. The intersecting verse's elements always turn out to stand for, to signify, and to speak of something other than that to which they openly refer. Nothing says what it means. Everything important speaks elliptically, allegorically, and symbolically. All statements carry deeper meaning, which belongs to other statements altogether. The profound sense of the base verse emerges only through restatement within and through the intersecting verse—as if the base verse spoke of things that we do not see on the surface.

People who see things this way do not call a thing as it is. They have become accustomed to perceiving more or less than is at hand. Perhaps that was a natural mode of thought for the Jews of this period, so long used to calling themselves God's first love, yet now seeing others claiming that same advantaged relationship with greater worldly reason. The radical disjuncture between the way things were and the way Scripture said things were supposed to be and would some day become surely imposed an unbearable tension. It was one thing for the slave born to slavery to endure. It was another for the free man sold into slavery to accept that same condition. The vanquished people had lost its city and its Temple and had produced another nation from its midst to take over its Scripture and much else; it could not bear too much reality. So the defeated people found refuge in a mode of thought that trained vision to see things otherwise than as the eyes perceived them. Among the diverse ways by which the weak and subordinated accommodate to their circumstance, the one of iron-willed pretense in life is most likely to yield the mode of thought at hand: things never are what they seem because they cannot be.

Reading one thing in terms of another, the builders of the document systematically adapted for themselves the reality of the Scripture, its history and doctrines. They transformed that history from a sequence of one-time events, leading from one thing to another, into an ever-present mythic world. No longer was there one Moses, one David, or one set of happenings of a distinctive and never-to-be-repeated character. Now whatever happened of which the thinkers proposed to take account had to enter and be absorbed into that established and ubiquitous pattern and structure founded in Scripture. It was not that biblical history repeated itself. But biblical history was no longer a story of things that had happened once, long ago, and pointed to one moment in the future. Rather it became an account of things that happen every day in an ever-present mythic world.

We turn from the mode of thought to the message of the document for the age of its formulation, the fourth and early fifth centuries. The recurrent message may be stated in a single paragraph:

God loves Israel, and so gave them the Torah, which defines their life and governs their welfare. Israel is alone in its category, so what is a virtue to Israel is a vice to the nation, life-giving to Israel, but poison to the Gentiles. Israel sins, but God forgives that sin, having punished the nation on account of it. Such a process has yet to come to an end, but it will culminate in Israel's complete regeneration. Meanwhile, Israel's assurance of God's love lies in his many expressions of special concern for even the humblest and most ordinary aspects of the national life: the food the nation eats, and the sexual practices by which it procreates. These life-sustaining, life-transmitting activities draw God's special interest, as a mark of his general love for Israel. Israel must achieve its life in conformity with the marks of God's love. These indications also signify the character of Israel's difficulty, namely, subordination to the nations in general but to the fourth kingdom, Rome, in particular. Both food laws and skin diseases stand for the nations. The social category of sin is also collective and brings about collective punishment. Bad treatment of people by one another, gossip, and small-scale thuggery draw down divine penalty. The nation's fate therefore corresponds to its moral condition. The moral condition emerges not only from the current generation. Israel's richest hope lies in the merit of the ancestors, thus in the scriptural record of the merits attained by the founders of the nation, those who originally brought it into being and gave it life. The world to come upon the nation is so portrayed as to restate these same propositions. Merit overcomes sin, and doing religious duties or supererogatory acts of kindness will win merit for the nation that does them. Israel will be saved at the end of time, and the world to follow will be exactly the opposite of this one. Much that we find in the account of Israel's national life recurs in slightly altered form in the picture of the world to come.

The one-time events—the flood, Sodom and Gomorrah, the patriarchs and the sojourn in Egypt, the exodus, the revelation of the Torah at Sinai, the golden calf, the Davidic monarchy and the building of the Temple, Sennacherib, Hezekiah, and the destruction of northern Israel, Nebuchadnezzar and the destruction of the Temple in 586, the life of Israel in Babylonian captivity, Daniel and his associates, Mordecai and Haman—occurred over and over again. They served as patterns of sin and atonement, steadfastness and divine intervention, and equivalent lessons. We find, in fact, a fairly standard repertoire of scriptural heroes or villains, on the one side, and conventional lists of Israel's enemies and their actions and downfall, on the other. The boastful, for instance, included (in Lev. Rab. VII. VI) the generation of the flood, Sodom and Gomorrah, Pharaoh, Sisera, Sennacherib, Nebuchadnezzar, and the wicked empire (Rome)—contrasted to Israel, "despised and humble in this world." The four kingdoms recurred again and again, always ending with Rome, and with the repeated message that after Rome will come Israel. But Israel had to make this happen through its faith and submission to God's will. Lists of enemies rang the changes on Cain, the Sodomites, Pharaoh, Sennacherib, Nebuchadnezzar, and Haman.

The mode of thought brought to bear upon the theme of history remained exactly the same as before: list-making, with similar traits drawn together into lists based on common traits. The lists were repeated to make a single enormous point or prove a social law of history. The catalogues of exemplary heroes and historical events served a further purpose: they provided a model of how contemporary events were to be absorbed into the biblical pattern. Since biblical events exemplified recurrent happenings—sin and redemption, forgiveness and atonement—they lost their one-time character. Current events found a place within the ancient but eternally present pattern. No new historical events demanded narration because what was happening in the times of the framers of Leviticus Rabbah came under consideration through what was said about the past. This mode of dealing with biblical history and contemporary events produced two reciprocal effects. One was the mythicization of biblical stories, their removal from the framework of ongoing, unique patterns of history and sequences of events, and their transformation into accounts of things that happened all the time. The other was that contemporary events lost all of their specificity and entered the framework of established mythic existence. So the Scripture's myth happens every day, and every day produces reenactment of the Scripture's myth.

The message of Leviticus Rabbah attached itself to the book of Leviticus as if that book had come from prophecy and addressed the issue of salvation. It really came from the priesthood, however, and spoke of sanctification. Salvation would come through sanctification. The Messiah would come not because of what a pagan emperor did or because of Jewish action, but because of Israel's own moral condition. When Israel entered the right relationship with God, then God would respond to Israel's condition by restoring things to their proper balance. Israel could not and did not need to act so as to force the coming of the Messiah. Israel could attain the condition of sanctification by forming a moral and holy community and God's response would follow the established prophecy of Moses and the prophets. So the basic doctrine of Leviticus Rabbah was the metamorphosis of Leviticus. Instead of holy caste we deal with holy people. Instead of holy place, we deal with holy community in its holy land. The deepest exchange between reality and inner vision came at the very surface: the rereading of Leviticus in terms of a different set of realities from those to which the book related on the surface. No other biblical book would have served so well; it had to be Leviticus. Only through what the framers did with that particular book could they deliver their astonishing message and vision.

The complementary points of emphasis in Leviticus Rabbah—the age to come would come, but Israel had to reform itself beforehand—addressed the context defined by Julian, on the one side, and by the new anti-Judaic Christian policy of the later fourth and fifth centuries, on the other. The repeated reference to Esau and Edom and how they marked the last monarchy before God's through Israel underlined the same point: these truly form the worst of the four kingdoms, but they also come at the end. If we only shape up, so will history. We therefore grasp an astonishing correspondence between how people were thinking, what they wished to say, and the literary context—rereading a particular book of Scripture in terms of a set of values different from those expressed in that book—in which they delivered their message. Given the mode of thought, the crisis that demanded reflection, and the message found congruent to the crisis, we must find entirely logical the choice of Leviticus and the treatment accorded to it. So the logic and the doctrine prove to accord remarkably with the society and politics that produced and received Leviticus Rabbah.

THE TALMUD OF BABYLONIA

When people speak of "the Talmud," they do not mean the Talmud of the Land of Israel (the Yerushalmi) of about 400 C.E., but the Talmud of Babylonia (the Bavli) brought to closure about 600 C.E. This document, comprising discourses on thirty-seven of the Mishnah's sixty-two tractates (not all of them the same tractates that are dealt with by the Yerushalmi), constitutes the summa and the complete statement of the Judaism of the dual Torah as it was defined in its formative age. From the early seventh century when the Bavli was closed to the present day, the Judaism of the dual Torah has continued its long history always within the boundaries—mythic, symbolic, normative in theology and conduct alike—of that protean writing. Commentaries and commentaries upon commentaries, codes of law, authoritative ad hoc decisions (responsa)—these three kinds of writing expanded and developed the Bavli's basic principles.

Philosophers and theologians appealed not only to its authority, but to its doctrine. Lawyers and judges governed Israel, the Jewish people, by reference to the document read as a constitution. In some times and places, ordinary people expressed their love for God and the Torah by studying the lines of this writing. If there is one document that is Judaism, it is the Bavli. All of contemporary Orthodox Judaisms concur; Conservative and Reconstructionist Judaisms do not vastly differ except in detail; and Reform Judaism agrees in principle that the Bavli is a primary source of theological truth requiring exposition, if not invariably demanding assent.

Yet, in telling the history of this particular Judaism, it is difficult to point within the Bavli to developments of such originality and innovative character as to explain its influence. The foundation document should, after all, comprise the Yerushalmi, together perhaps with Genesis Rabbah and Leviticus Rabbah. Among those three compilations we can locate every important idea that the Bavli later set forth. Surely some of the principal Midrash-compilations should find a place alongside the Bavli as principal writings. Yet while all of these documents fall into the category of oral Torah, none has ever attained the stature, in the mind of the faith and the lives of the faithful, of the Bavli.

If we want to know why that is the case, we must ask what distinguishes the Bavli from any prior writing. The answer is simple. The Bavli's framers brought together within a single piece of writing both the Mishnah and its required amplification, and Scripture and its required amplification. They joined the written Torah, as they wished it to be read, and the oral Torah, as they proposed to lay it out. Within the pages that the Bavli's framers composed, they set forth in proportion and in place the one whole Torah of Moses, our rabbi, that (within their mythic framework) God had revealed at Sinai. The Bavli, therefore, represents a triumph of composition and conclusion, a classic comprising the classics. While much that its framers said was fresh and important on its own, and while they accomplished far more than a mere paraphrase and summary of received materials, their principal contribution lay not in innovation but in the authoritative re-presentation of what could now plausibly be called "the tradition."

By joining the whole and providing a reprise of all of the parts, the authorship of the Bavli imparted to the Judaism of the dual Torah the quality of tradition, something handed on from prophet to sage, as Mishnah tractate Abot represents matters. In the form of tradition, that fresh and remarkable system framed in the Yerushalmi and its associated writings would pass forward through the ages: new ideas once, established truth of Sinai now. The Bavli's definitive reshaping of the Judaism of the dual Torah constituted more than a work of literary legerdemain. In its pages we have far more than a mere reprise of what we find in the Yerushalmi and important Midrash-compilations. If, however, we wish to understand the chapter in the history of Judaism written in the Bavli, we must focus upon the accomplishment in formulation and redaction of received materials from the Mishnah, the Tosefta, the Yerushalmi, and the principal Midrash-compilations of the framers of the Bavli. That is where they made their mark, and that is, more importantly, why their document took priority over all others before *and afterward*.

What precisely did the authorship of the Bavli accomplish? If we want to know what and how people thought, we begin by asking how they organized what they knew and about the choices they made in laying out the main lines of the structure of knowledge. When we approach a document so vast and complex as the Bavli, resting as it does on a still larger and more complex antecedent corpus of writings, we do best to begin at the very beginning.

Before the time of the Bavli's authors, three principles of composition and redaction—Mishnah exegesis, Scripture exegesis, and biographical collection—flourished more or less in isolation from one another. How do we know? The first is fully exposed in the Talmud of the Land of Israel, the second in earlier compilations of scriptural exegeses. The third accounts for the available biographical composites. It is clear, therefore, that the antecedent authors of sizable passages (ten or twenty connected paragraphs) and redactors, before the age of the Bavli's own compositors, thought that the three things could be done fairly separately.

Accordingly, we must review the choices made by prior authorships in collecting, organizing, and laying out completed writings—for example, stories, comments on verses of Scripture, sayings, amplifications of paragraphs of the Mishnah and of the Tosefta in relationship to the Mishnah, and the like. What had others done and what did this authorship do? When the final organizers of the Talmud of Babylonia considered the redactional choices made by their predecessors, two appeared the most likely. First, the organizers might take up and arrange such materials as they had in their hands around the categories of Scripture—books or verses or themes—as had their precursors in bringing into being compositions made up of exegeses of Scripture (midrashim). Or they might follow the order of the Mishnah and compose a systematic commentary and amplification of Scripture, as had their precursors who created the Talmud of the Land of Israel a century or so before.

When they considered their task, however, they recognized that they had in hand a tripartite corpus of inherited materials awaiting composition into a final, closed document. First, they took up materials in various states and stages of completion that were pertinent to the Mishnah or to the principles or laws that the Mishnah had originally brought to articulation. Second, they received materials, again in various conditions, pertinent to the Scripture, both as the Scripture related to the Mishnah and also as the Scripture laid forth its own narratives. Finally, they had materials focused on sages. These were framed around twin biographical principles, either as strings of stories about great sages of the past or as collections of sayings and comments drawn together solely because the same name stood behind the sayings. No one had earlier compiled stories about holy men into biographies as had Christian authors ("gospels" or "lives of saints"). For many centuries to come, until the advent of the Hasidic revision of the dual Torah in the early nineteenth century, no one wrote lives of saints.

The framers of the Bavli decided to adopt and join in a single document the two redactional principles inherited from the antecedent century and to reject the one already rejected by their predecessors, even while honoring it. First, they organized the Bavli around the Mishnah. Thirty-seven tractates were given amplifications that

were in part commentaries, expansions, and generalizations, or
sustained speculative essays covering legal topics. Approximately 60
percent of the bulk of the Bavli tractates, in a probe I made of five of
the thirty-seven, serve as expansions of the Mishnah.

Second, they adapted and included vast amounts of antecedent
materials organized as scriptural commentary. They inserted these
whole and complete, not at all in response to the Mishnah's program.
Approximately 40 percent of the bulk of the Bavli comprises this kind
of material. In these passages the logic of redaction—what self-
evidently comes first, what obviously goes below—emerges from a
different sort of exegetical task than a Mishnah commentary. Here
people focused upon passages of Scripture as they drafted their
exegetical compositions. Verse-by-verse amplifications, in the model
of the treatment of the Mishnah's sentences and paragraphs, were
strung together.

Finally, while making provision for compositions built upon biographical principles, preserving strings of sayings from a given master
(and often a tradent [disciple] of a given master) and tales about
authorities of the preceding half millennium, they accomplished nothing new. That is, they never created redactional compositions of a
sizable order that focused upon given authorities, even though sufficient materials were at hand to do so.

In these three decisions—two concerning what to do and one
about what not to do—the final compositors of the Bavli indicated
what they proposed to accomplish: to give final form and fixed
expression, through their categories of the organization of all knowledge, to the Torah as it had been known, sifted, searched, approved,
and handed down, even from the remote past to their own day. In
our literary categories, then, the compositors of the Bavli were ency-
clopedists. Their creation became the encyclopedia of Judaism, its
summa, its point of final reference, its court of last appeal, its definition, its conclusion, its closure—so they thought and so said those
that followed to this very day.

Accordingly, the framers of the Bavli drew together the results
of three types of work that people prior to their own labors had
already created in abundance. Using the two I specified as definitive
redactional structures, the framers made them one document, the
Bavli, or, in the later tradition of Judaism, the Talmud. Whatever
the place and role of the diverse types of compositions circulating

before and in the time of the Bavli—compilations of scriptural exegeses, the Yerushalmi, not to mention the exegeses of pentateuchal laws
in Sifra and the Sifrés, the Tosefta, Pirqe Abot and Abot de R. Natan,
and on and on—the Bavli superseded all. It took pride of place. It laid
the final seal upon the past and defined not only what would succeed
for an unknown tomorrow but the very form, topical order, and
program of all that would pass into the hands of the future.

Since the first of the two Talmuds (the Yerushalmi) provided the
model for the way the Bavli's authorship would treat the Mishnah, let
us review its legacy. In many ways the Yerushalmi defined how the
Mishnah would be read in the Bavli. The Yerushalmi invariably does
to the Mishnah one of the following: (1) textual criticism; (2) exegesis
of the meaning of the Mishnah, including glosses and amplifications;
(3) addition of scriptural proof-texts regarding the Mishnah's central
propositions; and (4) harmonization of one Mishnah passage with
another such passage or with a statement of Tosefta. These four categories encompass all of the Yerushalmi's units of discourse that relate
to the Mishnah, 90 percent of the whole of the Yerushalmi. The first
two of these four procedures remain wholly within the narrow frame
of the Mishnah passage subject to discussion. The second pair take an
essentially independent stance vis-à-vis the Mishnah pericope at hand.

The Mishnah is read by the Yerushalmi as a composite of discrete and essentially autonomous rules—a set of atoms and not an
integrated molecule, so to speak. In this way the most striking formal
traits of the Mishnah are obliterated. More important, the Mishnah as
a whole and complete statement of a viewpoint no longer exists. Its
propositions are reduced to details. On occasion, the details may be
restated in generalizations encompassing a wide variety of other details
across the gaps between one tractate and another. This immensely
creative and imaginative approach to the Mishnah vastly expands the
range of discourse. But the first and deepest consequence is to deny
to the Mishnah its own mode of speech and its distinctive and coherent message. The authorship of the Bavli did no less. The Bavli's and
the Yerushalmi's framers differ in the treatment of history and biography. The Yerushalmi contains a number of statements that something
happened or narratives about how something happened. Stories about
and rules for sages and disciples, separate from discussion of a passage
of the Mishnah, also occur in the Yerushalmi. Preserved only parsi-

moniously in the Yerushalmi, these same kinds of materials make massive contributions to the Bavli. The difference, however, is in proportion and not in substance.

How about the comparison of the Bavli's treatment of passages of Scripture with the disposition of Scripture in Midrash-compilations? The categories for a Midrash-compilation's treatment of a scriptural book are four, of which the first two are closely related and the fourth of slight consequence. The first category encompasses close exegesis of Scripture, by which I mean a word-for-word or phrase-by-phrase interpretation of a passage. In such an activity, the framer of a discrete composition will wish to read and explain a verse or a few words of a verse of the Scripture at hand. The second category, no less exegetical than the first, is made up of units of discourse in which the components of the verse are treated as part of a larger statement of meaning rather than as a set of individual phrases, stichs requiring attention one by one. Accordingly, in this category we deal with wide-ranging discourse about the meaning of a particular passage, hence an effort to amplify what is said in a verse. The amplification may take a number of different forms and directions. But the discipline imposed by the originally cited verse of Scripture will always impose boundaries on discourse.

The useful third category encompasses units of discourse in which the theme of a particular passage defines a wide-ranging exercise. In this discussion the cited passage itself is unimportant; it is the theme that is definitive. Accordingly, we take up a unit of discourse in which the composer of the passage wishes to expand on a particular problem, which is merely illustrated in the cited passage. The problem, rather than the cited passage, defines the limits and direction of discourse. The passage at hand falls away, having provided a mere pretext for the real point of concern. The fourth and final category, also deriving from the Yerushalmi, takes in units of discourse shaped around a given topic but not intended to constitute cogent and tightly framed discourse on the topic. These units of discourse constitute topical anthologies rather than carefully composed essays.

The Bavli contains materials of these four types. In the nature of things, the Bavli's framers did not compose tractates around biblical books. But they did assemble enormous compositions on sustained passages of biblical books. The result is that in the pages of the Bavli, as much as in Midrash-compilations, we study Scripture in the way in which the sages wished Scripture to be read: as part of the Torah, the one whole Torah of Moses our rabbi.

The Yerushalmi and the collections of scriptural exegeses include compositions of already-worked-out units of discourse focused upon the Mishnah and Scripture respectively. Other such completed compositions deal with individual sages. The two cited components of the canon of Judaism as well as the Bavli contain a sizable quantity of sage units of discourse. These could have coalesced in yet a third type of book. Specifically, sayings and stories about sages could have been organized into collections of wise sayings attributed to various authorities (like Abot) on the one side, or brief snippets of biographies or lives of the saints on the other. No one made such compilations. But the Bavli's framers found ample space for them, proportionately and actually far larger than the accommodations for biographical materials supplied in the Yerushalmi and in the Midrash-compilations.

Accommodating biographical materials served the purpose of forming a complete and classic statement. For precisely the same modes of explanation and interpretation found suitable for the Mishnah and the Scripture served equally well for the sayings and doings of sages. That fact may be shown in three ways. First, just as Scripture supplied proof-texts, so deeds or statements of sages served as proof-texts. Second, just as a verse of Scripture or an explicit statement of the Mishnah resolved a disputed point, so also what a sage said or did might be introduced into discourse as ample proof for settling a dispute. Third, it follows that just as Scripture or the Mishnah laid down Torah, so also what a sage did or said laid down Torah. In the dimensions of the applied and practical reason by which the law unfolded, the sage found a comfortable place precisely in the categories defined by the Mishnah and Scripture.

An example of the kind of sustained discourse that appears in biographical materials produced by circles of sages follows. As these circles composed units of discourse about the meaning of a Mishnah passage, a larger theoretical problem of law, the sense of scriptural verse, or the sayings and doings of scriptural heroes seen as sages, so they composed the same for living sages themselves. In the simplest example, we see that two discrete sayings of a sage are joined together. The principle of conglomeration, therefore, is solely the name of the sage at hand. One saying deals with overcoming the impulse to do evil and the other with the classifications of sages' programs of learning. What the two subjects have in common is slight, but that fact meant nothing to the framer of the passage. He thought that compositions joined by the same tradent and authority—Levi and Simeon—should be made up.

Babylonian Talmud Tractate Berakhot 4.B. XXIII

A. Said R. Levi bar Hama and R. Simeon b. Laqish, "A person should always provoke his impulse to do good against his impulse to do evil,

B. "as it is said, 'Provoke and do not sin' (Ps. 4:5).

C. "If [the good impulse] wins, well and good. If not, let him take up Torah study.

D. "as it is said, 'Commune with your own heart' (Ps. 4:5).

E. "If [the good impulse] wins, well and good. If not, let him recite the Shema,

F. "as it is said, 'upon your bed' (Ps. 4:5).

G. "If [the good impulse] wins, well and good. If not, let him remember the day of death,

H. "as it is said, 'And keep silent. Sela' " (Ps. 4:5).

I. And R. Levi bar Hama said R. Simeon b. Laqish said, "What is the meaning of the verse of Scripture, 'And I will give you the tables of stone, the law and the commandment, which I have written, that you may teach them' (Exod. 24:12)?

J. " 'The tables' refers to the Ten Commandments.

K. " 'Torah' refers to Scripture.

L. " 'Commandment' refers to Mishnah.

M. " 'Which I have written' refers to the Prophets and the Writings.

N. " 'That you may teach them' refers to the Gemara.

O. "This teaches that all of them were given to Moses from Sinai."

The frame of the story at hand links A–H and I–O in a way unfamiliar to those accustomed to the principles of conglomeration in legal and biblical-exegetical compositions. In the former, a given problem or principle of law will tell us why one item is joined to some other. In the latter, a single verse of Scripture will account for the joining of two or more otherwise discrete units of thought. Here, one passage,

A–H, takes up Ps. 4:5, the other, I–O, takes up Exod. 24:12. The point of the one statement hardly goes over the ground of the other. So the sole principle by which one item has joined the other is biographical—a record of what a sage said about topics that are, at best, contiguous, if related at all. This example of how stories about sages were collected and organized in the Bavli suffices to show the importance assigned to tales of holy men in the Bavli. When, therefore, we understand how this document brought together a variety of different types of documents and materials and made them into one, we see in a detailed way the character of the framers' work.

Why did the framers of the Bavli not trouble with biographical tractates? We, of course, cannot answer that question by consulting diaries or notes or transcripts of discussions. Logic, however, suggests an answer. Either a teaching was true and authoritative wherever it was found and however it had reached the living sage, or a teaching was untrue and not authoritative. Scripture, the Mishnah, the sage—the three spoke with equal authority. True, one had to come into alignment with the other—the Mishnah with Scripture and the sage with the Mishnah. But it was not the case that one component of the Torah stood within the sacred circle and another beyond. Interpretation and what was interpreted, exegesis and text, belonged together. Once the Torah was deemed both written and oral, then one component of the Torah would remain wholly in unwritten form, not preserved in writing at all. By definition it could not be Scripture. But it also could not be the Mishnah or the Midrash-compilations. For, quite clearly, hundreds of years of writing down passages of the oral Torah had already passed. So the one component of the tripartite Torah—oral, written, living—that would remain in oral form would have to be the sage—living through time through the preservation in oral and not redacted form of the things he did and said. The sage then lived on in the life of the faithful—the never-to-be-written-down component of the Torah, enduring as long as the Torah would last, that is, through time immemorial.

That decision placed the sage at the center of the Torah, for the sage speaks with authority about the Mishnah and the Scripture. He therefore has authority deriving from revelation and may himself participate in the process of revelation. There is no material difference. Since that is the case, the sage's book, whether the Yerushalmi or the Bavli to the Mishnah or Midrash to Scripture, is Torah, that is, revealed by God. It also forms part of the Torah and is a fully canonical document. The sage is thus like Moses, "our rabbi," who received torah and wrote the Torah. While the canon was in three parts—Scripture, Mishnah, sage—the sage, in saying what the other parts meant and in embodying that meaning in his life and thought, took primacy of place. If no document organized itself around sayings and stories of sages, it was because that was superfluous. Why? Because all documents equally, whether Scripture, Mishnah, or Yerushalmi, gave full and complete expression regarding the deeds and deliberations of sages beginning with Moses.

Would that judgment have surprised the authorship of the Yerushalmi? Not at all. They too preserved stories of sages, if not in so prominent a position as did the Bavli's framers. There is only one important difference between the two Talmuds, but that difference suffices to explain the power of the Bavli to define the Torah. The distinction lies solely in the redactional character of the Bavli. The difference between the Bavli and the Yerushalmi is the Bavli's far more ample use of Scripture not only for proof, but for the redaction and organization of large-scale discourse. In the Bavli the Scripture serves alongside the Mishnah and is not much less than it in volume. Scripture and the Mishnah together in the Bavli define structure and impart proportion and organization. In the Yerushalmi, by contrast, Scripture forms an important component of the canon, but it does not dictate lines of order and main beams of structure. What difference does this distinction between the two Talmuds actually make?

The Bavli's complete union in its redactional substrate of the Mishnah and Scripture, encompassing also exemplary actions and sayings of sages, provided a summa of Judaism. The authorship of the Bavli thereby joined the two streams that, like the Missouri and the Mississippi rivers at St. Louis, had until its time flowed separately and distinct from one another within the same banks. The one stream coursing from the source of the Mishnah, and the other stream emanating from the source of Scripture had mingled only in eddies, at the edges. But the banks of the mighty river had been set from Sinai and, in the mythic dimension, the two streams had been meant to flow together as one river. In the Yerushalmi, Scripture found a place along the sides; the Mishnah formed the main stream. In the collections of scriptural exegesis (midrashim), Scripture had flowed by itself down the center, wholly apart from the Mishnah. In the Bavli, for the first time, the waters not only flowed together but mingled in the middle and in the depths, in common and sustained discourse. So the Bavli for the first time from Sinai (to speak within the Torah myth) joined together in a whole and complete way, in literary form and in doctrinal substance, the one whole Torah of Moses.

That is why the Bavli became the Torah par excellence, the Torah through which Israel would read both Scripture and Mishnah, the Torah all together, the Torah all at once, as God at Sinai had revealed it to Moses, our rabbi. It was because the Bavli's writers accomplished the near perfect union of Scripture and Mishnah in a single document that the Bavli became Israel's fullest Torah. That is why when the people of the Torah, Israel, the Jewish people, for the next fifteen hundred years, wished to approach the Mishnah, it was through the reading of the Bavli. That is why when that same people wished to address Scripture, it was through the reading of the Bavli. All the other components of the canon, while authentic and authoritative too, stood in line from second place backward, behind the primary reading of the Bavli. It is no accident that authentic avatars of the classical literature of Judaism even today learn Scripture through the Bavli's citations of verses of Scripture just as much as, commonly, they learn the Mishnah and assuredly interpret it exactly as the Bavli presents it.

It was for good reason that the Bavli has formed the definitive statement of Judaism from the time of its closure to the present day. The excellence of its composition, the mastery and authority of those who everywhere studied it and advocated its law, the sharpness of its exegesis and discussion, the harmonious and proportionate presentation of all details, these virtues of taste and intellect may well have secured for the document its paramount position. The Babylonian Talmud, moreover, incorporated a far broader selection of antecedent materials than any other document that reaches us out of Judaism in late antiquity, far more, for instance, than the Yerushalmi. This vast selection was so organized and assembled that systematic accounts of numerous important problems of biblical exegesis, law and theology alike, emerged. Consequently, the Bavli served from its closure as an encyclopedia of knowledge and as a summa of the theology and law of Judaism. The comprehensive character of the Bavli, in form and in substance, and its dependence upon the Scripture's and the Mishnah's redactional framework, gained for it the priority it would enjoy. No one had done what the Bavli did; no one had to do it again. The Torah was now complete.

THE DUAL TORAH: A REVIEW. FROM THE MISHNAH THROUGH THE BAVLI

The history of the formation of Judaism is the story of how the crisis precipitated by the Mishnah was resolved by the Bavli. The path of Torah through the ages, marked by the first six centuries of the Common Era, is straight and true, harmonious and linear; it is the story of the impact of the appearance of a holy book beyond Scripture upon the lives and thought of the people who deemed that book to be authoritative.

The advent of the Mishnah around 200 C.E. demanded that people explain the status and authority of the new document. The lines of structure emanating from the Mishnah led to the formation of a vast and unprecedented literature of Judaism. The explosive force of the return to Zion, in the time of Ezra, had produced the formation of the Torah book and much else. The extraordinary impact of the person and message of Jesus, among other things, had led to the creation of an unprecedented kind of writing in yet another sector of Israel's life. So, too, would be the case with the Mishnah, Israel's response to the disaster wrought by Bar Kokhba's calamity, the failed rebellion against Rome.

The reason the Mishnah, a philosophical essay rich in theoretical initiatives which also served as a law code, presented a stunning challenge to its age and heirs was its sponsorship in Israel's politics. To begin with, the Mishnah enjoyed the sponsorship of the autonomous ruler of the Jewish nation in the Land of Israel, namely, Judah the Patriarch. The result was that the Mishnah served purposes other than simple learning and speculative thought.

Whatever had been intended for it, at its very beginnings the Mishnah was turned into an authoritative law code, the constitution, along with Scripture (the Hebrew Scriptures, the written Torah), of Israel in its land. Accordingly, when completed, the Mishnah emerged from the schoolhouse and forthwith made its move into the politics, courts, and bureaus of the Jewish government of the Land of Israel. Men (never women, until our own day) who mastered the Mishnah thereby qualified themselves as judges and administrators in the government of Judah the Patriarch, as well as in the government of the Jewish community of Babylonia. Over the next three hundred years, the Mishnah served as the foundation for the Talmuds' formation of the system of law and theology we now know as Judaism. Exegesis of the Mishnah furthermore defined the taxonomy for hermeneutics of Scripture.

The vast collection constituted by the Mishnah therefore demanded explanation. What is this book? How does it relate to the (written) Torah revealed to Moses at Mount Sinai? Under whose auspices, and by what authority, does the law of the Mishnah govern the life of Israel? These questions, we realize, bear political as well as theological implications. To begin with, the answers emerge out of an enterprise of exegesis, of literature. The reception of the Mishnah followed several distinct lines, each of them symbolized by a particular sort of book. Each book, in turn, offered its theory of the origin, character, and authority of the Mishnah. For the next three centuries these theories would occupy the attention of the best minds of Israel, the authorities of the two Talmuds, and the numerous other works of the age of the seed time of Judaism.

We now know full well the two lines of expansion and development—theological, therefore also literary. One line from the Mishnah stretched through the Tosefta—a supplement to the Mishnah—and the two Talmuds, one formed in the Land of Israel (the Yerushalmi), the other in Babylonia (the Bavli), both serving as exegesis and amplification of the Mishnah. The second line stretched from the Mishnah to compilations of biblical exegesis of three different sorts. First, there were exegetical collections framed partly in relation to the Mishnah and the Tosefta, in particular Sifra on Leviticus, Sifré to Numbers, and Sifré to Deuteronomy. Second, exegetical collections were organized mainly in relation to Scripture, with special reference to Genesis Rabbah and Leviticus Rabbah. Third, exegetical collections focused on constructing abstract discourse out of diverse verses of Scripture but on a single theme or problem, represented by Pesikta de Rab Kahana.

This simple catalogue of the types, range, and volume of creative writing over the three hundred years from the closure of the Mishnah indicates an obvious fact. The Mishnah stands at the beginning of a new and utterly original epoch in the formation of Judaism. Like such generative crises as the return to Zion for the nation as a whole and the advent of Jesus for his family and followers, the Mishnah ignited in Israel a great burst of energy. The extraordinary power of the Mishnah, moreover, is seen in its very lonely position in Israelite holy literature of its time and afterward. The subsequent literature, for centuries to come, would refer back to the Mishnah or stand in some clear-cut hermeneutical relationship to it. But for its part, the Mishnah referred to nothing prior to itself—except (and then, mostly implicitly and by indirection) to Scripture. So from the Mishnah back to the revelation of God to Moses at Sinai—in the view of the Mishnah—lies a vast desert. But from the Mishnah forward stretches a fertile plain.

The crisis precipitated by the Mishnah therefore stimulated wide-ranging speculation, inventive experiments of a literary and (in the nature of things) therefore also of a political, theological, and religious character. The Yerushalmi's work of defining and explaining the Mishnah in relation to the (written) Torah, interpreting the meaning of the Mishnah, and expanding upon and applying its laws ultimately precipitated the making, also, of compilations of exegeses of Scripture. The formation of the Talmuds and scriptural-exegetical collections thus made necessary—indeed, urgent—extraordinary and original reflection on the definition of the Torah, through inquiry into the nature of canon and scriptural authority, the range and possibilities of revelation. The results of that work all together would then define Judaism from that time to this. So the crisis presented opportunity, and Israel's sages took full advantage of the occasion.

What was this crisis? As far as Judaism was concerned, revelation had been contained in the Hebrew Scriptures, later called the written Torah. True, God may have spoken in diverse ways. The last of the biblical books had been completed—as far as Jews then knew—many centuries before. How then could a new book claim status as holy and revealed by God? What validated the authority of the people who knew and applied that holy book to Israel's life? These questions defined the critical issue of formative Judaism from 200 to 600 C.E. The resolution of the problem defines Judaism today. Accordingly, the crisis precipitated by the Mishnah came about because of the urgent requirement of explaining what the Mishnah was in relation to the Torah of Moses; why the sages who claimed to interpret and apply the law of the Mishnah to the life of Israel had the authority to do so; and how Israel, in adhering to the rules of the Mishnah, kept the will of God and lived the holy life God wanted them to live.

Why should the Mishnah in particular have presented these critical problems of a social and theological order? After all, the Mishnah was hardly the first piece of new writing to confront Israel from the closure of Scripture to the end of the second century. Other books had found a capacious place in the canon of the groups of Israelites that received them and deemed them holy. The canon of some groups had made room for writings of apocryphal and pseudepigraphic provenance, so framed as to be deemed holy. The Essene library at Qumran encompassed a diverse group of writings, surely received as authoritative and holy, that other Jews did not know within their canon. So, as is clear, we have to stand back and ask why the Mishnah presented special and particularly stimulating problems. Why should the issue of the relation of the Mishnah to Scripture have proved so pressing in the circles of talmudic rabbis of the third, fourth, and fifth centuries? We have no evidence that the relation to the canon of Scripture of the Manual of Discipline, the Hymns, the War Scroll, or the Damascus Covenant perplexed the Teacher of Righteousness and the other holy priests of the Essene community. To the contrary, the Qumran documents appear side by side with the ones we know as canonical Scripture. The high probability is that to the Essenes the sectarian books were no less holy and authoritative than Leviticus, Deuteronomy, Nahum, Habakkuk, Isaiah, and the other books of the biblical canon that they, among all Israelites, revered.

The issue had to be raised because of the peculiar traits of the Mishnah itself. But the dilemma proved acute, not merely chronic, because of the particular purpose the Mishnah was meant to serve and because of the political sponsorship behind the document. As I have already indicated, the Mishnah provided Israel's constitution. It was promulgated by the patriarch—the ethnic ruler—of the Jewish nation in the Land of Israel, Judah the Patriarch, who ruled with Roman support as the fully recognized Jewish authority in the Holy Land. So the Mishnah was public, not sectarian, not merely idle speculation of a handful of Galilean rabbinical philosophers, though in structure and content that is precisely what it was.

The Mishnah emerged as a political document. It demanded assent and conformity to its rules where they were relevant to the government and court system of the Jewish people in its land. The Mishnah therefore could not be ignored and had to be explained in universally accessible terms. Furthermore, the Mishnah demanded explanation not merely in relation to the established canon of Scripture and apology as the constitution of the Jews' government, the patriarchate of second-century Land of Israel. The nature of Israelite life, its inability to distinguish as secular any detail of the common culture, made it natural to wonder about a deeper issue. Israel understood its collective life and the fate of each individual under the aspect of God's loving concern, as expressed in the Torah. Accordingly, laws issued to define what people were supposed to do could not stand by themselves; they had to receive the imprimatur of heaven, that is, they had to be given the status of revelation. To make its way in Israelite life, the Mishnah as a constitution and code demanded for itself a theory of beginnings at (or in relation to) Sinai, with Moses, from God. As I pointed out above, other new writings had proved able to win credence as part of the Torah, hence as revealed by God and so enjoying legitimacy. But they did so in ways not taken by the Mishnah's framers. How did the Mishnah differ?

In the view of all of Israel until about 200 C.E., God was understood to have revealed the divine word and will through the medium of writing. The Torah was a written book. People who claimed to receive further messages from God usually wrote them down. They had three choices in securing acceptance of their account. All three involved linking the new to the old. In claiming to hand on revelation they could (1) sign their books with the names of biblical heroes; (2) imitate the style of biblical Hebrew; or (3) present an exegesis of existing written verses, validating their ideas by supplying proof-texts for them. From the closure of the Torah literature in the time of Ezra, around 450 B.C.E., to the time of the Mishnah nearly seven hundred years later, we do not have a single book alleged to be holy and at the same time standing wholly out of relationship to the Holy Scriptures of ancient Israel. The pseudepigraphic writings fall into the first category, the Essene writings at Qumran into the second and third. We may point also to the Gospels, which take as a principal problem demonstrating how Jesus had fulfilled the prophetic promises of the Hebrew Scriptures and in other ways had carried forward and even embodied Israel's Scripture.

Insofar as a piece of Jewish writing did not find a place in relationship to Scripture, its author laid no claim to present a holy book. The contrast between Jubilees and the Testaments of the Patriarchs, with their constant and close harping on biblical matters, and the several books of Maccabees shows the differences. The former claim to present God's revealed truth, the latter, history. So a book was holy because in style, in authorship, or in (alleged) origin it continued Scripture, finding a place therefore (at least in the author's mind) within the canon, or because it provided an exposition on Scripture's meaning.

But the Mishnah made no such claim. It entirely ignored the style of biblical Hebrew, speaking in a quite different kind of Hebrew. It is silent on its authorship through sixty-two of the sixty-three tractates (the claims of Abot pose a special problem). In any event, nowhere does the Mishnah contain the claim that God had inspired the authors of the document. These are not given biblical names and certainly are not alleged to have been biblical saints. Most of the book's named authorities flourished within the same century as its anonymous arrangers and redactors, not in remote antiquity. Above all, the Mishnah contains scarcely a handful of exegeses of Scripture. These, where they occur, play a trivial and tangential role. Here is the problem of the Mishnah: different from Scripture in language and style, indifferent to the claim of authorship by a biblical hero or divine inspiration, stunningly aloof from allusion to verses of Scripture for nearly the whole of its discourse, yet authoritative for Israel.

So the Mishnah was not a statement of theory alone, telling only how things will be in the eschaton. Nor was it a wholly sectarian document, reporting the view of a group without standing or influence in the larger life of Israel. True, in some measure it bears both of these traits of eschatology and sectarian provenance. But the Mishnah was (and is) law for Israel. It entered the government and courts of the Jewish people, both in the motherland and also overseas, as the authoritative constitution of the courts of Judaism. The advent of the Mishnah therefore marked a turning point in the life of Israel. The document demanded explanation and apology.

The one thing a Jew in third-century Tiberias, Sepphoris, Caesarea, or Beth Shearim in Galilee could not do was ignore the Mishnah. True, one might refer solely to ancient Scripture and tradition and live life within the inherited patterns of the familiar Israelite religion-culture. But as soon as one dealt with the Jewish government in charge of everyday life—went to court over the damages done to a crop by a neighbor's ox, for instance—one came up against a law in addition to the law of Scripture, a document the principles of which governed and settled all matters. So the Mishnah rapidly came to confront the life of Israel. The people who knew the Mishnah, the rabbis or sages, came to dominate that life. Their claim, in accord with the Mishnah, to exercise authority and the right to impose heavenly sanction came to perplex. Now the crisis is fully exposed.

The Mishnah therefore made necessary the formation of the Talmuds, its exegetical companions. Within the processes of exegesis of the Mishnah came the labor of collecting and arranging these exegeses, in correlation with the Mishnah, read line by line and paragraph by paragraph. Those sorts of things the sages who framed the Talmuds had done to the Mishnah, they then did to Scripture. Within the work of exegesis of Scripture was the correlative labor of organizing what had been said verse by verse, following the structure of a book of the Hebrew Scriptures. The type of discourse and the mode of organizing the literary result of discourse suitable for the one document served the other as well. The same people did both for the same reasons. So to the Tosefta, Sifra, and the Yerushalmi alike, the paramount issue was Scripture, not merely its authority but especially its sheer mass of information. The decisive importance of the advent of the Mishnah in precipitating the vast exegetical enterprise represented by the books at hand emerges from a simple fact: the documents all focus attention on the Mishnah in particular. Two of them, the Tosefta and the Yerushalmi, organize everything at hand around the redactional structure supplied by the Mishnah itself.

The importance of the Bavli's distinctive contribution now becomes entirely clear. The Bavli carried forward a long-established enterprise, namely, the forging of links between the Mishnah and Scripture. But the organizers and redactors of the materials compiled in the Bavli did something unprecedented. They allowed sustained passages of Scripture to serve, as much as sustained and not merely episodic passages of the Mishnah served, as main beams in the composition of structure and order. In a single document, the Mishnah and Scripture functioned together and for the first time in much the same way. The original thesis, that the Mishnah depended upon the written Torah and that all of its statements were linked to proof-texts of Scripture, now gave way to its natural and complete fulfillment.

Once sets of verses of Scripture could be isolated and made to provide a focus of discourse, Scripture would join the Mishnah in a single statement, cut down and reshaped to conform to the model of the Mishnah.

So Scripture now joined the Mishnah in a new union, in mythic language, one whole Torah. In revising Scripture to recast it into that same discursive and rhetorical framework that defined how and where the Mishnah would serve, the authors—framers of larger-scale units of discourse, ultimate redactors alike—made their unique contribution. Imposing a literary and redactional unity upon documents so remarkably disparate in every respect as the Mishnah and Scripture, the Bavli's authors created something entirely their own but in no way original to them: Judaism in its final and complete statement, Judaism in conclusion. From this point forward, the Torah would expand and develop, but only by making its own and naturalizing within its realm initially alien modes of thought and bodies of truth. Of these, two must be taken into account: philosophy in the Greco-Islamic tradition and mysticism.

RABBINIC JUDAISM: ITS FORMATIVE HISTORY AND HOLY BOOKS

"Midrash" means explanation or interpretation of a verse of the Hebrew Scriptures. From the third through the seventh centuries, the sages of the Torah produced and collected explanations of certain books of the written Torah, the ones that are read in the synagogue, particularly the Pentateuch (the Five Books of Moses), and parts of the Torah that are read in the synagogue on special occasions as well. The Midrash-compilations collect comments on some of the books of the written part of the Torah and organize them for various purposes. Our selection covers compilations made early in the process of interpretation of the written Torah by the sages of the dual Torah, Sifré to Deuteronomy. The Sifré to Deuteronomy probably was completed by about 300. It shows us how, in Judaism, Scripture is turned into part of the Torah. In compilations such as this, the sages wrote with Scripture to make their statement.

Deuteronomy and
Sifré to Deuteronomy

JACOB NEUSNER

The fundamental rhetorical structure of Sifré to Deuteronomy is defined by verses of the book of Deuteronomy. These are cited, and then whole verses or clauses systematically dictate the arrangement of materials. The structure of the document, therefore, finds its definition in verses of the book of Deuteronomy. But the "commentary form" as structure plays a misleadingly paramount role, for the structure that dictates a form, or a language pattern, in fact sustains and holds together a wide variety of forms. Once the overall arrangement of a given sequence of units of thought is established through the base verse—that is, the verse of the book of Deuteronomy that stands at the head—we may find a variety of formalized patterns.

To be sure, as in Sifré to Numbers, one pattern, or form, is exegetical, in that we have a clause followed by a sentence or two that expand on that clause or impute meaning to it. This is "commentary form." The citation of a sentence of one document, followed by an arrangement of words, ordinarily as a simple declarative sentence, independent of that document, in the most primitive way defines the exegetical form. But that form may develop in a number of ways. What is important at the outset is the distinction between the fundamental structure of the document as a whole, which finds definition in the book of Deuteronomy, and the forms of patterned language within the whole units of thought that make up our composition. These forms sometimes do, and sometimes do not, appeal to phrases or sentences of the book of Deuteronomy as part of the rhetorical pattern at hand. So, in all, we must distinguish form from structure, for my claim that Sifré to Deuteronomy adheres to highly formalized patterns of language proves trivial if all I mean is that the document is structured around the book of Deuteronomy. This is something we knew when we opened it. In our search for regularities of language patterning, let us now work our way through Sifré to Deuteronomy, Pisqa 1 (i.e., chap. 1), to provide an example of the forms that characterize the document as a whole.

SIFRÉ TO DEUTERONOMY

Pisqa 1

> I:I
>
> 1.
>
> A. "These are the words that Moses spoke to all Israel in Transjordan, in the wilderness, that is to say in the Arabah, opposite Suph, between Paran on the one side and Tophel, Laban, Hazeroth, and Dizahab, on the other" (Deut. 1:1):
>
> B. ["These are the words that Moses spoke" (Deut. 1:1):] Did Moses prophesy only these alone? Did he not write the entire Torah?
>
> C. For it is said, "And Moses wrote this Torah" (Deut. 31:9).
>
> D. Why then does Scripture say, "These are the words that Moses spoke" (Deut. 1:1)?
>
> E. It teaches that [when Scripture speaks of the words that one spoke, it refers in particular to] the words of admonition.
>
> F. So it is said [by Moses], "But Jeshurun waxed fat and kicked" (Deut. 32:15).
>
> 2.
>
> A. So too you may point to the following:
>
> B. "The words of Amos, who was among the herdsmen of Tekoa, which he saw concerning Israel in the days of Uzziah, king of Judah, and in the days of Jeroboam, son of Joash, king of Israel, two years before the earthquake" (Amos 1:1):
>
> C. Did Amos prophesy only concerning these [kings] alone? Did he not prophesy concerning a greater number [of kings] than any other?
>
> D. Why then does Scripture say, "These are the words of Amos, [who was among the herdsmen of Tekoa, which he saw

concerning Israel in the days of Uzziah, king of Judah, and in the days of Jeroboam, son of Joash, king of Israel, two years before the earthquake]" (Amos 1:1)?

E. It teaches that [when Scripture speaks of the words that one spoke, it refers in particular to] the words of admonition.

F. And how do we know that they were words of admonition?

G. As it is said, "Hear this word, you cows of Bashan, who are in the mountain of Samaria, who oppress the poor, crush the needy, and say to their husbands, 'Bring, that we may feast'" (Amos 4:1).

H. ["And say to their husbands, 'Bring, that we may feast'"] speaks of their courts.

3.

A. So too you may point to the following:

B. "And these are the words that the Lord spoke concerning Israel and Judah" (Jer. 30:4).

C. Did Jeremiah prophesy only these alone? Did he not write two [complete] scrolls?

D. For it is said, "Thus far are the words of Jeremiah" (Jer. 51:64).

E. Why then does Scripture say, "And these are the words [that the Lord spoke concerning Israel and Judah]" (Jer. 30:4)?

F. It teaches that [when the verse says, "And these are the words that the Lord spoke concerning Israel and Judah" (Jer. 30:4)], it speaks in particular of the words of admonition.

G. And how do we know that they were words of admonition?

H. In accord with this verse: "For thus says the Lord, 'We have heard a voice of trembling, of fear and not of peace. Ask you now and see whether a man does labor with a child? Why do I see every man with his hands on his loins, as a woman in labor and all faces turn pale? Alas, for the day is great, there is none like it, and it is a time of trouble for Jacob, but out of it he shall be saved'" (Jer. 30:5–7).

4.

A. So too you may point to the following:

B. "And these are the last words of David" (2 Sam. 23:1).

C. "And did David prophesy only these alone? And has it furthermore not been said, "The spirit of the Lord spoke through me, and his word was on my tongue" (2 Sam. 23:2)?

D. Why then does it say, "And these are the last words of David" (2 Sam. 23:1)?

E. It teaches that, [when the verse says, "And these are the last words of David" (2 Sam. 23:1)], it refers to words of admonition.

F. And how do we know that they were words of admonition?

G. In accord with this verse: "But the ungodly are as thorns thrust away, all of them, for they cannot be taken with the hand" (2 Sam. 23:6).

5.

A. So too you may point to the following:

B. "The words of Qohelet, son of David, king in Jerusalem" (Qoh. 1:1).

C. Now did Solomon prophesy only these words? Did he not write three and a half scrolls of his wisdom in proverbs?

D. Why then does it say, "The words of Qohelet, son of David, king in Jerusalem" (Qoh. 1:1)?

E. It teaches that [when the verse says, "The words of Qohelet, son of David, king in Jerusalem" (Qoh. 1:1)], it refers to words of admonition.

F. And how do we know that they were words of admonition?

G. In accord with this verse: "The sun also rises, and the sun goes down . . . the wind goes toward the south and turns around to the north, it turns round continually in its circuit, and the wind returns again—that is, east and west [to its circuits]. All the rivers run into the sea" (Qoh. 1:5–7).

H. [Solomon] calls the wicked sun, moon, and sea, for [the wicked] have no reward [coming back to them].

We may now identify a very blatant form, one that we have not observed in either Sifra or Sifré to Numbers. It is the propositional form, one in which a variety of verses makes one important point. The passage proposes to demonstrate a philological fact, which is that, under the stated conditions, "words" refers in particular to words of admonition. The form is repeated and readily discerned. A verse is cited, and then a question addressed to that verse, followed by an answer that bears in its wake secondary expansion. The whole composition in each case in the composite rests upon the intersection of two verses, a base verse (at I.1, it is Deut. 1:1) and then a secondary verse that challenges the superficial allegation of the base verse (at I.1, the secondary verse is Deut. 31:9). This yields "it teaches that," followed by yet a third verse, this one proving the proposed proposition. That this form is indeed fixed and patterned is shown by the fivefold repetition. Clearly we have nothing like a commentary on a clause or a phrase of a verse. The opening word of Deuteronomy, "words . . . ," serves solely as a joining clause, allowing us to tack on the first of the five exercises—and the rest in its wake. We may classify the pattern as a mode of stating and developing a syllogism, aiming at proving a particular proposition concerning word usages. Standing by itself, it is simply a very carefully formalized syllogism that makes the philological point that the word "words of . . ." bears the sense of "admonition" or "rebuke." Five proofs are offered. We know that we reach the end of the exposition when, at I.5.H, there is a minor gloss, breaking the perfect form. That is a common mode of signaling the conclusion of discourse on a given point.

BASIC PROPOSITIONS
IN SIFRÉ TO DEUTERONOMY

In Sifré to Deuteronomy we find a highly propositional statement. To set forth the propositions paramount in this compilation, I begin with what seem primary—Israel's relationship with God and the responsibilities within that relationship. These encompass, first of all, the theme of Israel and God and the implications of the covenant. The basic proposition is that Israel stands in a special relationship with God, and that relationship is defined by the contract, or covenant, that God made with Israel. The covenant comes to particular expression in Sifré to Deuteronomy in two matters, the Land and the Torah. Each marks Israel as different from all other nations and as selected by God. In these propositions, sages situate Israel in the realm of heaven, finding on earth the stigmata of covenanted election and the concomitant requirement of loyalty and obedience to the covenant. These propositions find a place in the foreground of Sifré to Deuteronomy. When we come to Mekhilta attributed to R. Ishmael, we shall ask where, and how, these positions make their appearance.

God's Merciful Character

First comes the definition of those traits of God that our authorship finds pertinent. God sits in judgment of the world, and God's judgment is true and righteous. God punishes faithlessness, but God's fundamental and definitive trait is mercy. The basic relationship of Israel to God is God's grace for Israel. God's loyalty to Israel endures, even when Israel sins. When Israel forgets God, God is pained. Israel's leaders plead with God only for grace, not for their own merit. Correct attitudes in prayer derive from the need for grace, Israel having slight merit on its own account. Israel should follow only God, carrying out religious deeds as the covenant requires, in accord with the instructions of prophets. Israel should show mercy to others, in the model of God's merciful character.

The Basis for the Covenant

Second, the contract, or covenant, produces the result that God has acquired Israel, his creation. The reason is that, of all the nations, only Israel accepted the Torah, and that is why God made the covenant with Israel in particular. Why is the covenant made only with Israel? The Gentiles did not accept the Torah; Israel did, and that has made all the difference. Israel recognized God forthwith; the very peace of the world and of nature depends upon God's giving the Torah to Israel. That is why Israel is the sole nation worthy of dwelling in the palace of God and that is the basis for the covenant, too. The covenant secures for Israel an enduring relationship of grace with God. It cannot be revoked and endures forever. The covenant, the terms of which are specified in the Torah, has duplicate terms: If you do well, you will bear a blessing, and if not, you will bear a curse. That is the singular mark of the covenant between God and Israel. A mark of the covenant is the liberation from Egypt and that sufficed to impose upon Israel God's claim for their obedience. An important sign of the covenant is the possession of the land. Part of the covenant is the recognition of merit of the ancestors. God promised, in making the covenant, recognition for the children of the meritorious deeds of the ancestors. The conquest of the land and its inheritance are marks of the covenant, which Israel will find within its power because of God's favor. It is the highest and choicest mark of merit, inherited from the ancestors. All religious duties are important, those that seem trivial as much as those held to be weightier.

God always loves Israel. That is why Israel must carry out the religious duties of the Torah with full assent. Israel must be whole-hearted in its relationship with God. If it is, then its share is with God, and if not, then not. The right attitude toward God is love, and Israel should love God with a whole heart. But Israel may hate God. The reason that Israel rebels against God is its prosperity. Wealthy people become arrogant and believe that their prosperity derives from their own efforts. But that is not so, and God punishes people who rebel to show them that their prosperity depends on God. When Israel practices idolatry, God punishes them, through exile, for example, through famine, or through drought. Whether or not Israel knows or likes this fact, Israel has no choice but to accept God's will and fulfill the covenant.

The heaven and the earth respond to the condition of Israel and therefore carry out the stipulations of the covenant. If Israel does not carry out religious duties concerning heaven, then heaven bears witness against them. This especially concerns the Land of Israel. Possession of the land is conditional, not absolute. It begins with grace, not merit. It is defined by the stipulation that Israel observe the covenant, in which case Israel will retain the land. If Israel violates the covenant, Israel will lose the land. When Israel inherits the land, in obedience to the covenant and as an act of grace bestowed by God, it will build the Temple, where Israel's sins will find atonement. The conquest of the land itself is subject to stipulations, just as possession of the land, as an act of God's grace, is marked by religious obligations. If Israel rebels or rejects the Torah, it will lose the land, just as the Canaanites did because of their idolatry.

The land is not the only or the most important mark of the covenant. The most important is Israel's dedication to the Torah, which shows that Israel stands in a special relationship to God. The Torah is the source of life for Israel. It belongs to everyone, not only the aristocracy. Children should start studying the Torah at the earliest age possible. The study of the Torah is part of the fulfillment of the covenant. Even the most arid details of the Torah contain lessons, and if one studies the Torah, the reward comes both in this world and in the world to come. The possession of the Torah imposes the requirement on every male Israelite to study the Torah, which involves memorizing each lesson. This is a daily requisite. Study of the Torah should be one's main obligation, before anything else. The correct motive is not for the sake of gain, but for the love of God and the desire for knowledge of God's will. People must direct heart, eyes, and ears to teachings of the Torah. Study of the Torah transforms human relationships, so that strangers become the children of the master of the Torah whom they serve as disciples. However unimportant the teaching or the teacher, all is as if on the authority of Moses at Sinai. When a person departs from the Torah, that person becomes an idolater. Study of the Torah prevents idolatry. The Torah's verses may be read in such a way that different voices speak discrete clauses of a single verse. One of these will be the Holy Spirit, another, Israel, and so on.

THE HISTORY OF ISRAEL

This brings us to the relationship between Israel and the nations, hence to the meaning of history. The covenant, through the Torah of Sinai, governs not only the ongoing life of Israel but also the state of human affairs universally. The history of Israel forms a single, continuous cycle, in that what happened in the beginning prefigures what will happen at the end of time. Events of Genesis are reenacted both in middle history, between the beginning and the end, and also at the end of time. The personal traits of the tribal founders were passed on and so dictated the history of their families to both the here and now and also the eschatological age. Moses was shown the whole of Israel's history, past, present, and future. The times of the patriarchs are reenacted in the messianic day. This shows how Israel's history runs in cycles, so that events of ancient times prefigure events now. The prophets, beginning with Moses, describe these cycles. What has happened bears close relationship to what is going to happen. The prophetic promises, too, were realized in the times of the Temple, and will be realized at the end of time.

The periods in the history of Israel, marked by the exodus and wandering, the inheritance of the land and the building of the Temple, and the destruction, are all part of a divine plan. In this age— the third century—Rome rules, but in the age to come, marked by the study of the Torah and the offering of sacrifices in the Temple cult, Israel will be in charge. That is the fundamental pattern and meaning of history. The Holy Spirit makes possible actions that bear consequences only much later in time. The prefiguring of history forms the dominant motif in Israel's contemporary life, and the reenacting of what has already been forms a constant. Israel, therefore, should believe, if not in what is coming, then in what has already been. The very names of places in the land attest to the continuity of Israel's history, which follows rules that do not change. The main point is that while Israel will be punished in the worst possible way, Israel will not be wiped out.

But the cyclical character of Israel's history should not mislead. Events follow a pattern, but knowledge of that pattern, which is found in the Torah, permits Israel both to understand and also to affect its own destiny. Specifically, Israel controls its own destiny through its conduct with God. Israel's history is the culmination of Israel's conduct, moderated by the merit of the ancestors. Abraham effected a change in God's relationship to the world. But merit, which makes history, is attained by one's own deeds as well. The effect of merit, in Israel's standing among the other nations, is simple. When Israel enjoys merit, it gives testimony against itself, but when Israel has no merit, then the most despised nation testifies against it. But God is with Israel in time of trouble. When Israel sins, it suffers; when it repents and is forgiven, it is redeemed. For example, Israel's wandering in the wilderness took place because of its failure to attain merit. Sin is what caused the wandering in the wilderness. People rebel against Torah because they are prosperous. The merit of the ancestors works historically to Israel's benefit. What Israel does not merit on its own, at a given time, the merit of the ancestors may secure in any event. The best way to deal with Israel's powerlessness is through Torah study; the vigor of engagement with Torah study compensates for weakness.

It goes without saying that Israel's history follows a prescribed time; at the end of such a period of time, an awaited event will take place. The prophets prophesy concerning the coming of the day of the Lord. Therefore, nothing is haphazard, and all things happen in accord with a plan. That plan encompasses this world, the time of the Messiah, and the world to come, in that order. God will personally exact vengeance at the end of time. God also will raise the dead. Israel has overcome difficult times and can continue to do so. The task ahead is easier than the tasks already accomplished. Israel's punishment is only once, while the punishment to the nations will be unremitting. Peace is worthwhile and everyone needs it. Israel's history ends in the world to come or in the days of the Messiah. The righteous will inherit the Garden of Eden. The righteous in the age to come will be joyful. God acts in history and does so publicly, in full light of day. This is to show the nations who rules. The Torah is what distinguishes Israel from the other nations. The other nations had every opportunity to understand and accept the Torah, and all declined it; that is why Israel was selected. And that demonstrates the importance of both the covenant and the Torah, the medium of the covenant. The nations even had a prophet comparable to Moses. The nations have no important role in history, except as God assigns them a role in relationship to Israel's conduct. The nations are estranged from God by idolatry. That is what prevents goodness from coming into the world. The name of God rests upon Israel in greatest measure. Idolaters do not control heaven. The greatest sin an Israelite can commit is idolatry, and those who entice Israel to idolatry are deprived of the ordinary protections of law. As to the nations' relationships with Israel, they are guided by its condition. When Israel is weak, the nations take advantage; when Israel is strong, they are sycophantic. God did not apportion love to the nations of the world as he did to Israel.

Consider Israel at home, the community and its governance. A mark of God's favor is that Israel has (or has had and will have) a government of its own. Part of the covenantal relationship requires Israel to follow leaders whom God has chosen and instructed, such as Moses and the prophets. Accordingly, Israel is to establish a government and follow sound public policy. Its leaders are chosen by God. Israel's leaders, the prophets, for example, are God's servants, and that is a mark of the praise that is owing to them. They are to be in the model of Moses, humble, choice, select, well known. Moses was the right one to bestow a blessing, Israel's leaders were the right ones to receive the blessing. Yet all leaders are mortal, and even Moses died. The saints—holy persons—are leaders ready to give their lives for Israel. The greatest of them enjoy exceptionally long life. But the sins of the people are blamed on their leaders. The leaders depend on the people to keep the Torah, and Moses thanked them in advance for keeping the Torah after he died. The leaders were to be patient and honest, give a full hearing to all sides, and make just decisions in a broad range of matters. To stand before the judge is to stand before God. God makes sure that Israel does not lack for leadership. The basic task of the leader is both to rebuke and also to console the people. The rulers of Israel are servants of God. The prophets exemplify these leaders, in the model of Moses, and Israel's rulers act only on the instruction of prophets. Their authority rests solely on God's favor and grace. At the urging of God, the leaders of Israel speak, particularly words of admonition. These are delivered before the leaders die, when the whole picture is clear. Then people can draw the necessary conclusions. These words, when Moses spoke them, therefore covered the entire history of the community of Israel. But the Israelites can deal with the admonition and draw the correct conclusions. Repentance overcomes sin, as with the sin of the golden calf. The Israelites were contentious, nitpicking, litigious, and, in general, gave Moses a difficult time. Their descendants should learn not to do so. Israel should remain united and obedient to its leaders. When the Israelites are of one opinion on earth, God's name is glorified above. This survey of the propositions set forth in Sifré to Deuteronomy shows us that, were we to have to point to a single document for the representation of the Judaism of the dual Torah, it would have to be this one. That sets the standard for measuring the propositional character of other writings and shows us, by contrast, the ad hoc and episodic character of such propositions, independent of mere textual paraphrase, as may make their way into the pages of Sifra.

10

The Success of Rabbinic Judaism: From Ancient Times to the Nineteenth Century

WHY JUDAISM TRIUMPHED AMID CHRISTIANITY AND ISLAM

The Judaism of the dual Torah constructed for Israel a world in which the experience of the loss of political sovereignty and the persistence of the condition of tolerated subordination attested to the importance and centrality of Israel in the human situation. So the long-term condition of the conquered people found more than mere explanation in precisely the pattern that had first defined God's will in the Torah for Israel after the first catastrophe and restoration. That condition turned out to afford reassurance and make the truths of the system certain. The success of Judaism derived from this reciprocal process. On the one side, the Judaism of the dual Torah restated for Israel in an acutely contemporary form, in terms relevant to the situation of Christianity and Islam, the experience of loss and restoration, death and resurrection, that the first Scripture had set forth as a pattern. The people had attained a self-consciousness that continuous existence in a single place under a single government had denied others (and had denied Israel before 586, as the Yahwist and the Deuteronomist testify). Israel thus found a renewed sense of its own distinctive standing among the nations of the world.

But at the same time, that Judaism taught the Jews the lesson that its subordinated position itself gave probative evidence of the nation's true standing: the low would be raised up, the humble placed into authority, the proud reduced, and the world made right. So the Judaism of the dual Torah did more than reassure and encourage. It

269

acted upon and determined the shape of matters. That Judaism defined the politics and policy of the community for a long time. It instructed Israel on the rules for the formation of the appropriate world and it laid forth the design for the attitudes and actions that would yield an Israel that was subordinate and tolerated, on the one side, but also proud and hopeful, on the other. The Judaism of the dual Torah begin in the encounter with a successful Christianity and persisted in the face of a still more successful Islam. But for Israel that Judaism preserved because, long after the conditions that originally precipitated the positions and policies deemed normative, that same Judaism not only reacted to but also shaped Israel's condition in the world. Making a virtue of a policy of subordination that was not always necessary or even wise, the Judaism of the dual Torah defined the Jews' condition and set the limits to its circumstance.

The religion of a small, weak group, Judaism more than held its own against the challenge of triumphant Christianity and Islam. The reason for the success of the Judaism of the dual Torah was that the system answered the question of why God's people, in exile, held a subordinated but tolerated position within the world framed by the sibling-rivals, Ishmael and Isaac, Esau and Jacob. The appeal to exile accounted for the dissonance between present unimportance and promised future greatness: "today if only you will." So the question was urgent, and the answer self-evidently true. Here was the family of Abraham, Isaac, and Jacob: Israel. Now tolerated, sometimes oppressed, in exile—in time to come the family would come home to its own land. The road back was fully mapped out. People now had to remember who they were, where they were going, and what they had to do in order to get from here to there.

The framing of the world as a system of families—with Israel unique but Israel's siblings related to it—admirably accounted for the state of Israel. The way of life of the Judaism of the dual Torah, with its stress on the ongoing sanctification of the everyday, the worldview with its doctrine of the ultimate salvation of the holy people—these realized in concrete and acutely relevant form the fundamental system. The consequence was total and enduring success. So long as Christianity defined the civilization of the West and Islam the civilization of North Africa, the Near and Middle East, and Central Asia, Judaism in its fourth-century, classical statement triumphed in Israel,

the Jewish people, located amid Christianity and Islam. The questions
deemed urgent and the answers found self-evidently true defined the
world for Israel. In the West from the eighteenth century on, as part
of the secularization of politics and culture, Christianity lost its standing as a set of self-evident truths. Then in the same countries Judaism
in its classical statement also found itself facing competition from
other Judaisms: different systems, each one asking its distinctive,
urgent questions and producing its own self-evidently true answers.
For these other Judaisms neither questions nor answers bore any
relationship whatever to those of the received system, even when
they episodically exploited proof-texts drawn from the inherited holy
writings. In Christian lands it was only until the eighteenth century
that the Judaism of the dual Torah both set the standard for accepted
innovation and defined the shape and structure of heresy. From that
time on, continuator-Judaisms completed with essentially new and
unprecedented systems, which in no way stood in a linear and incremental relationship with the Judaism of the dual Torah.

In the Muslim countries, because the palpable self-evidence of
Islam never gave way but has defined reality in pretty much its own
way from the beginning to the present day, the equivalently obvious
standing of truth accorded by Jews to the received system of the
Judaism of the dual Torah for Israel endured. Judaism in the received
statement of the fourth century, as given its definitive version in the
Talmud of Babylonia in the seventh century, persisted from the beginning of Islam to the end of the life of Israel in the Islamic world in
1948. In Muslim countries whatever variations and developments
marked the history of Judaism from the fourth century to today
worked themselves out within the received system and its norms.

The reason for the difference between the uninterrupted history
of Judaism in the Islamic world and the diverse histories of Judaisms
in modern and contemporary Christendom lies in the different modern and contemporary histories of Islam—so long the victim of imperialism—and Christianity—equally long the beneficiary of the same
politics. In its fourth century formulation Judaism thrived within
imperial systems in accord with the conditions of its circumstance—
uninterruptedly in the one world, conditionally in the other. But the
reason was the same: Judaism explained for Israel its subordinated
but tolerated condition and, indeed, made that condition into God's

will. The acceptance of that condition in the heart as much as in the mind was part of the definition of virtue. In its version of the dual Torah, Judaism brought to its ultimate statement the original, scriptural Judaism of the Torah of Moses that was completed in the time of Ezra. The message of the Judaism of the dual Torah addressed precisely the situation envisaged by the original system: the people are special, its life is contingent, its relationship to the land is subject to conditions, and its collective life is lived at a level of heightened reality.

The outside world works out its affairs in order to accommodate God's will for Israel, and Israel has complete control of its relationship to the larger world—but in a paradoxical way. For what Israel must do is accept, submit, accommodate, and receive with humility the will and word of God in the Torah. The power to govern the fate of the nation rested with the nation, but only so far as the nation accorded that power to God alone. Were people perplexed about who is Israel? The Torah answered the question: God's people here and now, living out the holy life prescribed by God. Did people wonder how long that people would have to endure the government of Gentiles? The Torah addressed that issue: so long as God willed. The system laid emphasis upon the everyday as a sequence of acts of sanctification. It promised remission and resolution—salvation—in consequence of the correct and faithful performance of those acts of sanctification. The system therefore served to attest to the true status of Israel, small and inconsequential now, but holy even now and destined for great reward at the end of time.

The power of Judaism therefore lay in its remarkable capacity to define and create the world of Israel, the Jewish people. Israel understood that the nation that had ceased to be a nation on its own land and had once more regained that condition could and would once more reenact that paradigm. The original pattern imparted on events the meaning that made ample and good sense for Israel. That is why I have maintained that in the case of the Judaism of the dual Torah the social world recapitulated religion, and that religion did not merely recapitulate the givens of society.

In the mid-seventh century Islam found a powerful adversary in the Judaism of the dual Torah. After the death of Muhammad, Muslim armies swept over the Middle East and North Africa, subduing the great empire of Iran to the east and much of Byzantine Rome to the west, cutting across Egypt, Cyrenaica, and what we know as Tunisia and North Africa, and reaching into Spain. Ancient Christian bishoprics fell, as vast Christian populations accepted the new monotheism though they were not compelled to do so. We have no evidence that similar sizable conversions decimated the Jewish community. That Judaism stood firm. The reason is clear. Having dealt with the political triumph of Christianity, the system of the dual Torah found itself entirely capable of coping with the military (and political) victory of Islam as well. Indeed, given the apparent stability of the Jewish communities in the newly conquered Islamic countries and the decline of Christianity in those same, long-Christian territories—Syria, Palestine, Egypt, Cyrenaica, and the western provinces of North Africa, not to mention Spain—we observe a simple fact. The Judaism of the dual Torah satisfactorily explained the events of the day for Israel, while the Christianity triumphant through the sword of Constantine withstood the yet-sharper sword of Muhammad only with difficulty. One may surmise that the great Christian establishments of the Middle East and North Africa fell away on that account. Since Judaism and Christianity enjoyed precisely the same political status, the evident success of the one and the failure of the other attests to what the fourth-century sages had accomplished for Israel, the Jewish people.

The situation of Jews as tolerated minority in Christianity and Islam, and that of Christianity in Islam, likewise accorded subordinated but tolerated standing, meant that only a free, male Muslim enjoyed the rank of a full member of society.[1] Jews and Christians could accept Islam or submit; they could pay a tribute and accept Muslim supremacy but continue to practice their received religions. Bernard Lewis characterizes the policy toward the conquered people in these terms:

> This pattern was not one of equality but rather of dominance by one group and, usually, a hierarchic sequence of the others. Though this order did not concede equality, it permitted peaceful coexistence. While one group might dominate, it did not as a rule insist on suppressing or absorbing the others. . . . Communities professing recognized religions were allowed the tolerance

of the Islamic state. They were allowed to practice their religions
. . . and to enjoy a measure of communal autonomy.[2]

The Jews fell into the category of *dhimmis*, communities "accorded a
certain status, provided that they unequivocally recognized the primacy of Islam and the supremacy of the Muslims. This recognition
was expressed in the payment of the poll tax and obedience to a
series of restrictions defined in detail by the holy law."[3] The situation
of Judaism in Muslim countries therefore corresponded overall with
that in the Christian ones. In some ways, to be sure, it proved easier,
there being no emotional hostility directed against either Jews or
Judaism such as flourished in Christendom.[4] But the Jews were a
subject group and had to accommodate themselves to that condition,
just as they had learned to make their peace with the remarkable
success of Christianity in fourth-century Rome. And that brings us to
the question of the basis for the remarkable success of Judaism in its
classical form.

From the fourth century in Christendom, and from the seventh
in the Islamic world, Judaism enjoyed remarkable success in the very
world that it had both created and also selected for itself—the world
of Israel, the Jewish people. Both Islam and Christianity presented a
single challenge: the situation of subordination along with toleration.
The power of Judaism lay in its capacity to do two things. First, in its
classical statement, shaped in the fourth-century Talmud of the Land
of Israel (Yerushalmi) and then fully articulated by the sixth-century
Talmud of Babylonia (Bavli), Judaism presented doctrines that both
explained and drew renewal from the condition of subordination and
toleration. So the facts of everyday life served to reinforce the claims
of the system. Second, the same Judaism taught an enduring doctrine
of the virtues of the heart that did more than make Israel's situation
acceptable. The doctrine so shaped the inner life of Israel as to define
virtue in the very terms that were imposed by politics. In age succeeding age Israel recreated within the exact condition of humility
and accommodation that the people's political circumstance imposed
from without. So the enduring doctrine of virtue not only made it
possible for Israel to accept its condition, but also that same condition
in the psychological structure of Israel's inner life, so bringing political
facts and psychological fantasies into exact correspondence. Judaism

triumphed in Christendom and Islam because of its power to bring into union the heart and mind, inner life and outer circumstance, psychology and politics. The Judaism of the dual Torah not only matched the situation of Israel the conquered but (ordinarily) tolerated people, but also created that same condition within the psychological heritage of Israel. The condition was the acceptance of a subordinated but tolerated position, while awaiting the superior one.

A JUDAISM WITHIN
RABBINIC JUDAISM: HASIDISM

Hasidism was a mystical movement that took shape in the eighteenth century and came to fruition in the nineteenth and twentieth centuries. What is most interesting about this movement was its power to reinforce the observance and study of the Torah. That fact is astonishing, given the fresh character of the doctrines of the movement, on the one side, and the powerful opposition precipitated by it, on the other. The power of the original system to absorb diverse viewpoints and novel doctrines and matters of emphasis and make them its own finds testimony in the ultimate character of Hasidism. The mystic circles in Poland and Lithuania among whom Hasidism developed in the eighteenth century carried on practices that marked them as different from other Jews—for example, special prayers and distinctive ways of observing certain religious duties. The first among the leaders of the movement of ecstatics and antiascetics was Israel b. Eliezer Baal Shem Tov, "the Besht," who worked as a popular healer. From the 1730s on, he undertook travels and attracted to himself circles of followers in Podolia, Poland, and Lithuania, and elsewhere. When he died in 1760 he left behind not only disciples but also a broad variety of followers and admirers in southeastern Poland and Lithuania. Leadership of the movement passed to a succession of holy men, about whom stories were told and preserved. In the third generation, from the third quarter of the eighteenth century into the first quarter of the nineteenth, the movement took hold and spread. Diverse leaders called *zaddikim*, who were holy men and charismatic figures, developed their own standing and doctrine.

Given the controversies that swirled about the movement, we might expect that many of the basic ideas were new. But that was hardly the case. The movement drew heavily on available mystical books and doctrines, which from medieval times onward had won a place within the faith as part of the Torah. Emphasis on a given doctrine on the part of Hasidic thinkers should not obscure the profound continuities between the modern movement and its medieval sources. To take one example of how the movement imparted its own imprint on an available idea, the Menahem Mendel of Lubavich, noted that God's oneness—surely a given in all Judaisms—meant more than that God is unique. It meant that God is all that is.

> There is no reality in created things. This is to say that in truth all creatures are not in the category of something or a thing as we see them with our eyes. For this is only from our point of view, since we cannot perceive the divine vitality. But from the point of view of the divine vitality which sustains us, we have no existence and we are in the category of complete nothingness like the rays of the sun in the sun itself. . . . From which it follows that there is no other existence whatsoever apart from his existence, blessed be he. This is true unification.[5]

Since all things are in God, the suffering and sorrow of the world cannot be said to exist. So to despair is to sin.

Hasidism laid great emphasis on joy and avoiding melancholy. Like their earlier counterparts in the medieval Rhineland, the Hasidim of modern times maintained that the right attitude must accompany the doing of religious deeds: the deed could be elevated only when carried out in a spirit of devotion. The doctrine of Hasidism further held that "in all things there are 'holy sparks' waiting to be redeemed and rescued for sanctity through man using his appetites to serve God. The very taste of food is a pale reflection of the spiritual force which brings the food into being."[6] Before carrying out a religious deed, the Hasidim would recite the formula, "For the sake of the unification of the Holy One, blessed be he, and his shekhinah [presence in the world]." On that account they were criticized. But the issues were defined by the fundamental pattern of life and the received worldview contained in the holy canon of Judaism. Hasidism therefore constituted a Judaism within Judaism—distinctive, yet in its major traits so closely related to the Judaism of the dual Torah as to be indistinguishable except in trivial details.

But one of the details mattered a great deal, and that was the doctrine of zaddikism—the doctrine of the holy man as mediator. The zaddik, holy man, had the power to raise the prayers of the followers and to work miracles. The zaddik was the means through which grace reached the world, the one who could control the universe through his prayers. The zaddik would bring humanity nearer to God and God closer to humanity. The Hasidim were well aware that this doctrine of the zaddik—the pure and elevated soul that could reach to the realm of heaven in which only mercy reigns— represented an innovation. So Jacobs:

> But if such powers were evidently denied to the great ones of the past how does the zaddik come to have them? The rationale is contained in a parable attributed to the Maggid of Mezhirech. . . . When a king is on his travels he will be prepared to enter the most humble dwelling if he can find rest there, but when the king is at home, he will refuse to leave his palace unless he is invited by a great lord who knows how to pay him full regal honors. In earlier generations only the greatest of Jews could attain to the holy spirit. Now that the *Shekhinah* [divine presence] is in exile, God is ready to dwell in every soul free from sin.[7]

Although it was apparently a complete innovation, the doctrine of the zaddik in fact carried forward a theme of the Zohar, a mystical document of the thirteenth century. The principal figure of that document, Simeon b. Yohai, an important rabbi in talmudic times, was seen by the Hasidim as the model for the veneration offered to the zaddik. In that way they linked themselves to the most ancient past of what to them was the Torah.[8] Nahman of Bratslav was identified with Simeon b. Yohai and was held by his disciples to have formed the reincarnation of the talmudic authority. The conclusion drawn from that fact, Green points out, is not the one that would distinguish the zaddik and his followers from the rest of Judaism: "Nahman was very cross with those who said that the main reason for the *zaddik*'s ability to attain such a high level of understanding was the nature of his soul. He said that this was not the case, but that everything depended first and foremost upon good deeds, struggle, and worship. He said explicitly that everyone in the world could reach even the highest rung, that everything depended upon human choice."[9] While the zaddik was a superior figure, a doctrine such as that of Nahman brought the Hasidic movement into close touch with the rest of Jewry, with its stress on the equal responsibility of all Israel to carry on the work of good deeds and worship (not to mention study of the Torah). What was special became its most appealing trait. So Green describes the legacy of Nahman of Bratslav, citing the record of the master's last great message: " 'Gevalt! Do not despair!' He went on in these words: 'There is no such thing as despair at all!' He drew forth these words slowly and deliberately, saying, 'There is no despair.' He said the words with such strength and wondrous depth that he taught everyone, for all generations, that he should never despair, no matter what it is that he has to endure." Green notes that the master had left "the example of a man who had suffered all the torments of hell in his lifetime, but had refused to give in to ultimate despair."[10] Rightly seeing this as emblematic of the master, we may also note how thoroughly in agreement the authors of the Yerushalmi, Genesis Rabbah, and Leviticus Rabbah found themselves. That is what I mean when I call Hasidism a Judaism within Judaism: it was both a restatement of the familiar in a fresh idiom and a reconsideration of the profane under the aspect of the holy.

By the 1830s the original force of the movement had run its course, and the movement, which had begun as a persecuted sect, now defined the way of life of the Jews in the Ukraine, Galicia, and central Poland, with offshoots in White Russia and Lithuania, on the one side, and Hungary on the other. The waves of emigration from the 1880s on carried the movement to the West, and in the aftermath of World War II, to the United States and the Land of Israel as well. Today the movement forms a powerful component of Orthodox Judaism, and that fact is what is central to our interest. For by the end of the eighteenth century, powerful opposition, led by the most influential figures of East European Judaism, characterized Hasidism as heretical. Its stress on ecstasy, visions, and miracles of the leaders and its enthusiastic way of life were seen as delusions, and the veneration of the zaddik was interpreted as worship of a human being. The stress on prayer, to the denigration of study of the Torah, likewise called into question the legitimacy of the movement. In the war against Hasidism the movement found itself anathematized, its books burned, and its leaders vilified: "They must leave our communities with their wives and children . . . and they should not be given a night's lodging; . . . it is forbidden to do business with them and to intermarry with them or to assist at their burial."

Under these circumstances, the last thing anyone could have anticipated was that Hasidism would find a place for itself within what was later considered Orthodoxy. But it did. For example, one of the most influential and important organizations within contemporary Orthodoxy, Agudat Israel, finds its principal membership in Hasidim. The acceptance of the movement came about through the development within Hasidism of centers of study of the Torah. The joining of Hasidic doctrine with the received tradition legitimated what had begun outside of that tradition altogether (or at least outside in the view of those who deemed themselves insiders). The first Hasidic center of Torah study came into being in the mid-nineteenth century, and by the end of that time the Lubavich sect of Hasidism had founded still more important centers. What had begun as a heretical movement had within the span of a century gained entry into the centers of the normative faith, and within another century had come to constitute the bulwark of that faith. I can imagine no greater testimony to the remarkable power and resilience of the Judaism of the dual Torah than the capacity of that system to make a place for so vigorous and original a movement as Hasidism.

HERESIES AGAINST RABBINIC JUDAISM: KARAISM VERSUS THE ORAL TORAH

The heresies generated by the Judaism of the dual Torah present still more striking evidence of the power of the received system to thrive. Judaism in its ascendancy also defined the limits of heresy, imposing its values upon the contrary-minded statements of the age. One heresy rejected the doctrine of the dual Torah, while another rejected the doctrine of the sage-Messiah. In the age of the dominance of the Judaism of the dual Torah, we look in vain for evidence that the system faced heresies essentially alien to its structure and system. From the fourth to the nineteenth centuries in Christendom, and to the mid-twentieth century in the Muslim world, Judaic "heresies"[11] commonly took up a position on exactly the program and agenda of the Judaism of the dual Torah. What made a heresy heretical was its rejection of one or another of the definitive doctrines of the norm. In the nineteenth- and twentieth-century West, by contrast, new Judaisms—not merely heresies cleaved out of the old—took shape wholly outside of the system and structure of the old Judaism. That fact attests to the contemporary world's systemic change of monumental proportions.

We consider two systemic heresies, each addressing a fundamental plank in the platform of the Judaism of the dual Torah: (1) Karaism, which denied the myth of the dual Torah, and (2) Sabbateanism, which rejected the doctrine of the Messiah as defined in the classical system and created a new doctrine within the received structure and system—a Messiah outside of the law. I cannot think of two more characteristic components of the Judaism of the dual Torah than its belief in the oral Torah, on the one hand, and its expectation of a Messiah who would master and carry out the teachings of the Torah of Sinai, on the other. Both of these heresies took exactly the opposite position of the Judaism of the dual Torah, thereby not only challenging that Judaism but also testifying to its power to define reality for all Israel. As in our consideration of the Judaisms within Judaism, we take up both medieval and early modern phenomena in order to show the uninterrupted and uniform history of Judaisms from the fourth to the nineteenth centuries. Karaite Judaism flourished in medieval times, and the Sabbatean system in the early modern age. Thus the correspondence between the systemically harmonious Judaisms and the systemically contradictory ones is exact.

The indicative trait of the Judaism of the dual Torah was the doctrine that, at Sinai, God had revealed the Torah to be transmitted through two media, written and oral. Focusing upon that central belief, Karaism denied that God had revealed to Moses at Sinai more than the written Torah and explicitly condemned belief in an oral Torah. Karaism took shape in the eighth century, beginning after the rise of Islam, and advocated the return to Scripture as against tradition, including rabbinic tradition. The sect originated in Babylonia in the period following the formation of the Talmud of Babylonia, on the one side, and the rise of Islam, on the other. In his classic account of the matter, Zvi Ankori explains the origin of the movement as follows:

> The forceful promotion of talmudic legislation by the central Jewish institutions under Muslim domination . . . could not but

call forth defiance in the distant peripheries of the Jewish Diaspora. Claiming to be the last link in an uninterrupted chain of oral transmission, the central Jewish administration, residing in Babylonia, considered itself the only legitimate heir and sole competent interpreter of that unique national experience: the lawgiving communication at Sinai. . . . The protest against the central Jewish authorities did perforce assume the form of opposition to the Oral Law which was embodied in the Talmud and effectively enforced by the exilarchic office and the continuous activity of . . . lawmakers. Indeed, regional customs, rites and observances persisted in the fringe areas of Jewish Dispersion in spite of their having been ordered out of existence by the levelling action of Babylonian talmudic legislation. In reaffirming adherence to these practices, the forces of protest would register their dissatisfaction with the exilarchic and [sages'] administration and repudiation of its legal and social policies which were identified with the talmudic legislation.[12]

Ankori judges that the dynamics of sectarian life found definition "within or against its normative environment."[13] For our purpose that observation proves critical, for it was the dual Torah that defined, in doctrinal and mythic terms, the normative environment.

The movement itself claimed to originate in biblical times and to derive its doctrine from the true priest, Zadok. The founder of the movement then recovered that original Torah. The founder, Anan b. David, imposed rules concerning food that were stricter than those of the rabbis, and he in other ways legislated a stricter version of the law than the talmudic authorities admitted. Ankori says of Anan:

Anan ben David led the forces of anti-Rabbanite rebellion out of the remote frontiers of the Muslim-dominated Jewish Dispersion into the heart of exilarchic and geonic [sages, that is rabbinic-talmudic] domination. Until that time open defiance was in evidence only in the outlying provinces of the Caliphate in which Muslim heterodoxy was thriving also. Anan's answer to the challenge of disillusionment with militant Palestino-centric messianism was national asceticism anchored in the diasporic community of the pious. . . . Anan's widely heralded fundamentalism and exclusive reliance on the letter of the Written Law are largely a misnomer. Rather, his was an ex post facto attempt to read into the Bible (the full twenty-four volumes of it and not the Pentateuch alone) the customs and observances already practiced by the sectarians. . . . Normative leadership in Babylonia, awakened to the danger of sectarian subversion in its own home while campaigning for the extension of Babylonian jurisdiction over all provinces of the Jewish dispersion, must have struck back with all its force.[14]

By the ninth century the movement was firmly established. From the seventh to the twelfth centuries the main centers were located in Baghdad, Nehavend, Basra, and Isfahan and elsewhere in Iran, and there were centers of the faith in the holy land and Egypt as well. Later on the movement moved its focus to the Byzantine Empire, especially in the twelfth through sixteenth centuries. In the seventeenth and eighteenth centuries it moved to Poland and nearby regions, and in the nineteenth and twentieth centuries it was found in the Crimea. What makes the movement interesting is its principle: "Search thoroughly in the Torah and do not rely on my opinion," so said Anan. The Scriptures formed the sole principle of the law.

Overall, in its formative century, the Karaite Judaism formed "a conglomeration of various anti-talmudic heresies." Exhibiting differences among themselves, they claimed that the differences proved their authenticity: "[The Rabbanites, that is, the talmudic rabbis and their heirs] believe that their laws and regulations have been transmitted by the prophets; if that was the case, there ought not to exist any differences of opinion among them, and the fact that such differences of opinion do exist refutes their presumptuous belief. We on the other hand arrive at our views by our reason, and reason can lead to various results."[15] The principal that predominated was that Scriptures were to be studied freely, independently, and individually. No uniformity of view could then emerge. Given the stress of the Judaism of the dual Torah on the authority of the Talmud and related canonical documents, we could not expect a more precise statement of the opposite view. Each party considered the other to be Jews, until the eighteenth century, but in the nineteenth century in the Russian Empire they were treated as distinct from one another. Karaites took the title "Russian Karaites of the Old Testament Faith."

On that account the Germans spared their lives during World War II. But after the rise of the state of Israel, the Karaites in Islamic lands moved to the state of Israel, where seven thousand of them live today.[16]

The principal doctrine that the Bible serves as the sole source of faith and law made a place for tradition. But it was to be kept subordinate. The emphasis lay not on the consensus of sages, characteristic of the Judaism of the dual Torah, but on the individual's task of finding things out for himself. Anan, the founder, said exactly that. So the doctrine balanced the principles of "rigidity and immutability of tradition" and "an absence of restrictions on individual understanding of the Scriptures."[17] The anarchy that resulted yielded ground to systemization later. Heller and Nemoy list the four principles for the determination of the law: (1) the literal meaning of the biblical text; (2) the consensus of the community; (3) the conclusions derived from Scripture by the method of logical analogy; and (4) knowledge based on human reason and intelligence.

Apart from the rejection of the oral Torah, one would look in vain for important differences in creed. God is the sole Creator, and God made the world out of nothing; God is uncreated, formless, incomparable in unity, incorporeal, unique; God sent Moses and the prophets, and gave the Torah through Moses, to which there will be no further complement or alteration; the dead will be raised on a day of judgment; there is reward and punishment, providence, freedom of will, and immortality of the soul; and God will send a Messiah when Israel in exile has been purified. The followers of the oral Torah would have found themselves entirely at home in these principles of the faith. On the other hand, the calendar did distinguish the Karaites from the other Jews, since the Karaites developed their own calendar and therefore observed holy occasions on different days from those selected by the rabbanites. Some minor details of the law of ritual slaughter differed, and the rules of consanguineous marriage are stricter than those of the rabbanites. In structure the liturgy does not vastly differ from that of the rabbanites: the Shema is recited, the Torah is read, and so on. So the fundamental point of heresy was simple: the authority of the oral tradition. The Karaites claimed that their Torah conveyed the pure faith of Moses, and the belief in a dual revelation was the point that separated them permanently from the

Judaism of the dual Torah. This was made explicit in the beginning, though later on Karaites could admit, "Most of the Mishnah and the Talmud comprises genuine utterances of our fathers, and . . . our people are obligated to study the Mishnah and the Talmud."[18] But that was the issue that had led to the original division.

HERESIES AGAINST RABBINIC JUDAISM: SABBATEANISM VERSUS THE SAGE-MESSIAH

From the perspective of our search for a theory for the entire history of Judaism, what is important about the Sabbatean movement, a seventeenth-century messianic movement organized around the figure of Shabbetai Zevi (1626–1676)[19] is a simple fact. The Sabbatean movement defined the Messiah not as a sage who kept and embodied the law, but as the very opposite. The Torah defined the framework of debate. Sabbateans responded with the Messiah as a holy man who violated the law in letter and in spirit. In positing a Messiah in the mirror image of the sage-Messiah of the Judaism of the dual Torah, the Sabbatean movement, like Karaism, paid its respects to the received system. Gershom Scholem finds the power of the movement in its link to earlier doctrines of the Jewish Kabbalah, in which the hope for the Messiah was joined to mystical religious experience, thus, in Scholem's language, "introducing a new element of tension into the Kabbalah, which was of a much more contemplative nature." The Kabbalah that took shape in the sixteenth century, associated with the name of Luria and the locale of Safed, linked the doing of the religious duties of the Torah, the recitation of prayer, and the messianic hope. Specifically, the link is drawn as follows:

> All being has been in exile since the very beginning of creation and the task of restoring everything to its proper place has been given to the Jewish people, whose historic fate and destiny symbolize the state of the Universe at large. The sparks of Divinity are dispersed everywhere . . . but are held captive by . . . the power of evil and must be redeemed. This final redemption . . . cannot be achieved by one single messianic act, but will be effected through a long chain of activities that prepare the way.[20]

The Jews' redemption through the Messiah will serve as "external symbols of a cosmic process which in fact takes place in the secret recesses of the universe." The doctrine of the sixteenth-century Kabbalists, that the final stages of redemption were now near, made the Judaic world ready for the messianic figure who came to the fore in 1665.

Shabbetai Zevi, born in Smyrna/Ismir in 1626, mastered talmudic law and lore and enjoyed respect for his learning even among his opponents. A manic-depressive, during his manic periods he deliberately violated religious law with actions called, in the doctrine of his movement, "strange or paradoxical actions." In depressed times he chose solitude "to wrestle with the demonic powers by which he felt attacked and partly overwhelmed." During a period of wandering in Greece and Thrace, he placed himself in active opposition to the law, declaring the commandments to be null and saying a benediction "to Him who allows what is forbidden." In this way he distinguished himself even before his meeting with the disciple who organized his movement, Nathan of Gaza. In 1665 the two met and Nathan announced to Shabbetai that Shabbetai was the true Messiah. This independent confirmation of Shabbetai's own messianic dreams served, in Nathan's doctrine, "to explain the peculiar rank and nature of the Messiah's soul in the kabbalistic scheme of creation."[21] In May 1665, Shabbetai announced that he was the Messiah, and various communities, hearing the news, split in their response to that claim. Leading rabbis opposed him, but others took a more sympathetic view. Nathan proclaimed that the time of redemption had come. In 1666 the grand vizier offered Shabbetai Zevi the choice of accepting Islam or imprisonment and death. On 15 September 1666, Shabbetai Zevi converted to Islam.

Nathan of Gaza explained that the apostasy marked a descent of the Messiah to the realm of evil, outwardly to submit to its domination but actually to perform the last and most difficult part of his mission by conquering that realm from within.[22] The Messiah was engaged in a struggle with evil, just as in his prior actions in violating the law he had undertaken part of the labor of redemption. The apostate Messiah then formed the center of the messianic drama, meant to culminate soon in the triumph. Until his death in 1672, Shabbetai Zevi carried out his duties as a Muslim and also observed

Jewish ritual. He went through alternating periods of illumination and depression, and in the former periods he founded new festivals and taught that accepting Islam involved "the Torah of grace," as against Judaism, "the Torah of truth." Scholem summarizes the doctrine as follows:

> In a way, every soul is composed of the two lights, and by its nature bound predominantly to the thoughtless light which aims at destruction, and the struggle between the two lights is repeated over and over again in every soul. But the holy souls are helped by the law of the Torah, whereas the Messiah is left completely to his own devices. These ideas . . . responded precisely to the particular situation of those who believed in the mission of an apostate Messiah, and the considerable dialectical force with which they were presented did not fail to impress susceptible minds.[23]

The Sabbatean movement persisted for another century or so. Some believers joined Islam and others reverted to Judaism. The mainstream of followers persisted in the antinomianism of the founder and took the view that the "new spiritual or Messianic Torah entailed a complete reversal of values. . . . This included all the prohibited sexual unions and incest." The story of Sabbateanism, both in the life of Shabbetai and Nathan and afterward, carries us far afield. The one consequential fact for the history of Judaism lies in the trait of the system that defined it as a heresy. The messianic doctrine that had stood at the head of the Judaism of the dual Torah—the Messiah as sage and master of the law—found as its counterpart and heretical opposite the doctrine of the Messiah as master of the law but at the same time the quintessential sinner in committing those very sins that the law designated as sinful. The Messiah, who was to come to fulfill and complete the law, ended up denying it. From the viewpoint of the Judaism of the dual Torah there can have been no greater heresy than that. Only when we encounter the Judaisms of the twentieth century, wholly out of phase with the received system of the dual Torah, shall we appreciate the full power of the received system to dictate to heretical groups the terms and doctrines of their heresies, for the doctrine of the dual Torah created Karaism and the sage-Messiah defined Sabbateanism.

THE POWER AND PATHOS
OF JUDAISM

In the nineteenth century the Judaism of the dual Torah found for itself adaptations and continuations. In the twentieth century, for the first time since the fourth, the same Judaism met with competition from Judaisms that defined themselves—their terms and classifications—wholly out of relationship with those of the Judaism of the dual Torah. The new Judaisms no longer fell into the category of heresies of the received one. They asked different questions and proposed as valid answers that had no bearing upon the issues of the dual Torah. The Judaism of the dual Torah exercised power for so long as people found its questions urgent and its answers obvious and beyond the need for argument. The same Judaism ceased to define the system for substantial communities of Jews when those questions gave way to others and those answers became irrelevant.

The power of Judaism derived from the world as it was defined by its rivals and heirs, Christianity and Islam. Christianity and Islam formulated the questions that Christianity, Judaism, and Islam would confront. The pathos of the Judaism of the dual Torah derived from its incapacity to address questions that lay totally outside of its powers of imagination. But those were the questions of the twentieth century, and no religious worldview and way of life would prove able to cope with them. When humanity lost the vision of itself as having been created in the image of God, "in our image, after our likeness," then Judaism, Islam, and Christianity had to fall silent. For the great religions of Scripture took as their critical question what it meant for humanity to be in God's image, after God's likeness. The power of Judaic religious systems, like that of Christian and Islamic religious systems, was the same as the pathos of the three faiths of Abraham. Their strength—the transcendent vision of humanity—also marked their weakness; the measure of trivial humanity, there to be murdered in its masses. The death of Judaism, where it died, formed a chapter in this century's tale of civil war within humanity, first in the West in World War I, and then in the world in World War II and afterward. But our task is to tell only that small paragraph in the history of Judaism that attests to the larger meaning in the story of humanity.

Since the Judaism of the dual Torah faced significant competition only in the West,[24] let us speak of Christendom in particular as we approach modern and contemporary times. The critical Judaic component of the Christian civilization of the West spoke of God and God's will for humanity, and what it meant to live in God's image, after God's likeness. So said the Judaism of the dual Torah, and so said Christianity in its worship of God made flesh. So that message of humanity in God's image, of a people seeking to conform to God's will, found resonance in the Christian world as well: both components of the world, the Christian dough and the Judaic yeast, bore a single message about humanity.

The powerful religious traditions of the West—the Christian and the Judaic—lost their voice in the nineteenth century and their echo in the twentieth. The twentieth century raised the inevitable issues of class and nation-state as bases for the bureaucratization of the common life. It did not ask what it meant to form one humanity in the image of one God. Asked to celebrate the image of humanity, the twentieth century created an improbable likeness of humanity: mountains of corpses. The Judaism of the dual Torah fell understandably silent when it confronted the twentieth century's framing of the inexorable question, What is man? In such a world as this, what was there to say?

NOTES

1. Bernard Lewis, *The Jews of Islam* (Princeton: Princeton University Press, 1984), p. 8.

2. Ibid., pp. 19–20.

3. Ibid., p. 21.

4. Ibid., p. 32.

5. Cited by Louis Jacobs, "Basic Ideas of Hasidism," *Encyclopaedia Judaica* 7:1404.

6. Jacobs, "Basic Ideas," col. 1405.

7. Ibid., col. 1406.

8. Arthur Green, *Tormented Master: A Life of Rabbi Nahman of Bratslav* (Tuscaloosa: University of Alabama Press, 1979), p. 12.

9. Ibid., p. 14.

10. Quoted in ibid., p. 265.

11. I treat heresy as an inappropriate but necessary word. Within the diversity of Judaisms, none can be more or less authentic than any other. Descriptively, a heresy becomes a heresy when it takes up a position on an issue defined by a dominant Judaism that is different from the position of

that Judaism. It thus conforms the dominance of the paramount system of the time and place.

12. Zvi Ankori, *Karaites in Byzantium* (New York: Columbia University Press, 1959), pp. 1–3.

13. Ibid., p. 9.

14. Ibid., pp. 14, 17, 21.

15. Al Kirkisani, quoted by Joseph Elijah Heller and Leon Nemoy in "Karaites," *Encyclopaedia Judaica* 10:766.

16. Heller and Nemoy, "Karaites," col. 777.

17. Ibid.

18. Ibid., col. 781.

19. Gershom G. Scholem, "Shabbetai Zevi," *Encyclopaedia Judaica* 14:1219–1254. All quotations and citations are from this article.

20. Ibid., col. 1220.

21. Ibid., col. 1224.

22. Ibid., col. 1238.

23. Ibid., col. 1243.

24. The impact of imperialism on Judaism in the Islamic world cannot be ignored, e.g., in French Algeria and Morocco. But Islam overall retained its self-evident standing as revealed truth, and the Judaism of the colonized world of Islam thrived, as did Islam. The development in the French colonies of a Francophone Israel affected only the urban middle and upper classes while the larger numbers were essentially untouched by Western secularism. Neither Reform nor Orthodoxy in their Western formulations found any counterpart in the colonial period of Islam.

11

The Advent of New Judaisms in the Nineteenth and Twentieth Centuries

THE FALL OF JUDAISM AND THE RISE OF JUDAISMS

In modern times in the West, although not in Muslim countries, the long-established system of Judaism formed in ancient days lost its paramount position. That received Judaic system was built on the experience of exile and return as it had been modified in the oral Torah to encompass the sanctification of the life of the people as the condition of the salvation of the nation at the end of time. It now competed with, and even gave way to, a number of new Judaisms. Some of these new Judaisms stood in direct continuation with the received system, revering its canon and repeating its main points. For our theory of the history of Judaism, Reform and Orthodoxy exemplify the Judaisms of continuation. Others utterly rejected the mythic structure and system of the Judaism of the dual Torah. For our examples we take Zionism and American Judaism. These heretical systems outside of the system of the dual Torah amply demonstrate the power of the pattern of the Torah of Moses, for both of them recapitulate the same pattern of exile and return that the original system laid forth, the one explicitly, the other structurally. American Judaism, the single Judaic system most remote from the Judaism of the dual Torah, simply replicated the original paradigm, in its categorical structure of Holocaust and Redemption. And that fact presents its own puzzle, since both categories, holocaust and redemption, in no way conformed to the actual events of the lives and social experience of the Jews who found in those categories the meaning of their lives both individually and as an Israel.

That is why the paramount question before us is not why the received system underwent modification, restatement, or, in some instances, total rejection in favor of discontinuous and fresh statements altogether. Our question does not concern the myth and ritual, the worldview, and the way of life of the Judaism of the dual Torah—or the continuity and change that affected that myth. Rather, our inquiry addresses the power of the structure of experience and expectation that sustained the Judaism of the dual Torah. We want to know whether and how the new Judaisms of modern times recapitulated the experience and viewpoint of the original Torah.

We shall find that, whether continuous with the Judaism of the dual Torah or quite distinct from it, the Judaic systems of our age adopted as their perspective the same pattern: exile and return, alienation and restoration. The single Judaism most remote from the received tradition in its canon and in its identification of definitive experience, American Judaism, in its deep structure of Holocaust and Redemption repeated in acutely contemporary terms the original pattern. What people expected to happen is what they thought happened—whether it did or not, and whether what they thought served their interest or violated it. When we consider religion as an independent variable, a world-creating power on its own, we may point to American Judaism as a stunning instance of how a religion defined what was not there and then led to its formation and realization, not in imagination alone but also in politics and society.

While I see no such thing as Judaism, but only Judaisms, there is, nonetheless, a pattern that has tended to characterize all Judaisms. The Judaic systems of the nineteenth and twentieth centuries followed a pattern of suffering and atonement, in theological terms, or a dark age followed by enlightenment, in secular and political ones, that would not have surprised the framers of the Torah of Moses in the aftermath of the original experience created and recorded in the time of Ezra. But the details would have astonished the first and founding author, and in the unfolding of Judaism God lives in the details. Orthodoxy and Reform Judaism were new and interesting, although they made only slight modifications in the enduring system. Zionism and American Judaism recapitulated the original pattern in a remarkably faithful but at the same time fresh and original formulation.

Identifying points of change in modern times presents few problems. Under some circumstances people simply chose for themselves a set of questions different from those that had defined the West since the formation of Christendom in the age of Constantine. They also produced a set of self-evidently true answers. If I want to know what people find self-evident, I have to uncover the questions they confront and cannot evade. These questions dictate the program of inquiry and the answers follow after the fact. These questions raised by the continuator-Judaisms of the nineteenth century—Reform and later Orthodoxy—asked how one could be both Jewish and something else. The Judaism of the dual Torah had answered only the question of how to be Jewish. In making a place for that something else, that corner of life not affected by the labor of sanctification in the here and now aiming at salvation at the end of time, the continuator-Judaisms framed in a fresh and striking way the system received from the dual Torah. The questions answered by the new Judaisms of the twentieth century—Zionism and American Judaism—were how one could survive in body and in spirit in an age of total annihilation. The answers had nothing to do with sanctification and salvation. But they conformed in an exact way to the structure of experience that had originated in the imagination of the authors of the Torah of Moses: the pattern of exile and return (Zionism) or suffering and resolution (American Judaism).

Many have speculated on the reasons for the shift in the character of Jewry in modern times from the pattern that persisted from the fourth century through the eighteenth. But an important point of change was in the realm of politics. A political change in the circumstance of the Jews in central and western Europe as well as America demanded the rethinking of the theory of who is Israel and what it means to be Israel. For the original pattern had emerged out of an essentially political problem confronting the author of the Torah of Moses, and it had settled a political question. That pattern served in subsequent settings to create a politics in the form of a powerful and definitive myth of who was Israel. Then a stunning shift in the political circumstance of a Judaism in the West, beginning at the time of the American Constitution of 1787 and the French Revolution of 1789, affected Jews' thought about perennial questions.

What happened toward the end of the eighteenth century was the secularization of political life and institutions. Earlier modes of organizing matters had recognized, as political entities, groups and guilds and classes, and the Jews had found a place among them. In the hierarchical scheme, with church and monarchy and aristocracy in their proper alignment, other political entities likewise found their location. When the church was disestablished, the monarchy rejected, and the aristocracy no longer dominant in politics, the political unit (theoretically) became the undifferentiated individual making up the nation-state. Within that theory there was no room for Israel as a political unit, although (in theory at least) there might be room for the Jewish individual, in his rightful place alongside other undifferentiated individuals. That was the theory that produced a considerable crisis for the Judaism of the dual Torah.

In the aftermath of the changes in Western politics in the nineteenth century, Jews asked themselves whether and how they could be something else in addition to being Jewish. That something first invariably found expression in the name of the locale where they lived: whether France, Germany, Britain, or America. So, could one be both Jewish and German? The question found its answer in two givens: the received Judaism of the dual Torah, and certain clearly defined responsibilities imposed by "being German" or "being French."

The full force of the twentieth-century innovation of totalitarianism, whether Soviet Communist or German Nazi, also made its imprint upon the Judaic agenda. Where and how could the Jew endure? That question predominated. Its self-evident answer was not among Gentiles, but only in the Jewish state. This answer produced one Judaism for the Jews of the State of Israel and another quite different one for the Jews of the Western democracies. But at the threshold of the twenty-first century it was only in the Jewish state and in the Western democracies that Jews found themselves free to ask questions and answer them at all.

We see that sweeping changes in the political circumstances of Jews, as well as in their economic conditions, made urgent issues that had formerly drawn slight attention, and rendered inconsequential claims that had for so long demanded a response. The Jews had formerly constituted a distinct group. Now in the West they formed part of an undifferentiated mass of citizens, all of them equal before the law and all of them subject to the same law. The Judaism of the dual Torah had rested on the political premise that the Jews were governed by God's law and formed God's people. The two political premises—the one of the nation-state and the other of the Torah—scarcely permitted a reconciliation. The consequent Judaic systems,

Reform Judaism and Orthodox Judaism, had each addressed issues they regarded as acute and not merely chronic. In the nineteenth century they had alleged that they formed the natural next step in the unfolding of "the tradition," meaning the Judaic system of the dual Torah. The Judaic systems born in the twentieth century did not make that claim. But nevertheless they recapitulated the pattern, familiar from the very beginning of the Torah of Moses, that taught them what to expect and how to explain what happened.

First was Reform Judaism, which came to expression in the early part of the nineteenth century and made changes in liturgy and then in the doctrine and the way of life of the received Judaism of the dual Torah. Reform Judaism recognized that it was legitimate to make changes and regarded change as reform. Second was the reaction to Reform Judaism called Orthodox Judaism. In many ways it was continuous with the Judaism of the dual Torah, but in some ways it was as selective of elements of that Judaism as was Reform Judaism. Third came Zionism, which to begin with was a theory and a program for responding to the failure of the promise of the nineteenth century and its politics. Finally, in the final third of the twentieth century came American Judaism, a response to the catastrophe of the destruction of the bulk of European Jewry and to the messianic expectations associated with the creation of the Jewish state: hence Holocaust and Redemption.

A JUDAISM WITHIN
RABBINIC JUDAISM: REFORM

If I had to specify the single dominant concern of the framers of Reform Judaism, I should turn to the matter of the Jews' position, beginning in the eighteenth century, in the public polity of the several Christian European countries in which they lived. From the perspective of the political changes taking place from the American and French Revolutions onward, the received system of the Judaism of the dual Torah answered irrelevant questions and did not respond to acute ones. For the issue no longer found definition in the claims of regnant Christianity. A new question, emerging from forces not contained within Christianity, demanded attention from the Jews affected by those forces. For those Jews, the change derived from shifts in political circumstances. The issue confronting the new Judaism derived not from Christianity but from political change brought about by forces of secular nationalism, which conceived of society not as the expression of God's will for the social order under the rule of Christ and his church or his anointed king, but of the popular will for the social order under the government of the people and their elected representatives. This was a considerable shift. When society was no longer formed of distinct groups, each with its place, definition, language, and religion, but rather was formed of undifferentiated citizens (male, white, and wealthy, to be sure), then Jews in such a society needed to work out a very different sort of Judaism. The Judaism had to frame a theory of who is Israel that was consonant with the social situation of Jews who wanted to be different, but not so different that they could not also be citizens. Both Reform and Orthodoxy answered that question. Each rightly claimed to continue the received tradition, that is, the Judaism of the dual Torah. But Reform came first and answered forthrightly.

The most dramatic statement of that continuator-Judaism emerged from a meeting of Reform rabbis in 1885 in Pittsburgh. At that meeting the American Reform rabbinate made a declaration of its definition of Reform Judaism. To the Reform rabbis in Pittsburgh, Christianity presented no urgent problems. The open society of America did. The self-evident definition of the social entity, Israel, therefore had to shift. The supernatural entity, Israel, now formed no social presence. The Christian world, in which Christ had ruled through popes and emperors, kings had claimed divine right, and the will of the church had born multiform consequences for society, and in which Israel too had been perceived in a supernatural framework, no longer existed. Therefore the world at large no longer verified that generative social category of Israel's life, Israel as supernatural entity. And the problem of the definition of what sort of entity Israel did constitute, of what way of life should characterize that Israel, and what worldview should explain it—that problem produced a new set of urgent and unavoidable questions and self-evidently true answers, such as the ones stated in Pittsburgh.

Reform Judaism forthrightly and articulately faced the political changes that had redefined the conditions of Jews' lives and presented a Judaism fully responsive to those changes, but still closely tied to the inherited system of the dual Torah. For Reform Judaism in the nineteenth century, the full and authoritative statement of the system came to expression not in Europe but in America, at the assembly of Reform rabbis in Pittsburgh in 1885. At that meeting of the Central Conference of American Rabbis, the Reform Judaism of the age, by now about a century old, took up the issues that divided Judaism and made an authoritative statement on them that most people could accept.

The very fact that this Judaism could conceive of such a process of debate and formulation of a kind of creed tells us that this Judaism found urgent the specification of its systemic structure. It is also testimony to its mature and self-aware frame of mind. In the antecedent thousand years of the Judaism of the dual Torah we look in vain for equivalent convocations to set public policy. When statements of the worldview emerged in diverse expressions of the received system, they did not take the form of a rabbis' platform and did not come about through democratic debate on public issues. The worldview percolated upward and represented a rarely articulated and essentially inchoate consensus about how things really were and should have been. The contrast tells us not merely that Reform Judaism represented a new Judaism but also that the methods and approaches of Reform Judaism enjoyed their own self-evident appropriateness. And from that we learn how the qualities people found self-evidently right had changed over time.

The American Reform rabbis thus issued a clear and accessible statement of their Judaism. We want to know one thing in particular about this Judaism: its formulation of the issue of Israel as political circumstances defined it. For critical to the Judaism of the dual Torah was its view of Israel as God's people, a supernatural polity, living out its social existence under God's Torah. That basic conception engendered the way of life—one of sanctification—and the worldview, one of persistent reference to the Torah for both the rules of conduct and the explanation of conduct. The Pittsburgh platform stated:

> We recognize in the Mosaic legislation a system of training the Jewish people for its mission during its national life in Palestine, and today we accept as binding only its moral laws and maintain only such ceremonies as elevate and sanctify our lives, but reject all such as are not adapted to the views and habits of modern civilization. We hold that all such Mosaic and rabbinical laws as regular diet, priestly purity, and dress originated in ages

and under the influence of ideas entirely foreign to our present
mental and spiritual state. . . . Their observance in our days is
apt rather to obstruct than to further modern spiritual elevation.
. . . We recognize in the modern era of universal culture of heart
and intellect the approaching of the realization of Israel's great
messianic hope for the establishment of the kingdom of truth,
justice, and peace among all men. We consider ourselves no
longer a nation but a religious community and therefore expect
neither a return to Palestine nor a sacrificial worship under the
sons of Aaron nor the restoration of any of the laws concerning
the Jewish state.

I cannot imagine a more forthright address to the age. The Pittsburgh
platform took each component of the system in turn. Who is Israel?
What is its way of life? How does it account for its existence as a
distinct, and distinctive, group? Israel was once a nation, but today is
not a nation. It once had a set of laws to regulate diet, clothing, and
the like. These no longer apply, because Israel now is not what it was
then. Israel forms an integral part of Western civilization. The reason
to persist as a distinctive group was that the group had its work to do,
namely, to realize the messianic hope for the establishment of a kingdom of truth, justice, and peace. For that purpose Israel no longer
constituted a nation. It now formed a religious community.

What that meant was that individual Jews lived as citizens in
other nations. Difference was acceptable at the level of religion, not
nationality, a position that fully accorded with the definition of citizenship for the Western democracies. The worldview laid heavy
emphasis on an as yet unrealized but coming perfect age. The way of
life admitted to no important traits that distinguished Jews from
others, since morality forms a universal category that is applicable in
the same way to everyone. The theory of Israel formed the heart of
matters, and what we learn is that Israel constituted a "we." The Jews
continued to form a group that, by its own indicators, held together
and constituted a cogent social entity. It was also a truth declared
rather than discovered, and the self-evidence of the truth of the statements competed with the self-awareness characteristic of those who
made them. For they recognized the problem that demanded attention: the reframing of a theory of Israel. No more urgent question
faced the rabbis, because they lived in a century of opening horizons,

in which people could envision perfection. World War I would change all that, also for Israel. By 1937 the Reform rabbis, meeting in Columbus, Ohio, would reframe the system, expressing a worldview quite different from that of the half century before.

Let us summarize the program of urgent issues and self-evident responses that constituted the first and most important of the new Judaisms of the nineteenth century. Questions we find answered fall into two categories: first, why "we" do not keep certain customs and ceremonies but do keep others; second, how "we relate to the nations in which we live." So the system of Reform Judaism explained both why and why not, the mark of a fully framed and cogent Judaism. The affirmative side covered why the Jews would persist as a separate group, and the negative side accounted for the limits of difference. These two questions deal with the same urgent problem: working out a mode of Judaic existence compatible with citizenship in America. Jews did not propose to eat or dress in distinctive ways. They sought a place within "modern spiritual elevation . . . universal culture of heart and intellect." They imputed to that culture the realization of "the messianic hope." And, explicitly the Jews no longer constituted a nation, but belonged to some other nation(s). If I had to specify a single self-evident proposition taken fully into account by this Judaism it is that political change had changed the entirety of "Judaism," but that Judaism had the power to accommodate to that change. So change formed the method of dealing with the problem, which was change in the political and social standing the Jews had enjoyed. So Reform Judaism formed a Judaic system that confronted immense political change and presented a worldview and way of life to an Israel redefined by the change. The Reformers maintained that change was all right because historical precedent had proved that change was all right. But change had long defined the constant in the ongoing life of the Judaism of the dual Torah.

The Reformers made much of change in liturgy. And they were right, but for the wrong reasons. The mythic being of the received liturgy had entailed the longing, in the imagination of the nation, for a return to Zion, for the rebuilding of the Temple, and for reconstitution of the bloody rites of animal sacrifice. These political propositions had formed a critical plank in the response to the Christian view that Israel's salvation had occurred in times past and had ended with Israel's rejection of the Christhood of Jesus. In response, the dual

Torah had insisted on future salvation, at the end of time. For ages from the original exile in 586 B.C.E., the Jews had appealed to a Scripture that explained why they had lost their land, their city, their Temple, and their cult, and told them what they had to do to get them back. Jews knew who they were. They were a nation in exile. So when the early changes included rewording the liturgy so as to diminish the motifs of the return to Zion and restoration of the cult, they signaled that much else had already undergone revision and that more would have to change as well. Reform ratified change already a generation old, proposed to cope with it, and reframed and revised the received tradition so as to mark out new outlines for self-evident truth.

For the nineteenth-century Jews of the West, the urgent problem was to define Israel in an age in which individual Jews had become something else, in addition to being Israel. Was Israel a nation? No, Israel did not fall into the same category as the nations. Jews were multiple beings: Israel in one dimension, part of France or Germany or America in another. But if Israel was not a nation, then what of the way of life that had made the nation different, and what of the worldview that had made sense of the way of life? These now formed the questions people could not avoid. The answers constituted Reform Judaism.

JUDAISM WITHIN
RABBINIC JUDAISM: ORTHODOXY

Orthodox Judaism is the Judaic system that mediates between the received Judaism of the dual Torah and the requirements of living a life integrated in modern circumstances. Orthodoxy maintains the worldview of the received dual Torah, constantly citing its sayings and adhering with only trivial variations to the bulk of its norms for everyday life. At the same time Orthodoxy holds that Jews adhering to the dual Torah do not have to wear distinctively Jewish clothing, may live within a common economy, need not practice distinctively Jewish professions, and may take up a life not readily distinguished from the life lived by people in general. So for Orthodoxy a portion of Israel's life may prove secular, in that the Torah does not dictate and so sanctify all details under all circumstances. Since the Judaism of the dual Torah presupposed not only the supernatural entity, Israel, but also a way of life that in important ways distinguished that supernatural entity from the social world at large, the power of Orthodoxy to find an accommodation for Jews who valued the received way of life and worldview and also planned to make their lives in an essentially integrated social world proves formidable. The difference between Orthodoxy and the system of the dual Torah therefore comes to expression in social policy: integration, however circumscribed, versus the total separation of the holy people.

Orthodoxy as an articulated system with its own organizations and social policy came into existence in mid-nineteenth-century Germany in response to Reform Judaism. It answered the same questions but gave different answers. Reform Judaism maintained that, because the Jews no longer constituted the holy people living its own distinct existence, but rather a religious group that was part of a larger nation-state, the distinctive way of life had to go. Orthodoxy held that the Torah made provision for areas of life in which a Jew could be something other than a Jew. In education, for example, the institutions of the Judaism of the dual Torah had commonly held that one should study Torah alone. Orthodoxy in the West included secular sciences in its curriculum as well. The Judaism of the dual Torah had ordinarily identified particular forms of dress as Judaic. Orthodoxy did not. In these and in other ways Orthodoxy formed a fresh statement of the Judaism of the dual Torah, and what made that statement distinctive is that it provided for a life lived legitimately outside of the Judaic one, as long as it never violated its norms. Adhering to the received system of the dual Torah differed from identifying with Orthodox Judaism mainly with respect to indicators such as clothing, language, and above all, education.

When Jews kept the law of the Torah as it dictated food choices and keeping the Sabbath, but sent their children to secular schools or to Jewish schools that included in the curriculum subjects outside of the Torah, they crossed the boundary between the received Judaism and the new Judaism of Orthodoxy. For the notion that science or German or Latin or philosophy deserved serious study, while not alien to important exemplars of the received system of the dual Torah, in the nineteenth century seemed wrong to those for whom the received system remained self-evidently right. Those Jews did not send their children to Gentile schools, and in Jewish schools they did not include in the curriculum anything other than Torah study.

The Reformers held that Judaism could change and that Judaism was a product of history. The Orthodox opponents denied that Judaism could change and insisted that Judaism derived from God's will at Sinai and was not historical and manmade but eternal and supernatural. In these two convictions, of course, the Orthodox recapitulated the convictions of the received system. But in their appeal to the traditional, they found some components of that system more persuasive than others. In their articulation of the view that Judaism formed a religion to be seen as distinct and autonomous of politics and society, they entered the same world of self-conscious belief that the Reformers had also explored.

In a sense, Orthodoxy was precipitated by Reform Judaism. The term *Orthodoxy* itself—though not the organized Judaism—first surfaced in 1795, and covers all Jews who believe that God revealed the dual Torah at Sinai and that Jews must carry out the requirements of Jewish law contained in the Torah as interpreted by the sages through time. Obviously, so long as that position struck Jewry at large as self-evident, Orthodoxy as a distinct and organized Judaism did not exist. It did not have to. Two events took place together: first, the recognition of the received system as Orthodoxy; second, the specification of the received system as religion.

The former of the two events came first: the view that the received system was "traditional" and "Orthodox." The identification of truth as tradition came about when the received system met the challenge of competing Judaisms. Then, on behalf of the received way of life and worldview addressed to supernatural Israel, people said that the Judaism of the dual Torah had been established of old, and it was the only way of seeing and doing things, it was how things had been and should be naturally and normally: tradition. But tradition is a category that contains within itself an alternative, namely, change, as in "tradition and change."

It is when the system lost its power of self-evidence that it entered the classification of tradition. And that came about when Orthodoxy met head-on the challenge of change become Reform. We understand why the category of tradition became critical to the framers of Orthodoxy when we examine the counterclaim. Just as the Reformers justified change, the Orthodox theologians denied that change was ever possible. Walter Wurzburger says: "Orthodoxy looks upon attempts to adjust Judaism to the 'spirit of the time' as utterly incompatible with the entire thrust of normative Judaism, which holds that the revealed will of God rather than the values of any given age are the ultimate standard."[1] The issue important to the Reformers was the value of what was called "emancipation," meaning the provision of civil rights to Jews. This issue defined the debate. Orthodoxy took up the issue precisely as the other side had framed it. When the Reform Judaic theologians took a wholly one-sided position of affirming emancipation, Orthodox theologians adopted the contrary view and denied its importance. If Reform made minor changes in liturgy and its conduct, Orthodoxy rejected even these that might have found acceptance under other circumstances. Saying prayers in the vernacular, for example, provoked strong opposition. But everyone knew that the prayers said in Aramaic were in the vernacular of the earlier age. The Orthodox thought that these changes were not reforms at all and represented only the first step of a process leading Jews out of the Judaic world altogether. As Wurzburger says, "The slightest tampering with tradition was condemned."

If we ask where the received system of the dual Torah prevailed and by contrast where Orthodoxy came to full expression, we may follow the spreading out of railway lines, the growth of new industry, the shifts in political status accorded to Jews and other citizens, the changes in the educational system, and the entire process of change, political, economic and social, demographic and cultural. Where the changes came first, Reform Judaism met them in its way and Orthodoxy in its way. Where change came later in the century, as in the case of Russian Poland, the eastern provinces of the Austro-Hungarian Empire, and Russia itself, there, in villages contentedly following the old ways, the received system endured. And in the age of mass migration from Eastern Europe to America and other Western democracies, those who experienced the upheaval of leaving home and country met the challenge of change by either accepting new ways of seeing things or in full self-awareness reaffirming the familiar ones: Reform or Orthodoxy. We may characterize the received system as a way of life and worldview wedded to an ancient peoples' homelands, the villages and small towns of central and eastern Europe. Orthodoxy was the heir of the received system as it came to expression in the towns and cities of central and western Europe and America. That rule of thumb allows us to distinguish between the piety of a milieu and the theological conviction of a self-conscious community.

When, therefore, we explain the beginnings of Reform Judaism by referring to political and economic change, we also understand the point of origin of distinct and organized Orthodoxy. The beginnings of Orthodoxy took place in the areas where Reform made its way, hence in Germany and in Hungary. In Germany, where Reform attracted the majority of many Jewish communities, the Orthodox faced a challenge indeed. Critical to the Orthodox theologians' conviction was the notion that Israel, all of the Jews, bore responsibility to carry out the law of the Torah. But in the hands of the Reform the community's institutions did not obey the law of the Torah as the Orthodox understood it. So in the end Orthodoxy took the step that marked it as a self-conscious Judaism. Orthodoxy separated from the established community altogether. The Orthodox set up their own organization and seceded from the community at large. The next step altogether prohibited Orthodox from participating in non-Orthodox organizations. Isaac Breuer, a leading Orthodox theologian, ultimately took the position that "refusal to espouse the cause of separation was interpreted as being equivalent to the rejection of the absolute sovereignty of God."[2]

The matter of accommodating to the world at large did not allow for as easy an answer as mere separation. The specific issue—integration or segregation—concerned preparation for life in the larger politics and economic life of the country. That meant secular education, involving not only language and science, but also history and literature, matters of values. Orthodoxy proved diverse, with two wings to be distinguished. One rejected secular learning as well as all dealing with non-Orthodox Jews. The other cooperated with non-Orthodox and secular Jews and accepted the value of secular education. That position in no way affected loyalty to the law of Judaism—belief in God's revelation of the one whole Torah at Sinai. The point at which the received system and the Orthodox split requires specification. In concrete terms we know the one from the other by their evaluation of secular education. Proponents of the received system never accommodated themselves to secular education, while the Orthodox in Germany and Hungary persistently affirmed it. That represented a remarkable shift, since the study of Torah—Torah, not philosophy—was central to the received system of the dual Torah.

Explaining where we find the one and the other, H. Katzburg works with the distinction we have already made, between an unbroken system and one that has undergone a serious break with the familiar condition of the past. He states:

> In Eastern Europe until World War I, Orthodoxy preserved without a break its traditional ways of life and the time-honored educational framework. In general, the mainstream of Jewish life was identified with Orthodoxy, while Haskalah [Jewish Enlightenment, which applied to the Judaic setting the skeptical attitudes of the French Enlightenment] and secularization were regarded as deviations. Hence there was no ground wherein a Western type of Orthodoxy could take root. . . . European Orthodoxy in the nineteenth and the beginning of the twentieth centuries was significantly influenced by the move from small settlements to urban centers . . . as well as by emigration. Within the small German communities there was a kind of popular Orthodoxy, deeply attached to tradition and to local customs, and when it moved to the large cities this element brought with it a vitality and rootedness to Jewish tradition.[3]

Katzburg's observations provide important guidance. He authoritatively defines the difference between Orthodoxy and tradition. So he tells us how to distinguish the received system, accepted as self-evident, from an essentially selective and therefore by definition new system, called Orthodoxy. In particular he tells us how to distinguish the one from the other; he tells us where to find the self-conscious affirmation of tradition that characterizes Orthodoxy but did not occur in the world of the dual Torah as it glided in its eternal orbit of the seasons and of unchanging time.

I find it difficult to imagine what the urban Orthodox might have done otherwise. They experienced change, they daily encountered Jews unlike themselves, and they no longer lived in that stable Judaic society in which the received Torah formed the given of life. Pretense that Jews faced no choices scarcely represented a possibility. Nor did the generality of the Jews in the West propose to preserve a separate language or to renounce political rights. So Orthodoxy made its peace with change, no less than did Reform. The educational program that led Jews out of the received culture of the dual Torah, the use of the vernacular, the acceptance of political rights, the renunciation of Jewish garments, education for women, abolition of the power of the community to coerce the individual—these and many other originally Reform positions characterized the Orthodoxy that emerged in the nineteenth century as another new Judaism.[4]

If we ask how new the Orthodox system was we find ambiguous answers. In conviction, in way of life, and in worldview, we may hardly call it new at all. For the bulk of its substantive positions found ample precedent in the received dual Torah. From its affirmation of God's revelation of a dual Torah to its acceptance of the detailed authority of the law and customs, from its strict observance of the law to its unwillingness to change a detail of public worship, Orthodoxy rightly pointed to its strong links with the chain of tradition. But Orthodoxy constituted a sect within the Jewish group. Its definition of the Israel to whom it wished to speak hardly coincides with the definition characteristic of the dual Torah. The Judaism of the dual Torah addressed all Jews, and Orthodoxy recognized that it could not do so. But Orthodoxy acquiesced in a situation that lay beyond the imagination of the framers of the Judaism of the dual Torah.

To claim that the Orthodox went in search of proof-texts for a system formed and defined in advance misrepresents the reality—but not by much. For once the system of a self-conscious and deliberate Orthodoxy took shape, much picking, choosing, and assigning of priorities would follow naturally. And the result was the same: a new system with a way of life much like the received one but readily differentiated; a worldview congruent with the received one, but with its own points of interest and emphasis; and, above all, a social referent, an Israel quite beyond the limits of the one posited by the dual Torah.

The distinction between the religious and the secular was lost on the received system of the dual Torah, which legislated matters we should today regard as entirely secular or neutral, for example, the institutions of state (king, priest, army). We have already noted that in the received system as it took shape in eastern and central Europe, Jews wore garments regarded as distinctively Jewish. Some important traits of these garments indeed derived from the Torah. Jews pursued sciences that only Jews studied, for example, the Talmud and its commentaries. In these and other ways the Torah encompassed all of the life of Israel, the holy people. The recognition that Jews were like others and that the Torah fell into a category into which other and comparable matters fell—that recognition was long in coming.

For Christians in Germany and other Western countries it had become commonplace to see religion as distinct from other components of the social and political system. While the church in Russia identified with the czarist state, and the church in Poland with the national aspirations of the Polish people, in Germany two churches, Catholic and Protestant, competed. The terrible wars of the Reformation in the sixteenth and seventeenth centuries, which had ruined Germany, had led to the uneasy compromise that the prince could choose the religion of his principality. From that self-aware choice, people understood that "the way of life and worldview" in fact constituted a religion, and that one religion might be compared with another. By the nineteenth century, moreover, the separation of church and state ratified the important distinction between religion, where difference would be tolerated, and the secular, where citizens were pretty much the same.

In the West, political consciousness reached the Judaic world only in the late eighteenth century for some intellectuals and in the nineteenth century for many others. There was a fundamental shift in the understanding and interpretation of the Torah. Among Orthodox as much as among Reform Judaism, it was now seen as "Judaism," an -ism along with other -isms. The creative power of the Jews who formed the Orthodox Judaic system was marked by their capacity to shift the fundamental category in which they framed their system. The basic shift in category is what made Orthodoxy a Judaism on its own and not simply a restatement of the received system of the dual Torah.

The received system, giving expression to the rules of sanctification of the holy people had entailed wearing Jewish clothing, speaking a Jewish language, and learning only, or mainly, Jewish sciences. But clothing, language, and education now fell into the category of the secular, while other equally important aspects of everyday life remained in the category of the sacred. As it came into existence in Germany and other Western countries, Orthodox Judaism therefore found it possible to accept the language, clothing, and learning of those countries by recognizing the category of the secular. And these matters serve openly to exemplify a larger acceptance of Gentile ways, not all, but enough of them to lessen the differences between the holy people and the nations. Political change of a profound order presented to Orthodox Jews the problem of how to separate and how to integrate. For Orthodox Jews as well as Reform Jews the answers required picking and choosing. Both Judaisms understood that some things were sacred while others were not. That understanding marked off these Judaisms from the system of the dual Torah.

Once the category shift had taken place, the difference was to be measured in degree, not kind. For Orthodox Jews maintained distinctive political beliefs that Reform Jews rejected: in the future coming of the Messiah and the reconstitution of the Jewish nation in its own land. But, by placing these convictions in the distant future, the Orthodox Jews nonetheless prepared for a protracted interim of life within the nation where they lived. Like the Reform Jews, they were different from their fellow citizens in religion, not in nationality as represented by citizenship. Orthodoxy, as much as Reform, signaled remarkable changes in the Jews' political situation and—more important—aspirations. They wanted to be different, but not so different as the received system would have made them.

Still, in its nineteenth-century formulation Orthodoxy laid claim to carry forward the tradition in continuous and unbroken relationship. That claim assuredly demanded a serious hearing, for the things that Orthodoxy taught, the way of life it required, the Israel to whom it spoke, and the doctrines it said had been revealed by God to Moses at Sinai all conformed more or less exactly to the system of the received Judaism of the dual Torah as people then knew. Is it not what it says it is, "just Judaism"? Yes, but "Judaism," Orthodox or otherwise, is not "Torah." Piety selected is by definition piety invented, and the theologians of Orthodoxy were a group of intellectually powerful creators of a Judaism. Their ideal, which they expressed as "Torah and secular learning," defined a new worldview, dictated a new way of life, and addressed an Israel different from the Judaism of the dual Torah. To those who received the dual Torah as self-evident, what the Torah did not accommodate was secular learning. As they received it, the Torah did not approve changes in the familiar way of life and did not know an Israel other than the one at hand. So the perfect faith of Orthodoxy sustained a wonderfully selective piety.

A JUDAISM OUTSIDE OF
RABBINIC JUDAISM: ZIONISM

Zionism came into existence with the founding of the World Zionist Organization in Basel in 1897. American Judaism in the Zionist formulation came to powerful expression in the aftermath of the 1967 War in the Middle East. Both Judaic systems answered profoundly political questions. Their agendas attended to the status of the Jews as a group (Zionism and American Judaism) and the definition of the Jews in the context of larger political and social change (Zionism). It follows that the urgent questions addressed by the twentieth-century Judaisms differed from those acute in the nineteenth century. In the twentieth century, powerful forces for social and economic change took political form, in movements meant to shape government to the interests of particular classes or groups—the working classes or racial or ethnic entities, for instance. The Judaic systems of the century responded in kind.

In that same century, the definition of citizenship, encompassing ethnic and genealogical traits, presented the Jews with the problem of how to find a place in a nation-state that understood itself in an exclusionary, racist way—whether Nazi Germany, nationalist Poland, Hungary, Rumania, or revanchist and irredentist France. Zionism declared the Jews "a people, one people," and proposed as its purpose the creation of the Jewish state. Later, in the 1960s, shifting currents in American politics—a renewed ethnicism and an emphasis on intrinsic traits of birth rather than ability—called into question Jews' identification with the democratic system of America as that system defined permissible difference. A Jewish ethnicism, counterpart to the search for roots among diverse ethnic groups, responded with a tale of Jewish uniqueness—unique suffering and unique Jewish ethnic salvation and redemption in the Jewish State. These movements addressed political questions and responded with essentially political programs. Zionism wanted to create a Jewish state, but American Judaism wanted the Jews to form an active political community on their own.

These Judaisms are not at all like the ones that were formulated in the nineteenth century. That is for two reasons. First, on the surface the Judaic systems of the twentieth century took up political, social, and economic, but not theological, questions. Second, while the nineteenth-century Judaisms addressed issues unique to Jews, public policy issues of the twentieth-century Judaic systems concerned everyone, not only Jews. Thus, none of the Judaisms of the twentieth century proves congruent in each detail of structure to the continuator-Judaisms of the nineteenth century. All of the new Judaisms intersected with comparable systems among other Europeans and Americans. American ethnic assertion is the genus and American Judaism the species. Accordingly, we move from a set of Judaisms that form species of a single genus—the Judaism of the dual Torah—to a set of Judaisms that have less in common with each other than with systems wholly autonomous of Judaic worldviews and ways of life. The reason is clear. The issues addressed by the Judaisms of the twentieth century and the crises that made those issues urgent did not affect Jews alone or even mainly. The common crises derived from (1) the reorganization of political entities that formed the foundation of nationalism and also Zionism, and (2) the reconsideration of the theory of American society that produced, along with the homogenization of American life, renewed interest in ethnic origins as well as American Judaism. So while the nineteenth-century Judaisms took their perspective from the dual Torah, Jews in the twentieth century had other things on their minds.

It is therefore not surprising that the Judaisms we consider now not only rejected propositions that were important in the Judaism of the dual Torah, as did Karaism and Sabbateanism, but they also defined themselves out of relationship with the categories and propositions of the received Judaism. Asking their own questions and answering them out of resources of their own choosing, they took shape more than a century after the initial separation of Reform and Orthodox Judaism from the received system of the dual Torah. The further we find ourselves from that original point of departure, the more attenuated become the links to that system. The two twentieth-century systems laid no claim to continue the Judaism of the dual Torah, in no way placed themselves in relationship to it, and implicitly denied all relevance to that Judaism. So in fact they formed heresies that in no way exhibited the claim or the mark of continuity. As a matter of form or convention, each claimed antecedents or even precedents, and all adduced proof-texts. But we find a new set of questions, a new body of proof-texts, and, above all, a new definition of imperatives confronting the Jews as a group.

The systems of the twentieth century, represented by Zionism and American Judaism, were discontinuous with the received system and found no urgency in such a self-conscious accounting, but treated their several compositions—worldviews and ways of life addressed to an identified Israel—as essentially self-evident. Appealing to fully formed systems of their own, the new Judaisms went in search not of the proof-texts, whether in literature or in history, that had been so critical to the Reform, Orthodox, and Conservative theologians, but of mere pretexts: rhetoric to conform to an available program. But the search enjoyed its own justification. Zionism and American Judaism did recapitulate what was essential in the texts in which they searched for validation. For both Judaisms took as the given precisely the pattern of the original Torah: Israel is special, the Land is held on condition, Israel's suffering bears meaning, and its salvation is promised and awaits fulfillment on account of what Israel will do.

The principal difference between the extrasystemic heresies of Zionism and American Judaism (as a system of Holocaust and Redemption) and the continuator-Judaisms of Reform and Orthodoxy derives once more from the facts of the Jews' political circumstance. This is a critical point of difference and demands some attention. Reform and Orthodoxy by all definitions fall into the category of religion. Zionism and American Judaism constitute political movements, focused upon political programs. They address an essentially political agenda, although both evoke myths, attitudes, and convictions commonly categorized as religious.

The Judaisms of the nineteenth century have a single point of origin. All of them take form in the world of intellectuals. All focus upon issues of doctrine and regard as important the specification of why people should do what they do, and how within their several definitions Israel should see the world and live life. The Judaisms of the twentieth century address questions not of intellect but of public policy. They regard collective action as important, not ideology, which they identify with propaganda, nor theology, which lies beyond their imagination altogether. That collective action works itself out through large-scale institutions of government, politics, and economics. In the categories of charisma and routine, of individual initiative through intellectual charisma and collective action through bureaucracy, the nineteenth century was the age of Judaisms of intellect, and the twentieth, of bureaucracy. For the Judaisms of the twentieth century all took shape in a world that required the gifts not of intellectuals (although the founders all were persons of substantial intellect and vision) but of organizers, people who could create large-scale institutions and organizations: unions, bureaucracies, and even (in Zionism) entire governments. What mattered to nineteenth-century Judaisms demanded the genius of individual minds: writers, scholars, and theologians. The reason for the shift stands near at hand: the urgent issues of the nineteenth century demanded attention to doctrine and individual deed: What should I think? What should I do? The critical concerns of the twentieth century focused upon public policy: How shall we survive? Where should we go? So the Judaisms of an age testified to the character and quality of the age. Jews could evade the intellectual issues of the nineteenth century, but the world forced the political crises of the twentieth on their attention. And that accounts for the difference between the one type of system and the other.

HERESIES OUTSIDE OF JUDAISM:
ZIONISM

Zionism constituted the Jews' movement of self-emancipation, responding to the failure of the nations' promises of Jewish emancipation. It framed its worldview and way of life for the Israel of its definition in response to a political crisis—the failure, by the end of the nineteenth century, of the promises of political improvement in the Jews' status and condition. Zionism called the Jews to emancipate themselves by facing the fact that Gentiles in the main hated Jews. Founding a Jewish state where Jews could free themselves of anti-Semitism and build their own destiny, the Zionist system of Judaism declared as its worldview this simple proposition: the Jews form a people, one people, and should transform themselves into a political entity and build a Jewish state.

Zionism began with the founding of the Zionist Organization in 1897, and reached its fulfillment and dissolution of its original form with the founding of the State of Israel in May 1948. Zionism began with the definition of its theory of Israel: a people, one people, in a secular sense. Then came the worldview, which composed of the diverse histories of Jews a single, singular history of the Jewish people, leading from the Land of Israel in exile back to the Land of Israel.

This component of the Zionist worldview constituted an exact recapitulation of the biblical narrative, even though it derived not from a religious but from a nationalist perspective. The way of life of the elitist or activist required participation in meetings, organizing within the local community, and attendance at national and international conferences—a focus of life's energy on the movement. Later, as settlement in Israel itself became possible, Zionism defined migration to the Land of Israel as the most noble way of living life, and the socialist wing of Zionism defined it as building a collective community (kibbutz). So Zionism presented a complete and fully articulated Judaism, and prior to its complete success in the creation of the State of Israel in 1948, one of the most powerful and effective of them all.[5]

It is self-evident that in Zionism we deal with a response to an essentially political situation. In modern times the word *Zionism* came into use in the 1890s, in the sense of a political movement of Jewish self-emancipation. The word *emancipation* had earlier stood for the Jews receiving the political rights of citizens in various nations. This self-emancipation turned on its head the entire political program of nineteenth-century Jewry. That shift alerts us to the relationship between Zionism and the earlier political changes of which Reform Judaism had made so much at the start of the century. Two things had occurred in the course of the nineteenth century to shift discourse from emancipation to self-emancipation: first, the disappointment with the persistence of anti-Semitism in the West; second, the disheartening failure to attain political rights in the East.

Jews therefore began to conclude that they would have to attain emancipation on their own terms and through their own efforts. The stress on Zionism as a political movement, however, came specifically from Theodor Herzl, a Viennese journalist who, in response to the rebirth of anti-Semitism he witnessed while covering the Dreyfus trial in Paris, discovered the Jewish problem and proposed its solution. To be sure, Herzl had earlier given thought to the problem of anti-Semitism, and the public anti-Semitism that accompanied the degradation of Dreyfus marked merely another stage in the development of his ideas. What Herzl contributed in the beginning was the notion that the Jews all lived in a single situation, wherever they were located, and therefore they should live in a single country, in their own state. Anti-Semitism formed the antithesis of Zionism, and anti-Semites, growing in strength in European politics, would assist the Jews in building their state and thereby also solve their "Jewish problem."

The solution entailed the founding of a Jewish state. That formed a wholly new conception, with its quite particular worldview and with its rather concrete and detailed program for the conduct of the life of the Jews. The Jews were now to become something that they had not been for the two thousand years of which Zionism persistently spoke: a political entity. The Judaism of the dual Torah had made no provision for a this-worldly politics, and no political tradition had sustained itself during the long period in which that Judaism had absorbed and transformed all other views and modes of life. In founding the Zionist Organization in Basel in 1897, Herzl said that he had founded the Jewish state, and that in a half-century the world would know it, as indeed the world did.

Three main streams of theory flowed abundantly and side by side in the formative decades. One, represented by Ahad Ha-Am, laid stress on Zion as a spiritual center to unite all parts of the Jewish people. Ahad Ha-Am and his associates emphasized spiritual preparation, ideological and cultural activities, and the long-term intellectual issues of persuading the Jews of the Zionist premises.[6]

Another stream, the political one, maintained from the beginning that the Jews should provide for the emigration of the masses of their nation from Eastern Europe. Eastern Europe was then entering a protracted stage of political disintegration and the Jews had long been suffering from economic dislocation. Herzl argued for their emigration to the Land of Israel—or somewhere, anywhere. He in particular placed the requirement of legal recognition of a Jewish state over the location of the state, and in doing so he set forth the policy that the practical salvation of the Jews through political means would form the definition of Zionism. Herzl stressed that the Jewish state would come into existence in the forum of international politics.[7] The instruments of state—a political forum, a bank, a mode of national allegiance, a press, and a central body and leader—came into being in the aftermath of the first Zionist congress in Basel. Herzl spent the rest of his life—less than a decade—seeking an international charter and recognition of the Jewish state.

A third stream of theory derived from socialism and expressed a Zionist vision of socialism, or a socialist vision of Zionism. The Jewish state was to be socialist, as indeed it was for its first three decades. In its earlier theoretical formulation (before its near-total bureaucratization), Social Zionism emphasized that a proletarian Zionism would define the arena for the class struggle within the Jewish people to be realized. The Socialist Zionists predominated in the settlement of the Land of Israel and controlled the political institutions for three-quarters of a century. They founded the labor unions, the large-scale industries, and the health institutions and organizations. They created the press and the nascent army—the nation. No wonder that for the first quarter-century after independence, the Socialist Zionists made all the decisions and controlled everything.

The Zionism that functioned as a Judaism draws our attention to the movement. In this regard Ahad Ha-Am made the explicit claim that Zionism would succeed Judaism (meaning the Judaism of the dual Torah). Arthur Hertzberg states:

> The function that revealed religion had performed in talmudic and medieval Judaism, that of guaranteeing the survival of the Jews as a separate entity because of their belief in the divinely ordained importance of the Jewish religion and people, it was no longer performing and could not be expected to perform. The crucial task facing Jews in the modern era was to devise new structures to contain the separate individuality of the Jews and to keep them loyal to their own tradition. This analysis of the situation implied . . . a view of Jewish history which Ahad Ha-Am produced as undoubted . . . , that the Jews in all ages were essentially a nation and that all other factors profoundly important to the life of this people, even religion, were mainly instrumental values.[8]

Hertzberg contrasts that statement with one made by Saadiah, a great philosopher, in the tenth century: "The Jewish people is a people only for the sake of its Torah." That statement of the position of the Judaism of the dual Torah contrasts with the one of Zionism and allows us to set the one against the other. Each can be classified as a Judaism, for each proposed to answer the same types of questions, and the answers provided by each enjoyed the same status of not mere truth but fact, and not mere fact but the just, and right, and appropriate fact.

As a Judaism entirely out of phase with the received system of the dual Torah, Zionism enunciated a powerful doctrine of Israel. The Jews form a people, one people. What made them one people and validated their claim to a state of their own was the central theme of the Zionist worldview. No facts of perceived society validated that view. Except for a common fate the Jews in no way formed one people. True, in Judaic systems they commonly did. But the Judaic system of the dual Torah and its continuators imputed to Israel a supernatural status, a mission, a calling, and a purpose. Zionism did not: the Jews were one people—that was all.

Zionist theory had the task of explaining how the Jews formed one people, and Zionist theory solved that problem in the study of Jewish history, read as a single and unitary story. The Jews all came from one place, had traveled together, and were going back to that same place as one people. Zionist theory therefore derived strength from the study of history, much as had Reform Judaism, and in time it generated a great renaissance of Judaic studies as the scholarly community of the nascent Jewish state took up the task at hand. The sort of history that emerged took the form of factual and descriptive narrative. But its selection of facts, its recognition of problems requiring explanation, its choice of what mattered and what did not—all of these questions found answers in the larger program of nationalist ideology. So the form was secular and descriptive, but the substance was ideological in the extreme.

At the same time, Zionist theory explicitly rejected the precedent of the Torah. It selected as its history not the history of the faith (of the Torah), but the history of the nation (Israel construed as a secular entity). Zionism defined episodes as history—linear history, Jewish history—and appealed to those strung-together events as vindication for its program of action. So we find a distinctive worldview that explained a particular way of life and defined the Israel to which it wished to speak. Like Reform Judaism, Zionism found the written component of the Torah more interesting than the oral. And in its search for a usable past, it turned to documents formerly neglected or treated as not authoritative, for example, the book of Maccabees. Zionism went in search of heroes unlike those of the present: warriors, political figures, and others who might provide a model for the movement's future. Instead of rabbis or sages, Zionism chose figures such as David, Judah Maccabee, and Samson. David the warrior king,

Judah Maccabee who had led the revolt against the Syrian Hellenists, and Samson the powerful fighter provided the appropriate heroes for a Zionism that proposed to redefine Jewish consciousness and to turn storekeepers into soldiers, lawyers into farmers, and corner grocers into builders and administrators of great institutions of state and government. The Judaism of the dual Torah treated David like a rabbi. The Zionist system of Judaism saw David as a hero in a more worldly sense: a courageous nation builder.

Yet the principal components of Zionism's worldview fitted comfortably within the pattern of the Torah of Moses. For that Torah held, for its own reasons based on genealogy, that the Jews form one people and should (when worthy) have the land back and build on it a state. It is not surprising that Zionism found in the writings about the return to Zion ample precedent for its program. It linked today's politics to something very like God's will for Israel in ancient times. Calling the new Jewish city Tel Aviv invoked the memory of Ezekiel's reference to a Tel Aviv, and that symbolized much else. Zionism would reconstitute the age of the return to Zion in the time of Ezra and Nehemiah, and so carry out the prophetic promises. The mode of thought was reminiscent of that of Reform Judaism, although Reform selected a different perfect world of mythic being, a golden age other than the one that for Zionism glistened so brightly.

Yet the points of continuity should not be overstated. For alongside the search of Scripture, Zionism articulated a very clear perception of what it wished to find there. What Zionism did not find, it deposited on its own. And that is what marked it as a heresy of its own systemic design: the celebration of the nation as a secular rather than a supernatural category, and imposition of the nation and its heroism in place of the heroic works of the supernatural God. A classic shift took the verse from Psalms, "Who will retell the great deeds of God," and produced "Who will retell the great deeds of Israel." And that only typifies the profound revision of Israel's history accomplished by Zionism. The earliest pronouncements of the Zionist movement were received in the Jewish heartland of Eastern Europe like the warning signal of the coming Messiah. But to the sages of the dual Torah, Zionism seemed to be blasphemy. God will do it or it will not be done. Considerable time would elapse before the sages of the dual Torah could make their peace with Zionism, and some of them never did.

The Zionist worldview explicitly competed with the religious one. The formidable statement of Jacob Klatzkin, a major Zionist theorist (1882–1948), provides a solid basis for comparison:

> In the past there have been two criteria of Judaism: the criterion of religion, according to which Judaism is a system of positive and negative commandments, and the criterion of the spirit, which saw Judaism as a complex of ideas, like monotheism, messianism, absolute justice, etc. According to both these criteria, therefore, Judaism rests on a subjective basis, on the acceptance of a creed . . . a religious denomination . . . or a community of individuals who share in a *Weltanschauung*. . . . In opposition to these two criteria, which make of Judaism a matter of creed, a third has now arisen, the criterion of a consistent nationalism. According to it, Judaism rests on an objective basis: to be a Jew means the acceptance of neither a religious nor an ethical creed. We are neither a denomination or a school of thought, but members of one family, bearers of a common history. . . . The national definition too requires an act of will. It defines our nationalism by two criteria: partnership in the past and the conscious desire to continue such partnership in the future. There are, therefore, two bases for Jewish nationalism—the compulsion of history and a will expressed in that history.[9]

Klatzkin's stress on "a will expressed in history" of course carries us back to the appeals of Reform and Conservative theologians to facts of history as precedents for faith. The historicism of Zionism fell into the same classification of thought. But for the theologians, the facts proved episodic and ad hoc, mere precedents. Zionists found it necessary to reread all the histories of Jews and to compose of them Jewish history, a single and linear system leading inexorably to the formation of the Jewish state. Klatzkin defined being a Jew not as something subjective but something objective: "land and language. These are the basic categories of national being."[10] That definition led directly to calling the Jewish state "the State of Israel," so making a clear statement of Zionism's doctrine of who is Israel.

As Klatzkin said, in contributing "the territorial-political definition of Jewish nationalism," Zionism offered a genuinely fresh worldview:

> Either the Jewish people shall redeem the land and thereby continue to live, even if the spiritual content of Judaism changes radically, or we shall remain in exile and rot away, even if the spiritual tradition continues to exist.[11]

It goes without saying that, like Christianity at its original encounter with the task of making sense of history, so Zionism posited that a new era began with its formation: "not only for the purpose of making an end to the Diaspora but also in order to establish a new definition of Jewish identity—a secular definition."[12] In this way Zionism clearly stated the intention of providing a worldview that would replace the worldview of the received Judaism of the dual Torah and would compete with all efforts of the continuators of that Judaism. Klatzkin states: "Zionism stands opposed to all this. Its real beginning is *The Jewish State* [italics his], and its basic intention, whether consciously or unconsciously, is to deny any conception of Jewish identity based on spiritual criteria."[13] Obviously, Klatzkin's was not the only voice. But in his appeal to history, in his initiative in positing a linear course of events of a single kind leading to one goal, the Jewish state, Klatzkin expressed the theory of history that would supply Zionism with a principal plank in its platform. The several appeals to the facts of history meant that the arena of scholarship as to what had "really" happened defined the boundaries for debate on matters of faith. Consequently the heightened and intensified discourse of scholars produced judgments not as to secular facts but as to deeply held truths of faith, identifying not correct or erroneous versions of things that had happened but truth and heresy, saints and sinners.

Until the massacre of the Jews of Europe between 1933 and 1945 and the founding of the State of Israel in 1948, Zionism remained very much a minority movement in Jewry. Jewish socialism and Yiddishism in the new nations of Eastern Europe and the New Deal in American Democratic politics attracted a far larger part of Jewry, and the former, though not the latter, formed a competing Judaic system. Before 1948 the Jewish population of the Land of Israel/Palestine had reached scarcely half a million, a small portion of the Jews of the world. In the United States and in Western Europe, Zionist sentiment did not predominate, even though a certain romantic appeal attached to the pioneers in the Land of Israel. Indeed until

1967 Zionism constituted one choice among many for Jews through-out the world. Since, at the present time, Jewry nearly unanimously attaches to the State of Israel the status of the Jewish state, affirms that the Jews form one people, concedes all of the principal proposi-tions of Zionism, and places the achievement of the Zionist program as the highest priority for Jewry throughout the world, we may say that today (but not a great many days before) Zionism forms a system bearing self-evident truth for vast numbers of Jews. This is because Zionism alone of the Judaisms of the nineteenth and twentieth cen-turies possessed the potential of accurately assessing the power of anti-Semitism and its ultimate destiny. Zionism turns out to have selected the right problem and to have given the right solution to that problem.

NOTES

1. *Encyclopaedia Judaica*, col. 1487.
2. *Encyclopaedia Judaica*, col. 1488.
3. Katzburg, *Encyclopaedia Judaica*, "Orthodoxy," col. 1490.
4. Samet, *Encyclopaedia Judaica*, "Neo-Orthodoxy," col. 957.
5. The Zionism of the post-1948 period faced a different set of issues and is not under discussion here.
6. S. Ettinger, "Hibbat Zion," in "Zionism," *Encyclopaedia Judaica* 16:1031–1178. Ettinger cited in col. 1041.
7. Arthur Hertzberg, "Ideological Evolution," in "Zionism," *Encyclopae-dia Judaica* 16:1044–45.
8. Ibid., col. 1046.
9. Ibid., p. 317.
10. Ibid., p. 318.
11. Ibid., p. 319.
12. Klatzkin, in ibid., p. 319.
13. Ibid.

RABBINIC JUDAISM: LAW, PHILOSOPHY, MYSTICISM, AND THEOLOGY

The Shulhan Arukh: Enduring Code of Jewish Law

ISADORE TWERSKY

Shulhan Arukh, a term taken from early rabbinic exegesis in the Midrash and applied to one of the most influential, truly epochal, literary creations of Jewish history, has a double or even triple meaning, and its use therefore necessitates precise definition or description. *Shulhan Arukh* is the title given by R. Joseph Karo (1488–1575) to a brief, four-part code of Jewish law that was published in 1565–66. The term *Shulhan Arukh* also designates a composite, collaborative work, combining this original text of R. Joseph Karo, a Spanish emigré from Toledo (1492) who lived and studied in Turkey and finally settled in Palestine in a period of turbulence, instability, and apocalyptic stirrings, with the detailed glosses—both strictures and supplements—of R. Moses Isserles (ca. 1525–1572), a well-to-do Polish scholar, proud of his Germanic background, who studied in Lublin and became de facto chief rabbi of Cracow in a period of relative stability and tranquillity. This unpremeditated literary symbiosis then generated a spate of commentaries and supercommentaries, brief or expansive, defensive or dissenting, from the *Sefer Me'irat 'Enayim* of R. Joshua Falk and the *Sefer Siftei Kohen* of R. Shabbetai ha-Kohen to the *Mishnah Berurah* of R. Israel Meir ha-Kohen. And the term *Shulhan Arukh* continued to be applied to this multidimensional, multigenerational, ever-expanding folio volume—a fact that attests to the resiliency and buoyancy of the halakhic tradition in Judaism. A person must, therefore, define his frame of reference when he purports to glorify or vilify, to acclaim or condemn—or, if he is able to avoid value judgments, to describe historically. The genuinely modest purposes of the following remarks are, first, to chronicle the emergence of the *Shulhan Arukh*, especially in its first and second meanings, and then to describe a few of its salient literary and substantive characteristics. "The rest is commentary," which we should go and study.

I

In the year 1522, R. Joseph Karo, a young, struggling, volatile, and ascetic scholar, having settled temporarily and discontentedly in Adrianople, Turkey, launched a massive literary project that would preoccupy him, sometimes at a frenetic pace, for over thirty years— twenty years in the composition and about twelve years in editorial revision and refinement. The stimulus was provided by the worrisome decline in scholarship—"and the wisdom of their wise men shall perish"—coming in the wake of the rigors and vicissitudes of exile, the endless turbulence of history, and the increasing human imperfection. The need was great for a comprehensive as well as authoritative guide that would stem the undesirable and almost uncontrollable proliferation of texts and provide a measure of religious uniformity in this period of great turmoil and dislocation. This would be accomplished, however, not by producing another compact, sinewy manual—a small volume such as the *Agur*, which R. Karo treats pejoratively—but by reviewing the practical halakhah in its totality. The oracular type of code, containing curt, staccato directives and pronouncements, was neither adequate nor reliable. It did not provide for intellectual stimulus and expansion of the mind, nor did it offer correct guidance in religious practice.

R. Joseph Karo's ambitious undertaking in the field of rabbinic literature, entitled *Bet Yosef* (House of Joseph), was thus motivated by the need to review "all the practical laws of Judaism, explaining their roots and origins in the Talmud" and all the conflicting interpretations concerning them. No extant work answered to this need. In order to avoid duplication or reducing it to a bare minimum, he decided to build his own work around an existing code that was popular and authoritative. He selected the *Turim* of R. Jacob b. Asher (ca. 1280– 1340) rather than the more famous and widespread *Mishneh Torah* of R. Moses b. Maimon, because the latter was too concise and monolithic, presenting, on the whole, unilateral, undocumented decisions, while the former was expansive and more interpretive, citing alternate views and divergent explanations. At this stage, then, the text of the *Turim* was only a pretext for his own work. His method was to explain every single law in the text, note its original source, and indicate whether the formulation found in the *Turim* was the result of consensus or was subject to dispute. He would, furthermore, explain the alternate interpretations and formulations that the *Turim* referred to but rejected. In addition, he would introduce and elucidate those views which the *Turim* had totally omitted from consideration. As a purely theoretical increment, he promised to examine and explain those views of predecessors—especially Maimonides—which were problematic or remained obscure despite the availability of such commentaries as the *Maggid Mishneh*. He would, incidentally, correct the text of the *Turim*, which suffered many scribal corruptions. That he intended his encyclopedic review of halakhah to be used as a study guide is indicated by his promise always to give exact bibliographical references in order to enable his readers to consult original texts or check quotations in their original contexts. However, having completed his panoramic presentation and almost detached, academic analysis of a law, he would regularly indicate the normative conclusion, for the "goal is that we should have one Torah and one law." The function of this massive work is thus twofold: to flesh out the bare-bones codifications that are too brief and uninformative, but preserve their sinewiness and pragmatic advantage by unequivocally stating the *pesak*, the binding regulation, in each case. Certitude and finality are among the top-priority items that will be guaranteed.

In connection with this, the author lays bare his judicial methodology, a methodology that was to be vigorously contested, as we shall see. The judicial process was complex. A talmudist could arrive at the normative conclusion by critically reviewing and appraising all arguments and demonstrations marshalled by his predecessors and then selecting the most cogent, persuasive view. His guide would be examination of underlying texts, relying, in the final analysis, upon his autonomous judgment and not on appeal to authority. This independent, assertive approach is unqualifiedly repudiated by R. Joseph Karo for two reasons: (1) it would be presumptuous to scrutinize the judgment of such giants as R. Moses b. Nahman, R. Solomon b. Adret, R. Nissim, and the Tosafists and then pass judgment on them—we are not qualified or competent; (2) even if the task were not beyond our powers and capacities, the process would be too long and arduous.

Forcefully underscoring his subservience and *apparently* forfeiting his
judicial prerogatives, he chose to arrive at the normative conclusion
in each case by following the consensus or at least the majority rule
of the greatest medieval codifiers—R. Isaac Alfasi (d. 1103), Maimonides (d. 1204), and R. Asher ben Yeḥiel (d. 1328). Contemporary
legislation, innovation, and native usage are given no role whatsoever—almost as if the law were all logic and no experience. In other
words, in the realm of commentary R. Joseph Karo was bold and
resourceful, while in the realm of adjudication he was laconic, almost
self-effacing.

At about the same time, in entirely different circumstances and
with a totally different motivation, R. Moses Isserles, born into comfort and affluence, son of a prominent communal leader who was
also a gentleman scholar and (for a while) son-in-law of the greatest
talmudic teacher in Poland (R. Shalom Shakna), also began to com-
pile an exhaustive commentary on the *Turim*. He reveals the immediate stimulus that led to his project: having been persuaded by friends
to assume rabbinic duties in Cracow—his youth, immaturity, and
unripe scholarship notwithstanding—he found himself deciding many
halakhic problems and issuing numerous judicial opinions. It was his
practice to turn directly to the Talmud and consult its authoritative
expositors, among whom he mentions R. Isaac Alfasi, R. Moses b.
Naḥman, and R. Asher b. Yeḥiel. He found, however, that he was
repeatedly subjected to criticism for having ignored the rulings of the
most recent scholars (e.g., R. Jacob Weil, R. Israel Isserlein, R. Israel
Bruna) who were really the progenitors of contemporary Polish Jewry
and gave it its creative and directive vital force. They introduced, inter
alia, many preventive ordinances and stringent practices that tended
to nullify early decisions, and as a result no picture of halakhah could
be true to life that did not reflect these resources, motifs, and developments. This put R. Moses Isserles in a bad light, and he and his
colleagues were, therefore, subjected to much severe criticism, the
validity of which he fully appreciated and accepted, as we shall see.

Impromptu, ad hoc review—and judicious, instantaneous application—of all this material, this panoply of interpretations and traditions, would be cumbersome, if not impossible. It therefore occurred
to R. Moses Isserles that the way out was to prepare a digest and
anthology of all opinions and record them alongside of a standard
code. The best book was the *Turim*, for its arrangement was very

attractive and useful, and it was easily intelligible to all. He set out, with great determination and commensurate perseverance, to implement this literary plan (he vividly describes his frenetic, indefatigable activity, without ease and without quiet). At a rather advanced stage of his work, he was electrified by the news that "the light of Israel, head of the exile" R. Joseph Karo had composed a comparable commentary on the *Turim*, the *Bet Yosef*, the excellence of which was immediately evident. R. Moses Isserles' anxiety was indescribable; just as he neared the hour of consummation, it appeared that his efforts and privations would turn out to be a wearying exercise in futility. He acknowledges—with what seems to be a blend of modesty and realism—that he could not hold a candle to R. Joseph Karo. However, shock did not lead to paralysis. His peace of mind and momentum were restored when, reassessing the situation, he realized that the field had not been completely preempted and that he was still in a position to make a substantive contribution.

There were three areas in which he could realign his material and operate creatively and meaningfully:

1. He would compress the material, almost encyclopedic in its present proportions, and present a more precise formulation of the law. Length, as Maimonides notes, is one of the deterrents of study. Nevertheless, R. Moses Isserles is somewhat apologetic at this point, because he was fully aware of the pitfalls of excessive brevity; indeed, it had been the codificatory syndrome—the rigidities and inadequacies of delphic manuals—that initially impelled him to disavow the methodology of existing codes. As a compromise, he determined to cite—not to reproduce or summarize—all sources, so that the inquisitive or dissatisfied but learned reader will be able to pursue matters further, while the less sophisticated and less talented reader will still benefit and not be able to argue that the material is too lengthy and complicated.

2. The *Bet Yosef* was too "classical," somewhat remote for Germanic-Polish Jewry: it failed to represent equally the more recent codifiers and commentators. His work, the *Darke Mosheh*, would do justice to them by incorporating their positions. It would reflect the historical consciousness of R. Moses Isserles and his colleagues who looked upon themselves as

heirs and continuators of the Ashkenazic tradition. On one
hand, therefore, the *Darke Mosheh* would be an abridgement
of the *Bet Yosef*, and, on the other, it would expand its scope.
Clearly, R. Moses Isserles had taken the words of his earlier
critics to heart.

3. Perhaps the most radical divergence between the two works
   appeared in the methodology of pesak (decision), formulating
   the normative conclusion and obligatory pattern of behavior.
   Unlike R. Joseph Karo, who cautiously claimed to follow the
   communis opinio, or majority rule, of early codifiers, and unlike
   those who would freely exercise independent judgment in
   arriving at practical conclusions, R. Moses Isserles adopted a
   third stance: to follow most recent authorities—*halakah
   ke-batra'e* (the law follows the latest authorities). This method
   would preserve established precedent and respect local custom. It is reflected stylistically in R. Moses Isserles' habit of
   underwriting the most valid view by adding "and this is
   customary" and then identifying the source or by noting can-
   didly "and so it appears to me." He is thus more independent
   and resourceful than R. Joseph Karo, though less so than
   R. Solomon Luria. In short, as R. Moses Isserles puts it in a
   rhetorical flourish, "And Moses took the bones of Joseph"—
   he adapted and transformed the essence of the *Bet Yosef* and
   abandoned the rest.

This ends the first chapter of our story in which R. Joseph Karo
made it to the press before R. Moses Isserles and forced the latter
to revise his initial prospectus in light of a changed literary reality.
What is, of course, striking is the remarkable parallelism and similarity of attitudes between these two talmudists, both seeking to
push back the frontiers of halakhic literature, both convinced of the
need to review individual laws in their totality and not rely upon
delphic manuals, and both selecting the same code (*Turim*) as their
springboard.

II

Ten years later, in the course of which the *Bet Yosef* spread far
and wide and his authority was increasingly respected, R. Joseph
Karo came full cycle in his own attitude toward the oracular-type

code. Having previously and persuasively argued against the utility and wisdom of the apodictic compendium, he now conceded its need and efficacy. He himself abridged the columinous *Bet Yosef*—"gathered the lilies, the sapphires"—and called his new work the *Shulhan Arukh* (prepared table), "because in it the reader will find all kinds of delicacies" fastidiously arranged and systematized and clarified. He was persuaded that the *Shulhan Arukh* would serve the needs of a diffuse and heterogeneous audience. Scholars will use it as a handy reference book, so that every matter of law will be perfectly clear and the answer to questions concerning halakhic practice will be immediate and decisive. Young, untutored students will also benefit by committing the *Shulhan Arukh* to memory, for even rote knowledge is not to be underestimated.

When the *Shulhan Arukh* appeared, it elicited praise and provoked criticism; the former could be exuberant, and the latter, abrasive. Some contemporaries needed only to resuscitate R. Joseph Karo's initial stance and refurbish his arguments against such works as the *Agur*. R. Moses Isserles' reaction moved along the same lines which had determined his reaction to the *Bet Yosef*. He could not—like R. Solomon Luria or R. Yom Tob Lipman Heller—take unqualified exception to the codificatory aim and form, for he had already, in his revised *Darke Mosheh*, aligned himself in principle with this tendency and had eloquently defended it. He could, however, press his substantive and methodological attack on Karo; the latter had neglected Ashkenazic tradition and had failed to abide by the most recent rulings, thereby ignoring custom, which was such an important ingredient of the normative law. Moreover, just as R. Joseph Karo drew upon his *Bet Yosef*, so R. Moses Isserles drew upon his *Darke Mosheh*; both, coming full cycle, moved from lively judicial symposium to soulless legislative soliloquy. If R. Joseph Karo produced a "set table," R. Moses Isserles spread a "tablecloth" over it. It is certain that the "table" would never have been universally accepted if it had not been covered and adorned with the "tablecloth." R. Moses Isserles' glosses, both strictures and annotations, were the ultimate validation of the *Shulhan Arukh*. The full dialectic has here played itself out, radical opposition to codes giving way to radical codification, almost with a vengeance; for the *Shulhan Arukh* is the leanest of all codes in Jewish history—from the *Bet Yosef* to the *Shulhan Arukh*, from the baroque to the bare.

It is not this dialectical movement per se that is novel or noteworthy, for this characterizes much of the history of post-talmudic rabbinic literature. Attempts to compress the halakhah by formal codification alternate with counter-attempts to preserve the fullness and richness of both the method and substance of the halakhah by engaging in interpretation, analogy, and logical inference, and only then formulating the resultant normative conclusion. Any student who follows the course of rabbinic literature from the Geonic works of the eighth century through the *Mishneh Torah* and *Turim* and on down to the *Shulhan Arukh* cannot ignore this seesaw tendency. The tension is ever present and usually catalytic. No sooner is the need for codification met than a wave of noncodificatory work rises. A code could provide guidance and certitude for a while but not finality. *'Arvak 'arva zarik*—"your bondsman requires a bondsman." A code, even in the eyes of its admirers, required vigilant explanation and judicious application. The heartbeat had constantly to be checked and the pulse had to be counted. It became part of a life organism that was never complete or static. What is striking, therefore, in the case of the *Shulhan Arukh* is that the dialectical movement plays itself out in the attitudes and achievements of the same person—"surfing" on the "sea of the Talmud," rising and falling on the crests of analysis and thoughts of argumentation, and then trying to "gather the water into one area," to construct a dike that would produce a slow, smooth flow of its waters. The *Shulhan Arukh* thus offers an instructive example of the dialectical movement in rabbinic literature as a whole.

This whole story is important, I believe, because it expands the historical background against which the *Shulhan Arukh* is to be seen and cautions against excessive preoccupation with purely sociological data, with contemporary stimuli and contingencies. It makes the *Shulhan Arukh* understandable in terms of the general history of halakhic literature and its major trends. It provides an obvious vertical perspective—that is, literary categories seen as part of an ongoing halakhic enterprise—to be used alongside of an, at best, implicit horizontal perspective—that is, historical pressures and eschatological hopes—for an explanation of the emergence of the *Shulhan Arukh*. This is strengthened by the striking parallelism between the literary careers of R. Moses Isserles and R. Joseph Karo; their historical situations, environmental influences, social contexts (in a phrase of contemporary jargon, their *Sitz-im-Leben*) are so different, but their aspirations and attainments are so similar.

III

When we come to gauge and appraise the impact of the *Shulhan Arukh*, it is idle to speculate whether R. Joseph Karo intended the *Shulhan Arukh* to circulate and be used independently, as a literary unit sufficient to itself, or to be used only as a companion volume together with the *Bet Yosef*. His intention has been disputed and variously construed. Some condemned those who studied the *Shulhan Arukh* in vacuo, thereby acquiring superficial acquaintance with halakhah, claiming that this contravened the author's intention. Others treated the *Shulhan Arukh* in a manner reminiscent of R. Joseph Karo's original attitude as found in the preface to the *Bet Yosef*. In this case, however, the original intention of the author is eclipsed by the historical fact, abetted or perhaps made possible by R. Moses Isserles' glosses, that the *Shulhan Arukh* and not the *Bet Yosef* became R. Joseph Karo's main claim to fame, and its existence was completely separate from and independent of the *Bet Yosef*. Commentators such as R. Abraham Gumbiner in the *Magen Abraham* effectively and irreparably cut the umbilical cord which may have linked the *Shulhan Arukh* with the *Bet Yosef*. What some literary critics have said about poetry may then be applied here: "The design or intention of the author is neither available or desirable as a standard for judging the success of a work of literary art." In our case, consequently, we should simply see what are some of the characteristics of the *Shulhan Arukh* and some of the repercussions of its great historical success.

Perhaps the single most important feature of the *Shulhan Arukh* is its unswerving concentration on prescribed patterns of behavior to the exclusion of any significant amount of theoretical data. The *Shulhan Arukh* is a manual for practical guidance, not academic study. This practical orientation is discernible in many areas and on different levels.

First of all, by initially adopting the classification of the *Turim*, R. Joseph Karo capitulated unconditionally to the practical orientation. The import of this becomes more vivid when we contrast the two major codes on this point. The *Mishneh Torah* is all-inclusive in scope, obliterating all distinctions between practice and theory, and devoting sustained attention to those laws and concepts momentarily devoid of practical value or temporarily in abeyance because of historical and geographical contingencies. Laws of prayer and of the Temple ceremonial are given equal treatment. Laws concerning the sotah, the unfaithful wife (abrogated by R. Johanan b. Zakkai in the first century), are codified in the same detail as the ever practical marriage laws. The present time during which part of the law was in abeyance was, in Maimonides' opinion, a historical anomaly, a fleeting moment in the pattern of eternity. The real historical dimensions were those in which the Torah and its precepts were fully realized, that is, the time after the restoration of the Davidic dynasty, when "all the ancient laws will be reinstituted . . . sacrifices will again be offered, the Sabbatical and Jubilee years will again be observed in accordance with the commandments set forth in the Law." The Oral Law was, therefore, to be codified and studied exhaustively. The *Turim*, on the other hand, addresses itself only to those laws that are relevant, to those concrete problems and issues whose validity and applicability are not confined either temporally or geographically. For while both Maimonides and R. Jacob b. Asher were of one mind in abandoning the sequence of the talmudic treatises and seeking an independent classification of halakhah, they differed in their goals: Maimonides sought to create a topical-conceptual arrangement that would provide a new interpretive mold for study and would also be educationally sound, while R. Jacob b. Asher was guided only by functionality and as a result was less rigorous conceptually. It involved a lesser degree of logical analysis and abstraction, and did not hesitate to group disparate items together. A code, according to this conception, should facilitate the understanding of the operative laws and guide people in translating concepts into rules of conduct.

The *Shulhan Arukh* adds a further rigorism to the practicality of the *Turim*. The *Turim's* practicality expresses itself in the rigid selection of material, in the circumscribed scope, but not in the method of presentation, which is rich, varied, and suggestive, containing as it does much textual interpretation and brief discussion of divergent views, while the functionality of the *Shulhan Arukh* is so radical that it brooks no expansiveness whatsoever. The judicial process is of no concern to the codifier; exegesis, interpretation, derivation, awareness of controversy—all these matters are totally dispensable, even undesirable, for the codifier. In this respect, the *Shulhan Arukh* has greater affinities with the *Mishneh Torah*, which also purports to eliminate conflicting interpretations and rambling discussions and to present ex cathedra legislative, unilateral views, without sources and without explanations. The fact is that the *Shulhan Arukh* is much closer to this codificatory ideal than the *Mishneh Torah*, which, after all, is as much commentary as it is code. One has only to compare, at random, parallel sections of the *Turim* and *Shulhan Arukh* to realize fully and directly, almost palpably, the extent to which the *Shulhan Arukh* pruned the *Turim*, relentlessly excising midrashic embellishments, ethical perceptions, and theoretical amplifications. It promised to give the "fixed, final law, without speech and without words." It left little to discretion or imagination.

There is yet another area in which this austere functionality comes to the surface—in the virtually complete elimination of ideology, theology, and teleology. The *Shulhan Arukh*, unlike the *Mishneh Torah* or the *Sefer ha-Rokeah*, has no philosophical or kabbalistic prolegomenon or peroration. The *Shulhan Arukh*—unlike the *Mishneh Torah* or the *Turim*—does not abound in extra-halakhic comments, guiding tenets and ideological directives. While the *Mishneh Torah* does reveal the full intellectualistic posture of Maimonides, the *Shulhan Arukh* does not even afford an oblique glimpse of the kabbalistic posture of R. Joseph Karo, who appears here in the guise of the civil lawyer for whom "nothing was more pointless, nothing more inept than a law with a preamble." He was concerned exclusively with what Max Weber called the "methodology of sanctification" which produces a "continuous personality pattern," not with its charismatic goals or stimuli, the ethical underpinning or theological vision which suffuse the halakhah with significance, guarantee its radical, ineradicable spirituality and thereby nurture the religious consciousness. The *Shulhan Arukh* gives the concrete idea, but omits what Dilthey called *Erlebnis*, the experiential component. In the *Shulhan Arukh*, the halakhah manifests itself as the *regula iuris*, a rule of life characterized by stability, regularity, and fixedness, making known to people "the way they are to go and the practices they are to follow" (Exod. 18:20). These specific, visible practices are not coordinated with invisible meaning or unspecified experience. One can say, in general, that there are two major means by which apparently trans-halakhic material has been organically linked with the halakhah proper: (1) construction of an ideational framework which indicates the ultimate concerns and gives coherence, direction and vitality to the concrete actions; (2) elaboration of either a rationale of the law or a mystique of the law which suggests explanations and motives for the detailed commandments. The *Shulhan Arukh*, for reasons of its own, about which we may only conjecture, attempts neither.

IV

This restrictive, almost styptic trait of the *Shulhan Arukh* was noticed—and criticized—by contemporaries, foremost among whom was R. Mordecai Jaffe (1530–1612), disciple of R. Moses Isserles and R. Solomon Luria and successor of R. Judah Loewe, the famous Maharal, of Prague. It is worth retelling the story of the composition of his major, multivolume work, known as the *Lebush*, inasmuch as it zeroes in on the radical functionality of the *Shulhan Arukh* and also briefly reviews the tense dialectic surrounding codification which we discussed above.

R. Mordecai Jaffe, a very articulate, sophisticated writer who was well acquainted with the contemporary scene, describes the enthusiastic reception accorded to the *Bet Yosef* because people imagined it would serve as a concise, spirited compendium, obviating the need for constant, wearisome recourse to dozens of rabbinic volumes in order to determine the proper halakhic course. He shared this feeling and heightened anticipation, but enthusiasm gave way to disillusionment as he realized that the *Bet Yosef* was anything but concise. Inasmuch as a comprehensive and compact compendium remained an urgent desideratum, he began a condensation of the *Bet Yosef* that would serve this purpose. External factors—an edict of expulsion by the Austrian emperor, which compelled him to flee Bohemia and settle in Italy—interrupted his work. In Italy, where so much Hebrew printing was being done, he heard that R. Joseph Karo himself had made arrangements to print an abridgement. Again he desisted, for he could not presume to improve upon the original author who would unquestionably produce the most balanced, incisive abridgement of his own work. R. Jaffe adds parenthetically—but with remarkable candor—that there was a pragmatic consideration as well: even if he persisted and completed his work, he could not hope to compete publicly with such a prestigious master as R. Joseph Karo—and to do it just for personal consumption, to satisfy his own needs, would be extravagant.

However, upon preliminary examination of the *Shulhan Arukh*—in Venice—he noted two serious deficiencies. First, it was too short and astringent, having no reasons or explanations—"like a sealed book, a dream which had no interpretation or meaning." He describes it as "a table well prepared with all kinds of refreshments, but the dishes are tasteless, lacking the salt of reasoning which makes the broth boil and warms the individual"—that is, lacking a minimum of explanatory and exhortatory material to embellish and spiritualize the bald halakhic directives. Second, it was almost exclusively Maimonidean, or Sephardic, and Ashkenazic communities could not, therefore, be guided by it—an argument that had been tellingly and uncompromisingly put forward by both his teachers (Isserles and Luria). Again he started work on a new composition which would fill the gap, and again he abandoned his plans in deference to R. Moses Isserles who was reported to have undertaken this task. When the full *Shulhan Arukh* appeared—the text of R. Joseph Karo and the glosses of R. Moses Isserles—he quickly realized that only the second deficiency had been remedied, that Ashkenazic halakhah had found a worthy and zealous spokesman, but the first deficiency remained—and this was glaring. Some measure of explanation was as indispensable for law as salt was for food. So, for the third time, he turned to producing a code which would (1) strive for a golden mean between inordinate length (the *Bet Yosef*) and excessive brevity (the *Shulhan Arukh*; and (2) explain, motivate, and spiritualize the law, often with the help of new kabbalistic doctrines.

In effect, R. Mordecai Jaffe—whose code was a potential but short-lived rival to the *Shulhan Arukh*—addressed himself to the problem which great halakhists, ethicists, philosophers, and mystics have constantly confronted: how to maintain a rigid, punctilious observance of the law and concomitantly avoid externalization and routinization. On one hand, we hear the echoes of Maimonides, R. Eleazar ha-Rokeah of Worms, and R. Menahem b. Zerah (author of *Zedah la-Derek*), who attempt to combine laws with their reasons and rationale, as well as R. Bahya ibn Pakuda, R. Jonah Gerondi, and R. Isaac Abuhab, to mention just a few of his predecessors. On the other hand, this tone continues to reverberate in the *Shulhan Arukh* of R. Shneur Zalman of Ladi, as well as in the writings of R. Isaiah Hurwitz and R. Moses Hayyim Luzzato, to mention just a few of his successors. The common denominator here is the concern that the halakhic enterprise always be rooted in and related to spirituality, to knowledge of God obtained through study and experience. All difficulties notwithstanding, it was generally felt that even when dealing with the corpus of practical, clearly definable law, an attempt should be made to express the—perhaps incommunicable—values and aspirations of religious experience and spiritual existence.

V

However, when all is said, it would be incorrect and insensitive to assert unqualifiedly that the *Shulhan Arukh*, that embodiment of halakhah which Jewish history has proclaimed supreme, is a spiritless, formalistic, even timid work. Its opening sentence, especially as elaborated by R. Moses Isserles, acts as the nerve center of the entire halakhic system and the fountain of its strength:

> A man should make himself strong and brave as a lion to rise in the morning for the service of his Creator, so that he should "awake the dawn" (Psalms 57:9) . . .
>
> "I have set the Lord always before me" (Psalms 16:8). This is a cardinal principle in the Torah and in the perfect (noble) ways of the righteous who walk before God. For man does not sit, move, and occupy himself when he is alone in his house, as he sits, moves, and occupies himself when he is in the presence of a great king; nor does he speak and rejoice while he is with his family and relatives as he speaks in the king's council. How much more so when man takes to heart that the Great King, the Holy One, blessed be He, whose "glory fills the whole earth" (Isaiah 6:3), is always standing by him and observing all his doings, as it is said in Scripture: "Can a man hide himself in secret places that I shall not see him?" (Jeremiah 23:24). Cognizant of this, he will immediately achieve reverence and humility, fear and shame before the Lord, blessed be He, at all times.

Law is dry and its details are burdensome only if its observance lacks vital commitment, but if all actions of a person are infused with the radical awareness that he is acting in the presence of God, then every detail becomes meaningful and relevant. Such an awareness rules out routine, mechanical actions; everything must be conscious and purposive in a God-oriented universe, where every step of man is directed toward God. Halakhah, like nature, abhors a vacuum; it recognizes no twilight zone of neutrality or futility. It is all-inclusive. Consequently, every action—even tying one's shoes—can be and is invested with symbolic meaning. Nothing is accidental, behavioral, purely biological. Even unavoidable routine is made less perfunctory. The opening paragraph of the *Shulhan Arukh* is thus a clear and resounding declaration concerning the workings and the searchings of the spirit. Its tone should reverberate throughout all the subsequent laws and regulations. It provides—as does also paragraph 231, which urges man to see to it that *all* his deeds be "for the sake of heaven"—an implicit rationale for the entire halakhah, but it is a rationale that must be kept alive by the individual. It cannot be passively taken for granted; it must be passionately pursued.

What I am saying, in other words, is that to a certain extent the *Shulhan Arukh* and halakhah are coterminous and that the "problem" of the *Shulhan Arukh* is precisely the "problem" of halakhah as a whole. Halakhah itself is a tense, vibrant, dialectical system which regularly insists upon normativeness in action and inwardness in feeling and thought. It undertook to give concrete and continuous expression to theological ideals, ethical norms, ecstatic moods, and historical concepts but never superseded or eliminated these ideals and concepts. Halakhah itself is, therefore, a coincidence of opposites: prophecy and law, charisma and institution, mood and medium, image and reality, the thought of eternity and the life of temporality. Halakhah itself, therefore, in its own behalf, demands the coordination of inner meaning and external observance—and it is most difficult to comply with such a demand and sustain such a delicate, highly sensitized synthesis.

There can be no doubt that R. Joseph Karo, the arch mystic passionately yearning for ever greater spiritual heights, could not have intended to create a new concept of orthopraxis, of punctilious observance of the law divorced, as it were, from all spiritual tension. While this may indeed have been one of the unintended repercussions of the *Shulhan Arukh*—while it may unknowingly have contributed to the notion, maintained by a strange assortment of people, that Judaism is all deed and no creed, all letter and no spirit—its author would certainly discountenance such an interpretation and dissociate himself from it. If the *Shulhan Arukh* only charts a specific way of life but does not impart a specific version or vision of meta-halakhah, it is because the latter is to be supplied and experienced independently. The valiant attempt of so many scholars to compress the incompressible, imponderable values of religious experience into cold words and neat formulae, alongside generally lucid halakhic prescriptions, did not elicit the support of R. Joseph Karo. Halakhah could be integrated with and invigorated by disparate, mutually exclusive systems, operating with different motives and aspirations, as long as these agreed on the means and directives. I would suggest that R. Mordecai Jaffe's parenthetical apology for his expansive-interpretive approach to halakhah—that every person spices food differently, that every wise person will find a different reason or taste in the law, and this reason should not be codified or legislated—may well be what prompted R. Joseph Karo, generally reticent about spiritual matters, to limit his attention to the concrete particularization of halakhah. This could be presented with a good measure of certitude and finality, but its spiritual coordinates required special and separate, if complementary, treatment.

As a personal postcript, or "concluding unscientific postcript," I would like to suggest that, if the Psalmist's awareness of "I have set God before me continually" (Ps. 16:8)—the motto of the *Shulhan Arukh*—is one of the standards of saintliness, then all *"Shulhan Arukh* Jews,"* all who abide by its regulations while penetrating to its essence and its real motive powers, should be men who strive for saintliness. But strive they must, zealously, imaginatively, and with unrelenting commitment.

The Mystical Element
in Judaism

ABRAHAM J. HESCHEL

THE MEANING
OF JEWISH MYSTICISM

There are people who take great care to keep away from the mists produced by fads and phrases. They refuse to convert realities into opinions, mysteries into dogmas, and ideas into a multitude of words, for they realize that all concepts are but glittering motes in a sunbeam. They want to see the sun itself. Confined to our study rooms, our knowledge seems to us a pillar of light; but when we stand at the door that opens out to the Infinite, we see how insubstantial is our knowledge. Even when we shut the door to the Infinite and retire to the narrow limits of notions our minds cannot remain confined. Again, to some people explanations and opinions are a token of wonder's departure, like a curfew after which they may not come abroad. In the kabbalists, the drive and the fire and the light are never put out.

Like the vital power in ourselves that gives us the ability to fight and to endure, to dare and to conquer, which drives us to experience the bitter and the perilous, there is an urge in wistful souls to starve rather than be fed on sham and distortion. To the kabbalists God is as real as life, and as nobody would be satisfied with mere knowing or reading about life, so they are not content to suppose or to prove logically that there is a God; they want to feel and to enjoy Him; not only to obey, but to approach Him. They want to taste the whole wheat of spirit before it is ground by the millstones of reason. They would rather be overwhelmed by the symbols of the inconceivable than wield the definitions of the superficial.

Stirred by a yearning after the unattainable, they want to make the distant near, the abstract concrete, to transform the soul into a vessel for the transcendent, to grasp with the senses what is hidden from the mind, to express in symbols what the tongue cannot speak, what the reason cannot conceive, to experience as a reality what vaguely dawns in intuitions. "Wise is he who by the power of his own contemplation attains to the perception of the profound mysteries which cannot be expressed in words."

The kabbalist is not content with being confined to what he is. His desire is not only to *know* more than what ordinary reason has to offer, but to *be* more than what he is; not only to comprehend the Beyond but to concur with it. He aims at the elevation and expansion of existence. Such expansion goes hand in hand with the exaltation of all being.

The universe, exposed to the violence of our analytical mind, is being broken apart. It is split into the known and unknown, into the seen and unseen. In mystic contemplation all things are seen as one. The mystic mind tends to hold the world together: to behold the seen in conjunction with the unseen, to keep the fellowship with the unknown through the revolving door of the known, "to learn the higher supernal wisdom from all" that the Lord has created and to regain the knowledge that once was in the possession of men and "that has perished from them." What our senses perceive is but the jutting edge of what is deeply hidden. Extending over into the invisible, the things of this world stand in a secret contact with that which no eye has ever perceived. Everything certifies to the sublime, the unapparent working jointly with the apparent. There is always a reverberation in the Beyond to every action here: "The Lord made this world corresponding to the world above, and everything which is above has its counterpart below . . . and yet they all constitute a unity"; "there being no object, however small, in this world, but what is subordinate to its counterpart above which has charge over it; and so whenever the thing below bestirs itself, there is a simultaneous stimulation of its counterpart above, as the two realms form one interconnected whole."

Opposed to the idea that the world of perception is the bottom of reality, the mystics plunge into what is beneath the perceptible. What they attain in their quest is more than a vague impression or a spotty knowledge of the imperceptible. "Penetrating to the real essence of wisdom . . . they are resplendent with the radiance of supernal wisdom." Their eyes perceive things of this world, while their hearts reverberate to the throbbing of the hidden. To them the secret is the core of the apparent; the known is but an aspect of the unknown. "All things below are symbols of that which is above." They are sustained by the forces that flow from hidden worlds. There is no particular that is detached from universal meaning. What appears to be a center to the eye is but a point on the periphery around another center. Nothing here is final. The worldly is subservient to the other-worldly. You grasp the essence of the here by conceiving its beyond. For this world is the reality of the spirit in a state of trance. The manifestation of the mystery is partly suspended, with ourselves living in lethargy. Our normal consciousness is a state of stupor, in which our sensibility to the wholly real and our responsiveness to the stimuli of the spirit are reduced. The mystics, knowing that we are involved in a hidden history of the cosmos, endeavor to awake from the drowsiness and apathy and to regain the state of wakefulness for our enchanted souls.

It is a bold attitude of the soul, a steadfast quality of consciousness, that lends mystic character to a human being. A man who feels that he is closely enfolded by a power that is both lasting and holy will come to know that the spiritual is not an idea to which one can relate his will, but a realm which can even be affected by our deeds. What distinguishes the kabbalist is the attachment of his entire personality to a hidden spiritual realm. Intensifying this attachment by means of active devotion to it, by meditation upon its secrets, or even by perception of its reality, he becomes allied with the dynamics of hidden worlds. Sensitive to the imperceptible, he is stirred by its secret happenings.

Attachment to hidden worlds holds the kabbalist in the spell of things more basic than the things that dominate the interest of the common mind. The mystery is not beyond and away from us. It is our destiny. "The fate of the world depends upon the mystery." Our task is to adjust the details to the whole, the apparent to the hidden, the near to the distant. The passionate concern of the kabbalist for final goals endows him with the experience of surpassing all human limitations and powers. With all he is doing he is crossing the borders, breaking the surfaces, approaching the lasting sources of all things. Yet his living with the infinite does not make him alien to the finite.

THE EXALTATION OF MAN

In this exalted world man's position is unique. God has instilled in him something of Himself. Likeness to God is the essence of man. The Hebrew word for man, *adam*, usually associated with the word for earth, *adamah*, was homiletically related by some kabbalists to the expression, "I will ascend above the heights of the clouds; I will be like *(eddamme)* the Most High" (Isa. 14:14). Man's privilege is, as it were, to augment the Divine in the world, as it is said, "ascribe ye strength unto God" (Ps. 68:35).

Jewish mystics are inspired by a bold and dangerously paradoxical idea that not only is God necessary to man but that man is also necessary to God, to the unfolding of His plans in this world. Thoughts of this kind are indicated and even expressed in various rabbinic sources. "When Israel performs the will of the Omnipresent, they add strength to the heavenly power; as it is said, 'To God we render strength!' " When, however, Israel does not perform the will of the Omnipresent, they weaken—if it is possible to say so—the great power of Him Who is above; as it is written "Thou didst weaken the Rock that begot thee" (Deut. 32:18). In the Zohar this idea is formulated in a more specific way. Commenting on the passage in Exod. 17:8, "Then came Amalek and fought with Israel in Rephidim," R. Simeon said: "There is a deep allusion in the name 'Rephidim.' This war emanated from the attribute of Severe Judgment and it was a war above and a war below. . . . The Holy One, as it were, said: 'When Israel is worthy below, My power prevails in the universe; but when Israel is found to be unworthy, she weakens My power above, and the power of severe judgment predominates in the world.' So here, 'Amalek came and fought with Israel in Rephidim,' because the Israelites were 'weak' (in Hebrew: *raphe*, which the Zohar finds in the name 'Rephidim') in the study of the Torah, as we have explained on another occasion." Thus man's relationship to God should not be that of passive reliance upon His Omnipotence but that of active assistance. "The impious rely on their gods . . . the righteous are the support of God." The patriarchs are therefore called "the chariot of the Lord." The belief in the greatness of man, in the metaphysical effectiveness of his physical acts, is an ancient motif of Jewish thinking.

Man himself is a mystery. He is the symbol of all that exists. His life is the image of universal life. Everything was created in the spiritual image of the mystical man. "When the Holy One created man, He set in him all the images of the supernal mysteries of the world above, and all the images of the lower mysteries of the world below, and all are designed in man, who stands in the image of God." Even the human body is full of symbolic significance. The skin, flesh, bones and sinews are but an outward covering, mere garments, even though "the substances composing man's body belong to two worlds, namely, the world below and the world above." The 248 limbs and 365 sinews are symbols of the 613 parts of the universe as well as of the 248 positive and 365 negative precepts of the Torah. Man's soul emanates from an upper region where it has a spiritual father and a spiritual mother, just as the body has a father and mother in this world. The souls that abide in our bodies are a weak reflection of our upper souls, the seat of which is in heaven. Yet, though detached from that soul, we are capable of being in contact with it. When we pray we turn toward the upper soul as though we were to abandon the body and join our source.

Man is not detached from the realm of the unseen. He is wholly involved in it. Whether he is conscious of it or not, his actions are vital to all worlds, and affect the course of transcendent events. In a sense, by means of the Torah, man is the constant architect of the hidden universe. "This world was formed in the pattern of the world above, and whatever takes place in this earthly realm occurs also in the realm above." One of the principles of the Zohar is that every move below calls forth a corresponding movement above. Not only things, even periods of time are conceived as concrete entities. "Thus over every day below is appointed a day above, and a man should take heed not to impair that day. Now the act below stimulates a corresponding activity above. Thus if a man does kindness on earth, he awakens loving-kindness above, and it rests upon that day which is crowned therewith through him. Similarly, if he performs a deed of mercy, he crowns that day with mercy and it becomes his protector in the hour of need. So, too, if he performs a cruel action, he has a corresponding effect on that day and impairs it, so that subsequently it becomes cruel to him and tries to destroy him, giving him measure for measure." Even what we consider potential is regarded as real and we may be held accountable for it: ". . . just as a man is punished for uttering an evil word, so is he punished for not uttering a good word when he had the opportunity, because he harms that speaking spirit which was prepared to speak above and below in holiness."

The significance of great works done on earth is valued by their cosmic effects. Thus, for example, "When the first Temple was completed another Temple was erected at the same time, which was a center for all the worlds, shedding radiance upon all things and giving light to all the spheres. Then the worlds were firmly established, and all the supernal casements were opened to pour forth light, and all the worlds experienced such joys as had never been known to them before, and celestial and terrestrial beings alike broke forth in song. And the song which they sang is the Song of Songs."

Endowed with metaphysical powers, man's life is a most serious affair; "if a man's lips and tongue speak evil words, those words mount aloft and all proclaim 'keep away from the evil word of so-and-so, leave the path clear for the mighty serpent.' Then the holy soul leaves him and is not able to speak: it is in shame and distress, and is not given a place as before. . . . Then many spirits bestir themselves, and one spirit comes down from that side and finds the man who uttered the evil word, and lights upon him and defiles him, and he becomes leprous."

Man's life is full of peril. It can easily upset the balance and order of the universe. "A voice goes forth and proclaims: 'O ye people of the world, take heed unto yourselves, close the gates of sin, keep away from the perilous net before your feet are caught in it!' A certain wheel is ever whirling continuously round and round. Woe to those whose feet lose their hold on the wheel, for then they fall into the Deep which is predestined for the evildoers of the world! Woe to those who fall, never to rise and enjoy the light that is stored up for the righteous in the world to come!"

THE EN SOF AND
HIS MANIFESTATIONS

Mystic intuition occurs at an outpost of the mind, dangerously detached from the main substance of the intellect. Operating as it were in no-mind's land, its place is hard to name, its communications with critical thinking often difficult and uncertain and the accounts of its discoveries not easy to decode. In its main representatives, the Kabbalah teaches that man's life can be a rallying point of the forces that tend toward God, that this world is charged with His presence and every object is a cue to His qualities. To the kabbalist, God is not a concept, a generalization, but a most specific reality; his thinking about Him full of forceful directness. But He who is "the Soul of all souls" is "the mystery of all mysteries." While the kabbalists speak of God as if they commanded a view of the Beyond, and were in possession of knowledge about the inner life of God, they also assure us that all notions fail when applied to Him, that He is beyond the grasp of the human mind and inaccessible to meditation. He is the En Sof, the Infinite, "the most Hidden of all Hidden." While there is an abysmal distance between Him and the world, He is also called All. "For all things are in Him and He is in all things . . . He is both manifest and concealed. Manifest in order to uphold the all and concealed, for He is found nowhere. When He becomes manifest He projects nine brilliant lights that throw light in all directions. So, too, does a lamp throw brilliance in all directions, but when we approach the brilliance we find there is nothing outside the lamp. So is the Holy ancient One, the Light of all Lights, the most Hidden of all Hidden. We can only find the light which He spreads and which appears and disappears. This light is called the Holy Name, and therefore All is One."

Thus, the "Most Recondite One Who is beyond cognition does reveal of Himself a tenuous and veiled brightness shining only along a narrow path which extends from Him. This is the brightness that irradiates all." The En Sof has granted us manifestations of His hidden life: He had descended to become the universe; He has revealed Himself to become the Lord of Israel. The ways in which the Infinite assumes the form of finite existence are called Sefirot. These are various aspects or forms of Divine action, spheres of Divine emanation. They are, as it were, the garments in which the Hidden God reveals Himself and acts in the universe, the channels through which His light is issued forth.

The names of the ten Sefirot are Keter, Hokhmah, Binah, Hesed, Geburah, Tiferet, Netsah, Hod, Yesod, Malkut. The transition from divine latency to activity takes place in Keter, the "supreme crown" of God. This stage is inconceivable, absolute unity and beyond description. In the following Sefirot, Hokhmah and Binah, the building and creation of the cosmos as well as that which divides things begins. They are parallel emanations from Keter, representing the active and the receptive principle.

While the first triad represents the transition from the Divine to the spiritual reality, the second triad is the source of the moral order. Hesed stands for the love of God; Geburah for the power of justice manifested as severity or punishment. From the union of these emanates Tiferet, compassion or beauty of God, mediating between Hesed and Geburah, between the life-giving power and the contrary power, holding in check what would otherwise prove to be the excesses of love.

The next triad is the source of the psychic and physical existences—Netsah is the lasting endurance of God, Hod His majesty, and Yesod the stability of the universe, the seat of life and vitality. Malkut is the kingdom, the presence of the Divine in the world. It is not a source of its own but the outflow of the other Sefirot; "of itself lightless, it looks up to the others and reflects them as a lamp reflects the sun." It is the point at which the external world comes in contact with the upper spheres, the final manifestations of the Divine, the Shekinah, "the Mother of all Living."

The recondite and unapproachable Self of God is usually thought of as transcendent to the Sefirot. There is only a diffusion of His light into the Sefirot. The En Sof and the realm of His manifestations are "linked together like the flame and the coal," the flame being a manifestation of what is latent in the coal. In the process of the emanation, the transition from the Divine to the spiritual, from the spiritual to the moral, from the moral to the physical, reality takes place. The product of this manifestation is not only the visible universe but an endless number of spiritual worlds which exist beyond the physical universe in which we live. These worlds, the hidden cosmos, constitute a most complex structure, divided into various grades and forms which can only be described in symbols. These symbols are found in the Torah, which is the constitution of the cosmos. Every letter, word or phrase in the Bible not only describes an event in the history of our world but also represents a symbol of some stage in the hidden cosmos. These are the so-called Raze Torah, the mysteries, that can be discovered by the mystical method of interpretation.

The system of Sefirot can be visualized as a tree or a man or a circle, in three triads or in three columns. According to the last image the Sefirot are divided into a *right* column, signifying Mercy, or light, a *left* column, signifying Severity, the absence of light, and a *central* column, signifying the synthesis of the right and left. Each Sefirah is a world in itself, dynamic and full of complicated mutual relations with other Sefirot. There are many symbols by which each Sefirah can be expressed, for example, the second triad is symbolized in the lives of each of the three patriarchs. The doctrine of Sefirot enables the kabbalists to perceive the bearings of God upon this world, to identify the Divine substance of all objects and events. It offers the principles by means of which all things and events can be interpreted as Divine manifestations.

The various parts of the day represent various aspects of Divine manifestation. "From sunrise until the sun declines westward it is called 'day,' and the attribute of Mercy is in the ascendant; after that it is called 'evening,' which is the time for the attribute of Severity. . . . It is for this reason that Isaac instituted the afternoon prayer (Minhah), namely, to mitigate the severity of the approaching evening; whereas Abraham instituted morning prayer, corresponding to the attribute of mercy."

The plurality into which the one Divine manifestation is split symbolizes the state of imperfection into which God's relation to the world was thrown. Every good deed serves to restore the original unity of the Sefirot, while on the other hand, "Sinners impair the supernal world by causing a separation between the 'Right' and the 'Left.' They really cause harm only to themselves, . . . as they prevent the descent of blessings from above . . . and the heaven keeps the blessings to itself." Thus the sinner's separation of the good inclination from the evil one by consciously cleaving to evil separates, as it were, the Divine attribute of Grace from that of Judgment, the Right from the Left.

THE DOCTRINE OF
THE SHEKINAH

Originally there was harmony between God and His final manifestations, between the upper Sefirot and tenth Sefirah. All things were attached to God and His power surged unhampered throughout all stages of being. Following the trespass of Adam, however, barriers evolved thwarting the emanation of His power. The creature became detached from the Creator, the fruit from the tree, the tree of knowledge from the tree of life, the male from the female, our universe from the world of unity, even the Shekinah or the tenth Sefirah from the upper Sefirot. Owing to that separation the world was thrown into disorder, the power of strict judgment increased, the power of love diminished and the forces of evil released. Man who was to exist in pure spiritual form as light in constant communication with the Divine was sunk into his present inferior state.

In spite of this separation, however, God has not withdrawn entirely from this world. Metaphorically, when Adam was driven out of Eden, an aspect of the Divine, the Shekinah, followed him into captivity. Thus there is a Divine power that dwells in this world. It is the Divine Presence that went before Israel while they were going through the wilderness, that protects the virtuous man, that abides in his house and goes forth with him on his journeys, that dwells between a man and his wife. The Shekinah "continually accompanies a man and leaves him not so long as he keeps the precepts of the Torah. Hence a man should be careful not to go on the road alone, that is to say, he should diligently keep the precepts of the Torah in order that he may not be deserted by the Shekinah, and so be forced to go alone without the accompaniment of the Shekinah." The Shekinah follows Israel into exile and "always hovers over Israel like a mother over her children." Moreover, it is because of Israel and its observance of the Torah that the Shekinah dwells on earth. Were they to corrupt their way, they would thrust the Shekinah out of this world and the earth would be left in a degenerate state.

The doctrine of the Shekinah occupies a central place in the Kabbalah. While emphasizing that in His essence "the Holy One and the Shekinah are One," it speaks of a cleavage, as it were, in the reality of the Divine. The Shekinah is called figuratively the *Matrona* (symbolized by the Divine Name *Elohim*) that is separated from the King (symbolized by the ineffable name *Hashem*) and it signifies that God is, so to speak, involved in the tragic state of this world. In the light of this doctrine the suffering of Israel assumed new meaning. Not only Israel but the whole universe, even the Shekinah, "lies in dust" and is in exile. Man's task is to bring about the restitution of the original state of the universe and the reunion of the Shekinah and the En Sof. This is the meaning of messianic salvation, the goal of all efforts.

"In time to come God will restore the Shekinah to its place and there will be a complete union. 'In that day shall the Lord be One and His Name One' (Zech. 14:9). It may be said: Is He not now One? no; for now through sinners He is not really One. For the Matrona is removed from the King . . . and the King without the Matrona is not invested with His crown as before. But when He joins the Matrona, who crowns Him with many resplendent crowns, then the supernal Mother will also crown Him in a fitting manner. But now that the King is not with the Matrona, the supernal Mother keeps her crowns and withholds from Him the waters of the stream and He is not joined with her. Therefore, as it were, He is not one. But when the Matrona shall return to the place of the Temple and the King shall be wedded with her, then all will be joined together, without separation and regarding this it is written, 'In that day shall the Lord be One and His Name One.' Then there shall be such perfection in the world as had not been for all generations before, for then shall be completeness above and below, and all worlds shall be united in one bond."

The restoration of unity is a constant process. It takes place through the study of the Torah, through prayer and through the fulfillment of the commandments. "The only aim and object of the Holy One in sending man into this world is that he may know and understand that Hashem (God), signifying the En Sof, is Elohim (Shekinah). This is the sum of the whole mystery of the faith, of the whole Torah, of all that is above and below, of the written and the oral Torah, all together forming one unity." "When a man sins it is as though he strips the Shekinah of her vestments, and that is why he is punished; and when he carries out the precepts of the law, it is as though he clothes the Shekinah in her vestments. Hence we say that the fringes worn by the Israelites are, to the Shekinah in captivity, like the poor man's garments of which it is said, 'For that is his only covering, it is his garment for his skin, wherein he shall sleep.' "

MYSTIC EXPERIENCE

The ultimate goal of the kabbalist is not his own union with the Absolute but the union of all reality with God; one's own bliss is subordinated to the redemption of all: "We have to put all our being, all the members of our body, our complete devotion, into that thought so as to rise and attach ourselves to the En Sof, and thus achieve the oneness of the upper and lower worlds."

What this service means in terms of personal living is described in the following way:

> Happy is the portion of whoever can penetrate into the mysteries of his Master and become absorbed into Him, as it were. Especially does a man achieve this when he offers up his prayer to his Master in intense devotion, his will then becoming as the flame inseparable from the coal, and his mind concentrated on the unity of the lower firmaments, to unify them by means of a lower name, then on the unity of the higher firmaments, and finally on the absorption of them all into that most high firmament. Whilst a man's mouth and lips are moving, his heart and will must soar to the height of heights, so as to acknowledge the unity of the whole in virtue of the mystery of mysteries in which all ideas, all wills and all thoughts find their goal, to wit, the mystery of *En Sof*.

The thirst for God is colored by the awareness of His holiness, of the endless distance that separates man from the Eternal One. Yet, he who craves for God is not only a mortal being, but also a part of the Community of Israel, that is, the bride of God, endowed with a soul that is "a part of God." Shy in using endearing terms in his own name, the Jewish mystic feels and speaks in the plural. The allegory of the Song of Songs would be impertinent as an individual utterance, but as an expression of Israel's love for God it is among the finest of all expressions. "God is the soul and spirit of all, and Israel calls Him so and says: (My soul), I desire Thee in order to cleave to Thee and I seek Thee early to find Thy favor."

Israel lives in mystic union with God and the purpose of all its service is to strengthen this union: "O my dove that art in the clefts of the rock, in the covert of the cliff" (Song of Sol. 2:14). The "dove" here is the Community of Israel, which like a dove never forsakes her mate, the Holy One, blessed be He. "In the clefts of the rock": these are the students of the Torah, who have no ease in this world. "In the covert of the steep place": these are the specially pious among them, the saintly and God-fearing, from whom the Divine Presence never departs. The Holy One, blessed be He, inquires concerning them of the Community of Israel, saying, "Let me see thy countenance, let me hear thy voice, for sweet is thy voice"; "for above only the voice of those who study the Torah is heard. We have learned that the likeness of all such is graven above before the Holy One, blessed be He, Who delights Himself with them every day and watches them and that voice rises and pierces its way through all firmaments until it stands before the Holy One, blessed be He."

The concepts of the Kabbalah cannot always be clearly defined and consistently interrelated. As the name of Jewish mysticism, "Kabbalah" (lit.: received lore), indicates, it is a tradition of wisdom, supposed to have been revealed to elect Sages in ancient times and preserved throughout the generations by an initiated few. The kabbalists accept at the outset the ideas on authority, not on the basis of analytical understanding.

Yet the lips of the teachers and the pages of the books are not the only sources of knowledge. The great kabbalists claimed to have received wisdom directly from the Beyond. Inspiration and Vision were as much a part of their life as contemplation and study. The prayer of Moses: "Show me, I pray Thee, Thy glory" (Exod. 33:18) has never died in the hearts of the kabbalists. The conception of the goal has changed but the quest for immediate cognition remained. The Merkaba mystics, following perhaps late prophetic traditions about the mysteries of the Divine Throne, were striving to behold the celestial sphere in which the secrets of creation and man's destiny are contained. In the course of the centuries the scope of such esoteric experiences embraced a variety of objectives. The awareness of the kabbalists that the place whereon they stood was holy ground kept them mostly silent about the wonder that was granted to them. Yet we possess sufficient evidence to justify the assumption that mystic events, particularly in the form of inner experiences, of spiritual communications rather than that of sense perceptions, were elements of their living. According to old rabbinic teachings, there have always been sages and saints upon whom the Holy Spirit rested, to whom wisdom was communicated from heaven by a Voice, through the appearance of the spirit of Elijah, or in dreams. According to the Zohar, God reveals to the saints "profound secrets of the Holy Name which He does not reveal to the angels." The disciples of Rabbi Simeon ben Yohai are called prophets, "before whom both supernal and terrestrial beings tremble in awe." Others pray that the inspiration of the Holy Spirit should come upon them. The perception of the unearthly is recorded as an ordinary feature in the life of certain rabbis. "When R. Hamnuna the Ancient used to come out from the river on a Friday afternoon, he was wont to rest a little on the bank, and raising his eyes in gladness, he would say that he sat there in order to behold the joyous sight of the heavenly angels ascending and descending. At each arrival of the Sabbath, he said, man is caught up into the world of souls." Not only may the human mind receive spiritual illuminations; the soul also may be bestowed upon higher powers. "Corresponding to the impulses of a man here are the influences which he attracts to himself from above. Should his impulse be toward holiness, he attracts to himself holiness from on high and so he becomes holy; but if this tendency is toward the side of impurity, he draws down toward himself the unclean spirit and so becomes polluted."

Since the time of the prophet Joel the Jews have expected that at the end of days the Lord would "pour out His spirit upon all flesh" and all men would prophesy. In later times, it is believed, the light of that revelation of mysteries could already be perceived.

The mystics absorb even in this world "something of the odor of these secrets and mysteries." Significantly, the Torah itself is conceived as a living source of inspiration, not as a fixed book. The Torah is a voice that "calls aloud" to men; she calls them day by day to herself in love . . . "The Torah lets out a word and emerges for a little from her sheath, and then hides herself again. But she does this only for those who understand and obey her. She is like unto a beautiful and stately damsel, who is hidden in a secluded chamber of a palace and who has a lover of whom no one knows but she. Out of his love for her he constantly passes by her gate, turning his eyes toward all sides to find her. Knowing that he is always haunting the palace, what does she do? She opens a little door in her hidden palace, discloses for a moment her face to her lover, then swiftly hides it again. None but he notices it; but his heart and soul, and all that is in him are drawn to her, knowing as he does that she has revealed herself to him for a moment because she loves him. It is the same with the Torah, which reveals her hidden secrets only to those who love her. She knows that he who is wise of heart daily haunts the gates of her house. What does she do? She shows her face to him from her palace, making a sign of love to him, and straightaway returns to her hiding place again. No one understands her message save he alone, and he is drawn to her with heart and soul and all his being. Thus the Torah reveals herself momentarily in love to her lovers in order to awaken fresh love in them."

THE TORAH—A MYSTIC REALITY

The Torah is an inexhaustible esoteric reality. To enter into its deep, hidden strata is in itself a mystic goal. The Universe is an image of the Torah and the Torah is an image of God. For the Torah is "the Holy of Holies"; "it consists entirely of the name of the Holy One, blessed be He. Every letter in it is bound up with that Name."

The Torah is the main source from which man can draw the secret wisdom and power of insight into the essence of things. "It is called Torah (lit.: showing) because it shows and reveals that which is hidden and unknown; and all life from above is comprised in it and issues from it." "The Torah contains all the deepest and most recondite mysteries; all sublime doctrines both disclosed and undisclosed; all essences both of the higher and the lower grades, of this world and of the world to come are to found there." The source of wisdom is accessible to all, yet only few resort to it. "How stupid are men that they take no pains to know the ways of the Almighty by which the world is maintained. What prevents them? Their stupidity, because they do not study the Torah; for if they were to study the Torah they would know the ways of the Holy One, blessed be He."

The Torah has a double significance: literal and symbolic. Besides their plain, literal meaning, which is important, valid and never to be overlooked, the verses of the Torah possess an esoteric significance, "comprehensible only to the wise who are familiar with the ways of the Torah." "Happy is Israel to whom was given the sublime Torah, the Torah of truth. Perdition take anyone who maintains that any narrative in the Torah comes merely to tell us a piece of history and nothing more! If that were so, the Torah would not be what it assuredly is, to wit, the supernal Law, the Law of truth. Now if it is not dignified for a king of flesh and blood to engage in common talk, much less to write it down, is it conceivable that the most high King, the Holy One, blessed be He, was short of sacred subjects with which to fill the Torah, so that He had to collect such commonplace topics as the anecdotes of Esau, and Hagar, Laban's talks to Jacob, the words of

Balaam and his ass, those of Balak, and of Zimri, and such-like, and make of them a Torah? If so, why is it called the 'Law of Truth?' Why do we read 'The Law of the Lord is perfect . . . The testimony of the Lord is sure . . . The Ordinances of the Lord are true . . . More to be desired are they than gold, yea, than much fine gold' (Ps. 19:8–11). But assuredly each word of the Torah signifies sublime things, so that this or that narrative, besides its meaning in and for itself, throws light on the all-comprehensive Rule of the Torah."

"Said R. Simeon: 'Alas for the man who regards the Torah as a mere book of tales and everyday matters! If that were so, we, even we, could compose a torah dealing with everyday affairs, and of even greater excellence. Nay, even the princes of the world possess books of greater worth which we could use as a model for composing some such torah. The Torah, however, contains in all its words supernal truths and sublime mysteries. Observe the perfect balancing of the upper and lower worlds. Israel here below is balanced by the angels of high, of whom it says: 'who makest thine angels into winds' (Ps. 104:4). For the angels in descending on earth put on themselves earthly garments, as otherwise they could not stay in this world, nor could the world endure them.

"Now, if thus it is with the angels, how much more so must it be with the Torah—the Torah that created them, that created all the worlds and is the means by which these are sustained. Thus had the Torah not clothed herself in garments of this world the world could not endure it. The stories of the Torah are thus only her outer garments, and whoever looks upon that garment as being Torah itself, woe to that man—such a one will have no portion in the next world. David thus said: 'Open thou mine eyes, that I may behold wondrous things out of Thy law' (Ps. 119:18), to wit, the things that are beneath the garment. Observe this. The garments worn by a man are the most visible part of him, and senseless people looking at the man do not seem to see more in him than the garments. But in truth the pride of the garments is the body of the man, and the pride of the body is the soul. Similarly the Torah has a body made up of the precepts of the Torah, called *gufe torah* (bodies, main principles of the Torah), and that body is enveloped in garments made up of worldly narratives. The senseless people only see the garment, the mere narrations; those who are somewhat wise penetrate as far as the body. But the really wise, the servants of the most high King, those who stood on Mt.

Sinai, penetrate right through to the soul, the root principle of all, namely to the real Torah. In the future the same are destined to penetrate even to the super-soul (soul of the soul) of the Torah. . . ."

How assiduously should one ponder over each word of the Torah, for there is not a single word in it which does not contain allusions to the Supernal Holy Name, not a word which does not contain many mysteries, many aspects, many roots, many branches! Where now is this "book of the wars of the Lord"? What is meant, of course, is the Torah, for as the members of the fellowship have pointed out, he who is engaged in the battle of the Torah, struggling to penetrate into her mysteries, will wrest from his struggles an abundance of peace.

THE MYSTIC WAY OF LIFE

A longing for the unearthly, a yearning for purity, the will to holiness, connected the conscience of the kabbalists with the strange current of mystic living. Being puzzled or inquisitive will not make a person mystery-stricken. The kabbalists were not set upon exploring, or upon compelling the unseen to become visible. Their intention was to integrate their thoughts and deeds into the secret order, to assist God in undoing the evil, in redeeming the light that was concealed. Though working with fragile tools for a mighty end, they were sure of bringing about at the end of time the salvation of the universe and of this tormented world.

A new form of living was the consequence of the Kabbalah. Everything was so replete with symbolic significance as to make it the potential heart of the spiritual universe. How carefully must all be approached. A moral rigorism that hardly leaves any room for waste or respite resulted in making the kabbalist more meticulous in studying and fulfilling the precepts of the Torah, in refining his moral conduct, in endowing everyday actions with solemn significance. For man represents God in this world. Even the parts of his body signify divine mysteries.

Everything a man does leaves its imprint on the world. "The Supernal Holy King does not permit anything to perish, not even the breath of the mouth. He has a place for everything, and makes it what He wills. Even a human word, yes, even the voice, is not void, but has its place and destination in the universe." Every action here below, if it is done with the intention of serving the Holy King, produces a "breath" in the world above, and there is no breath which has no voice; and this voice ascends and crowns itself in the supernal world and becomes an intercessor before the Holy One, blessed be He. Contrariwise, every action which is not done with this purpose becomes a "breath" which floats about the world, and when the soul of the doer leaves his body, this "breath" rolls about like a stone in a sling, and it "breaks the spirit." The act done and the word spoken in the service of the Holy One, however, ascend high above the sun and become a holy breath, which is the seed sown by man in that world and is called *Zedakah* (righteousness or loving-kindness), as it is written: "Sow to yourselves according to righteousness" (Hos. 10:12). This "breath" guides the departed soul and brings it into the region of the supernal glory, so that it is "bound in the bundle of life with the Lord thy God" (1 Sam. 25:29). It is concerning this that it is written: "Thy righteousness shall go before thee; the glory of the Lord shall be thy reward" (Isa. 58:8). That which is called "the glory of the Lord" gathers up the souls of that holy breath, and this is indeed ease and comfort for them; but the other is called "breaking of spirit." Blessed are the righteous whose works are "above the sun" and who sow a seed of righteousness which makes them worthy to enter the world to come.

Everything a man does leaves its imprint upon the world: his breath, thought, speech. If it is evil, the air is defiled and he who comes close to that trace may be affected by it and led to do evil. By fulfilling the divine precepts man purifies the air and turns the "evil spirits" into "holy spirits." He should strive to spiritualize the body and to make it identical with the soul by fulfilling the 248 positive and 365 negative precepts which correspond to the 248 limbs and the 365 sinews of the human body. The precepts of the Torah contain "manifold sublime recondite teachings and radiances and resplendences," and can lift man to the supreme level of existence.

The purpose of man's service is to "give strength to God," not to attain one's own individual perfection. Man is able to stir the supernal spheres. "The terrestrial world is connected with the heavenly world, as the heavenly world is connected with the terrestrial one." In fulfilling the good the corresponding sphere on high is strengthened; in balking it, the sphere is weakened. This connection or correspondence can be made to operate in a creative manner by means of *kawwanah* or contemplation of the mysteries of which the words and precepts of the Torah are the symbols. In order to grasp the meaning of those words or to fulfill the purpose of those precepts one has to resort to the Divine Names and Qualities that are invested in those words and precepts, the mystic issues to which they refer, or, metaphorically, the gates of the celestial mansion which the spiritual content of their fulfillment has to enter. Thus, all deeds—study, prayer and ceremonies—have to be performed not mechanically but while meditating upon their mystic significance.

Prayer is a powerful force in this service and a venture full of peril. He who prays is a priest at the temple that is the cosmos. With good prayer he may "build worlds," with improper prayer he may "destroy worlds." "It is a miracle that a man survives the hour of worship," the Baal Shem said. "The significance of all our prayers and praises is that by means of them the upper fountain may be filled; and when it is so filled and attains completeness, then the universe below, and all that appertains thereto, is filled also and receives completeness from the completion which has been consummated in the upper sphere. The world below cannot, indeed, be in a state of harmony unless it receives that peace and perfection from above, even as the moon has no light in herself but shines with the reflected radiance of the sun. All our prayers and intercessions have this purpose, namely, that the region from whence light issues may be invigorated; for then from its reflection all below is supplied." "Every word of prayer that issues from a man's mouth ascends aloft through all firmaments to a place where it is tested. If it is genuine, it is taken up before the Holy King to be fulfilled, but if not it is rejected, and an alien spirit is evoked by it." For example, "it is obligatory for every Israelite to relate the story of the Exodus on the Passover night. He who does so fervently and joyously, telling the tale with a high heart, shall be found worthy to rejoice in the Shekinah in the world to come, for rejoicing brings forth rejoicing; and the joy of Israel causes the Holy One Himself to be glad, so that He calls together all the Family above and says unto them: 'Come ye and hearken unto the praises which My children bring unto Me! Behold how they rejoice in My redemption!' Then all the angels and supernal beings gather round and observe Israel, how she sings and rejoices because of her Lord's own Redemption—and seeing the rejoicings below, the supernal beings also break into jubilation for that the Holy One possesses on earth a people so holy, whose joy in the Redemption of their Lord is so great and powerful. For all that terrestrial rejoicing increases the power of the Lord and His hosts in the regions above, just as an earthly king gains strength from the praises of his subjects, the fame of his glory being thus spread throughout the world."

Worship came to be regarded as a pilgrimage into the supernal spheres, with the prayerbook as an itinerary, containing the course of the gradual ascent of the spirit. The essential goal of man's service is to bring about the lost unity of all that exists. To render praise unto Him is not the final purpose. "Does the God of Abraham need an exaltation? Is He not already exalted high above our comprehension? . . . Yet man can and must exalt Him in the sense of uniting in his mind all the attributes in the Holy Name, for this is the supremest form of worship." By meditating upon the mysteries while performing the divine precepts, we act toward unifying all the supernal potencies in one will and bringing about the union of the Master and the Matrona.

Concerning the verse in Ps. 145:18, "The Lord is nigh to all them that call upon Him, to all that call upon Him in truth," the Zohar remarks that the words "in truth" mean in possession of the full knowledge which enables the worshiper perfectly "to unite the letters of the Holy Name in prayer. . . . On the achievement of that unity hangs both celestial and terrestrial worship. . . . If a man comes to unify the Holy Name, but without proper concentration of mind and devotion of heart, to the end that the supernal and terrestrial hosts should be blessed thereby, then his prayer is rejected and all beings denounce him, and he is numbered with those of whom the Holy One said, 'When ye come to see my countenance, who hath required this from your hand, to tread my courts?' All the 'countenances' of the King are hidden in the depths of darkness, but for those who know how perfectly to unite the Holy Name, all the walls of darkness are burst asunder, and the diverse 'countenances' of the King are made manifest, and shine upon all, bringing blessing to heavenly and earthly beings."

The lower things are apparent, the higher things remain unrevealed. The higher an essence is, the greater is the degree of its concealment. To pray is "to draw blessing from the depth of the 'Cistern,' from the source of all life. . . . Prayer is the drawing of this blessing from above to below; for when the Ancient One, the All-hidden, wishes to bless the universe, He lets His gifts of Grace collect in that supernal depth, from whence they are to be drawn, through human prayer, into the 'Cistern,' so that all the streams and brooks may be filled therefrom." The verse in Ps. 130:1, "Out of the depths have I called Thee," is said to mean not only that he who prays should do so from the depths of his soul; he must also invoke the blessing from the source of all sources.

THE CONCERN FOR GOD

The yearning for mystic living, the awareness of the ubiquitous mystery, the noble nostalgia for the nameless nucleus, have rarely subsided in the Jewish soul. This longing for the mystical has found many and varied expressions in ideas and doctrines, in customs and songs, in visions and aspirations. It is a part of the heritage of the psalmists and prophets.

There were Divine commandments to fulfill, rituals to perform, laws to obey—but the psalmist did not feel as if he carried a yoke: "Thy statutes have been my songs" (119:54). The fulfillment of the mitzvot was felt to be not a mechanical compliance but a personal service in the palace of the King of Kings. Is mysticism alien to the spirit of Judaism? Listen to the psalmist: "As the hart panteth after the water brooks, so panteth my soul after Thee, O Lord. My soul thirsteth for God, for the Living God; when shall I come and appear before God?" (42:2–3). "My soul yearneth, yea even pineth for the courts of the Lord; my heart and my flesh sing for joy unto the Living God" (84:3). "For a day in Thy courts is better than a thousand" (84:11). "In Thy presence is fulness of joy" (16:11).

It has often been said that Judaism is an earthly religion, yet the psalmist states, "I am a sojourner in the earth" (119:19). "Whom have I in heaven but Thee? And beside thee I desire none upon earth" (73:25). "My flesh and my heart faileth; but God is the rock of my heart and my portion forever" (73:26). "But as for me, the nearness of God is my good" (73:28). "O God, Thou art my God; earnestly will I seek Thee; my soul thirsteth for Thee, my flesh longeth for Thee in a dry and weary land, where no water is . . . for Thy lovingkindness is better than life. My soul is satisfied as with marrow and fatness; . . . I remember Thee upon my couch and meditate on Thee in the night-watches. . . . My soul cleaveth unto Thee, Thy right hand holdeth me fast" (63:2, 4, 6, 7, 9).

In their efforts to say what God is and wills, the prophets sought to imbue Israel with two impulses: to realize that God is holy, different and apart from all that exists, and to bring into man's focus the dynamics that prevail between God and man. The first impulse placed the mind in the restful light of the knowledge of unity, omnipotence, and superiority of God to all other beings, while the second impulse turned the hearts toward the inexhaustible heavens of God's concern for man, at times brightened by His mercy, at times darkened by His anger. He is both transcendent, beyond human understanding, and at the same time full of love, compassion, grief, or anger. The prophets did not intend to afford man a view of heaven, to report about secret things they saw and heard but to disclose what happened in God in reference to Israel. What they preached was more than a concept of Divine might and wisdom. They spoke of an inner life of God, of His love or anger, His mercy or disappointment, His interest or participation in the fate of Israel and other nations. God revealed Himself to the prophets in a specific state, in an emotional or passionate relationship to Israel. He not only demanded obedience but He was personally concerned and even stirred by the conduct of His people. Their actions aroused His joy, grief or disappointment. His attitude was not objective but subjective. He was not only a Judge but also a Father. He is the lover, engaged to His people, who reacts to human life with a specific pathos, signified in the language of the prophets, in love, mercy or anger. The Divine pathos which the prophets tried to express in many ways was not a name for His essence but rather for the modes of this reaction to Israel's conduct which could be changed by a change in Israel's conduct. Such a change was often the object of the prophetic ministry.

The prophets discovered the holy dimension of living by which our right to live and to survive is measured. However, the holy dimension was not a mechanical magnitude, measurable by the yardstick of deed and reward, of crime and punishment, by a cold law of justice. They did not proclaim a universal moral mechanism but a spiritual order in which justice was the course but not the source. To them justice was not a static principle but a surge sweeping from the inwardness of God, in which the deeds of man find, as it were, approval or disapproval, joy or sorrow. There was a surge of Divine pathos, which came to the souls of the prophets like a fierce passion, startling, shaking, burning, and led them forth to the perilous defiance of people's self-assurance and contentment. Beneath all songs and sermons they held conference with God's concern for the people, with the well out of which the tides of anger raged.

There is always a correspondence between what man is and what he knows about God. To a man of the *vita activa*, omnipotence is the most striking attribute of God. A man with an inner life, to whom thoughts and intuitions are not less real than things and deeds, will search for a concept of the inner life of God. The concept of inner life in the Divine Being is an idea upon which the mystic doctrines of Judaism hinge. The significance of prophetic revelation lies not in the inner experience of the prophet but in its character as a manifestation of what is in God. Prophetic revelation is primarily an event in the life of God. This is the outstanding difference between prophetic revelation and all other types of inspiration as reported by many mystics and poets. To the prophet it is not a psychic event, but first of all a transcendent act, something that happens to God. The actual reality of revelation takes place outside the consciousness of the prophet. He experiences revelation, so to speak, as an ecstasy of God, who comes out of His imperceivable distance to reveal His will to man. Essentially, the act of revelation takes place in the Beyond; it is merely directed upon the prophet.

The knowledge about the inner state of the Divine in its relationship to Israel determined the inner life of the prophets, engendering a passion for God, a sympathy for the Divine pathos in their hearts. They loved Israel because God loved Israel, and they frowned upon Israel when they knew that such was the attitude of God. Thus the marriage of Hosea was an act of sympathy; the prophet had to go through the experience of being betrayed as Israel had betrayed God. He had to experience in his own life what it meant to be betrayed by a person whom he loved in order to gain an understanding of the inner life of God. In a similar way the sympathy for God was in the heart of Jeremiah like a "burning fire, shut up in my bones and I weary myself to hold it in, but cannot" (20:9).

The main doctrine of the prophets can be called *pathetic theology*. Their attitude toward what they knew about God can be described as religion of sympathy. The Divine pathos, or as it was later called, the

Middot, stood in the center of their consciousness. The life of the prophet revolved around the life of God. The prophets were not indifferent to whether God was in a state of anger or a state of mercy. They were most sensitive to what was going on in God.

This is the pattern of Jewish mysticism: to have an open heart for the inner life of God. It is based on two assumptions: that there is an inner life in God and that the existence of man ought to revolve in a spiritual dynamic course around the life of God.

The Human Condition
after Auschwitz

EMIL L. FACKENHEIM

A midrash in Genesis Rabbah disturbs and haunts the mind ever more deeply. It begins as follows:

> Rabbi Shim'on said: "In the hour when God was about to create Adam, the angels of service were divided. . . . Some said, 'Let him not be created,' others, 'Let him be created.' . . . Love said, 'Let him be created, for he will do loving deeds.' But Truth said, 'Let him not be created, for he will be all falsity.' Righteousness said, 'Let him be created, for he will do righteous deeds.' Peace said, 'Let him not be created, for he will be full of strife.' What then did God do? He seized hold of Truth, and cast her to the earth, as it is said, 'Thou didst cast Truth to the ground.' " (Dan. 8:12)

No midrash wants to be taken literally. Every midrash wants to be taken seriously. Midrash is serious because its stories and parables address the reader; they are not confined to the past. It is religious because, while it may contain beauty and poetry, its essential concern is truth. And when, as in the present case, a midrash tells a story of human origins, the religious truth it seeks to convey is universal. Its theme is nothing less than the human condition as a whole.

Why does this midrash disturb and haunt us? Not simply because it is realistic rather than romantically "optimistic" about man. Midrash is always realistic. We are haunted because Truth is cast to the ground. This climactic part of the story (as thus far told) does not say that all is well, that the good Lord has the power, so to speak, of indiscriminately silencing all opposition. Were this its message, then Peace as well as Truth should be cast to the ground. That Truth alone is singled out for this treatment suggests the ominous possibility that *all* that might be said in favor of the creation of man is nothing but pious illusion; that Truth is so horrendous as to destroy *everything* for us unless we shun it, avoid it, evade it; that *only* after having cast Truth to the ground can God create man at all.

But then we ask: whom does God deceive? Surely one thing even God cannot do is, as it were, fool Himself. Are we the ones, then, who are fooled? Are we *radically* deceived in our belief that at least *some* of that which we undergo, do, are, is *ultimately* worthwhile—a belief we cannot endure?

But such a divine deception (if a deception it is) does not succeed. We can see through it. The midrashic author *knows* that Truth is cast to the ground. So do all the devout Jews who have read his story throughout the generations. But what is the effect of this knowledge? Can it be other than despair?

The midrash itself deals with this question when it repudiates despair. It ends as follows:

> Then the angels of service said to God, "Lord of the universe, how canst Thou despise Thy seal? Let Truth arise from the earth, as it is said, 'Truth springs from the earth.' " (Ps. 85:12)

Somehow it is possible for man to face Truth and yet to be. But do we know how? . . .

For many centuries . . . theologians would resort at once to the Word of God, with or without the help of ecclesiastical authority. Philosophers would affirm a human "nature" immune to the vicissitudes of history—an immunity which in turn guaranteed a timeless access to the True, the Good, and the Beautiful. And a long alliance between these two disciplines produced a firm stand in behalf of "eternal verities" against perpetually shifting "arbitrary opinion."

These centuries are past. Theologians (Jewish and Christian) should always have known that the Word of their God is manifest *in* history if it is manifest at all: because of the historical self-consciousness of contemporary man, this knowledge can now no longer be evaded. If nevertheless seeking refuge in the eternal verities of philosophy, they find that these, too, have vanished. For modern philosophy has found itself forced to abandon the notion of a permanent human nature—and along with this all timelessly accessible visions of the True, the Good and the Beautiful.

This fact is most profoundly if not uniquely manifest in the philosophies arising from the work of Immanuel Kant. These philosophies do not deny aspects of the human condition which remain more or less permanent throughout human history. Such aspects, however, are now confined to man's natural constitution. What makes man *human* (we are told) is neither given nor permanent, but rather the product of his own individual or collective activity. *Man qua man is a self-maker.* This formula sums up the deepest of all the many revolutions in modern philosophy. We may wish to quarrel with its central thesis. We may wish to qualify it. We may even wish to reject it outright. One thing, at any rate, seems for better or worse impossible—the return to the premodern philosophical wisdom.

Not so long ago theologians of liberal stamp greeted this revolution in philosophy with rejoicing. Who has not heard sermons (and in particular American sermons) about the "infinite perfectibility of man"? The notion of man as a self-maker seemed (and in some respects surely is) far more grandiose than the notion of a human nature given by another—even if this other was not (rather vaguely) "nature" or "the universe," but the Lord of Creation Himself. Add to this what was said above about the American tradition of optimism, and it is not surprising that for a considerable period of time all talk about "the nature of man" and "*the* True, *the* Good and *the* Beautiful" seemed in many circles to be timidly conservative, if not downright reactionary.

But now the crisis of American optimism has disclosed for us that the concept of man as a self-maker gives us grounds for apprehension and dread as well as for hope. The lack of a permanent nature may hold the promise that unforeseeable ways of human self-perfection are possible; since this lack is an unlimited malleability, however, it implies the possibility of unforeseeable negative as well as positive developments. And thus the specter comes into view that man, qua unlimited maker, may reach the point of making his whole world into a machine, while at the same time, qua infinitely malleable, himself being reduced to a mere part of the machine, that is, to a self-made thing. Nor is this possibility today a mere unsubstantial fancy confined to philosophers. For some of our futurologists have begun to conjure up a future in which man, the proud self-maker, will have lost control over the world he has made, and the reduction to self-made thinghood will be complete. Indeed, even popular consciousness is haunted by the prospect that the whole bold and exciting story of the one being in the universe capable of making his own nature—the story of the only truly *free* being—will come to an end, the pathos of which is matched only by its irony.

With prospects so terrifying, it is no wonder that some simply opt out of history; that others hanker after a simpler, more innocent past; and that, as if anticipating catastrophe, we are all tempted even now to deprecate indiscriminately all things human.

The philosopher may not yield to the temptations of escapism or indiscriminate despair. Nor may he simply throw in his lot with the futurologists, for (as we shall show at least in part) their entire approach calls for considerable philosophical suspicion. At this point, we shall be well advised to suspend the future and confine ourselves to the present. Is a genuinely *human* existence possible *even now*? Or, in order to make it possible, must we cast Truth to the ground? Must we suppress all knowledge of a future which is sure to come and force Truth to *stay* cast to the ground?

We have thus far made no reference to Jewish experience in this century. We do so at this point because the direst predictions any futurologist might make have already been fulfilled and surpassed at Auschwitz, Mauthausen, Bergen-Belsen, and Buchenwald. One shrinks from speaking of these unspeakable places of unique horror in any context which might invite false generalizations and comparisons. Yet one simple statement may safely be made. In the Nazi murder camps no effort was spared to make persons into living *things* before making them into dead things. And that the dead had been human when alive was a truth systematically rejected when their bodies were made into fertilizer and soap. Moreover, the criminals themselves had become living *things*, and the system, run by operators "only following orders," was well on the way toward running itself. The thoughtful reader of such a work as *The Holocaust Kingdom* reaches the shocking conclusion that here was indeed a "kingdom," that is, a society organized to a purpose; that, its organization near-perfect, it might in due course have dispensed with the need for a "king"; and that such was its inner dynamic and power for self-expansion that, given a Nazi victory, it might today rule the world.

This "society," however, was an anti-society, indeed, *the* modern anti-society par excellence: modern because unsurpassably technological, and anti-society because, while even the worst society is geared to life, the Holocaust Kingdom was geared to death. It would be quite false to say that it was a mere means, however depraved, to ends somehow bound up with life. As an enterprise subserving the Nazi war effort the murder camps were total failures, for the human and material "investment" far exceeded the "produce" of fertilizer, gold teeth and soap. The Holocaust Kingdom was an end in itself, having only one ultimate "produce," and that was death. . . .

Can either Nazism or its murder camps be understood as but one particular case, however extreme, of the general technological dehumanization? Or; (to use language which theologians are equipped to understand) does not a scandal of particularity attach to Nazism and its murder camps which is shied away from, suppressed or simply forgotten when the scandal is technologically universalized? To be sure, there have been "world wars"—but none like that which Hitler unleashed on the world. There have been (and are) "total" political systems—but none like Nazism, a truth suppressed when "fascism" is used as a generic term in which Nazism is included. And while there have been (and are) "cults of personality," there have been no Führers but only one Führer.

Nor is it possible to distinguish between the goals of Nazism-in-general, as one system, and those of the murder-camp-in-particular, as a second system subserving the first. In essence, Nazism *was* the murder-camp. That a nihilistic, demonic celebration of death and destruction was its animating principle was evident to thinkers such as Karl Barth from the start; it became universally revealed in the end, when in the Berlin bunker Hitler and Goebbels, the only true Nazis left, expressed ghoulish satisfaction at the prospect that their downfall might carry in train the doom, not only (or even at all) of their enemies, but rather of the "master race." The mind shrinks from systematic murder which serves no purpose beyond murder itself, for it is ultimately unintelligible. Yet in Nazism as a whole (not only in the murder camps) this unintelligibility was real. And except for good fortune this diabolical celebration might today rule the world.

Even this does not exhaust the scandalous particularity of Nazism. The term "Aryan" had no clear connotation other than "non-Jew," and the Nazis were not anti-Semites because they were racists, but rather racists because they were anti-Semites. The exaltation of the "Aryan" had no positive significance. It had only the negative significance of degrading and murdering the "non-Aryan." Thus Adolf Eichmann passed beyond the limits of a merely "banal" evil when, with nothing left of the Third Reich, he declared with obvious sincerity that he would jump laughing into his grave in the knowledge of having dispatched six million Jews to their death. We must conclude, then, that the dead Jews of the murder camps (and all the other innocent victims, as it were, as quasi-Jews, or by dint of innocent-guilt-by-association) were not the "waste product" of the Nazi system. They were *the* product.

Despite all necessary attempts to comprehend, the Nazi system in the end exceeds all comprehension. One cannot comprehend but only confront and oppose. We can here attempt to confront only one minuscule manifestation. When issuing "work permits" designed to separate "useless" Jews to be murdered at once from "useful" ones to be kept useful by diabolically contrived false hopes and murdered later, the Nazis on occasion issued two such permits to able-bodied Jewish men. One was untransferable and to be kept for himself; the other was to be given at his own discretion to his able-bodied father, mother, wife or one child. On those occasions the Nazis would not make this choice, although to do so would have resulted in a more efficient labor force. Jewish sons, husbands, and fathers themselves were forced to decide who among their loved ones was—for the time being—to live and who to die at once.

The mind seeks escape in every direction. Yet we must confront relentlessly the Nazi custom of the two work permits, recognizing in this custom not the work of some isolated sadists, but rather the essence of the Nazi system. . . . Had utility been the principle of Nazism it would not have left the choice between "useful" and "useless" Jews to its victims. Not utility (however dehumanized), but rather torture and degradation was the principle. Indeed, there is no greater contrast between the technological exaltation of utility (even when out of control) and a celebration of torture *contrary* to all utility when it is not incidental but rather *for torture's sake*. . . .

We cannot be sure how the ancient rabbis, were they alive, would respond to the death camps. We *can* be sure that they would not explain them away. In their own time, they knew of idolatry, and considered groundless hate to be its equivalent. They knew, too, that it could not be explained but only opposed. Alive today, they would reject all fatalistic futurological predictions as so many self-fulfilling prophecies which leave us helpless. Instead, they would somehow seek to meet the absolute evil of the death camps in the only way absolute evil can be met—by an absolute opposition on which one stakes one's life.

The authentic Jew after Auschwitz has no privileged access to explanations of the past. He has no privileged access to predictions of the future, or to ways of solving the problems of the present. He is, however, a witness to the world. He is a witness against the idolatry of the Nazi murder camps. This negative testimony is ipso facto also the positive testimony that man shall *be*, and shall be *human*—even if Truth should be so horrendous that there is no choice but to cast it to the ground.

The Jew in whom this testimony is unsurpassably manifest is the survivor of the two-work-permit custom. When the torture occurred he had no choice but compliance. Armed resistance was impossible. So was suicide. So was the transfer of his own work permit to another member of his family. Any of these attempts would have doomed the one member of his family who was to live. To save this one member, he was forced to become implicated in the diabolical system which robbed him of his soul and made him forever after innocently guilty of the murder of all his family except one member.

We ask: having survived (if survive he did), why did this Jew not seek blessed release in suicide? Choosing to live, why did he not seek refuge in insanity? Choosing to stay sane, why did he not do all he could to escape from his singled out Jewish condition but rather affirmed his Jewishness and indeed raised new Jewish children? How could even one stay with his God?

These are unprecedented questions. They require unprecedented responses. Why not suicide? *Because after the Nazi celebration of death life has acquired a new dimension of sanctity.* Why not flight into madness? *Because insanity had ruled the kingdom of darkness, hence sanity, once a gift, has now become a holy commandment.* Why hold fast to mere Jewishness? *Because Jewish survival after Auschwitz is not "mere," but rather in itself and without any further reasons or theological justifications a sacred testimony* to all mankind *that life and love, not death and hate, shall prevail.* Why hold fast to the God of the covenant? Former believers lost

Him in the Holocaust Kingdom. Former agnostics found Him. No judgment is possible. All theological arguments vanish. Nothing remains but the fact that the bond between Him and His people reached the breaking point but was not for all wholly broken. Thus the survivor is a witness against darkness in an age of darkness. He is a witness whose like the world has not seen.

We do not yet recognize this witness, for we do not yet dare to enter the darkness against which he testifies. Yet to enter that darkness is to be rewarded with an altogether astonishing discovery. *This may be an age without heroes. It is, however, the heroic age par excellence in all of Jewish history.* If this is true of the Jewish people collectively (not only of the survivor individually), it is because *the survivor is gradually becoming the paradigm for the entire Jewish people.*

Nowhere is this truth as unmistakable as in the State of Israel. The State of Israel is collectively what the survivor is individually— testimony on behalf of all mankind to life against death, to sanity against madness, to Jewish self-affirmation against every form of flight from it, and (though this is visible only to those who break through narrow theological categories) to the God of the ancient covenant against all lapses into paganism.

We ask: having survived, why did the survivor not seek both safety and forgetfulness among such good people as the Danes, but rather seek danger and memory in the nascent and embattled State of Israel? Indeed, why do not even now Israeli Jews in general, survivors or no, flee by the thousands form their isolated and endangered country, in order that they might elsewhere find peace and safety— not to speak of the world's approval? Why do they hold fast to their "law of return"—the commitment to receive sick Jews, poor Jews, oppressed Jews, rejected by the immigration laws of every other state? A world which wants no part of Auschwitz fails to understand. Indeed, perpetuating anti-Semitism, despite Auschwitz or even because of it, it often does not hesitate to resort to slander. Yet the truth is obvious: the State of Israel is a collective testimony against the groundless hate which has erupted in this century in the heart of Europe. Its watchword is *Am Yisrael Chai*—"the people of Israel lives." Without this watchword the State of Israel could not have survived for a generation. It is a watchword of defiance, hope and faith. It is a testimony to all men everywhere that man shall be, and be human—even if it should be necessary to cast Truth to the ground.

And now, astoundingly, this watchword has come alive among the Jews of the Soviet Union. What makes these Jews affirm their Jewishness against the overwhelming odds of a ruthless system, when they could gain peace and comfort by disavowing their Jewishness? Though we can only marvel at their heroism and not understand it, its mainspring is obvious enough. No American Jew has experienced the Holocaust as every Russian Jew has experienced it. Hence every Russian Jew must have felt all along that to be denied the right to his Jewishness is not, after what has happened, a tolerable form of discrimination or prejudice but rather an intolerable affront; it is, as it were, a secular sacrilege. And if now these Jews increasingly dare to convert secret feeling into pubic action, it is because of the inspiration incarnate in the State of Israel.

Is heroism in evidence among ourselves, the comfortable, mostly middle-class Jews of North America? In order to perceive any trace of it, we must break through the false but all-pervasive categories of a world which does not know of Auschwitz and does not wish to know of it.

In America this is a time of identity crises. Among these there is a specific Jewish identity crisis which springs from the view that a Jew must somehow achieve a "universal" transcendence of his "particular" Jewishness if he is to justify his Jewish identity. Thus it has come to seem that a Jew shows genuine courage when he rejects his Jewish identity, or when he at least seeks a "universal" justification of that identity by espousing all noble except Jewish causes. And the North American Jewish hero may seem to be he who actually turns against his own people, less because he seeks the creation of a Palestinian Arab state than because he seeks the destruction of the Jewish state.

Such may be the appearances. The truth is otherwise. Just as the black seeking to pass for white has internalized racism, so the Jew joining al-Fatah has internalized anti-Semitism, and this is true also (albeit to a lesser degree) of the Jew espousing all except Jewish causes. Where is the universalism in this exceptionalism—a "universalism" which applies to everyone with one exception—Jews? There is only sickness. To the extent to which the world still wants the Jew either to disappear or at least to become a man-in-general, it still has the power to produce Jews bent on disappearing, or at least on "demonstrating" their exceptionalist "universalism."

These may seem harsh judgments. They are necessary because Jewish identity crises such as the above have become a surrender to Auschwitz. For a Jew after the Holocaust to act as though his Jewishness required justification is to allow the possibility that none might be found, and this in turn is to allow the possibility, after Hitler murdered one third of the Jewish people, that the rest should quietly pass on. But merely to allow these possibilities is *already* a posthumous victory for Hitler. It is *already* an act of betrayal. And the betrayal is as much of the world as of the Jewish people.

Is there any trace of Jewish heroism among ourselves? The question transcends all conventional distinctions, such as between old and young, "right" and "left," and even "religious" and "secular." The North American Jewish hero is he who has confronted the demons of Auschwitz and defied them. It is the Jew who has said "No!" to every form, however mild or disguised, of anti-Semitism without and self-rejection within. It is the Jew at home in his Jewish skin and at peace with his Jewish destiny. It is the Jew who is whole.

But if this is the age of heroism in the history of the Jewish people, it is, after all, also an age of unprecedented darkness in world history, and Jewish heroism itself is possible only at the price of perpetually verging on despair. The question therefore arises what meaning the Jewish *Am Yisrael Chai* (the people of Israel lives) might have for contemporary man.

One shrinks from so large a question for two opposite reasons. At one extreme, the singled-out Jewish testimony may all-too-easily dissipate itself into a vacuous and thus cheap and escapist universalism. At the other extreme, it may express its universal significance at the false price of deafness to quite different, and yet not unrelated testimonies, such as might come from Vietnam, Czechoslovakia and Bangladesh. Perhaps one avoids both dangers best by concretizing the question. Earlier we dwelt on the American tradition of optimism that is now in a state of crisis, and stressed that, while much in this optimism was always false, America itself would be lost if American optimism were wholly lost. What may the Jewish *Am Yisrael Chai* reveal about American optimism? What was always false about the American Dream? What—if anything—remains true?

Always false was precisely the "dream." The innocence that produced that dream is lost. If the saving of America were dependent upon the recapturing of the innocence and the dream there would be no hope. However, the midrash which has furnished the text for the present discourse is not the product of a dream. Truth may be cast to the ground. The midrashic author *knows* that it is cast to the ground. He knows, too, that in the end Truth must rise again from the earth.

When dreams are shattered men are wont to seek refuge in wishful thinking. Our age is no exception. In a half-hearted version, collective make-believe is manifest in our current, self-enclosed, middle-class apotheosis of psychoanalysis. (Within its sober bounds, that discipline gives limited help to disturbed individuals, and quite possibly we are all disturbed. Expanded into systematic wishful thinking, it turns into a panacea for all the ills of our world.) In a radical version, collective make-believe is manifest in a self-enclosed ideologizing which would refashion all reality in its own image, while being itself out of touch with reality.

Being self-enclosed, collective make-believe can survive for a long period of time. Yet its nemesis is sure to come, and by dint of its greater honesty it is the radical version that is bound first to experience it. To be sure, ideology seeks to refashion reality. Being divorced from reality, however, it in fact refashions only ideology, and the conflict between ideality and reality in the end becomes so total as to result—when Truth springs from the earth—in despair.

Is despair, then, the only *truthful* outcome? Arthur Schopenhauer wrote as follows:

> Death is the great reprimand which the will to life, or more especially the egoism which is essential to it, receives through the course of nature; and it may be considered as a punishment for our existence. Death says: thou are the product of an act which should not have been; therefore to expiate it thou must die.

Once the sentiment expressed in this passage was attractive only to idle drawing room speculation. Today one can detect on every side a veritable fascination with every kind of negation and death itself. Once the denial of the will to live could seem to be a noble rejection of "egoism." Today it stands revealed as the foe, nothing short of obscene, of a will to live which, far from "egoistic," is a heroic act of defiance. And the revelation is nowhere as manifest as in the survivor of the Nazi custom of the two work permits. He is not blind to the shadows of death but has walked through its valley. He does not cling to life but rather affirms it by an act of faith which defies comprehension. He relives, in a form without precedent anywhere, that great "nevertheless" which has always been the secret of the enigmatic optimism of Judaism. His testimony is a warning to men everywhere not to yield to death when Truth springs from the earth. It is an admonition to endure Truth and to choose life. It is a plea, anguished and joyous, to share in a defiant endurance which alone reveals that Truth, despite all, remains the seal of God.

The Jewish Consensus

BEN HALPERN

What holds the Jews together? How has the Jewish people survived? These are perennial questions—that is, they keep cropping up in new forms after we have all got good and tired of them in their old forms. Who among us that remembers the era before the creation of the State of Israel has not lost patience with the argument whether the Jews were a nation or a religion? No one today will find an audience for this debate, framed in these terms. That there is a Jewish nation can hardly be denied after the creation of the State of Israel. That American Jews enjoy the status of a religious community is a commonplace accepted by everyone. We have settled our old debate over whether the Jews are a nation and not a religious community, or a religious community and not a nation, by proving both opposing views to be true. That is to say, we have settled it paradoxically. The result is that by demonstrating both of the opposing views, we have proved that neither can really answer the underlying question. What at bottom *does* hold the Jews together and how *do* the Jews survive? Now that we have a Jewish nation, pure and simple, in one place, and a Jewish religious community, pure and simple, in another place, it becomes even more puzzling and even more important to know what holds these two together and on what principles they can achieve survival in common.

Thus, we are confronted with a problem which persists even though solutions have been demonstrated for the old terms in which it was once formulated. What usually happens in such cases has happened in this case, too. We are now involved in new debates over terms, including some that were not controversial before, or less sharply so, and others that did not seem at all pertinent before. Having ceased to argue whether the Jews are a nation or a religious community, ideologists concerned with Jewish unity and survival in the new circumstances argue over what is a Zionist and who is a Jew. It is interesting to note that much the same situation exists for those who are professionally concerned not with preserving the Jews but only with understanding them.

"Nation" and "religious group," the terms most common in other ideological debates, are far from being the only conceptions whose application to the Jews has puzzled academic analysts. The Jews have been round pegs inserted in such square holes as "ethnic group," "national minority" or "minority group," "culture" and "sub-culture," "civilization" or "fossil" remains of a civilization, not to speak of "pariah" and "world conspiracy." It will perhaps be only rattling the Jews around in another ill-fitting box to see how they meet the measure of one more set of conceptions. But there may also be some gain in our understanding—both of the Jews and of the conceptions.

Among the peculiar facts concerning the peculiar Jewish people was their success in maintaining a law without a state, a structure of legitimacy without specific sanctions, authority without an organized hierarchy, social discipline without visible controls, and a capacity to perform certain collective political acts without a government. Obviously, some least common denominator of social cohesion and social order must have been at work. The word "consensus," a term used perhaps more widely than any other and defined perhaps less precisely than any other by all schools of political and social science, may be taken to represent that least common denominator. In what sense, then, and to what extent do the Jews have a consensus that unites them and singles them out? What is meant "operationally," as the social scientists say, by this term, and how far are we able to observe the various processes of "consensus" in operation among the Jews?

It is immediately apparent, incidentally, that this question is likely to be differently answered today, after the creation of the State of Israel, than before it, and that still other answers might have been given in even earlier times. In fact, it is one of those questions that we should only think of owing to the outdating of older ways of putting the perennial questions concerning Jewish survival since the rise of [the State] of Israel.

Zionism, crowned by success in creating the State of Israel, bears the authentic hallmark of a truly historic event; everything looks different before and after it in the field of its operation. It is a watershed that divides the lines of thought by which we understand the course of Jewish history. The Zionist movement was essentially an attempt to solve the Jewish problem—that is, to secure Jewish survival—by establishing a new basis of Jewish consensus. This implies, of course, that there was an older, pre-Zionist basis of Jewish consensus, different from the one the Zionists proposed to establish, which had been undermined. It also raises the questions whether any Jewish consensus would exist at all if the Zionist goal failed to be attained, and whether the Jewish people could then survive. Finally, now that the Jewish state has been established by Zionism, the question is forced upon us whether a new basis of Jewish consensus has thereby been established; and if this question should be answered in the negative, then the nature of the Jewish consensus—if not the whole question of Jewish survival—has at any rate become open and fluid this side of the Zionist watershed.

It is fairly clear what constituted the basis of the old Jewish consensus which the Zionists thought to be in collapse and which they hoped to replace. A common tradition of religious law, common rituals and religious practices, a common education in the Hebrew language and literature, and a common religious mythos of the divine, cosmic significance of the exile of the Jewish people and of the coming redemption in Zion—these were values in which Jews throughout the world shared universally.

Common values universally shared that bind a people together: such a description might almost serve as a technical definition of the term "consensus." But we should be careful what conclusions we draw from any definition; certainly, from this one. One conclusion looks so obvious that it appears unreasonable to doubt it; yet even this conclusion is unsafe. If certain laws, rituals, linguistic and literary traditions, together with the myth of exile and redemption, were the universal values that bound the Jews together, then with their loss, the Jewish people should have disintegrated. But these values *were* lost, and the Jews did *not* fall apart. Perhaps we should put the point in a more realistic and less hypothetical way. In the nineteenth century, values which had been universal among traditional Jewry still continued to be shared—but only by part of the Jews. There were some who no longer shared them, yet these dissenters continued to be regarded as Jews by the remainder who preserved the old values;

and they themselves felt that they belonged to a single community with the traditionalist Jews of their own time and of past generations. If we assume that the traditional values which were universal among Jews in older generations still defined the Jewish "consensus," then it was a "consensus" that could bind together only part of the Jews— those who now began to call themselves Orthodox. Yet, we know that a Jewish community continued to exist comprising, in addition to the Orthodox, not only Reform or Liberal Jews but agnostics and atheists, all calling themselves Jews and accepted by the others as Jews. Apparently there must have been a different "consensus" binding them together—that is, a set of values that were *universally* shared among all the Jews.

One of the most striking aspects of the modern Jewish problem is that it is so difficult to define the values of the Jewish "consensus." What well-defined values, after all, could be shared by a traditional Jew from the Carpathians or from Yemen and by an American Jewish undergraduate in an Ivy League college who is worried about his identity crisis? Instead of wasting time on the effort to define such values positively, let us ask ourselves a different question: Is it necessary for all values to be well-defined? When I am hungry, do I have to want something specific to eat before I can want anything at all to eat? This hardly seems to be so in our common experience. In fact, it is rather odd and unusual to be seized with a hankering for something specific. A woman may suddenly say she *must* have strawberries or pickles, but we are likely to explain this as a symptom of a physiological disturbance. Money, power, prestige, leisure, fun—many of the normal values men want—are quite general, nonspecific, even abstract. It is entirely possible, and even the usual thing, for a whole people to share a universal value that is not merely indefinite but negative—a value like freedom, for instance—and that nonetheless very effectively binds them together.

If we look again at the traditional values that bound the Jewish people together because they shared them universally before the nineteenth century, it appears that these values themselves were far from being rigidly defined. What was the most striking thing, first of all, about the cohesion and the survival over millennia of traditional Jewry? It was the fact that they were united and survived *without* many of the shared values that are generally believed to hold a normal people together and constitute essential parts of the consensus of comparable groups. Moses Mendelssohn made a great point, in his time, of the distinction of Judaism among the historic world religions as a faith without dogmas, or with only those essential beliefs which any rational man—the Eskimo, to name a notable example—must necessarily accept. The rational faith of Jewish monotheism—or of liberal deism, which men like Mendelssohn believed amounted to virtually the same thing—contained those beliefs which were essential to establish the bonds of morality universal among all men, not the bonds of a consensus universal only among Jews. It was the religious law, according to Mendelssohn, not any specific dogmas, that constituted the shared values of the Jewish consensus.

This, let us note, introduces a new element into the discussion. A consensus based on a shared dogma or belief is quite a different thing from a consensus based on a shared law. A dogma or belief is by nature defined; but it is in the nature of a law to be stated as a rule—that is, to be general, or indefinite. When people are bound together by a shared belief, it is necessary that they agree on a definition of the value they hold in common before they unite and so long as they remain united. When they disagree on definitions, their consensus has vanished and their union disintegrates—if it was really based on no more than a shared belief. But when the consensus that binds people together consists of sharing a common rule of law, they are free to disagree on definitions over a wide range of values. What unites them is an agreement to abide by certain *procedures* in settling their disagreements.

The shared value of such a consensus may be defined only in one respect—in specifying the rules by which people are to settle their most serious arguments, those that threaten to separate them. But when people have been living together for long enough, they may go well beyond this bare minimum and codify many other values upon which they are universally agreed, and which they include in their consensus. Traditional Jewry left many values and even procedures undefined that other peoples and other sects felt it necessary to define as part of their consensus. Not only did Judaism have few dogmas, but the Jewish law was backed by little or no executive power, and the Jewish courts and community had little or no hierarchial authority. On the other hand, over the course of centuries the customs of Jewish communities and the learned decisions on cases brought before scholarly, influential rabbis produced a multitude of minutely defined values, compiled in elaborate codes of behavior, the most widely accepted being the *Shulhan Arukh*.

Now let us recall what was the complaint of the nineteenth-century dissenters from traditional Jewry, especially those who sought a new basis for the Jewish consensus. They made the really astonishing accusation that the Jews had lost their consensus. They said that the Jews no longer had any sense of obligation, of loyalty, of fellow feeling, even among themselves, but were only a disorganized collection of egoists. Because they were frightened and oppressed egoists, it is true that they clung together in self-defense. Moreover, they were oppressed not only by the Gentile world, that still applied medieval restrictions against the Jews, but also by their own superstitious submission to the rabbis. The *Shulhan Arukh*, then, and the entire institutional structure of religious law and education, that were the universal values of the traditional Jewish consensus, were attacked by these critics from a rather unexpected angle. Even though the traditional institutions commanded universal obedience among the Jews of their times—with the exception of the dissenters, a small minority of so-called enlightened Jews—the modernist critics denied that the tradition represented a Jewish consensus. Obedience to it, they claimed, was mechanical or even compelled: that is, without the conviction—or, to use a more current terminology, the sense of identification—that a true consensus requires.

One could say a great deal about the accuracy of this criticism, but what interests us in this connection are some further observations about the nature of social consensus that is implied. These implications, needless to say, were not drawn by the Jewish Enlightenment of the late eighteenth, early nineteenth century. For they were not contemporary political sociologists. But for anyone reading it today the somewhat ambivalent defense of the Jews by a man like Mendelssohn is quite revealing. The Jews, he said, had few dogmas, and their consensus was not founded on universal beliefs, but on universal practices prescribed by religious law. On the other hand, he and his group were opposed to the rule of the rabbis and the power of excommunication upon which the Jewish consensus of his time rested; and from time to time they argued that there was no real Jewish consensus at all, only a mechanical or coerced obedience. This implies, first, that a consensus demands conviction, not only compliance even when it is based not on universal beliefs but on universal practices, on rules of law and agreements regarding procedures for collective decision. It also implies that a rule of law which becomes rigidly codified tends to lose its value as an element of consensus. In fact, a free commitment to live together regardless of disagreements probably requires elastic rules of law. . . .

What sort of consensus is involved here, where men are bound together in a community of fate? What kind of common values distinguish this union? It is certain, at any rate, that what binds them together more resembles the shared value of common rules of law and procedure than the shared value of common beliefs. Only because they are constantly involved in the consequences of each other's acts need each care what the other wants. A consensus based on common beliefs is not essential, only a consensus on common actions or abstentions from action.

A further point must be made, however. A community of fate can be a community that is not bound together at all, only thrown together. Men may be in the same boat, but only if and when they want to act, need they agree; if they simply share the same plight in total passivity, they need not even communicate, let alone agree.

To share a common fate in total isolation from each other is, of course, an imaginary idea rather than a condition one is likely to encounter in reality. But it is not nearly so imaginary to think of a community whose sole bond of consensus is their awareness that they are in the same boat. Such a community will not seek a course of common action, and thus will not build up the kind of active consensus which the Zionists prescribed as the solution of the Jewish problem. They will not even share with each other their understanding of the common fate by speaking to each other in the idiom of a common religious tradition, as pre-modern Jewry could, or of a national literary tradition, as proponents of secular *Yiddishkeit* (Jewishness) desired. Yet passing one another with faces averted or with brief nods and smiles, the members of this community, thrown together by fate, will be bound together by a consensus, too—a consensus of shared sensitivity. It is hard to imagine a common denominator of consensus more minimal than this. This, however, is the bond of union freely accepted by a whole school—a school, perhaps, in the same sense as a school of fish, but nevertheless a school of young Jewish intellectuals in our own time and country. It is, also, if one may believe reports, a common condition among many of the current generation of young Jewish college students.

For the present purposes, we must stop at this point. To have spun out the analysis of Jewish consensus to such a fine-drawn minimum does not, of course, mean that the actual kinds and degrees of consensus in the community are adequately described by the least common denominator. The Jews, in this country and throughout the world, are bound together, and for that matter thrown together, by many different kinds of circumstances, affecting various parts of the community in different ways and degrees. What binds some alienates others. The unity some desire others oppose with hostility or boredom.

I have no doubt whatever that the social scientists who speak of "consensus" with such innocent confidence that they know what they are saying would benefit from a close study of the complex nature of consensus in the always-odd Jewish case. Those who seek to preserve Jewish unity and give more conviction and substance to the Jewish consensus have much too difficult a task to be greatly aided by such a rough mapping of this terrain. But it doesn't hurt, when pulling an oar, to look around once in a while and see who else is in the boat.

PART THREE

THE JEWISH PEOPLE AND THE TORAH

12
Defining Judaism

THE PROBLEM OF DEFINITION AND
HOW IT HAS BEEN EVADED

If by "Judaism" we mean anything any Jews anywhere have ever believed about God, their society, and the meaning of life, then there is not now and there never has been a single Judaism. Nor is there a linear and harmonious history of a single Judaism. Taken all together, Jews have believed everything and its opposite about the critical components of a religion: God, community, and the holy way of life. It follows, therefore, that no one can write a history of Judaism, short or long. It is the simple fact that the history of Judaism that is continuous, unitary, and uniform never took place and cannot be told. In any single era there has been, as today there is, diversity; and, over time, there has been only change. So whence *the* Judaism that will have its continuous and harmonious history written? As one recent book (that nevertheless purports to write *the* history of Judaism) says explicitly, "Judaism has been and continues to be a dynamic and pluralistic religion with a common core of faith that has changed and adapted to the time, spirit, and conditions of the varying cultures and ages it has encountered."[1] Clearly a "common core of faith" that changes and adapts over time loses whatever "core" it had to begin with.

Anyone who imagines that "faith" in a propositional sense (expressed in words about God, revelation, the character of the social entity that is holy, and the like) can remain the same over thousands of years in a vast range of languages and cultures must tell us precisely how words can ever remain so stable and uniform as to say the same thing in so many different ways—and how we are to find out what that one thing is. Only a theological formulation, not a descriptive and factual one, can sustain such a conviction. But theology in historical form, while commonplace, deceives. For it does not deliver what it promises, and it distorts what it purports to provide. It is bad history and bad theology: bad history because it is fabricated; bad theology because it is unarticulated.

I do not mean to suggest that people who recognize changes over time and space and over long stretches of human experience draw the correct conclusion, that is, that there is no single Judaism, and therefore there can be no continuous and harmonious history of Judaism (or, I should imagine, any other religion of dimensions and endurance). Rather, they may announce that there is no continuity, but then they proceed to tell the story of a continuous and unfolding religion by picking and choosing in any given age what sustained Judaism for that moment and, more importantly, omitting reference to what did not. In this manner the historian settles the claim of normativity and religious truth. But the act of choice in the guise of mere description represents a theological judgment, not a historical one. The most current example of how people recognize and then deny the diversities that require us to speak only of Judaism admits "the continuity of the entire historical process." Then, talking of change and adaptation, the same writer proceeds to narrate a single, continuous tale of one unitary Judaism over time.

In the example at hand, which is representative of an entire genre of writing histories of the Jews or of Judaism, the author treats "proto-Judaism" (ca. 2000—400 B.C.E.), surveying in sequence (as though the biblical narrative were an account of historical events in order) the time of the patriarchs, Moses, judges, monarchy; Judaism after the Babylonian exile (400 B.C.E.—70 C.E.), rabbinic Judaism, the medieval era, philosophy and mysticism; proto-modernity (the influence of the Renaissance on Judaism, the Protestant Reformation and Judaism); the modern and contemporary periods (Reform, traditionalist opposition to Reform, Neo-Orthodoxy; Hasidism, Judaism in North America; Zionism, the Holocaust, and the State of Israel), then Judaism distilled: doctrines, ethics, ritual. All of these things, however, do not add up to one thing; they remain many, diverse, and incoherent.

Furthermore these categories are not really similar or alike. Some of these subjects are not religious but political (Zionism, for instance); some of them are ethnic and secular (the Holocaust); and some of them do not even focus upon Judaism at all (the influence of the Renaissance, an odd choice indeed, since most Jews lived where the Renaissance never reached). The repertoire of topics is wildly incoherent because the categories are unlike one another in their very form. In fact, in their basic convictions, they contradict one another. So the representation of a single, linear, harmonious Judaism from 2000 B.C.E.[!] to the present is in no sense historical.

As a next logical step we must ask: Then what of the histories of the Jews? If, as I have suggested, there is no one Judaism, then surely there must be a single Jewish people, and one can certainly write a history of that people, if not of its religion. The subject, "Jewish history," however, is as difficult to justify as "the history of Judaism." The conception that there is a single, unitary, and continuous history of the Jews is a commonplace, but each time someone attempts to tell that story, the same process of normative selection gets underway. Paul Johnson's *History of the Jews*[2] is a striking example of the difficulty of making sense of a single, unitary history of the Jews. The author perceives the Jews as having a "separate and specific identity earlier than almost any other people which still survives," and he thus believes that the Jews have a separate and single specific identity which they have maintained. He does not explain what he means by "identity." At the center of his book, however, is the premise that a single group, which everywhere and at all times exhibited the same indicative traits, formed a single unitary and linear history with a beginning, middle, and, so far, a happy end.

The composition of such a continuous, unitary history of the Jews, like the formation of a single history of Judaism, constitutes a theological act. For speaking descriptively, we cannot identify such a single group with fixed and ubiquitously uniform traits. To Johnson everything Jewish relates to everything else Jewish, with slight regard to circumstance and context. Johnson's notion of a single, linear "Jewish history," which he can tell as story, expresses not theology but ideology. His story is one of blood and peoplehood that represents a single group where there have been many, and he works out a single linear history where there has been none.

For most of their history prior to 586 B.C.E. Jews lived in various countries. Each country and its Jews worked out their own localized history, whether in the Land of Israel (Palestine) or Babylonia, whether in Morocco or Spain, Iraq or Tunisia, or France or the United States. The histories of such diverse groups of Jews cannot be linked together into a single linear and unitary history, that is, into a story that we can tell in a simple sequence: first came France, then the United States. Each history, whether Babylonian from 586 B.C.E. to 1949 or American from 1964 to the present, holds together on its own terms and tells its own distinct and distinctive story. Sewing these histories together into a continuous story yields "first they went there, then they went there," an itinerary followed by only a few.

Histories of Judaism and histories of the Jews that pick and choose and do not say so represent the intellectual version of a theology and an ideology. The theology is an essentially secular-ethnic one, and the ideology is Zionist-nationalist. These joined constructions answer critical and important questions for Jews regarding whence they have come and where they are heading and what their life together means. The neat picture painted by a single, linear, and unitary history conveys a message of proportion, sense, and order. But alas, such a one-level history selects a little and leaves out a lot. There is not now nor has there ever been a single Judaism. Nevertheless one Judaism has predominated for a long time. There is not now nor has there ever been a single "Jewish identity," which Jews have uniformly preserved unchanged from some mythic beginning to this morning. One history covering all Jews, beginning to the present, has never existed. But a single ideology does indeed demand the rehearsal of a single history and, in the service of contemporary ethnic celebration, such a history performs well.

That has not been so in the pages of this book. Here, for merely descriptive reasons, I have identified a single Judaism or Judaic system among many, and we have considered the reality today and the history of that Judaism that exhibits definitive traits of continuity, harmony, cogency, and uniformity. It is a Judaism that puts forth an enduring symbolic structure, that absorbs within that structure all manner of accretions, changing and accommodating what is new to conform to its enduring system, drawing strength from what fits, gaining vigor through rejecting what does not.

A single symbol does remain constant; what happens to that symbol over time proves coherent; and we can establish criteria for inclusion and also exclusion. By appeal to the symbol of Torah as one Judaism defined that symbol and referred to it, we can tell *the history of the Judaism of the Torah,* which is, in fact, the Judaism that has predominated from the age in which it took shape to our own day— and which gives every evidence of flourishing into the century that will commence shortly.

DEFINING BY IDENTIFYING AN INTEGRATING SYMBOL: "THE TORAH" AS THE DEFINITION OF JUDAISM

Different groups of Jews have, over time, framed for themselves diverse Judaisms, each with its generative symbol, worldview, way of life, and definition of themselves as "Israel," as noted earlier, one wonders how there can be a single, unitary, harmonious, and continuous history of Judaism or of the Jews. As I have explained, the simple answer is that there cannot be such a history. But there can be, in brief sketch, the history of the Judaism that proved normative over time and that today defines the terms for all other Judaic systems. And that Judaism does have a continuous, linear, and unitary history because, by appeal to its critical symbols, we may account for all developments that took place within its framework, and we may also exclude from consideration all Judaisms that did not. When we do, we find ourselves tracing a continuous path from the point of origin to the present day.

This Judaism may be delineated in a simple and clear way, in a definition that includes only this Judaism and excludes all others. It is the one and only one that appealed for its generative symbol to "the Torah," meaning God's revelation to Moses at Sinai. Other Judaisms appealed to the Mosaic legislation (submission to the authority of the Torah of Moses at Sinai marks all Judaisms as Judaic and excludes all other religions as not-Judaic). But this is the one that claimed a particular form and tradition to have originated at Sinai, a version of Moses' Torah that no other Judaism accepted. Furthermore, it is the sole Judaism that defined its way of life so as to sanctify the here and now, and that framed its worldview around salvation at the end of time with the coming of the Messiah.

Among all Judaisms, moreover, it is unique in its catholic definition of "Israel," that is, the social entity that realized in the here and now the worldview and way of life of the system. Other Judaisms, the Essene Judaism of the Dead Sea Scrolls, for example, proved exclusive, and defined as "Israel" only a very few persons, that is, its own adherents. But the Judaism we are delineating defined "Israel" in the broadest possible way to encompass all Jews bearing genealogical ties, through the mother, to the family of Abraham, Isaac, and Jacob and, paradoxically, all persons who accepted the Torah and its disciplines from late antiquity to our own day. It excluded not sinners but only those who denied the most fundamental principles of the worldview, for instance, that the belief in the resurrection of the dead (which many Judaisms affirmed) derived from the Torah.

This definition of "Israel" in the following surely means to extend to their outermost limits the boundaries of "Israel":

M. Sanhedrin 10:1

A. All Israelites have a share in the world to come,

B. as it is said, "Your people also shall be all righteous, they shall inherit the land forever; the branch of my planting, the work of my hands, that I may be glorified" (Isa. 60:21).

C. And these are the ones who have no portion in the world to come: (1) He who says that the resurrection of the dead is a teaching which does not derive from the Torah, (2) or that the Torah does not come from Heaven; or (3) an Epicurean.

In context the exclusions prove few, and the inclusions prove many. Moreover, this formulation of matters proves emblematic for the range of concern of the Judaism at hand: inclusive, welcoming, vastly proselytizing within the ethnic group on behalf of its particular reading of the life of the group.

True, there were other Judaisms before, and there have been and now are other Judaisms in modern times, each of which has framed its symbolic system and ordered its social entity without perpetual appeal to the Torah—Zionism and the Judaism of Holocaust and Redemption, to take two modern instances; or the Essene Judaism known from the Dead Sea Scrolls, to take an ancient one. From the point at which the Judaism that focused upon the Torah took the field, however, all known heresies defined themselves against it, and all other Judaisms took shape in relationship to it. That is a mark of its paramount and definitive status, hence its normative character in its time.

When there was a heresy, it identified as its critical issue a primary concern of this Judaism, and rejected that doctrine. One important example: in early medieval times in the Islamic world, a Judaism took shape called Karaism. Its principle position was that the writings that the normative Judaism called "the oral Torah" were not divine in origin and did not go back all the way to Sinai in a chain of tradition through oral formulation and oral transmission. Only the written Torah, what we know as the Pentateuch, or the Five Books of Moses, carried God's authority. Karaism therefore represents a heresy defined in terms of and over against the Judaism that predominated.

When there was a major new development as, for instance, the formation of a rich mystical life, the framers and founders identified their ideas with the Torah of the Judaism that was normative. Accordingly, the authorities of the Torah contributed their names as authors of writings much later on, or as authorities in those writings, so that the new and unprecedented system of thought and piety legitimated itself by appeal to the established Judaism. The Zohar, a great work of mystical theology and piety, claimed to tell the story of Simeon b. Yohai and other ancient rabbis and thus found a place for the new doctrines in the old Torah. As such, the Zohar represents a new development that defined itself within the established symbolic structure of the established Judaism. By contrast, in the nineteenth and twentieth centuries, Judaisms took shape that did not appeal to the symbols and social order defined by the Torah at hand—Zionism is one example; the Judaism of Holocaust and Redemption (matching the destruction of European Jewry from 1933 to 1945 with the formation of the State of Israel in 1948) is another.

When a Judaism has the power to dictate the terms of both its opposition (heresies) and its innovation, extension, and expansion, it occupies the center and defines the norm. From late antiquity to the present, there has been and is now only one such Judaism. In terms of religion, it is today the only religious formulation of a Jewish system—worldview, way of life, definition of the social entity, "Israel"—that circulates. There are secular Jewish systems that compete—Zionism (the doctrine that Jews form a political entity and should have a state) and Israelism (centering of Jewish life in the

State of Israel and its affairs), as one example; ways of life and world-views that center upon culture or politics, as another. As far as a group of Jews understand themselves in terms that people in general classify as religious—appeal to God, revelation, categories of sanctification and salvation—the only Judaism (in numerous variations to be sure) is the one that speaks about the Torah and reads as canonical the holy books identified with the Judaism of the Torah.

A REVIEW OF
THE HISTORY OF JUDAISM

Let me conclude with some specific definitions of the categories I use in dealing with the problem of the diversity of Judaisms within Judaism. Instead of "religion" we speak of "religious system," and a religious system comprises three components:

1. A worldview, explaining who people are, where they come from, and what they must do. In general, what a Judaism defines as "the Torah" will contain this worldview.
2. A way of life, expressing in concrete deeds that worldview and linking the life of the individual to polity. This is what a Judaism sets forth as the things a person must do, as, for instance, halakhah in the Judaism of the dual Torah describes that holy way of life.
3. A particular social group—in the case of a Judaic system, an "Israel"—to whom the worldview and way of life refer. All Judaisms define that social group by saying who and what is "Israel."

A Judaic system, a Judaism, comprises a worldview, a way of life, and a group of Jews who hold the one and live by the other. When we speak of a Judaism, therefore, we point to a given world-view, way of life, and social group that have coalesced in a definitive way. How do we discern that occasion of coalescence? We look for appeal to a striking and distinctive symbol, something that expresses the whole all together and all at once. For the symbol—whether visual or verbal, whether in gesture or in song or in dance, or whether even in the definition of the role of woman—will capture the whole and proclaim its special message: its way of life, its worldview, its definition of who is Israel. In the case of a Judaism, such a generative symbol may derive from the word "Torah," meaning God's revelation to Moses at Sinai. Or it may come to concrete form in the word "Israel," meaning God's holy people. Or, of course, the generative symbol may come to concrete expression in the conception of God. All Judaisms define God, Torah, and Israel. If we trace the way in which a Judaic system works out its conceptions of these over time, we can indeed follow the history of that Judaism.

Let us now review the Judaism of the dual Torah from late antiquity to modern times in the context of the history of religion. To begin with, simple statement of fact suffices to summarize my characterization of this history of (a) Judaism. As we have seen, the norm-setting position of that Judaism was such that, until the nineteenth century, all heresies within Judaism, schisms and fissures in the social fabric, defined themselves against the system of the dual Torah. All secondary expansions, revisions, developments, and modes of renewal that came to expression adopted the mythic structure and much of the canonical writings of that same Judaism. Consequently the history of Judaism from late antiquity to modern times proves cogent, since we can find a place for all later Judaic systems until the late nineteenth century either within or in contrast to that one Judaism and its system.

Within this picture, we may then identify four periods in the history of Judaism(s):

1. the age of diversity, in which many Judaic systems flourished, from the period of the formation of the Hebrew Scriptures around 586 B.C.E. to the destruction of the Second Temple in 70 C.E.;
2. the formative age, from 70 C.E. to the closure of the Talmud of Babylonia, around 600 C.E.;
3. the classical age, from late antiquity to the nineteenth century, in which that original definition dominated the lives of the Jewish people nearly everywhere they lived; and
4. the modern age, from the nineteenth century to our own day, when an essentially religious understanding of what it means to be Israel, the Jewish people, came to compete among Jews with other views and other symbolic expressions of those views.

The Age of Diversity (586 B.C.E.–70 C.E.)

In this first period there were various Judaisms, that is, diverse compositions of a worldview and a way of life that people believed represented God's will for Israel, the Jewish people. During this long age of nearly five hundred years, a number of different kinds of Judaism, that is, systems with a worldview and a way of life defining who is and who is not "Israel," or who is and who is not truly an heir to Scripture and its promises and blessings, came into being. During that time, too, the Judaism of the dual Torah came into being and competed for Jews' loyalty with those other Judaisms.

The Formative Age of Judaism (70–640 C.E.)

The formative period is divided into two parts, each designated by the documents that preserve the systems that took shape in that time.

1. 70–200 C.E. The first stage is represented by the Mishnah, a philosophical law code, around 200 C.E. in consequence of the destruction of the Second Temple and the defeat of Bar Kokhba three generations later, emphasizing sanctification. The question addressed by the mishnaic system was where and how Israel remained holy even without its holy city and temple.

2. 200–600 C.E. The second stage is marked by the Talmud of the Land of Israel, around 400 C.E., also called the Yerushalmi or Jerusalem Talmud, an amplification and expansion of the Mishnah in the aftermath of the rise to political power of Christianity, presenting a dual emphasis on both sanctification and salvation. The question taken up by the talmudic system—the dual Torah in its first definitive statement—was when and how holy Israel would be saved, even with a world in the hands of the sibling of Israel, Esau=Christendom, and later on in the power of the sibling, Ishmael=Islam, as well. A second Talmud, also serving to explain the Mishnah, took shape in Babylonia and reached closure around 600 C.E. This other Talmud, called the Talmud of Babylonia, or the Bavli, drew into itself a vast range of materials, treating both the Mishnah and Scripture, and presented the definitive statement of Judaism then to now.

The Classical Period of Judaism (640–1789)

A measure of the remarkable success of the Judaism of the dual Torah is readily at hand. In 640, shortly after the closure of the

Talmud of Babylonia, Islam swept across the Middle East and North Africa which, by that time, had been Christian for half a millennium. The Christian ocean evaporated as vast once-Christian populations accepted Islam. Yet the small but deep pools of Judaisms scarcely receded. That Judaic system that accounted for and made tolerable Judaic subordination in the here and now explained this new event. Christianity, however, which had triumphed by the sword of Constantine, fell before the sword of Muhammad. On the other hand, the same Judaic system flourished into the nineteenth century in Eastern Europe and down to the middle of the twentieth century for the great Judaic communities in Muslim countries, which is to say, it remained the self-evident answer to the urgent question.

The Modern and Contemporary Scene (1789–)

In modern times, the diversity characteristic of the period of origins has once again come to prevail. Now the symbolic system and structure of the Judaism of the dual Torah has come to compete for Jews' attention with other Judaic systems and with a widely diverse range of symbols of "other than Jewish" origin and meaning.

This account of Judaism has presented a single field-theory serviceable for the history of religion, a theory meant to deal with the diversity of Judaic systems (Judaisms) and to explain the character of every Judaism that has emerged through time. The same theory allows us to predict the shape of any Judaisms that will come into existence in the future. This same approach can serve for the study of Christianity, Islam, Buddhism, and other constructs that hold together diverse data within the structure of an "ism." That is how the history of the Judaism of the dual Torah may serve as an example for our consideration of the other components of the history of humankind's religions.

The reason is that this field-theory points to a particular selection and interpretation of events of a distinctive sort. The character of that selection then imposes its singular shape upon all systems—in our case, Judaisms—that follow it, then to now. These events—loss of the Land, return to the Land, which we remember are events that are identified as important happenings, selected but not experienced by any one person or generation or group—are understood to stand for exile, identified with everything people find wrong with their life, and return, marking what people hope will happen to set matters right. So each Judaism identifies what is wrong with the present and promises to make things tolerable now and perfect in the indeterminate future.

The inquiry into the generative paradigm and its definitive power may prove exemplary. How so? Any Judaism therefore stands for the identification by a social entity of a situation to escape, overcome, survive. Why does a Judaism succeed in perpetuating itself? Because the repeated pattern of finding the world out of kilter (exile) but then making it possible to live for the interim in that sort of world, that generative paradigm perpetuates profound resentment. Why here? Why us? Why now? To the contrary—and this is the resentment— why not always, everywhere, and forever? So a Judaic religious system recapitulates a particular resentment. In this way each Judaism relates to other Judaisms and religious systems. Each one in its own way and on its own will address and go over that same pattern, all addressing the same original experience. That is why a sequence of happenings, identified as important history and therefore a paradigmatic event, is recapitulated in age succeeding age, whether by one Judaism in competition with another or by one Judaism after another. But, as a matter of systemic fact, no Judaism recapitulates any other, though each goes over the same paradigmatic experience.

A further lesson we have learned for the study of a religion is to ask about the social entity to which and for which that religion speaks. If you agree that religion is public and social, then we start to study a religion by asking who holds that religion, where, when, and under what political circumstances. This emphasis upon the social world of religion leads us to want to know about the way in which a religion defines its social entity: the urgent questions facing that religious group, the self-evidently valid answers pertinent to its social and political circumstance.

When we identify Judaisms in one period after another, we begin by trying to locate, in the larger group of Jews, those social entities that see themselves and are seen by others as distinct and bounded, and that further present to themselves a clear account of who they are and what they do and why they do what they do: the rules and their explanations, their Judaism. This approach to the study of Judaism as a religion has rested on the simple premise that religion always is social and therefore also political, a matter of what people do together, not just what they believe in the privacy of their hearts.

No Judaic system can omit a clear picture of the meaning and sense of the category "Israel." Without an *Israel*, a social entity in fact and not only in doctrine, we have not a system but only a book. And a book is not a Judaism; it is only a book, except after the fact. A Judaism for its part addresses a social group, an Israel, with the claim that that group is not merely an Israel but Israel, Israel *in nuce*, Israel in its ideal form, Israel's saving remnant, the State of Israel, the natural next step in the linear, continuous history (progress) of Israel, everything, anything—but always Israel. So a Judaism or a Judaic system constitutes a clear and precise account of a social group, the way of life and worldview of a group of Jews, however defined.

A third lesson for the history of religions attends to diversity within a given religion or religious tradition. All religions encompass vast diversity and variety. If we pretend that Buddhism or Christianity or Islam represent single, unitary, harmonious religions, all representing the outcome of a continuous tradition formed in an incremental history, we obscure the reality of Christianities, Islams, and Buddhisms. But how are we to deal with the differences within large and distinct families of religions: the varieties of Christianities, Islams, Buddhisms, and Judaisms? Here we have had a case in point, in our working out the requirements of the theory that denies that there is now or ever was a single Judaism.

True, there is no linear and incremental history of one continuous Judaism, with a beginning, middle, and end, for there has never been Judaism, only Judaisms. But there is a single paradigmatic and definitive human experience, which each Judaism reworks in its own circumstance and context. In the case of all Judaisms, it is the experience of exile and return. In a broader sense, therefore, the present field-theory of the history of a particular religious tradition that comprises a variety of expressions may be summarized in the propositions that generalize on the case of Judaisms:

1. No religious system (within a given set of related religious systems) recapitulates any other (among that same set of closely related religious systems).

2. But all religious systems (within a given set) recapitulate
resentment. A single persistent experience for generation after
generation captures what, for a particular group, stands for
the whole of the human condition: everything all at once, all
together, the misery and the magnificence of life.

What we did for Judaism was to look into the Scripture common to all Judaisms and ask about the paradigm of human experience
embedded in the deepest structure of that document. But that does
not mean all Judaisms paraphrase one system. Recapitulating the
story of the religion does not help us understand the religion. By
contrast, identifying the point of origin of the story does. For the story
tells not what happened on the occasion to which the story refers
(the creation of the world, for instance) but how long afterward
and for their own reasons people want to portray themselves. The
tale therefore recapitulates that resentment, that obsessive and troubling point of origin, that the group wishes to explain, transcend,
transform.

Then how are diverse "versions," or in my language, systems,
formed into one system? That is, how may we speak of not only
Judaisms but Judaism? The reason is that every Judaic system takes
as urgent a set or questions deemed inevitable and demanding
answers. In one way or another the questions within a single and
singular paradigm have persisted as the center of system after system.
They turn on the identity of the group, they rest on the premise that
the group's existence represents choice and not a given of nature or
necessity. That obsessive self-awareness, a characteristic trait, masks a
deeper experience that evidently defines for one generation after
another and for one group of Jews after another that ineluctable
question that collectively the group must answer. Why among the
settled peoples of time the Jews, along with the Chinese and
the Armenians among the oldest peoples of continuous historical
existence on the face of the earth, should not have determined for
themselves answers to the question of self-identification, is for us to
find out. To begin with, we recognize that the question is not a given,
that other groups satisfactorily account for themselves and go on to
other questions, and that the critical tension in the life of Jews' groups
deriving from perplexity about the fundamental datum of group
existence presents a surprise and a puzzle.

Let me spell out this theory, accounting for the character and definition of all of the diverse Judaisms that have taken shape since the destruction of the First Temple of Jerusalem in 586 and the return to Zion, building of the Second Temple of Jerusalem, and writing down of the Torah, a process completed in 450 B.C.E. Since the formative pattern imposed that perpetual, self-conscious uncertainty, treating the life of the group as conditional and discontinuous, Jews have asked themselves who they are and invented Judaisms to answer that question. Accordingly, on account of the definitive paradigm affecting their group-life in various contexts, no circumstances have permitted Jews to take for granted their existence as a group.

Looking back on Scripture and its message, Jews have ordinarily treated as special what, in their view, other groups enjoyed as unconditional and simply given. Why the paradigm renewed itself is clear: this particular view of matters generated expectations that could not be met, hence created resentment—and then provided comfort and hope that made possible coping with that resentment. Promising what could not be delivered, then providing solace for the consequent disappointment, the system at hand precipitated in age succeeding age the very conditions necessary for its own replication.

It is therefore possible to classify all Judaisms as a single species of the genus religion, for all of them used some materials in common and exhibited some traits that distinguished all of them from other species of the genus religion, making of them a single species. Specifically each Judaism retells in its own way and with its distinctive emphases the tale of the Five Books of Moses, the story of a no-people that becomes a people, that has what it gets only on condition, and that can lose it all by virtue of its own sin. That is a terrifying, unsettling story for a social group to tell of itself, because it imposes acute self-consciousness, chronic insecurity, upon what should be the level plane and firm foundation of society. That is to say, the collection of diverse materials joined into a single tale on the occasion of the original exile and restoration because of the repetition in age succeeding age also precipitates the recapitulation of the interior experience of exile and restoration—always because of sin and atonement.

The power of all Judaisms to precipitate and then assuage resentment forms a useful point at which to conclude, because it forms a theory of the nature of religion that can be tested in the study of other religions, besides Judaism. That thesis about the nature of religion is as follows: religion recapitulates resentment. I mean two things, one psychological, the other political. In psychological terms, a generation that reaches the decision to change (or to accept or to recognize the legitimacy of change) expresses resentment of its immediate setting and therefore its past, its parents, as much as it proposes to commit itself to something better, the future it proposes to manufacture. In political change each Judaism addresses a political problem not taken up by any other and proposes to solve that problem. So when, in the second of the three theses, I say that the urgent question yields its self-evidently true answer, my meaning is this: resentment—whether at home or in the public polity—produces resolution. The two, when joined, form a religious system, in this context, a Judaism.

At issue when we study religion, therefore, are two things. First, we ask how religious ideas relate in particular to the political circumstances of the people who hold those ideas. Religion as a fact of the practical life of politics constitutes a principal force in the shaping of society and imagination alike, while politics for its part profoundly affects the conditions of religious beliefs and behavior. So one thing we should want to know when we study a religion, as we have seen in our study of Judaism(s), is how a stunning shift in the political circumstance of a religion affects that religion's thought about perennial questions.

But there is a second, more homely consideration. The one thing that the world at large does not always realize in contemplating the Jews is how much they enjoy being Jewish. Part One of this book underlines that fact. Through most of the past, and today, they have always had, and now have, the choice: to be or not to be Jewish. (Only during the Judeocide carried out by the Germans between 1933 and 1945, when all Jews were condemned to death, was there no choice.) And, through the ages, nearly all Jews, nearly all the time, said yes to their origins and commitments. They wanted to be Jewish even though that meant being different from majorities wherever they lived outside of the Jewish state. They chose to be Jewish even though that has meant suffering discrimination under Muslim, Christian, and secular governments. Were it not for a hundred generations of affirmation, the Jews would have perished, just as Abraham worried, right in the beginning:

After these things the word of the Lord came to Abram in a vision, "Fear not, Abram, I am your shield; your reward shall be very great." But Abram said, "O Lord, God, what will you give me, for I continue childless, and the heir of my house is Eliezer of Damascus?" And Abram said, "Behold, you have given me no offspring, and a slave born in my house shall be my heir." (Gen. 15:1–3)

At the very beginning of Israel, the Jewish people, the patriarch Abraham worried for the future of the people, and, from then to now, Jews have thought of themselves, generation by generation, as possibly the last Jews on earth, "the ever-dying people," in the profound insight of the late Simon Rawidovicz, a great philosopher of Judaism at Brandeis University (d. 1957). But the Jews survived, endured, triumphed—not the ever-dying people, but the ever-affirming people. And if you want to know why, consider the Torah through the ages, because that is the reason.

NOTES

1. Phillip Sigal, *Judaism: The Evolution of a Faith*, rev. and ed. by Lillian Sigal (Grand Rapids: Wm B. Eerdmans, 1989), 1. Additional passages from this are cited below.
2. Paul Johnson, *A History of the Jews* (San Francisco: Harper & Row, 1987).

HOW ENCYCLOPEDIAS
DEFINE JUDAISM

Judaism,
Encyclopaedia Judaica

LOUIS JACOBS

JUDAISM: THE RELIGION, PHILOSOPHY,
AND WAY OF LIFE
OF THE JEWS

Definition

The term Judaism is first found among the Greek-speaking Jews of the first century C.E. (*Judaismes*, see 2 Macc. 2:21; 8:1; 14:38; Gal. 1:13–14). Its Hebrew equivalent, *Yahadut*, found only occasionally in medieval literature (e.g., Ibn Ezra to Deut. 21:13), but used frequently in modern times, has parallels neither in the Bible (but see Esth. 8:17, *mityahadim*, "became Jews") nor in the rabbinic literature. (The term *dat Yehudit*, found in Ket. 7:6, means no more than the Jewish law, custom, or practice in a particular instance, e.g., that a married woman should not spin or have her head uncovered in the street.)

The Term "Torah." The term generally used in the classical sources for the whole body of Jewish teaching is Torah, "doctrine," "teaching." Thus the Talmud (Shab. 31a) tells the story of a heathen who wished to be converted to the Jewish faith but only on the understanding that he would be taught the whole of the Torah while standing on one leg. Hillel accepted him, and in response to his request replied: "That which is hateful unto thee do not do unto thy neighbor. This is the whole of the Torah. The rest is commentary. Go and study." Presumable if the Greek-speaking Jews had told the story they would have made the prospective convert demand to be taught Judaism while standing on one leg.

Modern Distinctions between "Judaism" and "Torah." In modern usage the terms "Judaism" and "Torah" are virtually interchangeable, but the former has on the whole a more humanistic nuance while "Torah" calls attention to the divine, revelatory aspects. The term "secular Judaism"—used to describe the philosophy of Jews who accept specific Jewish values but who reject the Jewish religion—is not, therefore, self-contradictory as the term "secular Torah" would be. (In modern Hebrew, however, the word *torah* is also used for "doctrine" or "theory," e.g., "the Marxist theory", and in this sense it would also be logically possible to speak of a secular *torah*. In English transliteration the two meanings might be distinguished by using a capital *T* for the one and a small *t* for the other, but this is not possible in Hebrew which knows of no distinction between small and capital letters.)

A further difference in nuance, stemming from the first, is that "Torah" refers to the eternal, static elements in Jewish life and thought while "Judaism" refers to the more creative, dynamic elements as manifested in the varied civilizations and cultures of the Jews at the different stages of their history, such as Hellenistic Judaism, rabbinic Judaism, medieval Judaism, and, from the nineteenth century, Orthodox, Conservative, and Reform Judaism. (The term *Yidishkeyt* is the Yiddish equivalent of "Judaism" but has a less universalistic connotation and refers more specifically to the folk elements of the faith.)

It is usually considered to be anachronistic to refer to the biblical religion (the "religion of Israel") as "Judaism" both because there were no Jews (i.e., "those belonging to the tribe of Judah") in the formative period of the Bible, and because there are distinctive features which mark off later Judaism from the earlier forms, ideas, and worship. For all that, most Jews would recognize sufficient continuity to reject as unwarranted the description of Judaism as a completely different religion from the biblical.

THE ESSENCE OF JUDAISM

The Hebrew writer Ahad Ha-Am (*Al Parashat Derakhim*, 4 [Berlin ed. 1924], 42) observed that if Hillel's convert (see above) had come to him demanding to be taught the whole of the Torah while standing on one leg, he would have replied: " 'Thou shalt not make unto thee a graven image, nor any manner of likeness' (Exod. 20:4). This is the whole of the Torah. The rest is commentary," that is, that the essence of Judaism consists in the elevation of the ideal above all material or physical forms or conceptions.

Ahad Ha-Am's was only one of the latest attempts at discovering the essence of Judaism, its main idea or ideas, its particular viewpoint wherein it differs from other religions and philosophies. This is an extremely difficult—some would say impossible—task, since the differing civilizations, Egyptian, Canaanite, Babylonian, Persian, Greek, Roman, Christian, Muslim, with which Jews came into contact, have made their influence felt on Jews and through them on Judaism itself. It is precarious to think of Judaism in monolithic terms. Developed and adapted to changing circumstances throughout its long history, it naturally contains varying emphases as well as outright contradictions. Belief in the transmigration of souls, for example, was strongly upheld by some Jewish teachers and vehemently rejected by others. Yet the quest has rarely ceased for certain distinctive viewpoints which make Judaism what it is. Some of these must here be mentioned.

Talmudic Attempts to State Essence. In a talmudic passage (Mak. 23b–24a) it is said that God gave to Moses 613 precepts, but that later seers and prophets reduced these to certain basic principles: David to eleven (Ps. 15); Isaiah to six (Isa. 33:15–16); Micah to three (Micah 6:8); Isaiah, again, to two (Isa. 56:1); and, finally, Habakkuk to one: "The righteous shall live by his faith" (Hab. 2:4). This would make trust in God Judaism's guiding principle.

In another passage the second-century rabbis ruled at the council of Lydda that although the other precepts of the Torah can be set aside in order to save life, martyrdom is demanded when life can only be saved by committing murder, by worshiping idols, or by offending against the laws governing forbidden sexual relations (e.g., those against adultery and incest). The historian Heinrich Graetz (in *Jewish Quarterly Review,* 1 (1889), 4–13) deduces from this ruling that there are two elements in the essence of Judaism: the ethical and the religious. The ethical includes in its positive side, love of mankind, benevolence, humility, justice, holiness in thought and deed, and in its negative aspects, care against unchastity, subdual of selfishness and the beast in man. The religious element includes the prohibition of worshiping a transient being as God and insists that all idolatry is vain and must be rejected entirely. The positive side is to regard the highest Being as one and unique, to worship it as the Godhead and as the essence of all ethical perfections.

Maimonides' Thirteen Principles. In the twelfth century, Maimonides (commentary to the Mishnah, on Sanh., ch. Ḥelek [10]) drew up thirteen principles of the Jewish faith. These are: (1) belief in the existence of God; (2) belief in God's unity; (3) belief that God is incorporeal; (4) belief that God is eternal; (5) belief that God alone is to be worshiped; (6) belief in prophecy; (7) belief that Moses is the greatest of the prophets; (8) belief that the Torah is divine; (9) belief that the Torah is unchanging; (10) belief that God knows the thoughts and deeds of men; (11) belief that God rewards the righteous and punishes the wicked; (12) belief in the coming of the Messiah; (13) belief in the resurrection of the dead.

A close examination of Maimonides' thought reveals that his principles are far more in the nature of direct response to the particular challenges that Judaism had to face in his day than conclusions arrived at by abstract investigation into the main ideas of Judaism. The third principle, for instance, is clearly directed against cruder notions of deity which were popular among some talmudists in Maimonides' day. (Maimonides' contemporary critic, Abraham b. David of Posquières, while believing with Maimonides that God is incorporeal, refuses to treat a belief in God's corporeality as heretical since, he says, many great and good Jews do entertain such a notion because they are misled by a literal understanding of the anthropomorphic passages in Scripture and the rabbinic literature; see Maimonides, Yad, Teshuvah, 3:7). The seventh principle seems to be aimed against the Christian claims for Jesus and the Muslim claims for Muhammad. The ninth principle similarly serves as a rejection of the Christian and Muslim claim that Judaism had been superseded (see S. Schechter, *Studies in Judaism,* 1 (1896), 147–81).

Reactions to Maimonides. Joseph Albo (*Sefer ha-Ikkarim,* 1:26) reduces Maimonides' principles to three basic ones: (1) belief in God; (2) belief that the Torah is divine; (3) belief in reward and punishment; while Isaac Arama *(Akedat Yizḥak,* Gate 55) reduces them to: (1) belief in *creatio ex nihilo;* (2) belief that the Torah is divine;

(3) belief in the hereafter. On the other hand Isaac Abrabanel *(Rosh Amanah,* 23) is out of sympathy with the whole enterprise of trying to discover the basic principles of Judaism in that it implies that some parts of the Torah are less significant than others. Similarly, the six-teenth-century teacher David b. Solomon ibn Abi Zimra writes: "I do not agree that it is right to make any part of the perfect Torah into a 'principle' since the whole Torah is a principle from the mouth of the Almighty. Our sages say that whoever states that the whole of the Torah is from heaven with the exception of one verse is a heretic. Consequently, each precept is a principle and a basic idea. Even a light precept has a secret reason beyond our understanding. How, then, dare we suggest that this is inessential and that fundamental?" (Radbaz, Resp. no 344).

Modern Trends. In modern times two new factors have been operative in the search for the essence of Judaism, one making the task more difficult, the other more urgent. The first is the rise of the Wissenschaft des Judentums movement in the nineteenth century. This had as its aim the objective historical investigation into the sources and history of Judaism. Its practitioners succeeded in demon-strating the complexity of Jewish thought and the fact that it devel-oped in response to outside stimuli, so that there could no longer be any question of seeing Judaism as a self-contained unchanging entity consistent in all its parts. The second new factor was the emancipa-tion of the Jew and his emergence into Western society, calling for a fresh adaptation of Judaism so as to make it viable and relevant in the new situation. The historical movement had demonstrated the devel-oping nature of Judaism and seemed, therefore, to offer encourage-ment to those thinkers who wished to develop the faith further in accord with the new ideals and challenges. Yet this very demonstra-tion made it far more difficult to detect that which is permanent in Judaism when so much is seen to be fluid and subject to change. Among modern thinkers, Leo Baeck was so convinced that the quest was not futile that his book carries the revealing title, *The Essence of Judaism* (1948). Acknowledging the rich variety of forms and differing phenomena in Judaism's history, Baeck still feels able to declare: "The essence is characterized by what has been gained and preserved. And such *constancy,* such *essence,* Judaism possesses despite its many varie-ties and the shifting phases of its long career. In virtue of that essence they all have something in common, a unity of thought and feeling, and an inward bond."

The Concept of "Normative Judaism." Jewish thinkers who hold that an essence of Judaism can be perceived tend to speak of "normative Judaism," with the implication that at the heart of the Jewish faith there is a hard, imperishable core, to be externally preserved, together with numerous peripheral ideas, expressed to be sure by great Jewish thinkers in different ages but not really essential to the faith, which could be dismissed if necessary as deviations.

Unfortunately for this line of thinking no criteria are available for distinguishing the essential from the ephemeral, so that a strong element of subjectivity is present in this whole approach. Almost invariably the process ends in a particular thinker's embracing ideas he holds to be true and valuable, discovering these reflected in the tradition and hence belonging to the "normative," while rejecting ideas he holds to be harmful or valueless as peripheral to Judaism, even though they are found in the tradition. Nor is the statistical approach helpful. An idea occurring very frequently in the traditional sources may be rejected by some thinkers on the grounds that it is untrue or irrelevant, while one hardly mentioned in the sources may assume fresh significance in a new situation, to say nothing of the difficulties in deciding which sources are to be considered the more authoritative. The absurdities which can result from the "normative Judaism" approach can be seen when, for example, contemporary thinkers with a dislike for asceticism, who wish at the same time to speak in the name of Judaism, virtually read out of the faith ascetics such as Baḥya ibn Paquda and Moses Ḥayyim Luzzatto (see, for instance, Abba Hillel Silver, *Where Judaism Differed* (1957), 182–223).

Recognition of Constant Ideas. However, if due caution is exercised and no exaggerated claims made, the idea of a normative Judaism is not without value in that it calls attention to the undeniable fact that for all the variety of moods in Judaism's history there does emerge among the faithful a kind of consensus on the main issues. It has always been recognized, for instance, after the rise of Christianity and Islam, that these two religions are incompatible with Judaism and that no Jew can consistently embrace them while remaining an adherent of Judaism. The same applies to the Far Eastern religions.

This, of course, is very different from affirming that there are no points of contact between Judaism and other faiths, or no common concerns. Nor has the idea of a Judaism divorced from the peoplehood of Israel ever made much headway, even in circles in which the doctrine of Israel's chosenness is a source of embarrassment. Nor does Jewish history know of a Torah-less Judaism, even though the interpretations of what is meant by Torah differ widely. The most important work of Jewish mysticism, the Zohar, speaks of three grades or stages bound one to the other—God, the Torah, and Israel (Zohar, Lev. 73a–b). Historically considered it is true that Judaism is an amalgam of three ideas—belief in God, God's revelation of the Torah to Israel, and Israel as the people which lives by the Torah in obedience to God. The interpretation of these ideas has varied from age to age, but the ideas themselves have remained constant.

Old Habits Die Hard:
Judaism in
The Encyclopedia of Religion

WILLIAM SCOTT GREEN

Two bad habits plague the study of Judaism. The first is the inveterate reduction of Jewish religion to the Hebrew Scriptures. The second is the assimilation of Jewish religion to Jewish peoplehood and Jewish history. Both habits of mind fundamentally misrepresent Judaism, though in different ways, and both frustrate the integration of Judaic data into the study of religion. Astonishingly, both of them pervade the treatment of Judaism in *The Encyclopedia of Religion*.

The first habit equates Judaism with the Hebrew Scriptures. It has two variations, one Christian, the other Jewish. Since both are prevalent in *The Encyclopedia of Religion*, it will help to survey them briefly. At its most vulgar, the Christian form relegates Judaism to an ancient, pre-Christian text and denies Jewish religion any vitality beyond it. At its most refined, the Christian form acknowledges a Jewish religion beyond the Bible but assumes that Jewish Scripture embodies Judaism's characteristics. Either way, Judaism emerges as tantamount to the "Old Testament," at best secondary in importance to the religion that allegedly supplanted it in the New. On the other side, the Jewish version of this habit depicts biblical religion not as the precursor but as the earliest form of Judaism and posits a direct continuity between them. On this view, Judaism alone correctly understands the Hebrew Scriptures and is the authentic heir to the legacy of Israel. Common to both variations of this habit are the categories "biblical Judaism" and "post-biblical Judaism," which are alleged to differ from one another in degree, but not in kind.

To identify the Hebrew Bible as Judaism is a confusion of categories that mistakes Scripture for religion. The Hebrew Scriptures are indeed Judaism's Scripture, and no one denies that some parts constitute a kind of template for some aspects of Judaic theology and practice. But Jewish religion is historically, morphologically, mythically, and ritually different from—and in some crucial respects even discontinuous with—the religion of ancient Israel mandated in Scripture. The texts that give Judaism its distinctive cast and shape are the rabbinic documents, all of which are postbiblical and none of which has the status of Scripture within Judaism. They represent, define, and determine the character of Jewish religion more than does anything written in the Hebrew Scriptures. The conflation of Judaism and Jewish Scripture may validate basic and legitimate Judaic and Christian theological positions, but it obscures the contours, and hence the integrity, of Judaism as a religion.

The second habit fuses the study of Judaism with the study of Jewish institutional and communal life and thereby confounds the history of Judaism with the history of the Jews. It reflects the ideological conviction—especially appealing in modern times—that all Jews can and should understand themselves as a single people bound together by a common political and social history that extends backwards, unbroken, from the present to ancient Israel. No one denies that nearly everywhere Jews have constituted a distinct social group. No one denies that, like every religion, Judaism developed within concrete social and political conditions and cannot be fully understood independent of the circumstances of the people who practiced it. But these factors do not justify equating Jewish religion with whatever Jews did or do together to preserve their collective identity. Although all who practice and affirm Judaism are Jews, not all Jews affirm(ed) and practice(d) Judaism. This habit of mind subsumes Judaism under Jewish social identity and mistakes ethnicity for religion.

Because these two habits depict Judaism as epiphenomenal—as the offshoot of Scripture or ethnicity—they thwart the use of Judaic materials as routine components in the study of religion. They make the issue of religion secondary and thus are incongruous to the stated goals of *The Encyclopedia of Religion.*

In his foreword, Joseph Kitagawa explains the *Encyclopedia's* aim as follows:

The editors agreed with [editor-in-chief Mircea] Eliade that the basic methodology underlying our encyclopedia should be that of the history of religions (*Religionswissenschaft*), which consists of two dimensions, historical and systematic. In this framework, the historical dimension depends upon a mutual interaction between the histories of individual religions . . . and the history of *religion*—myths, symbols, rituals, and so on. The systematic task consists of phenomenological, comparative, sociological, and psychological studies of religion. (Eliade's particular contribution here has been termed the "morphological" study of religion.) (1:xv)

The program is reflected in the *Encyclopedia's* Synoptic Outline of Contents (16:97–127), which divides entries on all subjects into two primary categories, "The Religions" and "History of Religion." Entries on discrete religions are subdivided into "Principal Articles," "Supporting Articles," and "Biographies," and entries on the history of religion are separated into "Religious Phenomena," "Art, Science, and Society," and "The Study of Religion."

Since entries that deal with Judaic data appear in both primary categories and throughout the *Encyclopedia's* major divisions and subdivisions, several editors had responsibility for how Judaism is presented. No evidence suggests any systematic effort to bring work on Judaism in one division into conformity with work on Judaism in the others, and entries often differ sharply from one another in tone and emphasis. Occasionally, entries on Judaism—even within a single division—contradict one another. Very few articles on the "historical" dimension of Judaism employ the categories of the study of religion to describe or interpret the data they present. Thus, most fail to exhibit the "mutual . . . interaction . . . between . . . religions and . . . *religion*" that is supposed to mark the *Encyclopedia* as distinctive. The entries on the "systematic" dimension of religion tend to limit discussion of Judaism to the Hebrew Scriptures or, in a surprising number of instances, to exclude Judaism altogether, even when its data would have been exemplary. With some notable exceptions, the entries on Judaism in the *Encyclopedia* fail to meet even the editors' own announced standards.

The Synoptic Outline of Contents lists 15 discrete principal articles, 85 supporting articles, and 116 biographies under the heading

"Judaism." Since the principal articles evidently are to form a foundation for, or perhaps an introduction to, the others, it is best to begin with them.

PRINCIPAL ARTICLES

The principal articles consist of "an overview," seven articles on the history of Judaism in what an editor's note (8:127) calls "major regions of the Diaspora" (inexplicably, Judaism in the State of Israel is ignored in this section), two entries on Jewish studies (one covering the years 1818–1919, the other 1919 to the present), four entries on the modern forms of Judaism (Conservative, Orthodox, Reconstructionist, and Reform), and an article on Jewish people.

The entry entitled "An Overview" is impressive for its scope, erudition, and occasional eloquence, and it exhibits an admirable sensitivity to the varied positions of contemporary Jewish religious denominations. But its usefulness is severely diminished because it eschews the categories of the study of religion in favor of a different approach. Instead of supplying a critical definition or morphology of Judaism, which would have helped readers distinguish Jewish religion both from other religions and from other Jewish activities, the entry offers the following agenda:

> This article describes postbiblical Judaism in terms of the evolving expression of the Jewish people's covenant with God, understood in liberal religious terms. (8:129)

The entry does not define the key term "covenant" or explain the placement of it as a distinguishing variable of Jewish religion. (The *Encyclopedia's* entry on "Covenant" is no help. Ironically—but typically for the *Encyclopedia*—it discusses covenant in the "Old Testament," at Qumran and in the New Testament, and in Christian theology and church history, but ignores Judaism.) More important, the last clause of this programmatic sentence should have disqualified this entry from an encyclopedia of religion because "liberal religious terms" are normative rather than descriptive. They are terms of apology rather than analysis. Describing Judaism in "liberal religious terms"—which is like describing Christianity in Unitarian-Universalist terms—undermines the study of Judaism as a religion in two ways. First, it imposes on Judaism—especially ancient Judaism—anachronistic categories that highlight the religion's least distinctive traits and suppress its most distinctive ones. Second, particularly when discussing modern Judaism, it blurs the distinction between what is religion and what is not.

Before briefly illustrating these problems, it will help to establish a proper historical framework. At the outset of its inaugural section ("From the Bible to Rabbinic Judaism"), the entry claims that "we have little hard data by which to trace the progress from biblical to rabbinic Judaism, despite some help from the biblical Book of Daniel" (8:129). Actually, we have lots. The Apocrypha, Pseudepigrapha, the Qumran Scrolls, the writings of Josephus, rabbinic traditions about Pharisees and Sadducees, the New Testament, inscriptional records, and recent archeological finds—none of which the entry mentions, and all of which are more relevant than Daniel—supply "hard data" about the different Judaisms that flourished in the Land of Israel during the so-called Second Temple period. Although none of these testifies explicitly about the origins of rabbinic Judaism, they display the Judaic options available in antiquity and thereby establish a reasonably certain historical and religious context for rabbinism's formation and emergence.

In a section entitled "Way of the Rabbis," the entry divides rabbinic Judaism into three categories: responsibility of the individual; family in rabbinic Judaism; and Jewish community and Jewish people. These may reflect the interests of contemporary liberal Judaism, but they seriously misrepresent the emphases of the rabbinic texts themselves. As a consequence, the entry ignores these prominent characteristics of rabbinic Judaism: purity/impurity, the transfer of women, the holiness of the Land of Israel, the Torah-scroll as a sacred object, the supernatural abilities of rabbis, the sage as "living Torah," the collectivity of rabbinic literature, the conflict between the authority of Scripture and that of reason, and the union of sanctification and salvation.

Instead of highlighting these, the entry begins its description of rabbinic Judaism with a discussion of androcentrism, which concludes:

> The rabbis did assign women a comparatively high personal and communal status. Nonetheless, by egalitarian standards, the dif-

ferentiation of women's duties from those of men, which are
viewed as the norm, imposes on women a loss of dignity and
worth. (8:130)

By egalitarian standards, nearly every religion "imposes on women a
loss of dignity and worth," so this observation, though correct, reveals
nothing particular about rabbinism. More important, the facile
condemnation of rabbinic sexism obscures a distinctive trait of rabbinic religion. The third Order of the Mishnah is entitled "Women"
(Nashim), and in the Babylonian Talmud—rabbinism's most authoritative document—it occupies nearly one-fifth of the whole. The transfer of women is a self-declared preoccupation of rabbinic religion, but
the rabbinic construction of gender and conception of gender relations—beyond a cursory nod to the conventional realms of home and
family (8:131–32)—are overlooked in this entry. Surely the issue of
women reveals more about Judaism than the distinction between the
"promise and problem" of liberal Judaism and the "promise and problems" of Orthodoxy (8:142, 143). (Given the prominence of this issue
here, it is ironic that the *Encyclopedia's* entry "Androcentrism" neglects
Judaism, save for a reference to the Shekinah.)

The entry's second point about rabbinism is that it was
democratic:

The troubling issue of sexism aside, rabbinic Judaism is remarkably democratic. It calls all Jews to the same attainable virtues:
righteousness in deed, piety of heart, and education of the mind.
. . .The sacred elite, the rabbinate, remains open to any man
and recognizes no substantial barriers between rabbis and other
Jews. (8:130)

Again the imposition of "liberal religious terms" yields an unillu-
minating description. Which religion calls its followers to unrigh-
teousness, impiety, and ignorance? This depiction misses the ritual
totalization—in action, speech, and thought—that defines rabbinic
halakhah. Moreover, it mistakes the absence of a religious hierarchy
and central authority for democracy. Although in principle any Jewish male could join rabbinism's religious elite (as is the case in any
religion without a caste system or dynastic priesthood), rabbis sharply
differentiated themselves from the ordinary Jews among whom they

lived—and thus objectified their claims to authority and leadership—by distinctive speech and dress, by supererogatory piety, and by assertions that their knowledge of Torah gave them supernatural powers. Finally, rabbis in no way constituted a "sacred" class. If they had, the barrier between them and other Jews would have been more than "substantial"; it would have been, as in the case of the Israelite priesthood, absolute.

From the perspective of liberal religion it may appear that rabbinic Judaism was mainly a matter of "an ethnic group's unique covenant with God and its consequences for the lives of the individuals who constitute the group" (8:131) and that "the rabbis exhibited a clear-cut sense of the unity and identity of the Jewish people, who were the sole recipients of God's law and thus bore unique witness to God" (8:133), but rabbinic literature shows these assessments to be oversimplifications. "The Jewish people" is a modern conception. Rabbinic literature speaks of "Israel," a social metaphor that rabbis themselves defined and circumscribed. Thus, rabbinic Judaism excluded from membership in "Israel," either in this world or the next, categories of people—from Samaritans to sectarians—who were not Gentiles and whom we would regard, ethnically, to be Jews. It also included Gentile proselytes in the category "Israel" and compared to the high priest those Gentiles who fulfilled Torah. Indeed, as the entry itself notes (8:135), some sages granted "righteous" Gentiles a place in the "world to come" (a view made normative by Maimonides)—the very redemption rabbinism denied to impious Jews. Religion and ethnicity were not coessential, and conformity to the sages' Torah was the ultimate arbiter.

The imposition of "liberal religious terms" also affects the entry's description of time and theology in rabbinism. The entry interprets what it calls "Jewish time" as consisting of "three interrelated dimensions": the "personal" (rites of passage), the "annual-historical" (Sabbath and yearly festivals), and the "eschatological" (the time of the Messiah). It notes that rabbinic Judaism infused new meanings into the Israelite agricultural festivals of Passover, Shavu'ot, and Sukkot, but deems these meanings "historical": "Thus, the undeviating cycle of the year becomes a reminder and renewal of the Jewish people's unique historical experience" (8:133). Attention to the *Encyclopedia*'s stated purpose would have helped here. The history of religion demonstrates that the themes and events evoked by these rites and festi-

vals—creation, paradise, and exodus from Egypt, the revelation to
Moses at Sinai—are neither personal nor historical, but paradigmatic
and, therefore, mythic. These Judaic rituals and holy days exhibit a
pattern common to many religions. They confer sense and meaning
on contingent autobiography and history by connecting them to the
perduring realm Eliade called "sacred time." None of this is discussed
in the entry.

To the liberal eye, Israelite religion and rabbinic Judaism appear
equally unliberal, so critical distinctions between them are difficult to
discern. Although this entry speaks of rabbinism's "mix of continuity
and creativity" (8:120) and acknowledges its "creative development"
and its "reverent continuity with the past," the section titled "Beliefs
of the Rabbis" emphasizes "the primacy of continuity in rabbinic
belief" (8:134), which yields the following judgment:

> the rabbis did not see the loss of the Temple as a disaster requir-
> ing major theological reconstruction; rather, they found it a con-
> firmation of the Bible's teaching. . . . Continuing the faith of the
> Bible as they understood it, the rabbis indomitably transcended
> profane history. (8:134)

It is correct that rabbinic Judaism saw the hand of God in the Temple's second destruction, which it could not regard as a gratuitous
caprice. But after the debacle of the Bar Kokhba rebellion—which
signalled precisely the enduring loss, not merely the temporary
absence, of the Temple and its cult—rabbis generated the "major theological reconstruction" this statement denies. To take one obvious
example, the Mishnah developed an unprecedented theology of sanctification, which located the power to effect holiness in the motiva-
tions and intentions of the ordinary Israelite—defined, of course, in
rabbinic terms—to which God himself responded. Moreover, the claim
that rabbis follow the Bible "as they understood it" is no argument for
continuity. Church fathers did the same thing, with dramatically different results. At issue is *how* rabbis read Scripture, *how* they understood it, and *how* they made it speak with a rabbinic voice—all of
which the entry neglects.

The entry's treatment of the pietistic, mystical, and philosophic
developments in medieval and early modern Judaism is more disci-

plined than its handling of the rabbinic period, as are its discussions of modern Jewish philosophy. But in its description of the impact of modernity on Judaism, the normativity and advocacy of its "liberal religious terms" are all too evident. If, in the entry's own terms, readers are to understand Judaism as the "evolving expression of the Jewish people's covenant *with* God" (italics added), how are they to comprehend secular Jewish activities—which by definition do not involve God—as manifestations of Jewish religion? How are they to make sense of the following claim?

> The interplay between Judaism and modernity can best be illus-
> trated by the devotion of Jews to interpersonal relationships.
> American Jews today express the longstanding rabbinic com-
> mitment to family and community by their disproportionate
> involvement in the helping professions (such as teaching, social
> work, and psychotherapy) and their intense concern for family
> relationships. In these areas they demonstrate a dedication lack-
> ing in their observance of the halakic dietary law and laws gov-
> erning sexual relations between spouses. They seem now to
> believe that sanctifying life, their covenant goal, now requires
> giving these general human activities priority in Jewish duty.
> (8:141–42)

This argument seems to suggest that the career choices of modern Jews are somehow religiously determined. If so, shall we also see
the hand of God in the disproportionate involvement of Jews in the
American entertainment and movie industry, in the international dia-
mond trade, and among the cabbies of London? Alternatively, the
argument may mean to say that some values that earlier developed in
Judaism persist in the modern secular Jewish community. Even if
that be so—and it is notoriously difficult to demonstrate convinc-
ingly—by which analytic criterion do we classify the current expression of those values as religion? If, as the entry later suggests, "high
culture" is the " 'Torah' of secular Jews" (8:143), if "being politically
informed and involved" is for Jews "the modern equivalent of a
commandment" (8:144), what would count as not Torah, as not
commandment? If secularity is evidence of religion, what can these
terms mean?

The overarching difficulty with this principal article on Judaism is that it commits the bad habit of confusing religion with ethnicity. As a consequence, it vitiates religion, the very phenomenon the encyclopedia was constructed to explain.

The seven historical/geographical entries cover the following topics: Judaism in the Middle East and North Africa to 1492, Judaism in the Middle East and North Africa since 1492, Judaism in Asia and Northeast Africa, Judaism in Southern Europe since 1500, and Judaism in the Western Hemisphere. As a group, these entries do not formally distinguish Jewish religion from the Jewish institutional and social histories of the periods and regions they cover, so the degree of explicit attention to religion varies from entry to entry.

The most disciplined in the focus on religion is the article on Asia and Northeast Africa, which is especially useful for its discussion of the religious rituals of the Falashas and the Jews of Cochin, and the entry on Northern and Eastern Europe to 1500. The latter neatly describes the emergence of the *hasid* (pietist) and Talmud scholar as representatives of new Judaic ideals, and it offers a concise and insightful description of the shift from the eleventh century to the twelfth:

> The righteous self-image, the reverence for the dead martyrs, German Hasidism, and the scholasticism of the tosafists were part of a twelfth-century transformation of classical Judaism into a "traditional" Ashkenazic Judaism. (8:183)

Regrettably, this observation, which would have made a fine focus for the entry as a whole, is not developed.

The entry on the Middle East and North Africa to 1492 limns important developments in post-talmudic Judaism and offers a nicely detailed discussion of Judaic philosophy. Interested readers will regret that it does not say more about what the responsa literature reveals of the Judaism(s) of lay communities or about how the commentaries to the Mishnah and Talmud influenced the reception and understanding of these documents.

The four remaining entries in this category are exercises in Jewish history rather than the history of Judaism. The entry on Judaism in Southern Europe draws a helpful distinction between popular religious practices and the "idealized religion of the intellectual leadership" (8:172). Focusing on the latter, it provides a short and solid cultural history of Jewish intellectual and literary life that stresses the emergence of new forms of literature and the impact of non-Jewish culture on the cultural life of Jews. The article on the Middle East and North Africa since 1492 deals primarily with historical questions of Jewish political and legal status, demography, and community organization. It offers brief treatments of Joseph Karo, Isaac Luria, and Shabbetai Tsevi. The entry on Judaism in Northern and Eastern Europe since 1500 combines the social and political history of the Jews in Europe with a summary treatment of major religious developments: Hasidism, *musar*, Reform, and Neo-Orthodoxy. The last entry in the set, on Judaism in the Western Hemisphere, focuses heavily on cultural history and treats Jewish religion organizationally rather than morphologically. Surprisingly, it has little to say about the peculiarity of the American context. Curiously, it pays excessive attention to American rabbinical seminaries, as if the history of American Judaism took place in them. A difficulty of these four in particular is the absence of a theory that correlates Jewish history and Jewish religion.

The two entries on "Jewish Studies" are aptly titled. They discuss the emergence and development of modern "Jewish scholarship"—on all Jewish subjects, from art to sociology—in Europe, America, and the State of Israel. The first entry covers the years 1818 to 1919 and deals primarily with the *Wissenschaft des Judenthums*. The second lists periodicals, institutions, and scholars in the three regions from 1919 to the present. Inexplicably, it ignores such figures as George Foot Moore and Erwin Ramsdell Goodenough, who did so much to integrate Judaism into American scholarship on religion. Since neither entry exhibits much interest either in the study of Judaism within the study of religion or in the study of Jewish religion as a subfield in Jewish studies, both belong in some other encyclopedia.

The entries on Orthodox, Reform, Conservative, and Reconstructionist Judaism are clear, concise, and informative. The first enriches with sociological insight its focus on Orthodoxy's theology and halakhah. It deftly surveys the varied trends within Orthodoxy and helps both to dispel the misconception that Orthodoxy is an antimodern monolith and to explain its persisting vitality. The second, on

Reform Judaism, highlights matters of belief and ritual and supplies a disciplined historical narrative that tracks the shift in Reform's focus from well-defined theology to "ethnic survival" (12:262). The article on Conservative Judaism describes the movement's institutional developments and surveys its short roster of "conceptual components" (positive-historical Judaism, Zionism, revelation, religious education). It notes that Conservatism's key notion of "catholic Israel" has acquired an increasingly elitist connotation but doubts that the halakhic decisions of the Rabbinical Assembly's Committee on Jewish Law and Standards play any "decisive role" in the lives of Conservative congregations (4:67–68). The entry on Reconstructionism expertly demonstrates the intellectual coherence and sociological realism that distinguishes the naturalist ideology of the movement's founder, Mordechai Kaplan, from both Reform and Conservative thought. Although Kaplan held that "Judaism is for the sake of the Jewish people" (12:225), his conception of Judaism as a "religious civilization" integrates, but does not confuse, a theory of peoplehood with a theory of religion.

The entry "Jewish People" discusses "the nature of Jewish corporate identity, from the biblical period to the present" (8:30). For the reasons specified above, this monolithic conception is both anachronistic and misleading, particularly as a principal article on Judaism. The authentic religious categories "Torah" or "Israel"—both of which, by contrast, are native to Judaic literature and liturgy of all regions, periods, and groups—would have been far superior choices. (Amazingly, the *Encyclopedia* has no article on "Israel" at all.) Because the entry fails to distinguish Judaic reflection on "Israel" from the social and political circumstances of the Jews, it lacks a consistent perspective. Thus, the qualified observation that "medieval Judaism did not become a multinational *religion* in the sense that Christianity or Islam did" (8:36) (italics added) becomes, one paragraph later, a claim for the "mononational character of the Jewish people" and, still later, for "the national unity of the Jews" (8:38)—a very different matter, which the entry's own listing of the "wide diversity of Jewish subcultures" in the Middle Ages renders doubtful. The confusion of ethnicity with religion robs this entry of analytical coherence.

Despite the strengths of some individual entries, the principal articles as a whole do not effectively introduce the morphology and history of Judaism to the "educated, nonspecialist readers" (1:xiii) for whom the *Encyclopedia* is intended. Fortunately, a number of excellent supporting articles perform that essential task.

SUPPORTING ARTICLES

The entry titled "Rabbinic Judaism in Late Antiquity" supplies a proper morphology of rabbinic religion by focusing on the myth of Torah, the different expressions of that myth in rabbinic writings, messianism, and the figure of the rabbi. The entries "Mishnah and Tosefta" and "Midrash and Aggadah" highlight and effectively explicate the native categories of classical Judaic literature and show how the texts work. The entry "Talmud" rightly draws attention to the "role of law" and the "role of study and intellect" as two major foci of "talmudic religion." Regrettably, it contains no illustration of a page of the Babylonian Talmud and says far too little about the character of talmudic dialectic.

Enough good cannot be said about the exemplary entries titled "Premodern Philosophy" and "Modern Thought," which appear as subdivisions of the larger category "Jewish Thought and Philosophy." The first is an unpretentious, lucid, and engaging discussion of Judaic philosophy from Sa'dyah to the Italian Renaissance. After defining "medieval" as a "style of thought" "shaped by philosophy and prophecy," the entry admirably conveys the force and excitement of medieval philosophical argument and shows its pertinence to the history of Judaism. Its sections on Sa'dyah and Maimonides are especially useful. The entry on modern thought is equally fine. It focuses on "modern Jewish religious thought," which it defines not merely chronologically but as "meditations by Jews about Judaism and Jewish destiny that take place within—or at least seek to take into account—the cognitive process distinctive of the modern world" (8:70). The entry is a masterful and illuminating survey of major Judaic thinkers from Moses Mendelssohn to Emmanuel Levinas. Its discussions of the historicist ideology of the *Wissenschaft des Judenthums* and its effect on the study of Judaism as a religion, and of the relationship of Zionism and Jewish religion, are particularly strong.

The supporting articles also contain a number of fine entries on discrete topics. The entry "Afterlife: Jewish Concepts" offers a concise, responsible, and broad survey of its topic. The article on "Amoraim" attempts to explain the contributions of this later generation of talmudic sages to rabbinic religion. (Its companion entry, "Tannaim," is more lexical and less informative.) The entry "Ashkenazic Hasidism" provides a clear picture of the value structure and "socioreligious program" of that movement. Likewise, the three entries that comprise the longer article on "Hasidism" skillfully show how Hasidic theology and ethics constitute a coherent Judaic system and describe the two major sectors within that movement. Also strong are the two entries on "Synagogue" ("History and Tradition" and "Architectural Aspects") and the article "Tosafot," which describes the scope and method of these important talmudic commentators.

The supporting articles also contain some unexpected disappointments. The entry on "Torah" is surprisingly diffuse. Instead of a disciplined program of inquiry into this central Judaic category, it offers a series of disjointed observations whose relevance to the topic of "Torah" *in Judaism* is not always clear. After a routine lexical survey of the term in the Hebrew Scriptures, the entry describes the contents of the Pentateuch and then discusses pentateuchal criticism, oddly jumping from rabbinic literature directly to the eighteenth century and the documentary hypothesis. It supplies a series of observations about Torah in rabbinic Judaism, medieval philosophy, and Kabbalah, and concludes with a section on the Torah scroll. It will be difficult for readers to learn from this entry about the rich array of religious meanings Torah came to acquire as a defining native category of Jewish religion. The entry "History: Jewish Views" is equally problematic. Although it devotes nearly half its space to ancient Israelite views of history, it virtually ignores the ahistorical preferences of the priests and the cult. Curiously, it identifies the liturgical use of biblical themes as a use of history and judges the chain of authority in Mishnah Abot to be "the most prominent essentially historic element of Pharisaic-rabbinic Judaism" (6:392). In so doing, it neglects important categories of the study of religion, such as myth and tradition, and makes it impossible for readers to distinguish history from any memory, fabrication, or use of the past.

The entry "Sanhedrin" provokes a question about the *Encyclopedia's* editorial procedures. The entry itself—an expertly critical, well-argued, and balanced review of all the evidence for this putative institution—concludes:

Thus the existence of a supreme governing body in Jerusalem called the Sanhedrin cannot be proven by the sources before us, and if it existed, it cannot be described. (13:63)

To this considered—and definitive—judgment, an editor has added an italicized comment:

[*For another view of the historicity of the Beit Din ha-Gadol and the Boule, see* Pharisees.]

But the entry "Pharisees" assumes as fact—and without argument— exactly what the one on Sanhedrin denies! Indeed, it not only claims that Pharisaic ideology "generated" the Sanhedrin, but even describes its membership and procedures. And to this description, an editor has added:

[*For another view of the Beit Din ha-Gadol, see* Sanhedrin.] (11:270)

Since, by logic, both these entries cannot be correct, what are readers to think? To make matters worse, the entry on "Pharisees" ends with yet another editor's note!

[*For another view of this period in Jewish history, see* Rabbinic Judaism in Late Antiquity.] (11:272)

These three entries come to different conclusions about the same data because "Pharisees" merely paraphrases the sources that the other two entries critically examine. Yet the *Encyclopedia* presents them as equivalent alternatives, as if the quality—indeed, the presence— of argument and the critical use of evidence counted for nothing in scholarship.

The remaining supporting articles, far too numerous to examine individually, are generally informative, competent, and accessible. As a rule, however, they describe their topics primarily within a Judaic framework and make no reference to the categories of the study of religion. This is unfortunate because in some cases the data and phenomena of Judaism constructively challenge the viability of those categories. For instance, the editors have classified the rites and practices of most religions into the categories "Domestic Observances" and

"Rites of Passage." For Judaism, however, this distinction is misleading because some rites of passage (circumcision, mourning practices) are or can be domestic observances as well.

Finally, it is worth noting that the themes of religious conflict and persecution appear to constitute a leitmotif in the *Encyclopedia*'s treatment of Judaism. Nearly forty-five pages are given to the topics of Christianity and Judaism; Anti-Semitism; Jewish-Christian Polemic; Muslim-Jewish Polemic; Persecution: Jewish Experience; The Holocaust: History; and The Holocaust: Jewish Theological Responses. All these entries are solid and expert—"Christianity and Judaism" is especially learned and intelligent—but there is too much duplication among them. Surely, this aspect of the history of Judaism could have been handled more efficiently. The amount of space devoted to Jewish theological responses to the Holocaust is disproportionate to the influence on Judaism of the thinkers the entry discusses (and sharply criticizes). Moreover, the absence of a comparable entry on Christian theological responses ignores at least a generation of serious Christian reflection on this problem and implies that the Holocaust is an issue only for Judaism.

BIOGRAPHIES

In the section on biographies the entries on medieval and modern figures are conventional and reliable. But—save for the article on Yohanan ben Zakkai—the entries on talmudic figures are uncritical paraphrases of stories about, or opinions of, individual rabbis drawn indiscriminately from various rabbinic documents. Since rabbinic literature avoids biography as a genre and fabricates tales about rabbis to illustrate idealized collective values rather than the facts of individual lives, the very assignment of such entries reflects a profound misunderstanding of rabbinism. The space given to these entries could better have been devoted to important Judaic figures, thinkers, and artists—some even highlighted elsewhere in the *Encyclopedia*—inexplicably absent here, such as Theodore Herzl, Ahad Ha-Am, A. D. Gordon, Solomon Maimon, Simon Dubnow, Walter Benjamin, Milton Steinberg, Nelly Sachs, S. Y. Agnon, and H. N. Bialik. Why the index lists the biographies of Spinoza and Wittgenstein under Judaism is a mystery that the entries themselves do not help to solve.

GENERAL ARTICLES

If the habit of confusing religion with ethnicity mars some major articles classified under "Judaism," the habit of reducing Judaism to the Hebrew Scriptures dominates the treatment of Judaism in the rest of the *Encyclopedia*. Indeed, the assumption that these two fields are continuous appears basic to the *Encyclopedia's* very conception. Primary responsibility for both subjects was assigned to a single editor.

When the entries in the categories of "Religious Phenomena," "Art, Science, and Society," and "Scholarly Terms" do not equate Jewish religion with the Bible, they exercise two other alternatives with respect to it. They either inappropriately ignore Judaism or grossly misrepresent it.

Again, it is impossible to deal with all of these individually, so some representative examples—listed, for convenience, alphabetically—will have to suffice.

The entry "Apostasy," in a section titled "Apostasy in Jewish Ritual Law," observes as follows:

> Apostasy needed to be legally regulated. "Whole Israel has a share in the world to come. . . . And these don't have a share in the world to come: whoever says 'There is no resurrection of the dead in the Torah' and 'There is no Torah from heaven,' and the Epicurean" (San. 10:1). About 100 c.e. the twelfth prayer of the so-called eighteen benedictions has been expanded by the *birkat ha-minim* ("the blessing over the heretics"): "For apostates let there be no hope. The dominion of arrogance do thou speedily root out in our days. And let Christians and the sectarians be blotted out of the book of the living." This amplification implies that apostates had earlier been cursed in Jewish divine service. Christian literature corroborates that after the fall of the temple Jews cursed Christians. (1:354)

There is not space here to correct all the mischief done by this paragraph. Perhaps it is enough to note that the rendering of Mishnah Sanhedrin 10:1 is both vulgar and inaccurate, *birkat ha-minim* does not mean "blessing over the heretics," the benediction cited is from the fourth century not the first, and the word in it translated here as

"Christians" means something else. Jewish liturgical cursing of Christians in antiquity is something John Chrysostom might have wished for, but there is scant evidence for it.

The entry "Authority" discusses Buddhism, Christianity, and Islam as "founded religions," treats "primitive" and "archaic" religions, but ignores Judaism (and Hinduism). Although rabbinic Judaism made benedictions into a virtual art form, and although the first tractate of the Mishnah and both Talmuds is entitled "Blessings," the entry "Blessing" discusses only the Hebrew Scriptures, Islam, and Christianity. Despite the extensive development of halakhic codes in Judaism—all of which are listed in the entry "Halakhah: History of"— the entry "Codes and Codification," under a section amazingly entitled "Jewish Codes," discusses only the Book of the Covenant and the "legal parts of Deuteronomy."

The entry "Charity" gives an incomplete account of Maimonides on charity and then observes:

> Notwithstanding occasional references to liberality toward the gentiles, in Jewish tradition "charity begins at home," and for many centuries the object of charity was the fellow Jew—the individual, the family circle, and the community. (3:222)

What this entry invidiously labels "occasional references to liberality toward the gentiles" is in fact an explicit talmudic injunction to give charity to the Gentile poor as to the Jewish poor (Babylonian Talmud, Gittin 61a). The article "Confession of Sins" bypasses Judaism, as does the long entry on the "Crusades," which has separate sections on Christian and Muslim "perspectives." The entry "Eschatology" discusses only the Bible and the Pseudepigrapha, and then moves on to Christianity. The entry "Faith" mentions Judaism in a section called "Faith-as-Obedience," but refers only to 1 Sam. 15:22. It supplies detailed examples from Confucianism, Christianity, Buddhism, and Islam. (Ironically, the entry "Obedience" barely mentions Judaism.)

Remarkably, Judaism finds no place in the entries on "Migration and Religion" and "Oral Tradition." This occurs despite the fact that migration, both forced and voluntary, accounts for many developments—and is a fundamental mythic theme—in Judaism; and the extensive literature about oral tradition in Judaism. Likewise, the major entry "Poetry and Religion," which has separate subentries on

Indian, Chinese, Japanese, Christian, and Islamic religions, makes no mention of Judaism. Surely a few pages could have been given over to a discussion at least of the Psalms in Judaic liturgy, the medieval *piyyutim*, Judah HaLevi, and the Nobel Prize winner Nelly Sachs.

One final example will conclude this sampling. The entry "Revelation" observes:

> The Judaism of the scribes (beginning with Ezra, fourth cent. B.C.E.) shows a tendency to regard revelation as closed and to see the prophetic movement as now past. The Jewish tradition generally accepted these positions. Only Jewish mysticism . . . regarded not only the once-for-all historical act of divine revelation but also the repeated mystical expressions of God as revelatory; the function of the latter is to bring out the implications of the historical revelation and make it intelligible. (12:360)

Even the slightest familiarity with some reliable secondary work on the theory of "oral Torah" in rabbinic Judaism would show how misleading this judgment is.

Although there are exceptions to these ignorant and neglectful entries—the article "Canon," for instance—and although there may be some not examined here that do a better job than these, the examples listed above should encourage readers to be very cautious about believing anything they read about Judaism in the general articles of *The Encyclopedia of Religion*.

This survey of the treatment of Judaism in *The Encyclopedia of Religion* provides no occasion to rejoice. It shows, grimly, that long-practiced habits of mind—within both Jewish studies and the study of religion—continue to exert a powerful and sinister influence on scholarship. With respect to the study of religion, Judaism remains largely a ghettoized subject. With respect to Judaism, the study of religion exhibits a field-wide and virtually systemic ignorance.

A Word to the Teacher:
Introducing Judaism

This is the first textbook designed to serve as the only textbook needed for an entire one-semester course on Judaism. It includes not only an exposition of the subject but also extensive anthologies by others—a broad variety of viewpoints on a single cogent problem: the description of Judaism through the ages. The book is designed for classroom teachers who are generalists in the area of religion and also for those who specialize in aspects of the study of religion other than Judaism. In these pages, both will find it possible to offer an introductory course on Judaism. This volume provides everything needed except what the classroom teacher alone can give: perspective, texts for analysis, a wide variety of viewpoints, and, above all, insight into the issues of a subject and guidance into making connection with those issues and current concerns. Readings that will provide necessary information, sources for analysis, various viewpoints and perspective make up the anthologies that serve the major units of the text. In explaining to students the main points of each chapter and in showing the connections between the propositions of the text and the complementary reading in the anthologies, in comparing and contrasting Judaism with other religions, in bringing to bear issues of general interest upon this exposition of a particular religion, teachers with specialties other than Judaism will find for themselves an important role through the medium of what is given in these pages.

My intent is to invite into the field of teaching about Judaism anyone who shares in the profession of the study of religion, to open this subfield to everybody who finds the subject interesting. And to those who may not know why Judaism is interesting for those investigating the nature of religion and its remarkable power in the world order, I mean to set forth the reason. The case I make is simple. Although Judaism attracts only a tiny proportion of religious people, it has been, and is today, a religion rich in examples of generally intelligible and important propositions about the character of religion: what it is, how it works, why it is critical to the life of humanity.

The textbook serves five subsidiary purposes. First, in the context of courses that introduce religion in general, for example, the theory of religion, Part One offers an account of the religious life of Judaism in America and Canada today, an account that draws upon the liturgy of the synagogue. The theory of a Judaism for home and family and a civil Judaism for the corporate community, worked out in Part One, will enrich such a course. The problem of defining a religion, addressed in chapter 13, presents a case study in that difficult problem in the theory of religion and of the study of religion.

Second, in the context of Bible introductory courses, Part Two provides an account of the Hebrew Scriptures in Judaism. Third, courses in New Testament and earliest Christianity will find in Part Two an introduction to the formation of Judaism in that same period and also to the literature of Judaism pertinent to the formative age of Christianity. Fourth, courses in Western civilization will find in chapters 11 and 12 an account of Judaism as it flourished in the medieval and modern West. Finally, courses in religion in the modern world will find in Parts One and Three a complete account of Judaism in modern and contemporary times. For all of these purposes, framed by specialists in other aspects of the study of religion or by generalists, this book should prove useful.

This book began because I needed it for my own teaching at the University of South Florida, but my real goal is to provide a book, the first book of its kind to enable specialists in the study of religions besides Judaism to teach interesting and coherent courses on Judaism. The book's success will be marked by colleagues' teaching results. From an introduction to Judaism I want my students to gain knowledge—through the example of Judaism—of how human beings are transformed by religion into something they would otherwise not have been, and of what religion is and accomplishes in this world. Part One accomplishes the first purpose, Part Two, the second. I believe that one byproduct of such an enhanced understanding of religion will be a sympathetic grasp of what it means to be a Jew and to live by Judaism in contemporary America. A second will be a deeper understanding of the extraordinary power of religion to shape lives and change the world.

The main points of each chapter are accompanied by sizable examples of words that Jews recite in certain settings. Students can then judge for themselves how these rites can make an impact upon the people and, in certain settings, affect and even enchant those who say them and who carry them out. The textbook also includes a substantial anthology. In addition to the exposition of the text are presentations of important subjects relevant to the narrative of the text but not covered in it. Since this textbook-anthology is addressed to nonspecialists in Judaism who wish to offer a course about Judaism, I have included in these pages everything that is needed for that task: all the information, together with propositions and arguments that can sustain the intellectual adventure of the classroom. Anyone who teaches courses in religion will find himself or herself at home here: the issues are those of the study of religion, only the cases are special to Judaism. The textbook and the anthologized materials are set forth so as to allow the teacher to (1) present a topic, with students reading an original source in English translation, and (2) relate the topic to the larger problem of religion that, in context, Judaism is meant to exemplify. The anthology not only contains complementary materials for a given topic, but also, and especially, introduces information that is relevant to a general theme but not covered in the textbook chapters, as well as viewpoints in addition to mine.

So while the basic theories of how Judaism is to be introduced, and of the shape and structure of the history of Judaism, are entirely my own, I have tried to provide a broad spectrum of opinion as well as a rich corpus of primary sources in English translation. In this way I hope to help nonspecialists in Judaism to present a rich and informative, accurate, and appreciative account of the Judaic religion. At the same time I also hope that studying Judaism will strike both teachers and students as more than the exercise of acquiring information about what Jews believe, do, or do not do. I want the study of this religion to produce discussions on questions of broad general interest on the whys of religion, not only the whats. This is a first effort, and there will be further editions. Hence letters to me, telling me how to make this a still more helpful medium for teaching the subject—introducing Judaism—will be very welcome, read, and used.

Accordingly, I mean to present all of the information, primary sources in English translation, and exposition of problems and ideas needed to make possible a fourteen-week college course, "Introduction to Judaism." Specifically, I hope that colleges whose religious studies departments have no specialist on Judaism—as well as Protestant, Roman Catholic, and Orthodox Christian seminaries, and churches and synagogues—will take up the subject to which I have devoted my life and find in that subject ideas and insights relevant to the study of religion and important in appreciating the importance of religion in the social order. The role of the nonspecialist teacher hardly requires explanation. All of us who are college teachers teach a great many things that we do not know firsthand and that are far outside of our own scholarly interests.

I realize that for many scholars and students of religion, courses in Judaism come under consideration because the study of the Bible, the Hebrew Scriptures and New Testament, draws attention to Judaism. Many, for instance, believe that the New Testament cannot be read without knowledge of Judaism of the same time and place, and most people recognize that the Hebrew Scriptures yielded not only Christianity but also Judaism, so that an appreciation of the power of the Bible to shape the civilization of the West requires attention to the minority- as well as the majority-faith. These motives for presenting, or taking, a course about Judaism serve only until the course begins. Then, in my view, the topic must take over. And that must mean that Judaism is to be studied in its own terms and not for "the Jewish background to the New Testament" or "the legacy of the Hebrew Scriptures." Judaism is a living religion, which takes over and transforms the lives of millions of Americans (not to mention Europeans, Latin Americans, and others around the world), and for those who are interested in religion in general, not only in Christianity in particular, Judaism presents on its own a religion well worth sustained attention. The reasons are spelled out in my opening note to the students who will use this book: Why study Judaism at all?

That is not to say that those who give or take a course on Judaism because of a special interest in the Bible will be disappointed. Much of Part Two is devoted to the way in which the Torah—the revelation of God to Moses, called "our rabbi," at Sinai—unfolded. The history of Judaism, which in its formative stages was contemporary with the very beginnings of the history of Christianity, is set forth in two aspects: the crisis that raised an urgent and critical issue, and the response that later came to expression in an important holy book.

THE TEXTBOOK AND THE ANTHOLOGY:
HOW THEY RELATE

The relationship between the anthology and the text complemented by it is spelled out as follows:

Part One
The Jewish People:
Judaism in the World Today

I start with contemporary Judaism in America because knowledge about and insight into religion and the world order today are important in the study of religion. Our students study with us in part because they want better to understand the social order that they enter, and they study a religion other than their own because they want to make sense of what is both present and unfamiliar. Hence when students study Judaism, we help them achieve their goals by emphasizing what is both most interesting and engaging, but also what is most relevant to the tasks of education: helping young people make sense of the here and now. In my view contemporary Judaism in America forms the most interesting body of data for our students, because there we see not what books say but what people do, and, further, we ask the questions that concern us when we study about any religion: Why do real people believe this religion? and Why do they live their lives in accord with its requirements and teachings? Thus, I devote more discussion to Part One than to Part Two, even though it would have been more conventional to commence with the past and the "facts" of books and beliefs and end with a lick and a promise for the present.

Chapters 1 to 4 present a condensation of the exposition of Judaism as a living religion in this country that is set forth in my book *The Enchantments of Judaism: Rites of Transformation from Birth through Death* (New York: Basic Books, 1987; University of South

Florida Studies in the History of Judaism; Atlanta: Scholars Press, 1991). I set forth how Judaism lives for American Jews at home, through the life cycle, in the synagogue, and in the Jewish community at large. The principal goals of this section are two. First, I want the students to grasp that Judaism is a living and vital religion that exercises the power of enchantment and transformation over the lives of real people—from the perspective of our students, other Americans, like but unlike themselves. The students learn, therefore, that there are different modes of religiosity, different ways by which people may be religious or express their deepest convictions besides the modes deemed conventional in American Protestant Christianity. Second, I want the students to recognize that a given religion may involve more than a single formulation. In chapter 4 I contrast the private and familial life of Judaism and the public and community life of the Jews, pointing out that quite distinct sets of symbols and myths prove operative. This requires the distinction, familiar in the study of religion, between the religion that serves at home and the one that takes place in the public square and is called "civil religion." Here students will recognize that just as there is a civil religion in America, so there is a corporate and communal Judaism, one that is public and that holds diverse people together. The contrast between the Judaism of home and family, deriving from the received Torah, and the Judaism of Holocaust and Redemption makes the point. This then yields recognition that in the world today some received rites and beliefs truly change people and others do not; and it raises the question of why a given rite works its enchantment, while another does not. That is a variation on the further question, Why does a religion work when it works, and why does it not work when it does not work?—a question that arises whenever we compare what the holy books say about a religion and its doctrines and practices with what the living generation that receives the holy books actually believes and does.

The anthology for Part One emphasizes descriptions of American Jews in relationship to Judaism. My interpretive essay raises the question that I think should interest students most of all. Judaism, they know, is a religion with a long history. How has America affected Judaism? What is Judaic and what is distinctively American in the American Judaism with which we begin this introduction to Judaism? This section is intended to raise the final questions for class discussion and debate in the first unit of the course.

Part Two
The Torah:
Judaism in Holy Books and in History

Drawing upon my *Self-Fulfilling Prophecy: Exile and Return in the History of Judaism* (Boston: Beacon Press, 1987; South Florida Studies in the History of Judaism, Atlanta: Scholars Press, 1990), this unit—the shank of the course—covers three subjects: the history of the formation of Judaism, the classical literature of Judaism, and the modern and contemporary age and its Judaisms. The questions that predominate are, Why does a given Judaism—here, rabbinic Judaism or "the Judaism of the dual Torah, oral and written"—enjoy the standing of self-evident truth for as long as it does (from the fourth century to the nineteenth)? and When and why does that same Judaism lose its power to compel assent when it does and for those for whom it does? These two questions—why does it work when it works, why does it not work when it does not work—belong together, for if we cannot answer the one, we cannot address the other. But at stake in dealing with both is a general theory of where, when, and why a given religious system serves or does not serve, and if students come with curiosity not about their own particular religion but about religion in general—religion and the social order—then that defines the fundamental and generative issue. That question, moreover, should divert attention from the questions pursued out of all context concerning the truth of religious allegations, the apologetics resting on well-rehearsed arguments. For ideas out of context are merely slogans. But in social context they form the mainbeams of society: the accepted truths, the self-evident propositions that shape attitudes and inform action.

The basic attitude that comes to expression in the position outlined here is expressed, in the context not of the history of religion but of the history of ideas, by R. Jackson Wilson:

> There can be no serious history of ideas that is not also the history of the social experience of the people who have them. Apart from that experience, where their meaning is grounded, ideas may have a chronology, but not a history.

Wilson writes not about the history of Judaism in the first century, but about the life of William Lloyd Garrison, the American abolitionist in the nineteenth century. But in these words he presents the challenge to all of us who find religion a critical force in the formation of world civilization. It is to relate religious ideas to the social experience of the people who hold and respond to those ideas—to relate, but not to reduce those ideas to that experience—so that we may better understand how religion works. My premise in Part Two, then, is that we better understand a religion when we can relate its ideas—theology, myth, holy books, modes of exegesis—to the social world of the people to whom those ideas proved self-evidently true, the right reply to the relevant question not of the day but of all eternity, as those people in the here and now experienced eternity.

Chapter 5, on the formation of the first Judaism or Judaic system, set forth in literary form in the Pentateuch (the Five Books of Moses), emphasizes that Judaism begins with the Pentateuch, and the Pentateuch comes to closure with Ezra, ca. 450 B.C.E. While biblical scholarship is nearly unanimous on that point, some students may find it difficult to make sense of the notion that the stories about Abraham, Isaac, Jacob, Moses and the exodus are to be read in the context of the final statement that sets them forth, which is the Pentateuch as we have it. This is not a course in Old Testament history, archeology, and religion, and it would not serve to challenge students' profoundly held convictions on those matters. The text need not offend people who take a different view of matters, and I like to think that students and teachers who read Scripture as an account of how events happened as composed by Moses will find the patience to see things in a different way—if only for the purpose of argument. The main point for this course is that the pentateuchal account explains the events of exile and return, and that explanation proved particularly formative in light of the destruction of the Second Temple in 586 B.C.E. and the return to Zion in the time of Ezra in 450. Bible-believing students and professors will find their faith strengthened by that observation, and nothing would please me more than their willingness to discover in matters of unbelief firmer grounds for belief. I do not imagine, to be sure, that the discussion of the contribution to the Pentateuch of J (the Yahwist) will make much sense. I introduce the Yahwist's perspective to provide a contrast with the Judaic system put forth by the Pentateuch as framed by the priestly editors in the end. If that brief section is troublesome, I would prefer that Bible-believing students simply move on; nothing else in this book will give offense, and much in these pages will prove illuminating, both for Bible-believers and for others. I certainly do not want this textbook to precipitate classroom debates on the veracity of Scripture, and I do want students of a variety of religious beliefs, as well as students who are not at all religious, to find this textbook interesting and educationally valuable.

The main point is that the Pentateuch is the first Judaic system (whether put forth by Moses or by Ezra), and that it explains, above all, that the possession of the Land is covenanted, that Israel's life is a gift, not a given, and that God's will for Israel may lead to exile by way of penalty for disloyalty to the covenant, as well as to restoration in response to Israel's repentance and reconciliation with God. Hence Judaism would become, from that point forward, a sequence of religious systems all built around the experiences of exile and return, alienation and reconciliation.

Drawing on my *Self-Fulfilling Prophecy. The Midrash: An Introduction. The Mishnah: An Introduction* (Northvale, N.J.: Jason Aronson, 1989); *The Midrash: An Introduction* (Northvale, N.J.: Jason Aronson, 1990); and *Torah through the Ages: A Short History of Judaism* (Philadelphia: Trinity Press International; and London: SCM, 1990), chapters 6 through 10 set forth the history and literature of rabbinic Judaism, which appeals to the myth of the dual Torah, oral and written, that was revealed to Moses at Sinai, including the written Torah, the Hebrew Scriptures known to Christianity as the Old Testament, along with the substantial exegetical literature contained in the Midrash-compilations of the first six centuries C.E.; and the oral Torah ultimately written down in the Mishnah and its two vast exegetical continuators, the Talmud of the Land of Israel (Yerushalmi) and the Talmud of Babylonia (Bavli), ca. 400 and 600 C.E., respectively. In these chapters, students of the New Testament and Christian origins will find out what they want to know about Judaism. A secondary purpose of this textbook anthology is to serve as a reading for the "Jewish background" week(s) of introductions to the New Testament. The anthology concentrates on the exegesis of Scripture in rabbinic Judaism (Midrash), because for class reading and discussion the substantive chapters amply cite passages of the Mishnah and the two Talmuds.

The Judaism that took shape in the first six centuries, rabbinic Judaism or the Judaism of the dual Torah, succeeded in its goals for a long time. The reasons for success and failure and examples of how religions make progress or seem to decline in attraction may be introduced in this context. The historical exposition of the success of the Judaism of the dual Torah is aimed at provoking thought on where, when, and why a religion works, and why it ceases to work or, at least, meets competition in the very group that it means to address. Given the changing characteristics of the religious scene today, the issue should provoke considerable thought in the classroom. Chapters 10 and 11 deal with Judaism from the completion of the formative age (ca. 600), to modern times. Chapter 10 provides an account of "what happened then," once the faith had taken shape and while it was the paramount and authoritative Judaism for nearly all Jews in the world, wherever they lived. The important question is, How do we know that a religious system predominates? The answer, I propose, is, when heresies find their definition within the symbolic structure of a given system. If you can dictate the issues for debate, then you dominate, whether or not your position then prevails.

The two fundamental points of rabbinic Judaism, as we see in chapters 6 to 9, are, first, that the Torah is in two parts, written and oral, and, second, that the master of the oral Torah, the sage, also will be the Messiah, so the Messiah is going to be a sage of the Torah. The two most important heretical movements in Judaism from ancient to modern times were Karaism, which rejected the doctrine of the oral Torah and claimed God revealed only the written Torah; and Sabbateanism, which held that the Messiah would not be a sage but a man who rejected the Torah in its entirety. These movements are described. Does that mean nothing new can be accommodated in a system that predominates? To the contrary, the mark of a system in control is its capacity to absorb and make its own what originates in other circumstances altogether. The example for Judaism is Hasidism, which began—so it is generally maintained—as a Judaism critical of the Judaism of the dual Torah but ended up a principal component of that same Judaism.

Chapter 11 then addresses the question of how, in the aftermath of the advent of a world order not defined by Christianity, in particular (within the experience of Jews) the period dating from the American Constitution of 1787 and the French Revolution of 1789, political conditions precipitated a new urgent question, one that the

Judaism of the dual Torah did not address and that Christianity in its long age of paramountcy had never required Jews to consider: How to be both Jewish and something else. In context, this was both Jewish and French, or British, or German, or American. And that simple shift, in which Jews found themselves in a new political circumstance, produced questions other than those that the rabbinic Judaism had so long answered with such remarkable power of persuasion.

The anthology for these two chapters fills in important gaps in the narrative, which focuses upon only primary questions. We begin with attention to a fundamental holy book of Judaism, the Code of Jewish Law that guides everyday life for contemporary adherents to Orthodox Judaism and that, further, formed the authoritative guide for nearly all practitioners of Judaism before the nineteenth century. The essay by Isadore Twersky introduces that classic. Abraham J. Heschel provides the portrait of Jewish mysticism. Since rabbinic Judaism in modern times encompasses important theological systems, we then proceed to a theological essay by the premier theological mind of our day, Emil L. Fackenheim, who writes on theology in general and the theology that emerged in the aftermath of the Holocaust in particular. Finally, the anthology ends with a profound meditation on the Jews and Judaism by the great social philosopher of Judaism, Ben Halpern.

Part Three
The Jewish People and the Torah

We close with the most difficult and important task—to sum up and put together everything we have learned. That strikes me as the work that all of us must do when we study a religion: in the end define what we mean by that religion. This book has presented two very distinct kinds of materials: Judaism as lived by the Jewish people in America ("Jewish Americans") and Judaism as defined by the Torah, the holy books of Judaism. At the same time, I also have underlined the fact that through history there have been many Judaisms, just as today we recognize in this country at least two distinct Judaisms, each with its own symbolic structure, myth, canon of holy books, and the like. How then do all things fit together? The final chapter—which draws on the opening and closing parts of my *Torah through the Ages: A Short History of Judaism* (Philadelphia: Trinity Press International; and London: SCM, 1990)—raises that question and offers material toward a useful definition.

But keep in mind that a definition is always for a given purpose, thus, "For the purposes of joining a synagogue, how is Judaism defined?" will produce a different answer than will the question, "For the purposes of becoming a citizen of the State of Israel, which accords automatic citizenship to all Jews, hence to all who profess Judaism, how is Judaism defined?" It seems to me that by the end of this book students will have been reflecting on the question of definition; and if the course succeeds, one mark will be that the students will carry over from their study of Judaism to their study of other religions, including Christianity, that same question. That is, of course, the point at which the academic study of religion shades over into the consideration of theological questions, an appropriate conclusion for a course about Judaism. The work, of course, concludes with a brief summary of the main points of the course, which will help students see Judaism whole and also in context.

The anthology for Part Three provides a laboratory experiment in defining Judaism. We take up two distinct approaches to the problem of defining Judaism for an encyclopedia, the cutting edge of knowledge. The first is the definition of Judaism supplied by Louis Jacobs for the article titled "Judaism" in the *Encyclopaedia Judaica* (1971). I present only the part of his article that defines Judaism. Students by now will have ample knowledge to discern the premises of Jacobs's definition, his appeal to (1) theology, and (2) a linear and continuous harmonious history of a single Judaism. Judaism is then given a theological definition. The solution to the problem of diversity is discovered in the notion that there were certain "essential" beliefs, and these beliefs are set forth in sequence, governing the unfolding of that single unitary "Judaism" that the author posits. This definition then is supposed to cover everything, leave out nothing, and hold the whole together. The second reading is William Scott Green's analysis of how the current *Encyclopedia of Religion* treats Judaism. Having taken this course to the conclusion, students will readily sympathize with Green's view that the new encyclopedia treats Judaism with a combination of ignorance and contempt. Here, too, Green points to the highly theological character of the description and the theological definition given by a leading Reform Judaic theologian.

At this point students may well wish to try their hand at defining Judaism for a variety of distinct purposes. If students emerge with a grasp of the whole and some detailed knowledge of the parts, then the study of Judaism will have made its mark on their ideas on the nature of religion, with special reference to its place in the social order and its impact upon world civilization.

POSTSCRIPT

Let me close by paraphrasing Wilson: There can be no serious history of a religion that is not also the history of the social experience of the people who believe and practice that religion. Apart from that experience, where their meaning is grounded, religious ideas may have a chronology, but no relevance to outsiders interested not in religions, but religion. And in my view we can understand the world only when we can make sense of religion in the world. Too much depends upon and is decided by religions for us to pretend, any longer, that we can explain what we see without knowing how beliefs inform and shape the world in which we live. Those who dismiss religion as a relic simply cannot hope to grasp the world today, let alone anticipate what is going to be tomorrow.

I hope that teachers and students who use this book will write to me at the Department of Religious Studies, University of South Florida, Tampa, Florida 33620, and tell me whether this fresh approach to teaching about Judaism—starting in the present, emphasizing the faith as lived and practiced in our own country, then turning to the classical writings and their historical context, and finally asking about how one might define Judaism—proved interesting and helped you meet your goals for this course. Suggestions you may have on how the book may be made of still greater educational use will be gladly received and much appreciated: What information did you need that was not provided? What works, what does not work? Which sections or readings were unclear or not engaging? Which sections did you find most interesting? In all, how can I do a better job?

Glossary

Ab, ninth of. Fast day commemorating five disasters that fell on that day: (1) the decree that those in the exodus of Egypt should not enter the Promised Land; (2) the destruction of the First Temple in 586 B.C.E.; (3) the destruction of the Second Temple in 70 C.E.; (4) the taking of Betar, where the rebels against Rome in 135 made their last stand; and (5) the ploughing up of Jerusalem after that same war in 136. The day stands for Israel's national disasters and is observed through fasting, prayer, and reading the book of Lamentations.

Adam. Adam, man.

Adamah. Earth.

Additional service (Heb. *musaf*). Corresponding to the additional offerings presented in the Temple on the Sabbath, festivals, and holy days, the additional service liturgy recounts the Temple offerings on those occasions.

Aggadah. Narrative. A native category of Judaism, aggadah, or lore, is defined in contrast to halakhah, law. Lore makes normative statements about matters of attitude and belief; law, about action and conduct. Aggadah takes Old Testament narratives and retells them to make exemplary points about right thinking and virtuous behavior.

Alenu. Prayer at the conclusion of morning and evening worship: "It is our duty to praise the Lord of all . . ."

Anti-Semitism. Hatred of Jews based on the belief that Jews form a race and inherit bad traits of character, personality, or culture.

Apocalyptic prophecy. Prophecy in the form of visions, rather than teachings of God to the prophet.

Apocrypha. Ancient Israelite writings not accorded a place in the canon, or approved list of documents, of the Hebrew Scriptures or "Old Testament."

Ashkenazic tradition. European or North African and Middle Eastern Jews. The principal cultural divisions of Jews throughout the world, and especially in the State of Israel, are between Ashkenazi and Sephardi Jews. A Jew whose origins are in central or eastern Europe is called Ashkenazi; one from Spain or Portugal is called Sephardi.

B.C.E. Before the Common Era (= B.C.).

Bar Kokhba War. Jewish war in the Land of Israel (Palestine) against Rome, fought from 132 to 135 C.E.

Bar/bat mitzvah. At puberty, a boy (bar) or girl (bat) becomes responsible for keeping religious duties. A bar mitzvah is a male who is responsible for observing the commandments; a bat mitzvah, a female. The bar/bat mitzvah is celebrated by calling the boy or girl to the Torah and having him or her read from the Torah and also read the passage of the Prophets read in the synagogue on a given Sabbath.

Bavli (Talmud of Babylonia). A compilation of clarifications and expansions of statements in the Mishnah. There are two Talmuds; one, completed in the Land of Israel ca. 400–500 C.E., is called the Talmud of the Land of Israel (in Hebrew, the Yerushalmi or Talmud of Jerusalem, even though it was not prepared in Jerusalem). The other is the Talmud of Babylonia (in Hebrew, the Bavli). It was concluded ca. 600 C.E. in Babylonia, a province at the western frontier of the Iranian Empire that corresponds to present-day Iraq. Both Talmuds are organized as commentaries to the Mishnah. They are, however, entirely autonomous documents, and the later Babylonian Talmud does not expand upon the earlier one but forms its own discussions in accord with its own program. The Talmud of the Land of Israel treats thirty-nine of the Mishnah's sixty-three tractates, the Talmud of Babylonia, thirty-seven of them.

Bayit. House.

Berit milah. Circumcision as a mark of the covenant between

God and Israel; the word *berit* means both covenant and circumcision.

Bet Yosef. House of Joseph, the title of a work on Jewish law.

Binah. Understanding.

Birkat ha-minim. A curse against heretics and schismatics.

Birkat hammazon. Blessing of food, recited after meals. See Grace after Meals.

C.E. Common Era (= A.D.).

Circumcision. Removing the foreskin of the penis as a mark of God's covenant with Israel.

Conservative Judaism. A religious movement in American Judaism that adheres to the law of the Torah and accepts the necessity of change in the law so as to make it possible to observe the Torah under the conditions of contemporary life.

Covenant. An agreement, or contract, between God and Israel, the Holy People, that binds each party to adhere to certain rules.

Day of Atonement. Yom Kippur, day of fasting and prayer in penitence for sin, observed five days prior to the first new moon following the autumnal equinox.

Days of Awe. The New Year (Rosh Hashanah) and the Day of Atonement (Yom Kippur), observing the creation of the world. A time of judgment in which God judges all humanity and decrees what will happen in the year to come; observed from the fifteenth to the fifth day prior to the first new moon following the autumnal equinox.

Dead Sea Scrolls. Writings of ancient Jews found in caves by the Dead Sea, widely believed to derive from the Essenes, an ancient Jewish sect.

Diaspora. Jews living outside of the Land of Israel, as citizens of the nations in which they dwell.

Dual Torah. Belief that God revealed the Torah to Moses at Sinai in two media, oral and written. The written part corresponds to what Christianity knows as the Old Testament; the Oral Torah came to be written down in the Mishnah and elaborated in various commentaries to the Mishnah, ultimately in the two Talmuds (the Talmud of the Land of Israel, the Talmud of Babylonia).

Eddammae. "I shall be like . . ."

Eighteen Benedictions (Shemoneh esre). The silent Prayer, recited morning, noon, and night, in the liturgy of Judaism, which consists of nineteen paragraphs, each ending with a blessing ("blessed are you, Lord, who . . .").

El Male Rahamin. "God, full of mercy"; prayer recited for the dead.

Elohim. God.

Emunah. Faith.

Erusin. Betrothal.

Essene Judaism. A Judaism formed in ancient times by Jews who lived in communities that observed laws of cleanness outside of the Temple where these laws generally applied, and who possessed beliefs of their own in addition to those held in common by other Jews.

Exegesis. The interpretation and explanation of the meanings of words and phrases in Scripture.

Exile and redemption. The belief that the Jews outside of the Land of Israel are living in exile, but the Messiah, when he comes, will redeem them from exile and bring them back to the Land of Israel, where they will live under the law of God and the rule of the Messiah.

Exodus. When, led by Moses, ancient Israel escaped from Egyptian slavery.

Ezrat nashim. The women's court in the Temple in ancient times and, by transfer, a place in which women recite their prayers separated from men.

First Temple. The temple built in Jerusalem by Solomon ca. 900 B.C.E., where the animal sacrifices required by the Torah were offered.

Five Books of Moses. Genesis, Exodus, Leviticus, Numbers, Deuteronomy.

Geburah. The divine attribute of power; the All-Powerful.

Genesis Rabbah. The systematic verse-by-verse reading of the book of Genesis, compiled ca. 400 against the background of the world-historical change represented by the conversion of the Roman Empire to Christianity. Rome now claimed to be Israel, that is, Christian and heir to the testament of the founders. Sages of Genesis Rabbah affirmed that Rome is Esau, or Moab, or Ishmael. That concession—Rome is a sibling, a close relative of Israel—represents an implicit recognition of Christianity's claim to share the patrimony of Judaism, to be descended from Abraham and Isaac. Sages in Genesis Rabbah represent Rome as Israel's brother, counterpart, and nemesis, the one thing standing in the way of Israel's and the world's ultimate salvation.

Gentile. Anyone not born in Israel, the Holy People (not to be confused with the modern State of Israel) covenanted with God at Sinai through the Torah; or anyone not converted to the religion Judaism.

Gittin. Mishnah tractate on writs of divorce: how they are prepared and delivered (chaps. 1–3); the law of agency in writs of divorce: receiving and handling it over (chaps. 6–7); stipulations and conditions in writs of divorce (chap. 7); invalid writs of divorce by reason of improper delivery, improper preparation, improper stipulations, or invalid witnesses (chaps. 8–9).

Gnosticism. A religious movement in ancient times whose adherents believed that people are saved by what they know, that is, by secret knowledge.

Grace after Meals. Birkat hammazon, the blessing recited after meals that praises God for the food that sustains, and for the gift of the holy land and its produce, and that asks for the rebuilding of Jerusalem.

Gufe torah. The basics, or essentials, of the Torah.

Habad. The first three letters of the Hebrew words for wisdom, understanding, and knowledge.

Haggadah. The narrative of exodus from Egypt, recited at the Passover seder.

Halakhah, Halakhot. "The way things are done," from Heb. *halakh* (go). More broadly, the prescriptive, legal tradition; the law; a final decision.

Halisah. The rite of removing the shoe. The surviving brother of a childless, deceased man is required either to marry his sister-in-law, that is, levirate marriage, or to undertake the rite of removing the shoe (halisah).

Hallel. Psalms of thanksgiving (Psalms 113—118) chanted in the synagogue on Tabernacles, Hanukkah, Passover, Pentecost, and New Moon.

Hashem. "The Name," that is, the name of God; God.

Hasidic Judaism, Hasidism. A Judaism that took shape in the eighteenth century around holy men, or tsaddiks (called "rebbes"), who were believed to stand in a special relationship to God and to mediate God's blessing to humanity. Stories about the doings of the rebbes were preserved.

Havdalah. The ceremony that marks the end of the Sabbath, at sunset on Saturday night, and the beginning of the ordinary work.

Havurah, Havurot. Fellowships of persons who share a common discipline and commitment in a holy way of life.

Heschel, Abraham Joshua (1907–1972). American Jewish theologian and scholar of Judaism, author of ten books on philosophy of religion and of Judaism, rabbinic theology, and Hasidism. Born in Poland, Heschel came to the United States in 1940, brought by Hebrew Union College, Cincinnati. He became Professor of Jewish Philosophy and Mysticism at the Jewish Theological Seminary of America in 1945. The most influential theologian of Judaism of the twentieth century, Heschel developed a method he called depth-theology. His principal books are *Man Is Not Alone: A Philosophy of Religion; God in Search of Man: A Philosophy of Judaism; The Prophets;* and *A Passion for Truth.* He took an active part in the civil rights movement and marched with Martin Luther King, Jr., in Selma, Alabama.

Hesed. Loving kindness. Acts beyond the strict requirement of the law.

High priest. The head of the priesthood of the Temple, who bears special responsibilities in preparing the animal sacrifices on the Day of Atonement in accord with Leviticus 16.

Hod. Glory.

Hokhmah. Wisdom.

Holocaust. The systematic murder of more than five million European Jews by the Nazis between 1935 and 1945.

Holy People. Israel, covenanted with God through the Torah revealed by God to Moses at Mount Sinai.

Huppah. Marriage canopy.

Israel. In Judaism the Holy People whom God first loved and to whom God gave the Torah, the Land of Israel, and much else. In the theology and canon of Judaism, the word "Israel" refers to the People and, by extension, may bear such qualifications as "Land of . . . ," "king of . . . ," and any number of other subordinate categories. When people, Jews or Christians, call themselves "Israel" and refer to that same group of which the Hebrew Scriptures or "Old Testament" speaks, they claim to embody the Israel chosen by God in the here and now. To be Israel in that sense generally involves one of three definitions of Israel: (1) the extended family of Abraham, Isaac, and Jacob, who was called Israel, hence Israel as a genealogy; (2) a people which, as a social entity, is unique and has no analogy to any other social entity, hence, a social entity that is sui generis, defined by the holy way of life and worldview characteristic of that social entity; and (3) a mixture of the two, that is, "Israel" as both family and a unique or singular nation defined not by genealogy but by taxic genus.

Jerusalem Talmud. See Yerushalmi.

Jewish state. The State of Israel, created in 1948 to provide a homeland for all Jews who wished to live there.

Jubilee Year. Every seventh year the land was to lie fallow, and at the end of seven such periods, that is, in the fiftieth year, the land was to lie fallow for two successive years; inherited land was to be returned to the family that had inherited it.

Judaism of Holocaust and Redemption. A Judaism that takes shape around two principal symbols: the identification of the destruction of the Jews of Europe (holocaust) and the founding of the State of Israel (redemption).

Kabbalah. Mystical doctrine.

Kabbalist. One who studies and practices mystical doctrine.

Kaddish. Prayer of sanctification and praise of God, recited at various points in the liturgy of Judaism, including as a memorial prayer for the dead.

Karaism. A sect in Judaism, formed ca. 700 by Anan Ken David, that rejected the authority of the Oral Torah and therefore rabbinic Judaism. Karaite Judaism did not accept that God revealed to Moses at Sinai an Oral Torah in addition to the Written Torah, and maintained that only the Written Torah—the Pentateuch— was valid for Judaism. The Karaite system of Judaism therefore accepted only the authority and law of the Pentateuch and applied that law in as literal a way as possible. Karaites rejected such customs as the observance of Hanukkah, the use of certain ritual objects, the rigid application of scriptural laws on the Sabbath, ritual cleanness, and consanguineous marriage. They prohibited the use of light and fire on the Sabbath and travel more than 2,000 yards beyond one's house. They required washing of the hands and feet and removal of the shoes before entering the synagogue or reading from the Torah. The liturgy of the Karaite synagogue also differed from that of the rabbinate one. Because they rejected the authority of the Oral Torah and the practices of rabbinic Judaism, the Karaites were declared schismatics, and marriage between them and rabbanite Jews ultimately was banned by the latter. They remained numerous in the Middle East and in the Russian Crimea until the twentieth century.

Kashrut. What is suitable or acceptable; applies to many aspects of life, including food.

Kawwanah. The proper intentionality, doing the right thing for the right motive.

Keter. Crown.

Ketubah. Marriage settlement, providing support for a woman if her husband divorces her or dies. Plural: ketubot.

Kibbutz. Collective farm in the State of Israel.

King of Kings. The most important king. In Judaism, God is called king of kings of kings.

Kol nidre. The prayer recited at the beginning of the Day of Atonement, relieving the worshiper of vows made to God during the prayer year.

Kosher. Suitable, fit.

Land of Israel. The Holy Land, also known as Palestine.

Levir. The surviving brother of a childless, deceased man; required either to marry his sister-in-law (levirate marriage) or to undertake the rite of removing the shoe (see halisah).

Levirate rules. Rules governing the union of the levir and the widow of the deceased childless brother.

Leviticus Rabbah. Compilation of comments on episodic verses of the book of Leviticus, formed into thirty-seven propositional composites. Unlike Genesis Rabbah, a verse-by-verse commentary, the paramount and dominant exegetical construction in Leviticus Rabbah is the base-verse/intersecting verse exegesis. A verse of Leviticus is cited (hence, base-verse), and another verse (the intersecting verse) from such books as Job, Proverbs, Qohelet, or Psalms is then cited. The latter, not the former, is subjected to detailed and systematic exegesis. But the exegetical exercise ends by leading the intersecting verse back to the base-verse and reading the latter in terms of the former.

Lubovitch. The most important Hasidic Judaism in the world today.

Maccabees. The Jewish family that fought against Syrian-Greek rule and in 167 B.C.E. restored the Jewish state in Jerusalem.

Magen Abraham. The shield of Abraham.

Malkut. Dominion; God's rule.

Mamzer (mamzerim). The child of a couple that is not permitted by the law of the Torah to marry, such as unions prohibited in Leviticus 18.

Matzoh. Unleavened bread eaten on Passover.

Mazel tov. Good luck; under a good star.

Mekhilta attributed to R. Ishmael. A Midrash-compilation of the sages of Judaism on parts of the book of Exodus, Mekhilta joins episodic commentary on verses with expositions of topics, defined by the themes of scriptural narrative or the dictates of biblical law. The authorities named derive from the period before 200, but the work of closure probably was accomplished in the third century C.E. It is made up of three kinds of materials: (1) ad hoc and episodic exegeses of some passages of Scripture; (2) propositional and argumentative essays in exegetical form, in which theological principles are set forth and demonstrated; and (3) topical articles, some of them sustained, many of them well crafted, about important subjects of the Judaism of the dual Torah.

Melog property. A wife's property that comes into a marriage which the husband may use and enjoy but must restore to the wife if he divorces her or dies.

Merkaba mystics. Mystics who envisioned God riding on a chariot (Merkabah) and conceived of a journey to heaven, along the lines of Ezekiel 1.

Middot. Mishnah tractate that describes the layout of the Temple: watch posts and gates (chap. 1); Temple mount (chap. 2); altar and porch (chap. 4); sanctuary and courtyard (chaps. 4–5).

Midrash. Exegesis of Scripture. Also applied to collection of such exegeses. Midrash-compilations exhibit distinctive traits. Seen individually and also as a group, they are connected, intersect at a few places but not over the greater part of their territory, and are not compilations but free-standing compositions. These documents emerge as sharply differentiated and clearly defined, each through its distinctive viewpoint, particular polemic, and formal and aesthetic qualities.

Midrashim. Compilations of Midrash-exegeses of Scripture.

Minhah. Prayer recited at twilight.

Minyan. Quorum for prayer; ten persons (in Orthodox Judaism, ten males).

Mishnah. A philosophical law-code promulgated by Judah the Prince ca. 200 C.E. The Mishnah is in six parts, comprising sixty-three tractates on agriculture laws, festival and Sabbath law, family and personal status, torts, damages, and civil law, laws pertaining to the sanctuary and to rules of ritual cleanness. Through details of the law, a philosophical system of hierarchical classification of this-worldly things is set forth, showing that many things derive from one, and one thing encompasses many; hence, the hierarchical unity of all being is set forth. The Mishnah's premise is that one God has generated many kinds and classes of things. It classifies and compares, finding the right rule for each matter and each important situation by determining whether one case is like or not like another. If it is like another, it follows the rule governing that other; and if not, it follows the opposite of that rule. In this way an orderly and logical way to sort chaos and discover the inner order of being generates the balanced, stable, and secure world described by the Mishnah. Historical events, when they enter at all, lose their one-time and unprecedented character and are shown to follow, even to generate, a fixed rule; events therefore are the opposite of eventful. This age and the age to come, history and the end of history play only a small role. Even the figure of the Messiah serves as a classification, namely, designation or anointment distinguishes one priest from another.

The Mishnah focuses upon the sanctification of Israel; sanctification means, first, distinguishing Israel in all its dimensions from the world in all its ways; second, establishing the stability, order, regularity, predictability, and reliability of Israel in the world of nature and supernature, in particular at moments and in contexts of danger. Danger means instability, disorder, irregularity, uncertainty, and betrayal. Each topic of the system as a whole takes up a critical and indispensable moment or context of social being. Through what is said about each of the Mishnah's principal topics, what the halakhic system as a whole wishes to declare is fully expressed. Yet if the parts severally and jointly give the message of the whole, the whole cannot exist without all of the parts, so well joined and carefully crafted are they. This brings us to a survey of the several parts of the system, the six divisions and their sixty-three tractates.

The Division of Agriculture, whose principal point is that the Land is holy because God has a claim both on it and on what it produces. God's claim must be honored by setting aside a portion of the produce for those for whom God has designated it. God's ownership must be acknowledged by observing the rules God has laid down for use of the Land. The Division is divided along two lines: (1) rules for producing crops in a state of holiness—tractates Kilayim, Shebiit, Orlah; and (2) rules for disposing of crops in accord with the rules of holiness—tractates Peah, Demai, Terumot, Maaserot, Maaser Sheni, Hallah, Bikkurim, Berakhot.

The Division of Appointed Times forms a system in which the advent of a holy day, such as the Sabbath of creation, sanctifies the life of the Israelite village by imposing on the village rules modeled on those of the Temple. The purpose of the system, therefore, is to bring into alignment the moment of sanctification of the village and the life of the home with the moment of sanctification of the Temple on those same occasions of appointed times. The underlying and generative theory of the system is that the village is the mirror image of the Temple. If things are done in one way in the Temple, they will be done in the opposite way in the village. Together the village and the Temple on the occasion of the holy day therefore form a continuum, a completed creation, thus awaiting sanctification.

The Division of Women defines the women in the social economy of Israel's supernatural and natural reality. Women acquire definition wholly in relationship to men, who impart form to the Israelite social economy. The status of women is affected through both supernatural and natural, this-worldly action. What man and woman do on earth provokes a response in heaven, and the correspondences are perfect. So women are defined and secured both in heaven and here on earth, and that position is always and invariably relative to men. The principal interest for the Mishnah is the points at which a woman becomes and ceases to be holy to a particular man, that is, when she enters and leaves the marital union. These transfers of women are the dangerous and disorderly points in the relationship of woman to man and, therefore, the Mishnah states, to society as well. The formation of the marriage comes under discussion in Qiddushin and Ketubot, as well as in Yebamot. The rules for the duration of the marriage are scattered throughout but derive especially from parts of Ketubot, Nedarim, and Nazir, on the one side, and the paramount unit of Sotah, on the other. The dissolution of the marriage is dealt with in Gittin, as well as in Yebamot. Important issues are the transfer of property, along with women, covered in Ketubot and to some measure in Qiddushin, and the proper documentation of the transfer of women and property, treated in Ketubot and Gittin. The critical issues, therefore, turn upon legal documents (such as writs of divorce) and legal recognition of changes in the ownership of property (for example, through the collection of the settlement of a marriage contract by a widow, through the provision of a dowry, or through the disposition of the property of a woman during the period in which she is married).

Within this orderly world of documentary and procedural concerns, a place is made for the disorderly conception of the marriage not formed by human volition but decreed in heaven, the levirate connection. Yebamot states that supernature sanctifies a woman to a man (under the conditions of the levirate connection). What it says by indirection is that man, like God, can sanctify that relationship between a man and a woman and can also effect the cessation of the sanctity of that same relationship. Five of the seven tractates of the Division of Women are devoted to the formation and dissolution of the marital bond. Of them, three treat what is done by man here on earth, that is, the formation of a marital bond through betrothal and marriage contract and the dissolution through divorce and its consequences: Qiddushin, Ketubot, and Gittin. One of them is devoted to what is done by woman here on earth: Sotah. And Yebamot, the greatest of the seven in size and in formal and substantive brilliance, deals with the corresponding heavenly intervention into the formation and end of a marriage: the effect of death upon both forming the marital bond and dissolving it through death. The other two tractates, Nedarim and Nazir, draw the two realms of reality, heaven and earth, into one as they work out the effects of vows, perhaps because vows taken by women and subject to the confirmation or abrogation of the father or husband make a deep impact upon the marital life of the woman who has taken them.

The Division of Damages comprises two subsystems that fit together in a logical way. One part presents rules for the normal conduct of civil society. These cover commerce, trade, real estate, and other matters of everyday intercourse, as well as mishaps, such as damages by chattels and persons, fraud, overcharge, interest, and the like, in that same context of everyday social life. The other part describes the institutions that govern the normal conduct of civil society, that is, courts of administration, and the penalties at the disposal of the government for the enforcement of the law. The two subjects form a single tight and systematic dissertation on the nature of Israelite society and its economic, social, and political relationships as the Mishnah envisages them. The main point of the first of the two parts of the Division is expressed in the sustained unfolding of the three Babas—Baba Qamma, Baba Mesia, and Baba Batra. That point is that the task of society is to maintain perfect stasis, to preserve the prevailing situation, and to secure the stability of all relationships. To this end, in buying and selling, giving and taking, borrowing and lending, it is important that there be an essential equality of interchange. No party in the end should have more than what he had at the outset, and none should be the victim of a sizable shift in fortune and circumstance. All parties' rights to, and in, this stable and unchanging economy of society are to be preserved. When the condition of a person is violated, so far as possible the law will secure the restoration of the antecedent status.

The Division of Holy Things speaks of the sacrificial cult and the sanctuary in which the cult is conducted. It presents a system of sacrifice and sanctuary: matters concerning the praxis of the altar and maintenance of the sanctuary. The praxis of the altar involves sacrifice and things set aside for sacrifice and so deemed consecrated. The topic covers these among the eleven tractates of the present Division: Zebahim and part of Hullin, Menahot, Temurah, Keritot, part of Meilah, Tamid, and Qinnim. The maintenance of the sanctuary (inclusive of the personnel) is dealt with in Bekhorot, Arakhin, part of Meilah, Middot, and part of Hullin. Viewed from a distance, therefore, the tractates divide themselves into the following groups (in parentheses are tractates containing relevant materials): (1) rules for the altar and the praxis of the cult: Zebahim, Menahot, Hullin, Keritot, Tamid, Qinnim (Bekhorot, Meilah); (2) rules for the altar and the animals set aside for the cult: Arakhin, Temurah, Meilah (Bekhorot); and (3) rules for the altar and support of the Temple staff and buildings: Bekhorot, Middot (Hullin, Arakhin, Meilah, Tamid). The law pays special attention to the matter of the status of the property of the altar and of the sanctuary, both materials to be utilized in the actual sacrificial rites, and property the value of which supports the cult and sanctuary in general. Both are deemed to be sanctified, that is, "holy things."

The Division of Purities presents a simple system in three principal parts: sources of uncleanness, objects and substances susceptible to uncleanness, and modes of purification from uncleanness. It tells the story of what makes a given object unclean and what makes it clean. The tractates on these several topics are (1) sources of uncleanness: Ohalot, Negaim, Niddah, Makhshirin, Zabim, Tebul Yom; (2) objects and substances susceptible to uncleanness: Kelim, Tohorot, Uqsin; and (3) modes of purification: Parah, Miqvaot, Yadayim. The Division of Purities treats the interplay of persons, food, and liquids. Dry, inanimate objects or food are not susceptible to uncleanness. What is wet is susceptible. So liquids activate the system. What is unclean, moreover, emerges from uncleanness through the operation of liquids, specifically, through immersion in fit water of requisite volume and in natural condition. Liquids thus deactivate the system. Thus, water in its natural condition is what concludes the process by removing uncleanness. Water in its unnatural condition, that is, water deliberately affected by human agency, is what imparts susceptibility to uncleanness to begin with. The uncleanness of persons, furthermore, is signified by body liquids or flux in the case of the menstruating woman (Niddah) and the *zab* (Zabim). Corpse uncleanness is conceived to be a kind of effluent, a viscous gas, which flows like liquid. Utensils receive uncleanness when they form receptacles able to contain liquid. In sum, we have a system in which the invisible flow of fluidlike substances or powers serves to put food, drink, and receptacles into the status of uncleanness and to remove those things from that status. Whether or not we call the system "metaphysical," it certainly has no material base but is conditioned upon highly abstract notions. Thus, in material terms, the effect of liquid is upon food, drink, utensils, and man. The consequence has to do with who may eat and drink what food and liquid, and what food and drink may be consumed in which pots and pans. These loci are specified by tractates on utensils (Kelim) and on food and drink (Tohorot and Uqsin).

The human being is ambivalent. Persons fall in the middle, between sources and loci of uncleanness, because they are both. They serve as sources of uncleanness. They also become unclean. The *zab*, suffering the uncleanness described in Leviticus 15, the menstruating woman, the woman after childbirth, and the person afflicted with the skin ailment described in Leviticus 13 and 14 are all sources of uncleanness. But being unclean, they fall within the system's loci, its program of consequences. So they make other things unclean and are subject to penalties because they are unclean. Unambiguous sources of uncleanness never also constitute loci affected by uncleanness. They always are unclean and never can become clean: the corpse, the dead creeping thing, and things like them. Inanimate sources of uncleanness and inanimate objects are affected by uncleanness. Systemically unique, man and liquids have the capacity to inaugurate the processes of uncleanness (as sources) and also are subject to those same processes (as objects of uncleanness).

Mitzvot. Commandments.

Mohel. A specialist in circumcisions.

Mosaic legislation. Laws given by God to Moses at Sinai.

Musar. Ethics.

Nag Hammadi. The place in Egypt where the Christian Gnostic library was found.

Nazir. Mishnah tractate on the Nazirite that pays special attention to the vow that he or she takes (chaps. 1–4); the offerings presented by a Nazirite at the end of the period of restriction (chaps. 4–5); restrictions on the Nazirite, grape and wine, haircut, corpse-uncleanness (chaps. 6–9).

Nedarim. Mishnah tractate on vows: the language of vows, euphemisms, language of no or limited effect (chaps. 1–3); binding effects of vows (chaps. 4–8); absolution of vows (chaps. 8–11), for example, by a father for the daughter and the husband for a wife (chaps. 10–11); vows not subject to abrogation (chap. 11).

Neo-Orthodoxy. "Modern Orthodoxy," a form of Judaism that maintains Jews can keep the Torah in the received manner and also live lives integrated into Gentile society. Neo-Orthodoxy rejects segregationism in Orthodoxy, which maintains Jews must live completely isolated from everybody else.

Netilat yadayim. The washing of hands prior to a meal, a cultic, not a hygienic washing.

Netsah. Eternity.

Nissuin. The stage at which a marriage is consecrated.

Oral Law. The oral part of the one, whole Torah revealed by God to Moses at Mount Sinai.

Orthodox Judaism. A set of Judaisms that adheres strictly to the law of the Torah.

Palestinian Talmud. See Yerushalmi.

Parashiyyot. Passages, chapters.

Passover (Pessah). The spring festival that commemorates the exodus of Israel from Egypt.

Pentateuch. The Five Books of Moses.

Pharisees (from Heb. *Parush*). Separatist. The Pharisees espoused prophetic ideals and translated them to everyday Jewish life through legislation. Distinctive beliefs according to Josephus: (1) immortality of the soul; (2) existence of angels; (3) divine providence; (4) freedom of will; (5) resurrection of the dead; (6) Oral Torah. Distinctive practices according to the Mishnah and certain passages in the Gospels of Mark and Matthew: observing cultic purity even at home, not only in the Temple; faithfully giving tithes and offerings from food; careful observance of the holiness of the Sabbath day.

Piyyutim. Poems used in synagogue liturgy.

Priestly Code. The passages of the Pentateuch assigned to the authorship of priests, for example, the book of Leviticus.

Promised Land. The Land of Israel, which God promised to give to Abraham and his descendants and which God gave to Israel.

Proof-text. A verse of Scripture cited to prove a proposition.

Pseudepigrapha. Writings assigned to the authorship of an ancient authority other than the persons who actually wrote them.

Qiddushin. Mishnah tractate on betrothals, with a general account of rules of acquisition of persons and property (chap. 1); procedures of betrothal (chap. 2); stipulations in a betrothal, doubts (chap. 3); castes (priest, Levite, Israelite, and other) and who may marry whom (chaps. 3–4).

Qumran. Site of the discovery of some of the Dead Sea Scrolls.

Rabbinic Judaism. The Judaism, formed in the first six centuries C.E., that believed that Moses revealed the Torah in two media— written and oral—and that the sages at any given time are those who are masters of that dual Torah and hence are to define the holy life of Israel.

Rabbis. Collective reference to the masters of the Oral Torah.

Ramah. A place in the Land of Israel.

Rashi. Rabbi Solomon Isaac, of Troyes, France (1040–1105), the first letters of whose name—R SH I—yielded the popular acronym, Rashi. He wrote the most influential commentaries in Judaism to the Hebrew Scriptures and the Babylonian Talmud. His reading of the two foundation documents of Judaism, the Written and the Oral Torah, forms the point of departure for all study. On the Hebrew Scriptures his commentary is eclectic, gathering and arranging received comments into authoritative interpretation. Since Rashi's commentary on the Torah is the one thing Jews study along with Scripture, Judaism's teachings about the Pentateuch are mediated to the pious through Rashi's selection and arrangement of the received tradition. On the Babylonian Talmud the commentary is pedagogical and analytical, explaining the sense of words and the meaning of passages. Since his commentary to the Babylonian Talmud is the primer that affords access to that document, here, too, what the pious learn about that authoritative document is defined by Rashi. Thus he defines the religious world of Judaism from his time to the present.

Raze Torah. Mysteries of the Torah.

Reconstructionist Judaism. A Judaism that believes that God is the power that makes for salvation, rather than a supernatural conception of God.

Redemption (Heb. *geullah*). In Judaism, redemption refers to the transformation of the status and condition of an individual (e.g., the restoring of freedom to a slave) and of the entirety of Israel (e.g., from subjugation to self-government). The "redeemer" could be one who ransomed a kinsman or restored to ownership property that had been inherited and then sold. The act of redemption then carries out familial responsibilities in which one member of a family is responsible to save or redeem another person or property belonging to that same family. God is called redeemer (Job 19:25: "I know that my redeemer lives") when he saves his people. Appearing as redeemer of Israel in the liturgy, God's action in removing Israel from Egypt is identified as one definition of redemption. Redemption is this-worldly and individual, but it is also to take place at the end of time, when God will redeem Israel from the bondage of exile and restore the Jews to the Land of Israel. The Land, too, will be redeemed at that time. Since its theory encompasses the language of redemption, modern Zionism, a political movement, is characterized as a secularized restatement in political terms of the received category.

Reform Judaism. A Judaism that believes Jews can and should live integrated lives but at the same time preserve their distinctive religious heritage.

Revelation at Sinai. At Mount Sinai, God gave ("revealed") the Torah to Moses.

Rosh Hashanah. The New Year, fifteen days prior to the first full moon after the autumnal equinox, celebrates the creation of the world and marks God's judgment of humanity for the coming year.

Roshei yeshivah. Heads of a yeshiva.

Sabbateanism. A Judaism that believed that Shabbatei Zevi, a seventeenth-century mystic, was the Messiah.

Sabbatical years. The seventh year, when the Land of Israel was left fallow.

Sadducees. A sect in Judaism that denied the resurrection of the dead. Rivals of the Pharisees in the time of Jesus.

Sanhedrin. The governing body.

Scribes. Masters of the Torah who were responsible for teaching the Torah and preparing legal documents.

Second Temple period. From 586 B.C.E. to 70 C.E.; began with the destruction of the First Temple of Jerusalem in 586 and the building of the Second Temple of Jerusalem about three generations later.

Seder. Order. A Passover banquet meal commemorating the exodus of Israel from Egypt.

Sefirah, Sefirot. Divine emanations.

Selah. A concluding word in a psalm; a period.

Sephardic. See Ashkenazic.

Seven Blessings. See Sheva berakhot.

Shabbat. The seventh day, the Sabbath, holy day of rest in commemoration of God's rest after creating the world in six days.

Shabos. See Shabbat.

Shavuot. Pentecost.

Shekinah. God's presence in the world.

Shema. "Hear, Israel, the Lord our God, the Lord is One."

Shemoneh esre. See Eighteen Benedictions.

Sheva berakhot. Seven Blessings recited under the marriage canopy in celebration of a wedding.

Shofar. Ram's horn, sounded on the New Year, the celebration of the New Moon, and certain other occasions.

Shomrei mitzvot. Those who keep religious duties.

Shulhan Arukh. The code of Jewish religious law by Joseph Karo. Published in 1565, the work covers (1) ritual obligations of everyday life from dawn to dusk; blessings, prayers, and observances of Sabbaths and festivals (*orah hayyim*); (2) laws governing the conduct of life and life passages, dietary laws, mourning, ethics, piety, and religious virtues, respect for parents, charity (*yoreh deah*); (3) laws of marriage, divorce, and other questions of personal status (*even haezer*); (4) civil law and institutions of the community of Judaism (*hoshen mishpat*). The Shulhan Arukh has been translated into all the languages in which Jews live and is consulted for daily guidance.

Sifra. Commentary to the book of Leviticus. For sizable passages, the sole point of coherence for the discrete sentences or paragraphs of Sifra's authorship derives from the base-verse of Scripture that is subject to commentary. A sizable portion consists simply of the association of completed statements of the Oral Torah with the exposition of the Written Torah, the entirety re-presenting the dual Torah received by Moses at Sinai as one whole Torah. Without the Mishnah or the Tosefta, Sifra's authorship would have had virtually nothing to say about numerous passages of the book of Leviticus. In order to do so, the authorship has constructed through its document, first, the sustained critique of the Mishnah's *Listenwissenschaft*, then, the defense of the Mishnah's propositions on the foundation of scriptural principles of taxonomy, hierarchical classification in particular.

Sifré to Deuteronomy. Verse-by-verse commentary to the book of Deuteronomy, maintaining that Israel stands in a special relationship with God and that that relationship is defined by the contract, or covenant, that God made with Israel. In Sifré to Deuteronomy, the covenant comes to particular expression in two matters—the Land and the Torah. Each marks Israel as different from all other nations, on the one side, and as selected by God, on the other. In these propositions, sages situate Israel in the realm of heaven, finding on earth the stigmata of covenanted election and the concomitant requirement of loyalty and obedience to the covenant. First comes the definition of those traits of God that the authorship finds pertinent: God sits in judgment upon the world, and God's judgment is true and righteous. God punishes faithlessness. Second, the contract, or covenant, produces the result that God has acquired Israel, which God created. The reason is that only Israel among all the nations accepted the Torah, and that is why God made the covenant with Israel. Why is the covenant made only with Israel? The Gentiles did not accept the Torah, while Israel did; and that has made all the difference. Israel recognized God forthwith; the very peace of the world and of nature depends upon God's giving the Torah to Israel. Sifré to Deuteronomy also presents an account of the structure of the intellect.

Sotah. A wife accused of adultery. Mishnah tractate on the ordeal inflicted upon the wife accused of adultery: invoking the ordeal (chap. 1); narrative of the ordeal (chaps. 1–3); rules of imposing the ordeal, exemptions, testimony (chaps. 4–6); rites conducted in Hebrew in addition to that involving the accused wife (chaps. 7–9); the anointed for battle and draft exempts (Deut. 20:1–9) (chap. 8); the rite of breaking the heifer's neck in connection with the neglected corpse (Deut. 21:1–9) (chap. 9).

Streimel. A fur hat worn by Hasidic Jews.

Sukkah. Booth erected in celebration of Sukkot.

Sukkah. Mishnah tractate devoted to the festival of Tabernacles: objects used in celebrating the festival, the Sukkah, the lulab and etrog (chaps. 1–3); rites and offerings on the festival (chaps. 4–5).

Sukkot. Festival of Tabernacles, the week from the 15th of Tishri, first full moon after autumnal equinox.

Tabernacle. See Sukkah.

Talmud. A commentary to the Mishnah; there are two Talmuds, each comprising the Mishnah and a commentary on the Mishnah produced from ca. 200 to 500 C.E. in rabbinical academies called *Gemara*. One Talmud was produced in Palestine, the other in Babylonia. From 500 C.E. on, the Babylonian Talmud was the primary source for Judaic law and theology. See Bavli; Yerushalmi.

Talmud of Babylonia. See Bavli.

Talmud of the Land of Israel. See Yerushalmi.

Tiferet. Glory.

Torah. God's revelation to Moses at Sinai. The word Torah bears number of meanings: (1) the Written Torah; (2) the one whole Torah, oral and written, revealed by God to our lord, Moses, at Sinai; (3) a particular thing, a scroll, containing divinely revealed words; (4) revelation in general; (5) a classification or rules, as in "the torah of . . . ," meaning "the rules that govern . . ."; (6) a particular act, namely, to study the Torah; (7) the status of a teaching, namely, deriving from the Torah as against deriving from the scribes.

Torah, Oral. The oral part of the Torah that at Sinai God gave to Moses. The Torah was in two media, oral and written; the oral part was formulated for memorization and handed on from master to disciple, in the model of God to Moses: "Moses received Torah at Sinai and handed it on to Joshua, Joshua to elders, and elders to prophets. And prophets handed it on to the men of the great assembly" [M. Abot 1:1]. Beginning with the Mishnah, ca.

200 C.E., the Oral Torah was committed to writing. Since the authorities of the Mishnah and related writings stood in the line of oral transmission of the Torah, what they said is accorded the status of Torah.

Torah, Written. The written part of the Torah revealed by God to Moses at Sinai; generally equivalent to the books of the Hebrew Scriptures (Pentateuch, Prophets, Writings).

Tosafists. Commentators to the Talmud's principal commentator, Rashi.

Tradent. One who is responsible for the wording and transmission of the teaching of a master.

Written Law. See Torah, Written.

Yarmulke. Skull cap worn by Conservative and some Reform Jews at prayer and by Orthodox Jews at all times, as a sign of respect for God.

Yebamot. Mishnah tractate on levirate marriages: establishing the levirate marital bond or severing the levirate bond through the rite of removing the shoe (chaps. 1–5); the special marital bond, marriage into the priesthood (chap. 6): when a woman may eat heave offering (chap. 6); who may eat heave offering (chaps. 7–8); severing the marital bond (chaps. 10–16); marital bonds subject to doubt (chaps. 10–11); severing the levirate bond through the rite of removing the shoe (chap. 12); severing the marital bond of a minor, the right of refusal (chap. 13); the infirm marital bond of a deaf mute (chap. 14); severing the marital bond through the death of the husband (chaps. 15–16).

Yerushalmi. Talmud produced in the Land of Israel, ca. 400 C.E., as a commentary to the Mishnah's first, second, third, and fourth divisions. It is made up mostly of amplification and extension of passages of the Mishnah. Approximately 90 percent of the document comprises Mishnah-commentary.

Yeshiva. Academy where the Torah, with special emphasis on the Talmud of Babylonia, is studied.

Yesod. Foundation.

Yihud. The unity of God.

Yom Kippur. See Day of Atonement.

Zaddikism. The reverence for the Zaddik in Hasidism.

Zedakah. "Righteousness" as concerns acts of philanthropy.

Zionism. The Jewish national movement, founded in Basel in 1897 by Theodore Herzl, that defined the Jews as a political entity with the goal of founding a Jewish state in Palestine. Fully successful in its political program, Zionism achieved its goal in 1948 with the creation of the State of Israel. Zionism as a political movement is closely associated with Judaism; its mythic categories derive from Judaism and are reworked in relationship to a political and messianic reading of the received Judaism. First, Zionism takes its name from the hill, Mount Zion, on which, in ancient times, the Temple of Jerusalem stood. Second, the paradigm for the political myth of Zionism is the cycle of the exile of the Jews from the Land of Israel in 586 B.C.E., and their return in the time of the Persians ca. 500 B.C.E. Jews living in the Land are redeemed; those outside are in exile. Third, Zionism invoked such messianic symbols as "the ingathering of the exiles," and claimed on its own behalf the realization of those symbols when Jews from various parts of the world emigrated to settle in the Jewish state.

Zionism therefore reinterpreted the received myths and symbols of Judaism in political terms. That constant reshaping of the received categories of Judaism explains why Zionists maintain that Zionism is the same as Judaism or is part of Judaism. They mean that the conception that the Jews form a people, one people, and that they have the right and duty to build a Jewish state in a particular place, which they call "the Land of Israel" (or Palestine) is intrinsic to the religion Judaism. The Zionist claim that "Zionism is Judaism" rests upon the fact the Zionism—return to the Land, (re)establish the Jewish state—indeed forms a critical component of the persistent paradigm of all Judaisms. The very structure of the first Judaic system, the one expressed by the authorship of the Pentateuch (the Five Books of Moses) assembled by Ezra in Jerusalem ca. 450 B.C.E., in fact took as its premise precisely the datum of Zionism, that the existential norm of Israel, the people, comes to full expression in its relationship to Israel, the Land. When, therefore, people say, "Zionism is Judaism," they express a view initially set forth by the Judaism of the pentateuchal authorship. That authorship set forth a Judaism that, to begin with, took as normative in Israel's experience the encounter with exile and return, therefore placing at the center of Judaic existence the relationship with the Land. Both the pentateuchal system of Judaism and modern and contemporary Zionism in all forms and all definitions concur that the right place for Israel, the Jewish people, is the Land of Israel. Other Judaisms have, of course, not concurred, among them, in practice, all versions of Judaism in the United States. In addition, the Zionist identification of the return to the Land and the founding of the state with the messianic promises of prophecy is rejected by various contemporary Judaisms, including important sectors of the Orthodox type of Judaisms in the State of Israel. But all Judaisms agree with contemporary political Zionism that the history of that people finds continuity and meaning in the relationship of the people to the Land. Since that conviction does characterize the pentateuchal system that is paradigmatic for all Judaisms, political Zionism has solid grounds to claim that, for its part, it is equivalent to (a) Judaism. The enlandisement of Judaism in the Pentateuch corresponds with the enlandisement of Zionism, and the choice of locale, the Land of Israel/Palestine, is, of course, the same.

Zionism originally considered the formation of the political entity, the Jewish state, critical, and the location to be peripheral; but within a decade of its founding, the World Zionist Organization decided that the Jewish state must be only in Palestine, and with that decision Zionism entered the framework of (a) Judaism. For the principal givens of the pentateuchal Torah's paradigm, namely, Israel's heightened sense of its own social reality, its status as an elected people standing in a contractual or covenantal relationship with God, in the pentateuchal system of Judaism all reach expression in the relationship of Israel to the Land of Israel. The enlandisement of Judaism in the territory called the Land of Israel explains why Zionism stands well within the Judaic system of the Pentateuch. The stress upon the locative character of Israel's existence forms the centerpiece of the pentateuchal system. Scripture said, in both the Torah and the prophetic-historical books, that Israel suffered through exile, atoned, attained reconciliation, and renewed the covenant with God as signified by the return to Zion and the rebuilding of the Temple. Although only a minority of "Israel" in fact had undergone those experiences, the Judaic system of the Torah made normative that experience of alienation and reconciliation. The original Judaism both raised and answered the question of exile and restoration. With the continuing authority of the Torah in Israel, the experience to which it originally constituted a profound and systematic response was recapitulated, age after age, through the reading and authoritative exegesis of the original Scripture that preserved and portrayed it: "Your descendants will be aliens living in a land that is not theirs . . . but I will punish that nation whose slaves they are, and after that they shall come out with great possessions" (Gen. 15:13–14). The pentateuchal system in its basic structure addressed, but also created, a continuing and chronic social fact of Israel's life. The generative tension, precipitated by the interpretation of the Jews' life as exile and return, persisted. With the persistent problem renewing for generation after generation that same resentment, the product of a memory of loss and restoration joined to the recognition in the here and now of the danger of a further loss, the priests' authoritative answer would not lose its power to persist and to persuade. In identifying alienation with exile, and reconciliation with return to the holy land, the pentateuchal Judaism formed a Zionist paradigm. Modern secular Zionism then restated that paradigm in concrete political terms and realized it through the State of Israel. That explains why Zionism is seen by much of contemporary Judaism to be integral to Judaism.

Index

Printed in the United States
1199500005B/70

9 780664 253486